CONTEMPORARY COLONIALITIES IN MEXICO AND BEYOND

Contemporary Colonialities in Mexico and Beyond

*Kathleen Ann Myers, Beth T. Boyd,
Pablo García Loaeza, Cara Anne
Kinnally, and Alejandro Mejías-López*

INTRODUCTION BY JUSTIN KNIGHT

UNIVERSITY OF TORONTO PRESS
Toronto Buffalo London

© University of Toronto Press 2024
Toronto Buffalo London
utorontopress.com
Printed in the USA

ISBN 978-1-4875-5121-6 (cloth)   ISBN 978-1-4875-5122-3 (EPUB)
                                   ISBN 978-1-4875-5123-0 (PDF)

Latinoamericana

Library and Archives Canada Cataloguing in Publication

Title: Contemporary colonialities in Mexico and beyond / Kathleen Ann Myers,
  Beth T. Boyd, Pablo García Loaeza, Cara Anne Kinnally, and Alejandro
  Mejías-López ; introduction by Justin Knight.
Names: Knight, Justin (College teacher), writer of introduction. | Container of (work):
  Myers, Kathleen Ann. Archaeology of coloniality.
Series: Latinoamericana (Toronto, Ont.)
Description: Series statement: Latinoamericana | Includes bibliographical references
  and index.
Identifiers: Canadiana (print) 20230525814 | Canadiana (ebook) 20230525881 |
  ISBN 9781487551216 (cloth) | ISBN 9781487551230 (PDF) | ISBN 9781487551223 (EPUB)
Subjects: LCSH: Popular culture – Mexico. | LCSH: Mexico – In mass media. |
  LCSH: Mexico – In literature. | LCSH: Mexico – In motion pictures. |
  LCSH: Mexico – Colonization – Social aspects. |
  LCSH: Mexican-American Border Region – Social aspects.
Classification: LCC F1210 .C66 2024 | DDC 306.0972 – dc23

Cover design: Louise OFarrell
Cover images: On the details page, the image is by Octavio Alonso Maya Castro, imported
from 500 px (archived version) by the Archive Team. This work is licensed under the CC
BY-SA 3.0 licence from "Colonial Mexico Urbanscape," Wikimedia Commons, https://
commons.wikimedia.org/w/index.php?curid=78766347. The background image is from
iStock.com/ivoris.

We wish to acknowledge the land on which the University of Toronto Press
operates. This land is the traditional territory of the Wendat, the Anishnaabeg, the
Haudenosaunee, the Métis, and the Mississaugas of the Credit First Nation.

This book has been published with the assistance of Purdue University and Indiana
University.

University of Toronto Press acknowledges the financial support of the Government of
Canada, the Canada Council for the Arts, and the Ontario Arts Council, an agency of
the Government of Ontario, for its publishing activities.

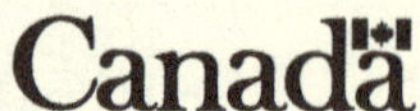

Contents

Illustrations

Acknowledgments

The co-authors acknowledge the generous funding provided by their respective institutions for this project. We thank Indiana University's College of Arts and Humanities Institute and Institute for Advanced Study for funding our initial workshops and seminar. The College of Liberal Arts at Purdue University provided funding for another workshop that allowed us to engage and receive feedback from members of the Purdue community. All this support gave us multiple opportunities to deepen our collaboration and to invite input from colleagues and students. The publication of our project received funding from Purdue University's Office of the Executive Vice President for Research, College of Liberal Arts' Publication Subvention Program, and School of Languages and Cultures. Additional funding was provided by Indiana University Research through the Grant-in-Aid Program and by West Virginia University's Eberly College of Arts and Sciences. We also thank the many colleagues and student-colleagues who added much to this collaborative project by offering encouragement, insights, and suggestions over the last three years. Finally, our thanks go to the reviewers and editors at the University of Toronto Press.

Chronology of Notable Dates and Events

1325	Mexico-Tenochtitlan is founded.
c1430	The *altepemeh* ("city-states") of Mexico, Tetzcoco, and Tlacopan form the Triple Alliance (aka the Aztec Empire).
1502	Moteuczoma Xocoyotzin ascends to power in Mexico-Tenochtitlan.
1519	The Spanish expedition led by Hernán Cortés reaches the Yucatan peninsula and sails up the Gulf of Mexico coast. The Villa Rica de la Vera Cruz is founded.
1521	After a three-month siege the Mexica ruler, Cuauhtémoc, is captured and Mexico-Tenochtitlan falls to allied Spanish and Indigenous forces.
1524	The first official delegation of Franciscan missionaries reaches Mexico City.
1535	The Viceroyalty of New Spain is established with Mexico City as its capital.
1551	Mexico's first university is founded by royal decree.
1560	A royal decree orders that the Indigenous population be settled in designated towns ("*congregaciones de indios*").
1571	The Holy Inquisition is officially established in New Spain.
1572	The Jesuit order founds its first chapter in New Spain.
1680	An Indigenous uprising in New Mexico eliminates the Spanish presence in the region until the early 1690s.
1681	A royal decree prohibits Spaniards, Blacks, and individuals of mixed descent from living in towns designated as *pueblos de indios*. A compilation of the laws of the Indies (four volumes) is published in Madrid.
1767	The Jesuit order is expelled from the Spanish Empire. Texts in which exiled Jesuits extol their homelands reinforce patriotic feelings.

1810   The Mexican path to independence begins with a call to arms by the priest Miguel Hidalgo y Costilla, who is considered today the father of the nation.

1821   Mexico declares independence from Spain.

1822   The new state is established as an empire under Agustín de Iturbide.

1824   Mexico becomes a federal republic, the United States of Mexico, modelled after the United States of America.

1833   Antonio López de Santa Anna becomes president and enacts centralist reforms.

1836   Texas declares independence from Mexico. In 1845 it is admitted as a state in the United States.

1846–8   The United States and Mexico engage in war. In the 1848 Treaty of Guadalupe Hidalgo, Mexico loses 525,000 square miles of land to the United States.

1854   Through the Venta de la Mesilla, or Gadsden Purchase, the United States acquires portions of present-day southern Arizona and New Mexico, thus establishing the current US-Mexico border.

1857   A new liberal constitution buttresses the separation of church and state.

1858–61   Mexico's War of Reform takes place, and the country is left bankrupt.

1862   France invades Mexico under the excuse of collecting the unpaid debt owed by Benito Juárez's liberal government.

1864–7   The Second Mexican Empire is ruled by Maximilian of Hapsburg.

1867   Maximilian is executed. Benito Juárez re-establishes the republic and remains president until his death in 1872.

1876   Porfirio Díaz becomes president. His time in power is marked by industrial development and violent repression, and the economic ties between the United States and Mexico grow.

1910–29   The Mexican Revolution begins with an uprising led by Francisco Madero against Porfirio Díaz and ends with the establishment of the Partido Nacional Revolucionario (PNR).

1916   The first feminist congress takes place in Mexico.

1917   Mexico adopts its current constitution.

1924   In the United States a border patrol is established, and the National Origins Act, or Johnson-Reed Act, places broad

	limitations on legal immigration, permanently imposing a restrictive quota system.
1926–9	The anticlerical policies of President Plutarco Elías Calles anger conservative Catholics and result in the Cristero War.
1929	With the goal of controlling and limiting the settlement of Mexicans, the US Immigration Act criminalizes undocumented border crossings.
1939	President Lázaro Cárdenas welcomes thousands of Spanish refugees. Mexico does not recognize the regime of Francisco Franco.
1942	The US Bracero Program, which allowed entry to Mexican farm workers, is established to address the labour shortage created by the Second World War.
1946	The PNR, changed to Partido de la Revolución Mexicana (PRM) in 1938 during the presidency of Lázaro Cárdenas, adopts its current name, Partido Revolucionario Institucional (PRI).
1953	Women obtain the right to vote.
1954	The so-called Mexican miracle begins, lasting until 1970.
1968	The Tlatelolco massacre occurs. Mexico hosts the Olympic Games.
1971	Luis Echeverría Álvarez becomes president. On 10 June a government-sponsored paramilitary group known as *los halcones* ("the hawks") attacks a peaceful student protest, in what is remembered as *El halconazo*.
1979	The first Gay Pride parade takes place in Mexico.
1985	A series of major earthquakes causes widespread destruction and kills thousands in Mexico City.
1988	Carlos Salinas de Gortari becomes president and begins pursuing neoliberal economic policies.
1992	Mexico joins the United States and Canada in the North American Free Trade Agreement (NAFTA).
1994	NAFTA goes into effect. An uprising of the Ejército Zapatista de Liberación Nacional (EZLN) occurs in the southern state of Chiapas.
1996	The government and the EZLN sign the San Andrés de Larráinzar Accords through which Indigenous communities are afforded greater autonomy.
2000	Vicente Fox of the Partido Acción Nacional (PAN) becomes president. This is the first time in seventy years that the PRI is not in power.

2001   A constitutional amendment defines Mexico as a single, indivisible nation that is pluri-ethnic and pluricultural in nature.

2006   Felipe Calderón (of PAN) becomes president. His government's war against the drug cartels leads to a significant escalation of violence across the country.

2012   The PRI returns to power when Enrique Peña Nieto becomes president.

2018   Andrés Manuel López Obrador (known as AMLO) of the left-leaning party Movimiento de Regeneración Nacional (MORENA) becomes president.

CONTEMPORARY COLONIALITIES IN MEXICO AND BEYOND

Introduction: Contemporary Mexican Coloniality

JUSTIN KNIGHT

During the past three decades a meaningful shift has occurred in Latin American Studies concerning the use of the term *colonial*. Until the early 1990s it was commonly invoked in reference to a historically specific mode of territorial administration in which Latin America was carved into distinct colonies that were formally possessed and governed by a variety of European powers, most notably Spain and Portugal. According to this historicist version of the story, colonialism in the region mostly receded over the course of the nineteenth century, giving way to the rule of independent territorial nation states. Patricia Seed's 1991 review essay in the *Latin American Research Review*, "Colonial and Postcolonial Discourse," registered a significant departure from this traditional understanding of colonialism by highlighting emerging trends in the fields of history, anthropology, and literary studies. By pivoting towards the discursive dimensions of colonial and postcolonial situations, Seed argued, Latin Americanist scholars had begun to reorient the field towards a broader critique of authority as practised not only in regimes of colonial administration but also in the exercise of state power after independence, in the concomitant formation of literary and cultural canons, and, by implication, in Western scholarly practices and knowledge creation in general. The colonial no longer was simply to be thought of as "out there" – in the distant past and its outmoded forms of political domination – but must be acknowledged as an integral component of politics, cultural production, and scholarly work in the present day.

In the years since Seed's article the colonial has come to function as one of the central thematic gathering places in the increasingly diverse and interdisciplinary field of Latin American Studies. Meanwhile, the predominant vocabulary on the topic has undergone a subtle yet consequential modification. We are by now much more likely to speak of a broader coloniality than colonialism per se, and the critical positions of postcolonial theory have themselves been subjected to a self-reflexive critique that goes by the name of *decoloniality*. Among the most influential currents in this development has been Walter Mignolo's work on the concepts of *colonial difference* and *locus of enunciation*, by which he attempts to register some of the particularities of Latin American history and culture that are consistently written out of traditional postcolonial studies. As Mabel Moraña, Enrique Dussel, and Carlos A. Jáuregui put it in their introduction to the influential volume *Coloniality at Large* (2008), "Latin American history challenges the concept of *post*coloniality from within" (11; italics in original). At least partly inspired by Mignolo's work, a generation of critics has set about demonstrating that the specificity of coloniality in the Americas holds up a mirror to postcolonial studies and shows the latter to be always already situated elsewhere, both geopolitically and epistemologically. It is based on histories of colonialism and decolonization that are more appropriate to Africa and Asia than to the Americas, for instance, and its methodologies consistently fail to account for distinctly Latin American forms of thought and knowledge production. The conclusion is therefore inescapable: postcolonial knowledge has itself been a colonizing force with respect to coloniality in the Americas. Indeed, to the extent that it is taken as a universal site of knowledge, it is so for all the "different local histories and embodied conceptions and practices of decoloniality" that might be deployed to "contest the totalizing claims and political-epistemic violence of modernity" (Walsh and Mignolo 1). It is questionable, under such conditions, whether postcolonial theory can articulate a coherent critique of colonial modernity at all – in Latin America or elsewhere.

Thus, as Jaime Hanneken has recently argued, "[d]ecoloniality is not … one variant of the postcolonial concept but is its meta-critique and conceptual correction" (8). In other words, it applies the postcolonial critique of colonial domination to the postcolonial itself. Decolonial theory should therefore be understood as a necessary turn propelled by demands that are internal to postcolonial critique, by which the latter is confronted with its own neocolonial relations of domination. Yet, as Hanneken points out, decolonial thinking must remain open to its own meta-critical interventions, or else it risks ossifying into an orthodoxy just as normative, and hence just as epistemologically colonizing, as those to which it responds. David Lehmann has seized upon this potential pitfall of the decolonial critique in his recent book, *After the Decolonial: Ethnicity, Gender and Social Justice in Latin America*. Lehmann argues that the commitment of decolonial scholars to racialized identity politics has channelled academic Latin Americanism's political potentiality into internecine battles within academia and severed the field from political movements on the ground. He proposes a new direction for Latin Americanist thought, one which, without abandoning the decolonial critique of racial and ethnolinguistic domination, reconnects it with notions of universalist justice that have been discarded for their complicity with Eurocentric enlightenment reason. The prospects for such a project, to say nothing of its political desirability, are beyond the scope of the present volume; however, Lehmann's diagnosis of the reasons for decoloniality's shortcomings goes to the heart of what is at stake here. He claims that the dominant view of this strain of thinking is that "Latin American society is characterized by a polarized and polarizing colonial apparatus of racialized domination that has existed *unchanged* for 500 years and infuses *all* relations of unequal power and status as well as the mindset of its population" (1; emphasis added). There is little to be done in the face of such monolithic and all-encompassing injustice, which Lehmann argues gives way to "a climate of despair and negativity" (1). Whether or not this critique is fair, it demonstrates the risks run by analyses of coloniality when they flatten their objects of study into simple expressions of changeless, unyielding forces of domination.

If Lehmann's call for a renewal of the drive towards universalist justice that suffused earlier Marxist and liberal currents in Latin Americanist thought constitutes one possible response to the dangers harboured within decoloniality, another possibility is suggested in the pages of this book. It springs from what Hanneken insists is a key feature of coloniality: "the irretrievability of the manifold particulars extinguished by colonial and neocolonial representations" (9). We are, in other words, never face to face with that which has been repressed by colonial relations of domination. Scholars of coloniality are instead left to register the effects of the erasures themselves within the various forms of representation at work in our colonial modernity, scholarly critique among them. To the extent that it is practised as a mode of retrieval and recognition of the repressed, colonial scholarship will always risks opening yet another avenue for neocolonial representation. Such an acknowledgment recasts both the problem and its potential overcoming as identified by Lehmann. It is not so much that decolonial theory lacks a notion of universal justice upon which to ground its political interventions, but that it risks misidentifying, and thus in a sense recolonizing, the very voices, demands, and cosmologies on whose behalf it claims to speak. In the present day, colonialists, along with post- and decolonial thinkers broadly, face the urgent challenge of elaborating a critique of coloniality that does not rest upon, and thereby reinforce, identity categories derived from colonial difference itself. More than a renewed commitment to the universalism of Marxist or liberal thought, the task will require a sustained interrogation of the irreducible specificity of the diverse sites at which the traces of colonial erasure might be registered.

The present volume endeavours to take up precisely this task. Rather than identify a set of entities under colonial erasure, it tracks the operations of coloniality itself across various forms of representation at work in nineteenth-, twentieth-, and twenty-first-century Mexico. Notable among these are politics, literature, film, web-based media content, and popular culture, to name but a few. In analyses that frequently resonate beyond the territorial boundaries of the present-day Mexican state, the diverse chapters presented here all explore the proposition that coloniality cannot be reduced to an inventory of themes – such as violence, domination, extraction, and political and economic subordination – which might be shown to repeat themselves and thus perpetuate an unchanging coloniality after the end of colonial rule. Rather, what is at stake is an intimate relationship between coloniality and modernity, whereby the latter internalizes and continually works through some of the core premises of the former. As Enrique Dussel has put it, "modernity as such was 'born' when Europe was in a position to pose itself against an other, … exploring, conquering, colonizing an alterity that gave back its image of itself" (66). The dialectic of modernity originates in the relationship between colonizer and colonized, giving rise to both "a rational 'concept' of emancipation" and, in Eurocentrism, "an irrational myth, a justification for genocidal violence" (66). For Dussel's politics of liberation, the emancipatory drive must transcend and negate the Eurocentric myth so that modernity might overcome its originary coloniality. Aníbal Quijano has advanced a similar notion of modernity's relationship to coloniality, specifically concerning the concepts of race and labour:

> Two historical processes associated in the production of [modern] space/time converged and established the two fundamental axes of the new model of power. One was the codification of the differences between conquerors and conquered in the idea of "race," a supposedly different biological structure that placed some in a natural situation of inferiority to others … The other process was the constitution of a new structure of control of labor and its resources and products. (533–4)

This system of racial differentiation and the appropriation of labour, as María Lugones points out in "The Coloniality of Gender," is built upon a persistent substrate of indifference to gendered violence, namely that perpetuated upon women of colour in colonized communities. Thus, deeply rooted structures of racial difference and the tendential subsumption of labour into the capitalist world market, each inaugurated in the colonial encounter and still operative in the modern world, expose an ongoing coloniality that continues to exercise its coercive power unevenly upon gendered and racialized bodies.

The insights of thinkers like Dussel, Quijano, and Lugones have proven essential for the field of Latin American Studies and for scholarly work on colonial modernity broadly. Their influence can be felt in recent work by scholars of colonial Latin America who have modified these perspectives in important ways. Daniel Nemser, for instance, argues that the colonial institution of racial differentiation cannot be reduced to the subjugation of one identity group by another based on arbitrary differences and must instead be understood as the production of such differences in the asymmetrical pursuit of a particular conception of the good. As he puts it, "race is a matter of making some people die more in order to make others live better" (11). It is thus as much a question of the valuation of life as of its devaluation, of necropolitics as a necessary by-product of the biopolitical administration of life itself in the social formations characteristic of colonial modernity. In other words, racial difference (and, following Lugones, one might add gender difference to this equation) is processual, and it therefore recurs in different identitarian configurations across distinct historical and geographic contexts. Orlando Bentancor has reworked the question of labour and resources in colonial Latin America along similar lines. Bentancor argues that Spanish colonialism in the Americas was not simply a matter of imposing a new regime of labour in the service of global capitalism; rather, this labour regime itself must be contextualized within the far-reaching metaphysical apparatus behind the colonial drive towards the transformation of raw material. Both the mineral resources and the Indigenous populations of the Americas were, from the standpoint of Spanish colonial projects, understood in terms of a "pure passive potential to receive an exemplary pattern or 'form' from above" (Bentancor 9). Mining and political administration were thus constituted as modes of looking after the ever-ready stores of (mineral and human) potential encountered in the colonies.

When conceptualized in such a manner, it becomes clear that coloniality does not simply survive – materially and/or thematically – in the modern world. Rather, as the privileged mode of caring for the distribution of life and death and the development of potentialities since the colonial encounter, modernity has only ever operated as an ongoing working out of certain premises of colonialism. It is in this sense that Peter Osborne has referred to the colonial as modernity's spatial reserve, "in each of the contradictory senses of the term 'reserve': (1) the sense of a reservation, a spatial delimitation that puts something aside, but also (2) in the sense of something that is held in reserve, as an as-yet-unrealised potential, something 'beyond' the actual" (76). In other words, it is the continual spatialization and re-spatialization of the colonial relation itself that nourishes modernity's temporal orientation towards the transcendence of the new. What appears to be a pure temporal form differentiating that which is current from that which is outdated – the modern and the tradition it must overcome, that is – in fact relies upon an original and still operative spatial distinction between colony and metropole, even if the differentiated terms and their order of priority may shift over time. The prime directive to actualize the historical present across a multiplicity of constitutively heterogeneous spaces, which lies at the heart of modern geopolitical reasoning broadly, can only become operational once spatial differences come to be coded as temporal ones, and vice versa. That which must be brought up to date at any given moment in history has always already been set aside by means of an original distinction that renders space and time legible as such. Spain's early colonial projects, aimed at the transformation of matter and the optimization of life, enact just such a mutually constitutive transposing of spatiality and temporality. As such, they might be thought of as one of the inaugural forms of the space-time of colonial modernity.

It is for precisely this reason that the present volume works from such a rich repository of artifacts that respond to colonial spatial schemas in one way or another. Mexico's unique and internally diverse histories of colonization and independence, not to mention subsequent neo-imperialist incursions, have left indelible marks on its territorial configuration and its spatial imaginaries – literary, political, or otherwise. And, remarkably, they have laid the spatializing groundwork for new and unforeseeable realms, like mass media and web-based social media platforms. Hence the underlying unity of the diverse chapters that follow. It is not so much that they all share a common vision of colonial spatiality in Mexico, but rather that they all identify sites at which spatial heterogeneities can be seen to arise from colonial modes of differentiation. They highlight urgent demands that have been registered in literature, film, news media, and popular culture in Mexico over the past two centuries, all of which vary immensely in terms of political orientation, aesthetic sensibility, religiosity, and mode of expression, among a host of other characteristics. What these divergent objects of study share in common is colonial difference itself. That is, they are all premised upon, and generally operate in reaction to, spatial configurations in which there is something separated off and held back as a potentiality yet to be realized. Such are the colonial conditions underlying Mexican history, beginning with the earliest encounters between Europeans and the populations living there at the time of their arrival and continuing through to the present day.

The Spanish colonization of present-day Mexico began in the early sixteenth century with a massive reconfiguration of existing territorial relations. Of course, the prevailing organization of land, populations, and resources at the time of Hernán Cortés's 1519 expedition was by no means static. What is now commonly referred to as the Aztec Empire was in fact a large and complex system of tribute, maintained through indirect rule and ritualistic warfare and centred on the hegemonic city-states built on and around Lake Tetzcoco: Tlacopan, Tetzcoco, and Mexico, which comprised the polities of Tlatelolco and Tenochtitlan. The latter had come to exercise a dominant role in the alliance, and in the Valley of Mexico broadly, by the turn of the sixteenth century. After the fall of Tenochtitlan in 1521, itself facilitated by alliances that Cortés had forged out of growing discontent among the Indigenous subjects of Tenochtitlan's rule, the diverse populations of Mesoamerica were increasingly organized under the umbrella term *indios*, eventually giving rise to an ideology of racial difference between European colonizers and colonized Indigenous populations. This racial ideology had as much to do with spatial organization and religious practice as with phenotype, however. The basic unit of pre-Columbian political cohesion, for instance, the *altepemeh* (often translated as "city-state"), was reorganized through systems like *encomienda* (the granting of territory and rights to Indigenous labour to Spanish *encomenderos*) and *congregación* (the forced resettlement of Indigenous populations into communities organized by the Spanish Crown and Catholic religious orders), which collapsed internal differences and antagonisms among Indigenous populations and consolidated their territories to facilitate their conversion to Catholicism and their assimilation into the colonial workforce. Although the ideological division of territory and populations into *repúblicas de indios* and *repúblicas de españoles* was never fully realized and eventually faded even from official discourses, these early efforts resulted in the creation of distinct spatial schemas wherein internally diverse populations came to be identified simply as *indios*. Crucially, the spaces associated with this supposedly homogenous Indigenous subject were defined by a mandate for transformation, both through religious conversion and through enforced labour in agricultural and mining projects. Eventually there emerged from these initial distinctions a complex system of *castas* ("castes") aimed at identifying people of mixed European, Amerindian, African, and Asian ancestry with reference not only to physical appearance but also to space and material culture. The famous eighteenth-century *cuadros de castas* ("caste paintings") register both the vast changes that had occurred since the early days of colonization and the persistence of space as a mediator of racial differentiation and the cultural imaginaries of colonial Mexico.

This structure proved to be an enduring element of subsequent Mexican history. The nineteenth century opened with a prolonged struggle for Mexico's independence from Spain, followed by a series of territorial transformations, including Central American independence, Texan independence, the secession and subsequent re-assimilation of the state of Yucatan, and finally the forced concession of territory to the United States. By 1848 more than half of the original territory claimed by the Mexican state was no longer under its control. In the north a new border would take shape over time as Mexico and the United States repeatedly drew and redrew a physical boundary that gradually became less porous and increasingly criminalized and militarized, at great cost to the lives and livelihoods of those residing in and moving through the region. Meanwhile, Mexico's political sphere in the early nineteenth century took shape around a contentious struggle for power between federalist and centralist factions with differing visions for the territorial and political organization of the nation. Morphing out of this struggle, there emerged a movement geared towards liberal political reforms and the separation of church and state, as well as a conservative movement allied with the Catholic Church in opposition to the constitutional reforms sought by liberals. The liberal faction, led by Benito Juárez, emerged victorious from a string of civil wars in the 1850s and set about instituting a series of laws known collectively as *La Reforma*. The process was interrupted, however, when Napoleon III of France used the Juárez government's unpaid foreign debt to justify an invasion and partial occupation of Mexico in 1862, establishing a short-lived monarchy that was supported by parts of the losing factions from the civil wars.

In the decades following the defeat of the French in 1867, Porfirio Díaz took control of the reins of government and held on to them until the early twentieth century. The Díaz government promised to bring modernization to Mexico under the slogan *Orden y progreso* ("Order and progress"). The version of progress pursued during the Porfiriato, as the years of Díaz's reign came to be known, tended to benefit urban elites and the wealthy landowning classes, while its emphasis on order – largely maintained by repressive deployment of the armed forces – kept at bay the rising tensions among the urban and rural poor. Though ostensibly a liberal himself, Díaz re-established relations with the Vatican and worked to reinstate many of the privileges of the Catholic Church. This state of affairs lasted until demands for Díaz's ouster erupted into open warfare in 1910. The series of conflicts collectively known as the Mexican Revolution, which lasted through much of the 1920s, registered a diverse array of demands from different sectors of the population. Perhaps the most enduring was the demand for a redistribution of the lands held by wealthy landowners and the Catholic Church. The revolution may have begun as a call for open elections and political liberalization, but it quickly became a struggle over rights of land tenure for rural Mexicans, mostly of mestizo and Indigenous descent. After years of shifting alliances and in-fighting among competing revolutionary factions, the victors formed a government around a new ruling party – later known as the Partido Revolucionario Institucional (Institutional Revolutionary Party, PRI) – which promised to carry out the popular reforms demanded during the revolution within a stable institutional framework. The first century of Mexican independence was thus punctuated by territorial conflicts that produced a continual dialectic of spatial configuration and reconfiguration, mediated by racial differences and distributions of wealth and power inaugurated during the colonial period.

The domestic political projects undertaken by the PRI governments that held power from the end of the Mexican Revolution until the turn of the twenty-first century were in many ways a continuation of this same process. In the name of modernization, successive PRI administrations introduced policies and projects aimed at transforming uneven urban and rural landscapes. Paradigmatic examples include the draining of lakes surrounding Mexico City and the subsequent incorporation of newly created land; uneven and incomplete efforts to carry out the agrarian reforms demanded by various factions during the revolution; and ongoing efforts to assimilate and incorporate Indigenous communities and their lands. Acting in accordance with the modernizing imperative to bring distinct parts of the country "up to date," these administrations drew from repertoires of spatial differentiation that are inherently colonial. Whether through ongoing agrarian reform or through the development of newly available lake-beds, the horizons of PRI policy and administration were constituted by uneven spaces marked as underdeveloped or lagging behind in relation to the putative present of modernity. Meanwhile, in the sphere of foreign policy, the post-revolutionary ruling party – especially under the presidency of Lázaro Cárdenas – greatly transformed the relationship between

Mexico and its former metropole. Taking an international stance against the 1936 fascist uprising that led Spain into a devastating civil war, Mexico welcomed thousands of exiles and temporarily became the seat of Spain's democratically elected government. In the following decades Mexico would stand out as one of the few countries that never recognized the Franco regime and continued to challenge its neo-imperialist discourse. The apparent contrasts between the PRI's (neocolonial) domestic and (anti-colonial) foreign policy are in fact exemplary of the curious perseverance of coloniality in the modern world: the overturning of the colonial and its perpetuation are but two sides of the same coin, for in either case the present becomes actionable precisely through spatial unevenness rooted in coloniality. The phenomenon itself – the actualization of the present by way of a colonial spatial reserve – did not come to a close with the ending of the PRI's electoral dominance in the twenty-first century, however. Subsequent administrations have contended with the power and territorial claims of non-state actors like multinational corporations and criminal enterprises, as well as shifting migratory patterns, the militarization of the border and criminalization of immigration in the United States, and enforcement policies that have radically transformed Mexico's geopolitical role vis-à-vis the rest of the Americas, to name only a few of the spatial transformations occurring in the twenty-first century. It remains painfully clear that the spatial differentiations characteristic of the present day – between Mexico, Central America, and the anglophone countries of North America, for instance, as well as those prevailing within Mexico itself – continue to actualize colonial legacies of race, gender, and labour exploitation.

The foregoing gloss of Mexican history may serve as a back-drop for thinking of the unity of the five chapters of this book. While each one takes contemporary (early-twenty-first-century) coloniality as its point of entry into the conversation, they often also examine artefacts that predate the revolution or deal with the decades of twentieth-century PRI rule. They span a variety of historical and geopolitical configurations that shed light on the continual negotiation of Mexico's own heterogeneous territoriality, its relationships with its neighbours to the north and the south, and its transatlantic links to Spain, the erstwhile colonial metropole. It is in precisely this regard that the diverse approaches and objects of analysis offered here coalesce into a common understanding of the colonial spatializations characteristic of modern Mexico. All five chapters demonstrate ways in which Mexican cultural producers, public figures, and media personalities find themselves enmeshed in and compelled to engage with local, regional, and transatlantic spatial networks that are inherently colonial. They are so, not only because they bear the unmistakable marks of their historical origins in Spanish colonialism but also because they engage in ongoing processes whereby the relations of coloniality, be they racialized, gendered, territorialized, or, more often, some combination of all three, are renegotiated and resignified in modern Mexico. The analyses yield potentially surprising insights into these processes. They suggest that contemporary coloniality in Mexico is by no means a simple reproduction of earlier colonial relations. Indeed, the latter are just as likely to persist in inverted or modified forms that, precisely by reshaping the colonial contours of the modern world, also reaffirm their inherent coloniality. The chapters of this book trace these modifications and reactivations of coloniality in present-day Mexico through detailed analyses of the sites in which they play out in literature, film, political discourse, mass media, and social media. The result is a series of studies that, taken together, disturb traditional notions of the relationship between the colonial and the modern, as well as that between colonizer and colonized, and thereby open up space for a more nuanced discussion of Mexican colonialities past, present, and future.

The first chapter centres on two canonical figures in twentieth- and twenty-first-century Mexican art and culture: José Emilio Pacheco and Alfonso Cuarón. It highlights the spatial dimensions of contemporary coloniality in Mexico City through close readings of two works set in the storied neighbourhood of Colonia Roma. The chapter opens by exploring the shifting urban geography of Mexico City as it has taken shape from the time of the Spanish conquest of Tenochtitlan through successive waves of reshaping and restructuring that continue to the present day. Within this broad perspective Pacheco's short semi-autobiographical novel *Las batallas en el desierto* (1980) is situated alongside Cuarón's feature-length film *Roma* (2018), which draws heavily on the filmmaker's autobiography for source material. Each work employs genre conventions in ways that call attention to the essential role of setting within narrative traditions that tend to privilege plot, characterization, and dialogue. As a result, they can be read today as reflections on the spatial practices of ongoing coloniality in Mexico. These readings challenge the notion that colonization was a discreet, temporally delimited process of territorial domination; on the contrary, they identify within the spatial practices of successive modes of political administration a continuous and internally conflictual process of reterritorialization through which colonial social relations reproduce themselves. In this sense, the first chapter offers an important framework for the book's interventions as a whole by interrogating contemporary coloniality not simply as a theme that recurs in the modern world but as a set of material and epistemological practices through which modernity itself takes shape as the development of potentialities that bear the marks of their origins in colonial encounters. It is thus not so much that modernity has yet to make a definitive break with its colonial past, but rather that each instantiation of the modern represents another turning of the colonial screw, so to speak.

Reading coloniality through Pacheco's and Cuarón's spatializing techniques demands engagement with several key theoretical issues. On a fundamental level, it requires a theorization of space that runs somewhat counter to the usual understanding of it as a uniform medium in which things exist and take place. Against this mostly implicit treatment of spatial uniformity, the opening chapter takes up questions raised by critical theorists like Henri Lefebvre, Michel Foucault, and Doreen Massey. In their own way, each of these writers challenges us to think of space as an overlapping domain of negotiation and conflict that is as heterogeneous as are the social formations within which it takes shape. These perspectives have had an important impact on Colonial Studies in recent years, notably in the work of Achille Mbembe and, in the field of Mexican Colonial Studies specifically, Daniel Nemser. To this growing dialogue the readings offered here contribute both another body of evidence and a fresh way of approaching the question. They remain attentive, on the one hand, to spatial multiplicity and the quotidian negotiations through which it takes shape and, on the other hand, to the often-violent modes of enclosure characteristic of territorial sovereignty, as well as to the intermingling of materiality and epistemology within both. Thus, the first chapter traces Mexico's colonial inheritance through sites and events that are not overtly colonial. And for precisely this reason, its readings of *Las batallas en el desierto* and *Roma* serve as a guide for reading contemporary coloniality through spatialization.

Chapter 2 carries forward the question of space in post-revolutionary Mexico, while shifting focus to regions outside of the capital city and to objects of study that conform less neatly to established genre conventions. Juan José Arreola's heterogeneous work of literary fiction *La feria* (1963) and Carlos Reygadas's experimental short film "Este es mi reino" (2010) each represent a single location in Mexico – a small town and a rural hacienda, respectively – as a layered assemblage that is constantly being formed and reformed by far-reaching historical forces. The chapter takes as its point of departure the long, uneven, and conflictual processes of land redistribution undertaken in the decades following the Mexican Revolution, arguing that both works situate twentieth-century struggles within centuries-long histories of conflict over the distribution of land. They both pursue this project by pushing form to its limits, thereby disturbing the hegemonic modes of representing Mexican history. The readings presented in the second chapter highlight this disruption by exploring the apocalyptic dimensions of both works in explicit contradistinction to narratives of revolution as a radical break with the past that is oriented towards the appearance of a new and more just social and political order. Delinking violent destruction from its utopian orientation as revolution, these readings call attention to a common substrate underlying both colonial and revolutionary violence. The thematization of apocalypse, it is argued, is what lends these two works the critical perspective from which to identify the inherently colonial conditions of possibility for modern spatial redistribution projects in isolation from the redemptive logic by which such projects justify themselves.

On the surface, the shift from revolution to apocalypse might seem to herald a renunciation of politics in favour of religious consolation. In fact, however, the readings presented in chapter 2 invite a broad reconsideration of the relationship between religion and politics in the modern era. Rather than breaking free from religious mystification by way of a progressive establishment of scientific reason, the chapter suggests that modernity internalizes some of the religious predicates it purports to overcome. In this way, it could be seen as an exploration of Walter Benjamin's insistence that the structure of promise inherent in modern revolutionary politics is derived from messianic religious formations. If, as Benjamin claims, revolutionary interventions tend to be motivated more by the memory of ancestors in chains than by the hope of liberated descendants – if, in other words, it is easier to say ahead of time what it is one must be emancipated *from* than to say what one must be emancipated *for* – then perhaps the apocalyptic, as a mode of ending above and beyond the calculable form of any new beginning, is present in at least equal measure to the messianic within the politics of revolutionary promise. These broad theoretical considerations set the stage for one of the book's key arguments concerning contemporary Mexican coloniality: its continued engagement with religion belies the traditional narrative of modernity as rational secularization. What comes to light in readings of *La feria* and "Este es mi reino," therefore, and what will be brought into even sharper relief in the chapters that follow, is that religious discourses articulated during colonization by no means disappear entirely, or even tendentially, in the wake of political independence and revolution. They are instead reinscribed at other levels, where they remain available as tools for the administration and contestation of political power in the modern nation state.

Chapter 3 brings some of the insights from the first two chapters to bear on newer modes of social interaction and cultural transmission through digitally mediated web platforms. It takes up two case studies: a viral video of a baby Jesus statue dancing the "Pasito perrón," posted by late-night-talk-show host Rolando Ávila in 2015, and a meme produced by the Querétaro-based, social-media account Tlacaélel in response to President Andrés Manuel López Obrador's (AMLO's) March 2019 demand for formal apologies from the Spanish crown and the Catholic Church for the Spanish conquest of Mexico. While the concerned responses of Catholic Church officials to Ávila's video could be said to stage a repetition of the colonial scene, the Tlacaélel meme operates through an inversion, identifying the colonial repetition within an overtly decolonial act. AMLO's demand, articulated on behalf of Mexico's Indigenous communities, implicitly posits an ideal anti-colonial indigeneity to which the widespread Catholic devotion among present-day Mexicans of Indigenous descent is decidedly heterodox. By calling attention to this situation, the Tlacaélel meme opens up the possibility of reading unexpected parallels between AMLO's anti-colonial deployment of state power and the inquisitorial resonances present in church officials' concerns over popular appropriation of the image in Ávila's viral video. The two instances reveal a similar mode of interaction between official discourse and popular response, in which the popular occupies a contestatory position constituted by the exclusion of that which is heterogeneous relative to the inherently normative operation of the official. The fact that this occurs even when the official position is explicitly anti-colonial demonstrates once again the unexpected forms in which coloniality reproduces itself in contemporary Mexican social life. The implications of this analysis, taken together with that of the first two chapters, reverberate broadly and begin to form a picture of just how deeply the material and epistemological structures of coloniality are embedded in modern social and political forms.

The third chapter contributes to ongoing work on this topic by exploring the theme of *lo popular* as an admixture of what is generally thought of under the rubric of everyday life and/or popular culture. The concept of popular culture mediates the chapter's engagement with the traditional archival research methodologies of Colonial Studies, as it insists on considering memes and viral videos alongside archival documents as texts in which to read the history of coloniality. In addition, it situates the popular structurally as a component part of the power structures through which coloniality reproduces itself. *Lo popular* is thus not treated simply as a passive substrate upon which hegemonic power relations are written; on the contrary, the chapter traces the emergence of the popular alongside the hegemonic as a necessary outcome of their mutually constitutive interactions. In this way, chapter 3 establishes a dialogue with the work of Ernesto Laclau and Chantal Mouffe on the processual and relational dimensions of hegemony and subalternity in modern social formations. The arguments advanced here emphasize the deep material and conceptual legacies of coloniality at the heart of the socio-political dynamics of modernity theorized by Laclau and Mouffe. In establishing this linkage, the third chapter also explores further some of the second chapter's fundamental questions about religion. It suggests that the logic of conversion developed during Spanish colonization subtends the modes of reception characteristic of the modern ideological state and that, therefore, the possibility of heterodox receptions of official discourses, once the motor of the Inquisition, continues to haunt the exercise of politics in twenty-first-century Mexico.

Picking up on these same far-reaching implications, chapter 4 pivots more explicitly towards the questions of pan-American geopolitics raised in each of the first two chapters. It takes into consideration a series of cultural objects – a travel book, a novel, and a feature film – that historicize the spatialization of race, nationhood, citizenship, and criminality in North America since the early nineteenth century. Broadly speaking, the chapter explores the colonial resonances of borders, which it positions among the tools by which modern territorial nation states attempt to assert control over the spatial distribution and movement of populations. Relative to the role of borders as signposts of territorial sovereignty, travel and border-crossing narratives constitute a privileged medium for exploring identities by means of differentiation, both from outsiders and from internal others. Lorenzo de Zavala's 1834 travel narrative *Viage a los Estados-Unidos del Norte de América* grapples with emerging geopolitical relations between the United States and Mexico in the first half of the nineteenth century. In the process Zavala employs a form of developmentalist historical reasoning articulated with emerging racial discourses about Mexico's Indigenous populations, a conceptual nexus that would crystalize into a new border ideology over the following century. The latter is registered in Daniel Venegas's 1928 satirical novel *Las aventuras de don Chipote, o Cuando los pericos mamen*, which highlights the racialization of the US-Mexico border in the early twentieth century and the concomitant criminalization of border crossing. What would have been unthinkable for Zavala, a Mexican criollo of European descent in the early days of independence, is that Mexico itself would come to occupy a place of racial otherness vis-à-vis the United States, a situation laid bare in Venegas's novel.

Finally, Diego Quemada-Diez's 2013 film *La jaula de oro* picks up the story in the twenty-first century, when Mexico has become something of a "vertical border" between the United States and the rest of Latin America, creating modes of displacement that operate unevenly across North and Central America and disturb codes of citizenship and belonging at a time when border ideologies and infrastructures seem to proliferate and harden in place. Taken together, these narratives speak to a complex history of racialization and criminalization by which the power structures of colonial spatialization have reproduced themselves within modern pan-American geopolitics, giving rise to a new coloniality at work within the territorializations of a global modernity mediated by transnational capital in the twenty-first century.

Chapter 4 traces the contours of this historical process by way of the conceptual framework of border studies. It situates contemporary migration issues within the practices of border thinking and travel narration as explored by Gloria Anzaldúa and Mary Louise Pratt. Anzaldúa's insistence on the mutual interdependence of selfhood and otherness as regulated by borders, and Pratt's insights on travel as a mode of identification through differentiation from presupposed others, establish a grounded framework for exploring hemispheric coloniality. The chapter highlights how the everyday experiences of people and communities in border spaces, and of those who travel across borders for one reason or another, bring about a variety of interactions with official geopolitical boundaries and the ideologies that ascribe meaning to them. Of course, the borders of territorial nation states are not the first such boundaries to have been instituted on the continent. Spanish colonial authorities had struggled since the earliest days of colonization to impose geographic boundaries on the migratory practices of a host of Indigenous populations in southwestern North America, a project carried over into the territorial consolidation of modern nation states from the nineteenth century to the present day. Over the centuries, however, the terms on which the boundaries are drawn and made to operate have evolved considerably. Colonial hierarchies, rearticulated into racial ideologies retroactively inscribed onto national identity and borders themselves, have come to define a modernity that is, in Pratt's terms, "neocolonial." If this is the case, however, it demands a critical reassessment of the centre/periphery spatial imaginary that continues to inform work on modernity's colonial heritage, including Pratt's. As the fourth chapter demonstrates, by the twenty-first century peripheral marginality is consistently reproduced throughout the geographic centres of global modernity in North America. Colonial distinctions continue to produce uneven exposure to vulnerability within the population but on other terms and within other spatializations. Our ability to account for the ongoing reproduction of coloniality in Mexico, and the Americas broadly, will require an engagement with this fundamental condition.

Chapter 5 brings the book to a close with a consideration of the symbolic relations between Mexico and Spain in the twenty-first century. Without flattening the vast internal differences within both Spain and Mexico, it identifies sites at which a mostly implicit, yet at times explicit, conflict over symbolic capital plays out, focusing on the politics of linguistic and cultural hegemony within the contested field of transatlantic Hispanism and Spain's uninterrupted institutionalization of Hispanidad. Among other conceptual registers, the chapter brings up Paul Gilroy's notion of "postcolonial melancholia," an incapacity to work through the loss of empire that in Spain takes the form of imperialist nostalgia. A particularly visible and pervasive manifestation of such melancholia is the "glottopolitics" at work in transatlantic Hispanism. Recent work in Hispanic linguistics has shown that, while linguists largely accept the notion that language is made up of multiple variants with no identifiable centre point, the prestige and symbolic power of different modes of expression within the Spanish-speaking world are subject to complex socio-political dynamics that produce deep inequalities. By bringing the glottopolitics of the everyday use of Spanish to bear on literary and film analysis, the chapter also implicitly dialogues with Pierre Bourdieu's treatment of the fields in which different kinds of power circulate. This becomes especially relevant as the chapter contextualizes its analysis within the politics of the Royal Spanish Academy (RAE), which continues to treat Castilian Spanish not as one regional variant of the language among many but as the norm of Spanish itself, in relation to which other variants deviate. The glottopolitics of the RAE find their expression in the fields of culture and politics as evinced in the success of novelist Arturo Pérez-Reverte's novels on the Spanish Empire and his foray into narcofiction, as well as in the ongoing refusal of most Peninsular politicians and academics to engage meaningfully with Spain's colonial history. The pervasiveness of such attitudes in Spain was made patently clear in the array of responses to AMLO's 2019 letter demanding an apology from the Spanish crown and the Catholic Church, responses that ranged from mildly defensive to outright affronted. Whatever intentions and politics might be identified behind AMLO's demand, its reception in Spain highlights a continued insistence on rallying to the defence of Spain's historical, linguistic, and cultural legacies vis-à-vis its former colonies.

Chapter 5 builds towards a reading of Mexican filmmaker Manolo Caro's Netflix-produced series *La casa de las flores*, released between 2018 and 2020. It argues that Caro's series attempts to imagine a future in which Mexico (and Spain) might overcome a colonial inheritance that has been passed down through generations in the form of repressive social structures; gendered, sexualized, and racialized violence and betrayal; and the unaddressed injustice of ingrained class differences. The chapter's analysis homes in on the linguistic politics of dialect and accent as a point of inflection at which to explore the series' treatment of this inheritance and the prospects for overcoming it. In pursuit of this reading, the chapter brings Caro's series into a productive dialogue with Pedro Almodóvar's 2004 film *La mala educación*. Refusing to yield to the narrative that Caro owes a debt of influence to the Spanish filmmaker, it contextualizes both works within the politics of historical memory and cultural hegemony characteristic of Hispanidad. While both emerge from a context in which Spain is positioned as the historic and linguistic centre of the Spanish-speaking world, Almodóvar's film, both in the process of its filming and in the final product itself, tacitly affirms this situation, whereas Caro's series points towards a potentially more productive critical engagement with these colonial legacies. Chapter 5 argues that the queering of gendered and linguistic normativity in Caro's series points towards possible avenues for acknowledging and remedying historic injustices in the name of better and more open futures. The sites of struggle explored here demonstrate that, however the spatial relationship between colony and metropole may have changed since the inauguration of Spanish colonialism in the Americas, the relationship itself continues to mediate the politics of linguistic and cultural prestige in the present day. Politics and cultural production in Mexico find themselves entangled in transatlantic networks of power and prestige, even as they are often explicitly aimed at overcoming the lingering effects of those very networks. It is for this reason, among a host of others explored in previous chapters, that Mexico's present and future continue to be routed through its colonial past.

What emerges from the interweaving of distinct perspectives and objects of study in these five chapters is a nuanced view of precisely how coloniality continues to mediate art, popular culture, and political discourse in present-day Mexico. This occurs not simply because the themes of colonialism continue to be brought up and reconsidered in contemporary contexts; if this were the case, it would be possible to imagine a future in which coloniality one day vanished from sight by dint of having been displaced by other topics. Rather, it is through the urgency with which new topics arise and demand our attention in the present, through the ongoing imperative to take action or undertake reflection and critique, that colonial spatializations continually re-emerge as the terrain upon which we are called to act and reflect. In other words, coloniality is the ground not only for the recurrence of the colonial but also for its overcoming, in such a way that it does not merely persist in the present but is also projected onto the future. The analyses contained in the chapters that follow bring this situation into view by considering objects of study that harbour within themselves a distinctly colonial inheritance, even though they most often make no explicit reference to Mexico's colonial period. Thus, in addition to the many contributions they make to the growing body of knowledge about Mexican coloniality, they may also serve as a guide for those who wish to explore the ways in which modernity, in Mexico and beyond, takes shape as an ongoing, constitutively incomplete working out of the spatio-temporal premises of the colonial.

Before turning to the chapters, a brief note is in order regarding the form of this book and the innovative process by which it was written and composed. Rather than a traditional collection of essays in an edited volume, *Contemporary Colonialities in Mexico and Beyond* is a collaborative work of scholarship. Each of the contributors has served as an interlocutor and editor for each of the others throughout the process, from the book's germinal stages in conference papers and informal conversations among colleagues to its final form. The irresistible spirit of collaboration even drew in the writer of this very introduction, who began as a research assistant. While each of the chapters is unmistakably the work of a single author, there are fewer contributors to this book than is common in a collection of essays, and the chapter lengths approximate those of scholarly monographs more closely than those of the shorter essays in many edited volumes. The result is a hybrid work, which offers a wide variety of case studies while sustaining a focused conceptual point of view. Each chapter brings distinct methodologies to bear on its objects of analysis in pursuit of a common objective: a deeper understanding of the colonial inheritance at work in the modern world as seen through contemporary Mexican literature, film, politics, and media. *Contemporary Colonialities in Mexico and Beyond* is thus a test case for a model of scholarship that is not common in the humanities but is a passion project for its contributors, who wish to see the dynamics of dialogue and exchange characteristic of academic life and scholarly work reflected in the field's publication practices.

WORKS CITED

Bentancor, Orlando. *The Matter of Empire: Metaphysics and Mining in Colonial Peru*. U of Pittsburgh P, 2017.

Dussel, Enrique. "Eurocentrism and Modernity (Introduction to the Frankfurt Lectures)." *Boundary 2*, vol. 20, no. 3, 1993, pp. 65–76.

Hanneken, Jaime. *Imagining the Postcolonial: Discipline, Poetics, Practice in Latin American and Francophone Discourse*. State U of New York P, 2015.

Lehmann, David. *After the Decolonial: Ethnicity, Gender and Social Justice in Latin America*. Polity, 2022.

Lugones, María. "The Coloniality of Gender." *Worlds and Knowledges Otherwise*, vol. 2, no. 2, 2008, pp. 1–17.

Moraña, Mabel, Enrique Dussel, and Carlos A. Jáuregui. "Colonialism and Its Replicants." *Coloniality at Large: Latin America and the Postcolonial Debate*, edited by Mabel Moraña, Enrique Dussel, and Carlos A. Jáuregui, Duke UP, 2008, pp. 1–20.

Nemser, Daniel. *Infrastructures of Race: Concentration and Biopolitics in Colonial Mexico*. U of Texas P, 2017.

Osborne, Peter. "Global Modernity and the Contemporary: Two Categories of the Philosophy of Historical Time." *Breaking Up Time: Negotiating the Borders between Present, Past and Future*, edited by Chris Lorenz and Berber Bevernage, Vandenhoeck and Ruprecht, 2013, pp. 69–84.

Quijano, Aníbal. "Coloniality of Power, Eurocentrism, and Latin America." *Nepantla: Views from South*, vol. 1, no. 3, 2000, pp. 533–80.

Seed, Patricia. "Colonial and Postcolonial Discourse." *Latin American Research Review*, vol. 26, no. 3, 1991, pp. 181–200.

Walsh, Catherine E., and Walter Mignolo. *On Decoloniality: Concepts, Analytics, Praxis*. Duke UP, 2018.

1 An Archaeology of Coloniality: José Emilio Pacheco's and Alfonso Cuarón's Colonia Roma

KATHLEEN ANN MYERS

Discussing his highly acclaimed film *Roma* (2018), which details life in middle-class Colonia Roma relative to the political repression and violence of the Partido Revolucionario Institucional (PRI) in 1970–1 Mexico City, Alfonso Cuarón explains that he chose this time and place in order to explore the spatiality of an ongoing class conflict that harkens back to colonial times. He argues, moreover, that the act of remembering this past prompts those of us who consume cultural commodities like his film to question our own culpability in perpetuating racial dynamics.[1] *Roma* takes place during the transition to Luis Echeverría Álvarez's presidency, and *Las batallas en el desierto* (1981), a best-selling novel by José Emilio Pacheco, recalls the memories of its narrator in this same Colonia Roma but decades before – towards the end of the authoritarian rule of Miguel Alemán Valdés (1951 and 1952) and the newly institutionalized PRI. The two presidencies function as bookends to the *milagro mexicano*: with Alemán's presidency there began a modernization process that led to unprecedented economic growth, which ended soon after Echeverría's term when the newly prosperous Mexico headed towards bankruptcy.[2]

Seemingly disparate in their presentation, the popular novel and the hit Netflix Original film both centre on domestic life as it unfolds in a quintessential middle-class neighbourhood in Mexico City during two key moments in Mexican history. As Pacheco's and Cuarón's

---

1 See the Netflix documentary *Road to Roma*. My deep thanks go to Nathan Douglas and Damián Solano Escolano, who provided valuable insight and commentary on this chapter. It further develops my article "An Archeology" on José Emilio Pacheco that was published in *Estudios Mexicanos*.

2 The *milagro mexicano* was portrayed as bringing political stability and economic growth to Mexico but it was also a period of increasing state violence. It ended in financial catastrophe in 1976 when the peso was devalued by 58 per cent.

protagonists navigate daily life within the socio-political spaces and conflicts that characterized those decades, we continually find references to quotidian social geographies plastered in PRI posters and developing in projects that seemed to monitor life, much like an Orwellian Big Brother.[3] Though the points of view by which we are projected into place differ – through the eyes of an adult narrator who looks back on his boyhood in *Las batallas en el desierto*, and through a camera lens that portrays a family's Indigenous nanny as part of a social landscape in *Roma* – I argue that both author and filmmaker select Colonia Roma in Mexico City as a site to excavate memories linked to PRI governance and thus to tell a story of the infrastructures of a continuing coloniality borne out of modernization processes.

In what follows I propose that the portrayals of racialized and spatialized interactions between classes in the novel and the film offer an archaeology of place, race, and modernity. As both Pacheco and Cuarón invite us to inhabit a recreated Colonia Roma in two different eras, they encourage us to uncover the memory and inner workings of socio-political systems and to interrogate a repression on the part of an enduring coloniality that continues to ignite debates about colonial legacies and contemporary coloniality. They depict how mid-twentieth-century modernization remapped space and class within what Aníbal Quijano describes as "the coloniality of power."[4] In other words, what these works register is an ongoing racialization of space that is made legible in the "refractory nature of those [colonial] practices of racial differentiation as they continue to inform the system of labor organization, laws, and political ideology" (Buscaglia-Salgado 109). Here I draw on the critical practice of spatial studies, looking beyond the flat representation of space, and instead study the multidimensionality of Pacheco's and Cuarón's works and how they highlight the key role of an active process of spatialization in modernity, predicated on colonial infrastructures of race and class. As Doreen Massey argues in *For Space*, a critical spatial approach allows us to examine the "potential geographies of our own social responsibility" (10). In this chapter I will examine the elaboration of social geographies in this best-selling novel and award-winning film and link the process to the phenomenon that historian Guy Beiner calls "social forgetting," which has to do with the continual resurfacing of private remembrances around histories largely

---

3 Orwell indirectly connects classism and state violence with self-proclaimed equalitarian revolutions, which can be summarized by the motto "We are all equals, but some are more equal than others."

4 See Quijano, "Coloniality of Power." See also Mignolo, *The Darker Side*.

suppressed by official narratives (15). In order to set the conceptual stage for the subsequent chapters in our volume, this chapter understands *Las batallas en el desierto* and *Roma* as points of interruption to the process of social forgetting, as works that allow absent histories to survive in the form of vernacular stories.

Both works also employ a fundamentally recursive temporal structure in order not only to return to the Colonia Roma but also, as we shall see in more detail below, to move beyond it. Pacheco's *Las batallas en el desierto* depicts a middle-class boy, Carlos, as he walks around the rapidly changing social landscape of Colonia Roma circa 1950. In Cuarón's film, through the eyes of a 1980s narrator who recalls his boyhood in the 1950s readers enter the same Colonia Roma, and at times the very same streets. Set some twenty years later, *Roma* separates the union of narrator and protagonist that characterizes Pacheco's novel as its camera lens follows an Indigenous live-in domestic worker, Cleo, as she performs her daily routines for an upper-middle-class family and, in one key scene, witnesses the 1971 Halconazo massacre that left about 120 people dead. In both cases, what appears first as private anguish begins to play out in the public sphere, as both Carlos's and Cleo's movements index a tacit social unrest that eventually erupts into violence that implicates not only the PRI state and US neocolonialist practices but also a class structure grounded on racialization.

We might therefore ask: Why do Pacheco and Cuarón not only centre their works in Colonia Roma but also return to events of earlier decades? And why have these works resonated so deeply with global audiences? One tentative answer is that these parallel narratives depict upper-middle-class families as they undergo dramatic change, wherein both protagonists must navigate the same neighborhood (known in Mexico City as *colonias*) whose history tells of space and race over centuries. Although the colonial spatial foundations date back to Hernán Cortés, Colonia Roma itself was not established until the early 1900s, when it was built over a former hacienda and kept separate from the largely Indigenous town of Aztacalco (originally a pre-Hispanic *altepemeh* given to Hernán Cortés in 1529 and later named Romita). Designed by the Porfiriato government to attract upper-class citizens who were leaving the old colonial city centre, Colonia Roma was part of an initiative to create modern areas that targeted specific social classes and were developed in large part by foreign companies. Established alongside public projects showcasing state history such as the elegant Paseo de la Reforma, this "new-world Rome" boasted modern European infrastructure with wide boulevards, Art Nouveau homes, and the first water-sewage treatment system in the area.[5] During the post–Second World War period an influx of lower-class migrants from rural Mexico and of refugees streamed into Mexico City and Colonia Roma, prompting many upper-class families to move out to newer, more distant colonias while government project housing was built in Roma. This population growth, paired with ambitious expansion projects, resulted in both an accelerated social change and a spike in urban violence. One of the most famous depictions of Colonia Roma / Romita during this period remains Luis Buñuel's film *Los olvidados* (1950), which portrays violence among a poverty-stricken generation that was betrayed by the post-revolutionary project. Steep social decline continued when the 1985 earthquake levelled many of the government public housing projects in the colonia and turned them to rubble.

The continual resignification of space on racial, cultural, and socio-economic terms in Colonia Roma offers a concrete and historically anchored space from which the artists explore patterns of socio-political change and attempt to counteract a process of social forgetting. It is through an immersion in personal stories, I argue, that both Pacheco and Cuarón allegorize a larger collective past and present, employing the formal techniques of their respective genres to privilege the role of space and place in a contemporary coloniality. Grounded as it is in acts of remembrance, this cinematic approach is a familiar one for Cuarón, for as Ignacio Sánchez Prado observes of the director's earlier film *Y tu mamá también* (2001), these personal memories "not only create a privileged perspective for the spectator ... [but] also question the very social world its spectators inhabit" (*Screening Neoliberalism* 190). At about the same time that Pacheco crafted his novel, moreover, literary and art critic John Berger argued that the new novelistic forms of the 1970s were helping to foreground the customary privileging of time and historicism, often at the expense of the key role of space. This new awareness, he posits, "is the result of our constantly having to take into account the simultaneity and extension of events ... Prophesy now involves a geographical rather than historical projection; it is space not time that hides consequences from us" (Berger 1974, quoted in Warf and Arias, 27). Pacheco and Cuarón not only inhabit the Colonia Roma as a place of social production but also explore the affordances of genre and of formal elements in the representation of a highly spatialized setting, inviting audiences to witness class conflict and to consider how spatialization produces and reproduces classism and racism over centuries.

---

5 For a history of Colonia Roma see Tavares López, *Colonia Roma*.

Technique is integral to theme as it foregrounds space as a constitutive of point of view.

To contextualize my readings of these vernacular stories of social forgetting and coloniality, I first explore historical practices and critical theories that connect spatialized racial practices with the development of colonialism and modernity. I then turn to a close reading of Pacheco's novel and, later, Cuarón's film, paying particular attention to the strategic depiction of space and social conflict. In particular, I suggest that the racial and class-bound category *indio* functions in each work as a public conscience for Mexico's cultural elite and bourgeois middle class. This use of the racial and conceptual category of the *indio* emerges first as a mirror for Pacheco's narrator and protagonist, Carlos; later it shifts wholly into the protagonist role as Cleo, the centre of Cuarón's cinematic portrayal.[6] In both works the tension between the socioeconomic spaces of the *indio* characters and those of the upper middle classes highlights a clash between two national post-revolutionary projects: a modernization as Americanization led by the elite "white" class, and the ideal of a mestizo nation built upon Mexico's Indigenous populations.[7] I conclude by suggesting the ways in which concepts such as social forgetting and geographies of responsibility help us ask new questions about how each artist implicates both their audiences and a state system in a contemporary coloniality.

The Colonial Triad: Space, Race, Modernity

Both *Las batallas en el desierto* and *Roma* trace topics that have long been issues within the early modern Spanish empire. When the Crown of Castile first established ideological communities and productive labour forces and resources in Las Indias, it began a process that would ultimately link space, race, and colonialism, forming a colonial triad. The *encomienda* system that controlled the Indigenous resources and

---

6   Although these categories of racialization have been often defined, Joshua Lund notes their referential ambivalence: mestizo and *indio* refer to subjects and communities as well as socio-historical processes. The category of the *indio* is "the outcome of a historical trajectory of identification that depends on a colonial gaze backed by force, a gaze that dialectically homogenizes (the monolithic Indian) while producing difference .... The Indian thus functions rhetorically as both emblem and social relation" ("The Mestizo State" 1431). In this essay I employ the original colonial nomenclature, *indio*, to connote its continued use over the centuries in different historical contexts and texts.

7   See also Contreras, *In the Shadow of the Giant.*

peoples in exchange for their evangelization began to rehearse in the Americas a series of practices that continue to suture relations of economic exploitation to the biopolitical imaginary of population. This initial process unified efforts between church and crown as it drew on a concept of *limpieza de sangre* (blood purity), including its familiar hierarchy between Europe's Old and New Christians. Soon other corollaries emerged, such as the *congregración*, *concentración*, and *reducción*, which moved originally separate ethnic and political groups into combined Indigenous communities under ecclesiastical control. One juridical corollary was the *empadronamiento*, which was first employed under the Roman Empire to control people and distribute space. The Crown refurbished the concept's civic infrastructure in order to define the *indio* as a subject pertaining to a communal land system rather than as a phenotype.[8] These new spatial formations segregated indigenous populations while functioning alongside new European-styled gridded cities for people of Spanish descent.[9] Thus, a historical process emerged by which colonial governance took shape through not only the occupation of territory and control of its inhabitants but also the reorganization of space and spatial practices.

Although the initial division and spatialization of groups into *repúblicas de indios* and *repúblicas de españoles* quickly broke down, by the end of the colonial period a central result of this spatialization of territory and colonial power was the creation of a homogenized Indigenous, or *indio*, subject. In an attempt to consolidate Indigenous ethnic groups and classes into a single category and thus consolidate colonial power, white Europeans and criollos created a complex system of racialization that developed into the *castas* or categories of mixed ancestry that included bloodlines from native America, Africa, and Asia. These *castas* soon became associated with certain spaces, material culture, and daily practices in New Spain. The most well-known visual representations of this consolidation are the eighteenth-century paintings known as the *cuadros de casta* (see fig. 1.1).[10]

---

8   With the laws of 1550–60, known as the *redistribución fiscal*, for example, all *altepetl*, regardless of ethnicity and language difference, became *pueblos de indios*, and all commoners ("*macehualtin*") and low-ranking nobles were categorized as *indios*, while the high-ranking nobles and *tlahtoque* became *caciques*. Each pueblo received a land share in a communal land system, and being *empadronado* within it became a de facto juridical definition of being *indio*, rather than a person being defined by phenotype. See Ouweneel and Hoekstra, "Las tierras de los pueblos de indios."

9   For a more detailed study of this centuries-long historical process in New Spain, see especially Nemser, *Infrastructures of Race*.

10   For additional work on the important relationships beween *estado*, *casta*, and *limpieza de sangre* see Martínez, *Genealogical Fictions* (especially 17–23); Hill, *Hierarchy, Commerce, and Fraud* (especially ch. 5, "Before Race"); and Saldaña-Portillo, *Indian Given*.

Figure 1.1. *Cuadro de Castas* (eighteenth century). This anonymous painting from colonial Mexico details the phenotypes and names of sixteen different castes recognized in eighteenth-century Mexico. The emphasis is on the biological combinations and customs resulting from the mixing of Indigenous, African, and European populations. From D.R. Instituto Nacional de Antropología e Historia, Mexico. This work is licensed under the CC BY-NC-ND 4.0 Licence.

Recently many theorists have called attention to spatial organization in early and late colonialism, considering it as the occupation of space and arrangement of people within it by Europeans in order for them to exploit local resources and labour forces. A notable theorist is Achille Mbembe, who observes that an important aspect of this process is "the manufacturing of a large reservoir of cultural imaginaries," the "writing on the ground [of] a new set of social and spatial relations" ("Necropolitics" 25–6). Drawing on Frantz Fanon's work, Mbembe points out that "the colonial state derives its fundamental claim of sovereignty and legitimacy from the authority of its own particular narrative of history and identity ... These imaginaries gave meaning to the enactment of differential rights to differing categories of people for different purposes within the same space; in brief, the exercise of sovereignty. Space was therefore the raw material of sovereignty and the violence it carried with it" (27). Literary scholar Joshua Lund further studies the development of this space-race-colonial relation but focuses on how it became intertwined with ideologies of modernity as nineteenth-century liberals reformulated ideas about "the colonization" of lands and Indigenous inhabitants.[11] In fact, Mexico's constitutions (1824, 1857, and 1917) tended to "disappear" Indigenous populations. It is only with the constitutional reforms in 2001 that the terms referring to *indio* or *indígena* reappear as an integral part of the nation.[12] The post-revolutionary state refocused this triad in order to create a centralized, ideological "mestizo state," built upon the assimilation of Mexico's Indigenous populations while continuing to define an essential link to its original populations.[13] Elaborating on Lund's work, colonial scholar Daniel Nemser details

---

11   Lund argues that the nineteenth-century liberal colonization program "became explicitly entangled with the articulation of a national conundrum that, by the end of the century, would have a generic name and a number of illustrious commentators: el problema del indio" (*The Mestizo State* 11). Unlike colonialism under the Spanish Empire, this nineteenth-century national project's land usage was "a developmental scheme thinly draped over a project of conquest, a state-sponsored version of what, around the same time, Marx would call 'primitive accumulation'" ("The Mestizo State" 1420).

12   The 2001 amendment adds to artículo 2º, "La Nación Mexicana es única e indivisible" (The Mexican nation is one and indivisible): "La Nación tiene una composición pluricultural sustentada originalmente en sus pueblos indígenas que son aquellos que descienden de poblaciones que habitaban en el territorio actual del país al iniciarse la colonización" (Mexico; "The Nation has a multicultural composition based originally on its Indigenous peoples, who are those descended from populations that inhabited the current territory of the country at the beginning of colonization").

13   Lund notes that *indigenismo* emerged in intellectual, governmental, and aesthetic ventures, and it pressed "the case for the Indian's formal equality, [but] ends with a de facto call for de-Indianization" ("The Mestizo State" 1430).

how early colonization practices over three centuries created an "infrastructure of race" that was "a powerful reminder that certain material structures and practices can endure the vicissitudes of history and politics. And if race itself has an infrastructural function, it may continue to operate in this way as well" (20). The colonial processes of "writing on the ground a new set of social and spatial relations" (Mbembe, "Necropolitics" 24) that had begun with the first wave of Europeans were in this way revised into new paradigms for a modern, urban utopia built upon the ideological project of the body politic defined, on the one hand, by its state of mestizaje and, on the other, by a corollary national imaginary: *mexicanidad*.

With its complex genealogy of race associated with certain projections of space and degrees of civilization and modernity, this basic triad continued to develop in the twentieth century. During this time the post-revolutionary state revived liberal reforms that sought to decrease the control of the Church while instituting economic, ideological, and cultural campaigns aimed at incorporating the *indio* into a secular national project. Mexico's post-revolutionary president Lazaro Cárdenas, for example, emphasized the need to acculturate *pueblos de indios* and build infrastructure in order to integrate them into the nation and national economy.[14] This was preceded by Minister of Culture José Vasconcelos's schema of a *"raza cósmica"* intended to constitute a superior race of mestizos and a strong, unified nation.[15] These mestizo statesmen promulgated a symbolic and literal "second conquest," arguing for processes of assimilation, civilization, and the bureaucratic management of population in order to bring about full national citizenship and a centralized mestizo state.[16] In this way the sustaining contradiction of government by monarchical power – a divine right embodied in the king that placed him above those whom he ruled and below the heavenly source from which the power emanated – came to be renewed for the modern age. A double move became necessary to buttress Mexico's claims to racial superiority against white Anglo-America, as well as the brand of commodity fetishism it had come to preach. Indigeneity was alternatively struck at, erased, or sublimated, and idealized into a pure genetic hybridity.

By the post–Second World War and the Cold War era and its push for modernization, US hegemony had resulted in a new coloniality of power that clashed with state-defined mestizaje and *mexicanidad*. As

---

14 See Cárdenas, "El problema indígena de México" (8–9).

15 See Vasconcelos, *La raza cósmica*.

16 Claudio Lomnitz-Adler details this ideological rhetoric of a second conquest and the accompanying narrative of needing to redeem the *indio*; see *Exits from the Labyrinth* (261–81).

theorist Nelson Maldonado-Torres elaborates, secularism and capitalism helped transfigure the ideology behind racial stratification, in which cultural practices that exhibited a high degree of Americanization became associated with civilization and modernity (71). Both *Las batallas en el desierto* and *Roma* explore this clash between a neocolonial modernity and a mestizo state ideology with reference to this age of Mexico City's exponential growth. At the time Vasconcelos was writing, Mexico City boasted 720,000 inhabitants. As land reform and structural economic change forced migration from the countryside, however, the population of Mexico City grew to nine million by 1970 and to fourteen million by 1980. These migratory waves challenged the idyllic bourgeois narrative of a post-revolutionary utopia, as a reality of violence and increased racial tensions pointed to the failure of the state project of modernization. The state's response to these changes continued to draw from the spatial playbook of colonialism.

The development of spatial theories that emerged out of the critique of the Western privileging of time and historicism can further help us view these ongoing colonial processes. In the same era of social unrest in Mexico that influenced Pacheco and Cuarón, French theorists Michel Foucault and Henri Lefebvre studied spatialization and social production. Foucault examined the organization of space as a key to capitalism and developed his theory of heterotopias to think about space as created. Meanwhile Lefebvre detailed how the production of space was not a concrete, objective entity but rather a combination of spatial practices, lived spaces, and representations. Drawing on these ideas, Latin American scholar Edward W. Soja advanced his concept of the "socio-spatial dialectic," or the triangular relationship among time, space, and social structures, arguing that while social processes shape and explain geographies, "geographies [also] shape and explain social processes and social action" (22).[17]

When Foucault developed his theory of biopolitics in the 1970s, he linked it to the way in which sovereign, and later state, regimes developed technologies to control populations through hierarchies that became the basis of racism. Arguing that racism as such first develops with colonization and genocide, he posits: "What in fact is racism? It is

---

17   This formulation of history as materially constructed is complicated by the porous nature of terms like *space* and *place*. In her influential work Doreen Massey warns against an easy dichotomy. In the general formulation, *place* is a product of acts or practices of spatialization, and *space* is the conceptual placeholder of all such spatializations. Yet in this framework, space, like time, would be neither thinkable nor experienceable as such; it would only come to us in the form of layered places constituted by the implicitly and explicitly spatializing dimensions of work, politics, consumption, and everyday life in general (11–12).

primarily a way of introducing a break into the domain of life that is under power's control: the break between what must live and what must die" (254). In other words, "the first function of racism [is] to fragment, to create caesuras within the biological continuum addressed by biopower" (255).[18] Later, in *Security, Territory, Population*, Foucault develops further the way in which over time biopolitical practices come to organize urban spaces. In so doing, he brings a concept of spatialization together with social practices, demonstrating their ongoing construction of racism.

Drawing on Foucault, Achille Mbembe examines how the construction of colonial space founds the biopolitics of racial stratification. He argues that these violent processes can evolve into "necropolitics," in which "to kill or to allow to live constitute the limits of sovereignty, its fundamental attributes. To exercise sovereignty is to exercise control over mortality and to define life as the deployment and manifestation of power" ("Necropolitics" 11–12). Key to this process, however, is that both private citizens' actions and state operations produce or reproduce the violence of this biopolitical stratification. With reference to the spatial practices that began in colonial Mexico, Daniel Nemser further ties together biopolitics and necropolitics – the differential exposure to life and death – with race and colonialism. He argues that pastoral care and extractive domination are "two expressions of a single modality of power" instituted with colonization and its spatialized practices (18).

In the modern Mexican state, racialized patterns of violence have tended to emerge at the sites of national anxiety – sites in which a pastoral racial cohesion has failed to attain the social relations promised, and social relations have been instituted instead by force of law. Several practices of the mid-twentieth-century PRI state in Mexico – and in particular, as Jean Franco notes in *Cruel Modernity*, the 1971 Halconazo massacre – exemplify this modality of modern power.[19] Similarly, state violence circumscribed to particular spaces and classes became the core of both Pacheco's and Cuarón's works. Yet as we shall now see in more detail, both artists go further than simply pointing to state violence; they implicate readers and viewers in an ongoing coloniality that is

---

18   Biopolitics refers to the political strategies and technologies used by the state to discipline individual bodies by intervening at the level of the population; see Foucault, *Society Must Be Defended* (239–63, especially 241–2). Foucault warns, "Once the State functions in the biopower mode, racism alone can justify the murderous function of the State" (256).

19   Franco writes: "Becoming modern meant overcoming underdevelopment by loosening the drag of those sectors of the population that were stigmatized as 'downstream,' 'unproductive,' 'traditional' ... That is why the urgency of modernization transposed racism into a different key and turned the indigenous from an exploited labor force into a negative and undesirable mass" (8).

built into both spatial practices and cultural metanarratives of Mexico and *mexicanidad*. A study of the spatial projections of racial difference reveals how Pacheco and Cuarón perform archaeological excavations of its socio-cultural and institutional evolution into a new coloniality of power in mid-twentieth-century Mexico.

Pacheco's Colonia Roma: Social Forgetting, Modernity, and the Coloniality of Space

Beginning with the sentence "Me acuerdo, no me acuerdo," through to the emphatic closing lines, "Demolieron la Colonia Roma ... terminó aquel país. No hay memoria del México de aquellos años," José Emilio Pacheco's *Las batallas en el desierto* depicts an inextricable link between place, social class, memory, and an emerging modernity in mid-twentieth-century Mexico City.[20] As the adult narrator, Carlos, recalls his youth, he evokes the material worlds and spatial racialization of classes at school and at the homes of his schoolmates as Mexico moved to modernize. Much of this modernity, he recalls, was based on new patterns of material and cultural consumption:

> Mientras tanto nos *modernizábamos*, incorporábamos a nuestra habla términos que primero habían soñado como pochismos en las películas de Tin Tan y luego insensiblemente se mexicanizaban: tenquíu, oquéi, uasamara, sherap, sorry, uan móment pliis. Empezábamos a comer hamburguesas, pays, donas, jotdogs, malteadas, áiscrim, margarina, mantequilla de cacahuate. La cocacola sepultaba las aguas frescas de jamaica, chía, limón. Los pobres seguían tomando tepache. Nuestros padres se habituaban al jaibol que en principio les supo a medicina. En mi casa está prohibido el tequila, le escuché decir a mi tío Julián. Yo nada más sirvo whisky a mis invitados: *hay que blanquear el gusto de los mexicanos*.[21] (11; emphasis added)

---

20   "I remember, I don't remember" (81); "they demolished the Roman Quarter ... That country was finished. There is no memory of the Mexico of those years" (116–17). Page numbers for all English-language translations of *Las batallas en el desierto* come from Katherine Silver's translation unless otherwise noted.

21   "In the meantime we modernized and incorporated into our vocabulary terms that had sounded like Chicanoisms when we had first heard them in the Tin Tan movies and then slowly, imperceptibly, they had become Mexicanized: *tenquiu, oquei, uasamara, sherap, sorry, uan moment pliis*. We began to eat *hamburguesas, pays, donas, jotdogs, malteadas, áiscrim, margarina, pinutbuter*. Fresh juice drinks of lemon, jamaica, and sage were buried by Coca-Cola. Only the very poor continued to drink *tepache*. Our parents soon got used to drinking *jaibol*, even though at first it had tasted to them like medicine. Tequila is prohibited in my house, I once heard my Uncle Julián say. I serve only whisky to my guests: we must whitewash the taste of Mexicans" (82–3).

As the protagonist, Carlos, and his family change daily habits, practices of consumption, languages, and residence over the course of the story, the author depicts a slow violence caused by post–Second World War Americanization and the politics of the ruling PRI. Through a series of indirect references, he suggests that this process was not far removed from the Porfiriato dictatorship that the Mexican Revolution had fought against. Commenting on the infrastructure and public monuments that had been inaugurated to herald a new modern era, the middle-aged narrator looks back on his youth and wryly quips that these all turned out to be *"un montón de piedras"* (a mountain of rubble). Yet the dynamic socio-economic processes of Americanization by which consumerism became the new culture, and culture became newly consumed, underscore a more lasting change: a new racialization supporting Mexico's bid for modernity.

While scholars often note Pacheco's frequent references to place in this new racialized modernity, none has studied how the spatialization of the scenes is the foundation upon which all the narrative layers are built.[22] Before we even know the name of our protagonist and narrator, he emphasizes his place of origin and that place seems to create destiny: "Ciudad en penumbra, misteriosa colonia Roma de entonces. Átomo del inmenso mundo, dispuesto muchos años antes de mi nacimiento *como una escenografía para mi representación*" (27; emphasis added).[23] Rather than simply refer to the quintessentially middle-class neighbourhood of Colonia Roma as a place (e.g., *un lugar, un escenario*), the narrator employs a theatrical term, *escenografía* ("scenography"), following ancient Greek drama tradition and the use of urban space to stage debates about social problems. Colonia Roma is the set in an urban drama, a stage for the characters within it. The concrete place is highlighted as a spatial index for the permutations of the impasses of modernity and the new process of "whitening" encouraged by capitalism, the new *"marcas de clase."* As noted, Colonia Roma was built under the Porfiriato government and over colonialized lands, in tandem with public projects such as the Paseo de la Reforma, an elegant boulevard designed to showcase state history by the erection of triumphant memorials to Columbus, Cuauhtémoc, and independence. Later, as the city's population explosion accelerated social change, Colonia Roma filled

---

22 See Epple, "De Santa a Mariana"; Barrantes, "Transformaciones seculares"; Ruiz, "El reverso del 'milagro mexicano'"; and Wolfenzon, *"Las batallas en el desierto."*

23 "A city immersed in semi-darkness: the mysterious Roman Quarter of those days. An atom in the immense world, prepared many years before my birth like a stage set for my performance" (93).

with migrants and immigrants, and the upper classes moved on to yet more exclusive areas of the city, such as Las Lomas de Chapultepec.

As the narrator reveals some of this remapping of space and class in mid-century Mexico, he showcases a stratification of legacies, ideals, and hegemony effected through biopolitical means. As noted earlier, the colonial process of what Mbembe calls "writing on the ground a new set of social and spatial relations" began early with accounts of conquest and colonization, such as those by Hernán Cortés and Bernal Díaz, depicting the city of Tenochtitlan as a place of wonder and civilization that was also menaced by a barbaric underbelly of "idolatrous" Mexica practices. The rewriting of space and race continued throughout the colonial period with works such as Bernardo Balbuena's epic "La grandeza mexicana" (1604), which further established the trope of backwards *indios* in relation to the new criollo elite. These narratives of identity were backed by various institutional sources of legitimacy and continued through the nineteenth and twentieth centuries.

Scholars have noted the relationship between material culture and modernity in Pacheco's novel but rarely delve into the specific use of place beyond linking it with the United States. Florence Moorhead-Rosenberg, for example, examines how Carlos's family becomes "entirely dominated by trademark United States cultural colonialism. Their economic journey can be mapped along various routes" (19). Moreover, as Saúl Jiménez Sandoval observes, "se sitúa en un espacio ya controlado por las fuerzas económicas de Estados Unidos que territorializan con una cultura y forma de ser disfrazadas bajo el velo de la modernización carente" (443).[24] Other scholars argue that *Las batallas en el desierto* is exemplary of the literary movement that critiqued the post-revolutionary project of a utopian city. Nestor García Canclini, for example, discusses the challenges of writing about the city as a whole and cites Pacheco's novel as an example. Rather than develop this connection, however, he focuses on how the novelist reveals the abject failure of this social promise and calls attention to fissures in the literary movement of Latin American Boom and its totalizing narratives.[25]

I contend that Pacheco's insistence on *escenografía* is critical to understanding the role of Colonia Roma as a place and reveals how the protagonist's recollections are as beholden to the places in which he situates them – places that largely no longer exist – as they are to how they exist in his own sense of memory. Carlos assembles and breaks

---

24   Barrantes links this to the original Spanish conquest, and Ruiz discusses it as a "vampire-like" relationship.

25   García Canclini, "Narrar la multiculturalidad."

down the staging of events and places to accommodate the vignettes that play through his mind, highlighting a sensation of place within the confines of current reality. This *escenografía* encapsulates how the past-present that Carlos is trying to reconstruct is a networked assemblage of founding ideologies and a persistent coloniality found in the infrastructures of race and class.[26] As Massey observes, "[s]pace can never be that completed simultaneity in which all interconnections have been established, and in which everywhere is already linked with everywhere else," for the production of space also includes "loose ends and missing links: For the future to be open, space must be open too" (11–12). We see these spaces and histories first within a public school, then in upper-, middle-, and lower-class neighbourhoods and homes, and finally along Colonia Roma's iconic avenues and plaza.

Public School: Conflicting Discourses of Race, Nation, and Modernity

Las batallas en el desierto begins in a public school that Carlos attends for less than a year while his father's soap factory is going under and before his father is hired by its American replacement. In the classroom we first witness the inability of his teacher, Mondragón, to combat the inherited racism and classism present in the public space, even though it was "una escuela de pelados. ... admiten al hijo de una cualquiera" (Pacheco, *Las batallas en el desierto* 43).[27] Echoing the conquest topoi of Mexico as a new world paradise filled with riches to develop Spanish colonialism, the school books depict Mexico as a "cornucopia" of resources that Alemanismo will use to develop a modern, urban Mexico:

> Para el impensable año dos mil se auguraba – sin especificar cómo íbamos a lograrlo – un porvenir de plenitud y bienestar universales. Ciudades limpias, sin injusticia, sin pobres, sin violencia, sin congestiones, sin basura.

---

26 I borrow this concept of networked assemblages of race and class from Jasbir K. Puar (who develops it from the work of Gilles Deleuze and Félix Guattari). In the conclusion to *Terrorist Assemblages* she articulates the concept thus: "As opposed to an intersectional model of identity, which presumes that components – race, class, gender, sexuality, nation, age, religion – are separable analytics and can thus be disassembled, an assemblage is more attuned to interwoven forces that merge and dissipate time, space, and body against linearity, coherency, and permanency" (212). Puar continues this encounter between the Deleuze-Guattarian assemblage and the biopolitics according to Foucault and Mbembe in *The Right to Maim*; see especially, "'Will Not Let Die': Debilitation and Inhuman Biopolitics in Palestine" (129–54).

27 "A school for beggars ... they admit the child of anybody" (104; translation modified).

> Para cada familia una casa ultramoderna y aerodinámica (palabras de la
> época) ... El paraíso en la tierra. La utopía al fin conquistada.[28] (10–11)

National textbooks mandated "obediencia, lengua nacional, y geografía," indoctrinating children into state hegemony, ethnonationalist
mexicanidad, and a territorial concept of Mexico. School children saw
the incumbent Miguel Alemán as "joven, sonriente, simpático, brillante,"[29] overseer of a national project similar to a panoptic Orwellian
Big Brother. They attended ribbon-cutting ceremonies for new infrastructure and monuments that were never finished, and heard about a
wealthy future for all. Observing the era from a distance of thirty years,
the narrator ironically juxtaposes this utopian propaganda with the actual corruption. The PRI's "utopia por fin conquistada" was, in fact, a
dual conquest; it was both an invasion from the north ("las compañías
norteamericanas invadieron el mercado nacional") and a state process
led by a president who sold out Mexico ("está chingando a México"
and was "robando hasta lo que no hay"; 45, 18).[30] Later, the novel closes
with an apocalyptic vision of the demolition of the city that he had
known.

The liberal urban maestro attempts to use the school as a social space
to unite Mexicans, to fight inherited classism and racism. He insists on
their common birthplace to unite them, on identity and *mexicanidad*:
"Udstedes nacieron aquí; son mexicanos" (13).[31] Mondragón directs
this comment to the Jewish and Arab students who are living the same
conflict as re-enacted by the other boys. Recess mimics ethnic wars:
their game "las batallas en el desierto" is based on the Arab-Israeli War
of 1948–9 and divides the boys into bands of Arabs and Jews, who now
fight each other in a modern variation of *moros y cristianos*. Now, however, it is *judíos* versus *moros*, the ethnic populations forced to convert to
Christianity or face exile in the early modern Spanish empire. The game
underscores how Mexico's period of rapid change was part of a long
history of multiple conquests, invasions, and subjugations and still was
in the aftermath of the long Mexican Revolution and the Cristero War.

---

28   "For a still unimaginable 2000, a future of plenitude and universal well-being was
     predicted, without specifying just how it would be achieved. Clean cities without
     injustice, poor people, violence, congestion, or garbage. Every family with an ultra-
     modern and aerodynamic (words from that era) house ... Paradise on earth. Finally,
     utopia will have been found" (82; translation modified).
29   "Young, smiling, personable, and brilliant."
30   "North American companies invaded the national market" (105); "fucking Mexico ...
     even stealing what isn't there to steal" (87).
31   "You were born here. You are Mexican" (83; translation modified).

The game depends on ethnic difference between two groups that have historically been dismantled in the Hispanic world. Yet, in the end, as the narrator notes: "Para mí, niño de la colonia Roma, árabes y judíos eran 'turcos'" (13).[32] Both groups are pitted against the Spanish, the white *cristianos*. Within this same school environment Carlos recalls the sons of an American industrialist who makes the Mexican people his "eternos aprendices" (23) and of a Japanese industrialist who will have "cuatro mil esclavos mexicanos" (14).[33] While Carlos is sensitive to the emerging geopolitical and ethnic relationships in the post–Second World War world, the liberal maestro tries in vain to resolve ethnic conflict on the basis of birthright citizenship.

Even as Pacheco evokes the historic Arab-Israeli War, he also offers new areas of colonization and conflict. Despite the rhetoric of equality espoused by the maestro, the Mexican state continued to support the racial structures of colonialism through the processes of Americanization. The situation Carlos and his friends encounter fails to suggest a path to easy victory over the overwhelming face of US influence and the PRI; it points, rather, to the longue durée of power and colonization as the play wars register allegorically what happens outside the school compound. While his teacher and school recall the liberal idealism according to which, regardless of social class, all pupils have the same rights and responsibilities, the inequalities re-emerge after school. The social contract of post-revolutionary Mexico encouraged forgiveness and forgetting. The maestro mandates: "No hereden el odio" (13).[34] The scene unveils the colonizing process of racism as inherited and transformed through the materiality of space and continues to inform divisions of race and class.

Using the school as a space to depict a past utopian dream and the present failure of the liberal project, the narrator notes that the maestro resigns himself to a future of more racism and war: "se preguntaba qué iba a ser de nosotros con los años, cuántos males y cuántas catástrofes aún estarían por delante." The narrator comments sarcastically as he posits, "[¿D]e ese horror quién puede tener nostalgia[?]" (60).[35] Widening his field of address with an interrogative, he includes

---

32 "For me, a child of the Roman Quarter, both Jews and Arabs were 'Turks'" (83).
33 "Eternal apprentices" (90); "four thousand Mexican slaves" (84).
34 "Don't pass on the hatred" (83).
35 "He asked himself what would become of us over the years, how many evils and catastrophes were we yet to witness" (84; translation modified); "who could feel nostalgic for that horror?" (117).

the readers, prompting them to interrogate their own complicity in the process. Beyond this final moment, the novel's constant shifts between (a grammatical) past, present, and future force the readers to navigate this wobbly field and to attempt to answer for themselves the questions about truth that go unanswered in the novel.

Mexico City's Colonias and the Spatialization of Class

Within this larger national narrative of social conflict built upon a tacit racism and classism, the narrator emphasizes the more circumscribed place of Carlos's home in Colonia Roma and the family's social class as "el lugar de enmedio" ("the place in between"). The young adolescent's brother underscores their shared situation with Colonia Roma's declining social status: "Somos puritito mediopelo, típica familia venida a menos de la colonia Roma: la esencial clase media mexicana" (43).[36] His mother, born into an elite Porfirista family that had migrated to Mexico City when their house was taken after the revolution, detests the post-revolutionary/capitalist city, especially Colonia Roma: "Odiaba la colonia Roma porque empezaban a desertarla las buenas familias y en aquellos años la habitaban árabes y judíos y gente del sur: campechanos, chiapanecos, tabasqueños, yucatecos" (21).[37]

Yet it is this very place of "el lugar de enmedio" that allows Carlos to access other social spaces. He visits the homes of three boys: two on either end of the class system and one who floats in the middle. This latter boy belongs nowhere and reflects, to a degree, Carlos's own unstable position in the middle class, a place from which he can compare himself to both a wealthy white boy and a poor *indio*. As the boy surveys the material culture, patterns of consumption, and behaviour of distinct classes, it provokes an assessment of his own place within the emerging biopolitical stratifications of class and race in the PRI state. He is a *flaneur*, a marginal observer who witnesses the city's modernization as he walks through it. These private viewings of the homes are always placed within the macrosystem of Mexico City's colonias, thus allowing us to witness the ways in which urban planning and its infrastructure of race deepen classism and racism.

---

36 "We are right where we belong: a typical Roman Quarter family on the way down: the essence of the Mexican middle class" (104).

37 "She hated the Roman Quarter because all the good families were beginning to move out and only Arabs, Jews, and Southerners – people from Campeche, Chiapas, Tabasco, Yucatan – were moving in" (89).

When Carlos visits the home of the American Harry Atherton (a boy he had known at his first school, the Colegio México, before moving to the public school), he surveys the new class at the pinnacle of this social hierarchy. Notably, the Atherton home is not in Colonia Roma but rather in the posh Colonia Las Lomas de Chapultepec, which was first established in the 1930s for Mexico City's elite and later expanded into Bosques de las Lomas when demand for mansions increased with the influx of foreigners with deep pockets. The Atherton home exudes material wealth with its pool, gym, billiard-room, and library, and it is here that Carlos first experiences racism in which he is the target. The adult narrator reconstructs a scene that he probably could not have understood at the time. The family speaks in English and makes racist comments about Carlos at the dinner table: "Sus padres no me dirigieron la palabra y hablaron todo el tiempo en inglés. Honey, how do you like the little Spic? He's a midget, isn't he?" (23). Later Harry comments on Carlos's poor table manners, unbefitting a well-bred person. A new language, racism, and class system emerge along with the developing neocolonialism of "transnacionales" who, as Carlos notes, "invadieron el mercado nacional" and colonized Mexicans as laborers within their own country, imposing English as the new language of socio-economic power (45). During the visit we learn that Harry only attends Roma's middle-class school so that he can meet his future employees. The privileged criollo class was being replaced not only by PRI's bureaucrats, referred to as "Ali Baba y sus 40 ladrones" (18) and "cacharros de la revolución" (25), but also by US entrepreneurs.[38] Soon after the visit Carlos and his father submit to the new power structure represented by an "inglés obligatorio" (41), feverishly learning English in order to work in "servicio de la empresa norteamericana" (53).[39] They adapt to modern, Americanized consumer culture and move out of Colonia Roma. The Athertons' lifestyle in Colonia Las Lomas becomes the new idealized model for an aspiring Mexican middle class.

When Carlos visits the socio-economically marginalized Colonia Doctores to secure class notes from his schoolmate Rosales, an *indio* on financial aid who had been bullied, we see how Carlos himself has already learned to instrumentalize his classmate. Rosales is not a person but a set of data to be used; he comments that Rosales is "un excelente alumno, el de mejor letra y ortografía, y todos lo utilizábamos para estos favores." Alternatively, he also calls Rosales "un indio pendejo"

---

38 "Ali Baba and the Forty Thieves" (86); "The Cub of the Revolution" (91).
39 "Mandatory English" (109); "in service of the North American company that had bought him out" (110; translation modified).

in a school skirmish (22–3; order modified).[40] The narrator lingers on a territorialization of poverty as he sketches the actual borders of the colonia where "los indios" Peralta and Rosales lived: "Ellos no pagaban colegiatura, estaban becados, vivían en las vecindades ruinosas de la colonia de los Doctores. La calzada de La Piedad, todavía no llamada avenida Cuauhtémoc, y el parque Urueta formaban la línea divisoria entre Roma y Doctores" (14).[41] Like other colonias in Mexico City, Doctores reveals a layered history. Still considered one of the most dangerous neighbourhoods, Colonia Doctores was originally called La Indianilla, after a group of Indigenous women who reportedly sold the land to an investor. Once it was developed, however, it was called Hidalgo to honour the hero of the War of Independence. Later, to reflect the presence of an important medical centre there, the name changed again to Doctores, and streets themselves were renamed to honour famous physicians. An archaeological layering of Indigenous lands, private investors and developers, ideological state naming, and popular vernacular usage comes to the fore when the adult narrator comments on the renaming of the street that forms the border of Doctores and Roma. The street, originally named after Río Piedad, a river that is now underground, was changed under the PRI to memorialize Cuauhtémoc, the heroic Mexica ruler who was the last to surrender to Cortés. The new name, Avenida Cuauhtémoc, establishes a border between middle-class Roma and the racialized poverty of Colonia Doctores. Reflecting on state practices of ideologically mapping sites of memory in order to contain ethnic/class stratification, the narrator deliberately comments on layers of street names and, in doing so, performs an archaeology of space, race, and the discourse of *mexicanidad*.

As Carlos crosses the border into Doctores, it seems to define his own place in the socio-economic construction of the city. He registers seeing raw sewage in the muddy streets, a traditional sleeping *petate* (mat) on Rosales's living-room floor, and quesadillas made with brain. This material culture and lack of infrastructure highlights the poverty of families living in Doctores. When Carlos shares a meal with Rosales, he reveals both the ironic relativity of social status and the ideological process by which one learns how social classes maintain clear

---

40 "An excellent student, the best in composition and spelling, and we all took advantage of him for things of this sort"; "[a] fucking Indian" (90–1; order modified).

41 "They did not pay tuition; they were on scholarship; they lived in the rundown neighborhood called the Doctors Quarter. The Highway of Piety – not yet renamed Cuauhtémoc Avenue – and Urueta Park formed the border line between the Roman Quarter and Doctors" (83–4).

boundaries by establishing difference and performing repulsion. Just as Harry had criticized Carlos's table etiquette, Carlos now remarks on being repulsed by Rosales's manners. The middle class, susceptible to change, was often assertive of its difference vis-à-vis the lower classes, frequently called *indios* whether they had Indigenous ancestry or not.

Whereas the liberal maestro insists, following in the lines of Benito Juárez, on a common identity shared by all (everyone is "mexicano"), Carlos's father teaches his son a different lesson about race, following an ethnonationalism made popular by Vasconcelos's concept of a "cosmic race." He instructs Carlos: "todos éramos indios aun sin saberlo ni quererlo."[42] Yet his use of a past tense that continues (imperfect) and a double negative (*sin … ni*) highlights an internal contradiction in how early post-revolutionary discourse constructed national identity. There continues to be an ambivalence at the centre of a culture that heralds the heroism of Cuauhtémoc in the conquest, while continuing to territorialize racial divisions that keep Indigenous Mexicans on the lowest rungs of society. Two national projects dependent upon the construction of race clash: the elite Europeanized/Americanized vision of a modern Mexico and the folkloric, national discourse of a *mexicanidad* based on Indigenous origins. Carlos's father, however, pointedly remarks on the relationship between racism and socio-economic class: "Si los indios no fueran al mismo tiempo los pobres nadie usaría esa palabra a modo de insulto" (22).[43]

Pacheco's novel depicts the blurring of race with class and how spatial production in the city reveals identity. The avenue that celebrates a Mexica hero doubles as the boundary for a poverty-stricken area of *indios*. The colonial construction of race through spatial and economic practices that first created the category of the *indio* has transformed, and it is now a derogatory term that equates economic class with what had already evolved as a phenotype or a racial category. In fact, the novel provides no clear ethnolinguistic or immigrant markers to indicate that Rosales is Indigenous; there is no mention of an Indigenous community, language, or relatives. Rather, middle-class schoolmates call him an *indio* due to his poverty and to the neighbourhood in which he lives. If Rosales were middle class or part of the political class, he most likely would have been considered a mestizo. The boundary between Colonia Roma and Colonia Doctores becomes a means of keeping socio-economic classes concentrated as it creates and reinforces urban spaces that uphold the biopolitical racial and class hierarchies supported by

---

42 "We are all Indians even if we do not know it or want to be" (90).
43 "If the Indians were not poor, no one would consider it an insult" (90).

state policies. Moreover, the PRI state utilizes these concrete boundaries to further insist on spatialization of race by creating imaginary links with a glorified historical past. The PRI renaming of the street to Cuauhtémoc underscores a dual process of appropriating Indigenous identity for the national project of a single *mexicanidad*, while at the same time associating the *indio* with poverty.

A visit to yet another classmate's home further complicates the relationship between infrastructures of space, race, and coloniality modernity. Born in the United States to an American father and a Mexican mother, Jim lives in an apartment building in Roma with his single mother, Mariana. She is a mistress to "el Señor," a high-ranking bureaucrat for Alemán, who Jim tells classmates is his father. It is the gap between where Jim lives and where a PRI bureaucrat and his family *should* live that makes Carlos question Jim's honesty: "Aún más indescifrable resultaba que Jim viviera con su madre no en una casa de Las Lomas, o cuando menos Polanco, sino en un departamento en un tercer piso cerca de la escuela" (18).[44] Inside Jim's simple apartment in Colonia Roma, however, the boy is seduced by the allure of Jim's Hollywood-like mother, a polyvalent figure who symbolizes both the wonders of American material culture and a lost innocence corrupted by capitalism. Many scholars view Mariana as an archetypical symbol of the Mexican nation during the *milagro mexicano*, but few examine how Pacheco's focus turns to her transnational son and the jarring physical and social spaces that the two occupy. The apartment features "muebles flamantes de Sears Roebuck," and Jim eats American sandwiches ("flying saucers") instead of Mexican tostadas.[45] Looking back in time, the narrator notes Jim's foreignness despite living in Mexico. He explains: "Los 'turcos' no me resultaban extraños como Jim, que nació en San Francisco y hablaba sin acento los dos idiomas" (13–14).[46]

Carlos's subsequent obsession with Mariana leads to his skipping school – using the excuse that he forgot his history book at her house – being caught, and then moving to a private school where, ironically, despite the lack of racial diversity, Carlos himself is the "foreigner" who has yet to learn the new language of colonization, English: "No había

---

44 "Even less comprehensible was that Jim would live with his mother in an apartment on the third floor near the school rather than in a mansion in Las Lomas, or at least in Polanco" (87).

45 "Garish furniture from Sears Roebuck" (91).

46 "The 'Turks' didn't seem as strange as Jim, who was born in San Francisco and spoke two languages without an accent" (83).

árabes ni judíos ni becarios pobres ni batallas en el desierto – aunque sí, como siempre, inglés obligatorio" (51).[47] He is now the other in a world evolving into Anglo-neocolonialism, which is underscored in his family as well. During these same months his father buys into the Americanization project and learns English to keep employed. Yet the American detergent company that takes over his Mexican-owned soap factory demotes him from owner to manager in the service of US interests. He is now in a relationship much like Harry Atherton was with his classmates ("eternos aprendices").

Taken together, these visits to distinct places within the city and with the social classes that were made to inhabit them reveal how *Las batallas en el desierto* positions Mexican identity (Carlos himself) and the *indio* Rosales relative to three socio-political processes: the Spanish colonial regime (conversion, acculturation, civilization as figures for Europeanization or whitening); Americanization (economic neoliberalism as "whitening" of tastes and consumptive practices); and the national narratives of liberalism and the post-revolution (a mestizo state with citizenship as a principle of formal equality that papers over material inequalities). The novel suggests a layering of racial, socio-economic, and colonial divisions, without necessarily privileging chronology. Rather, space becomes the key vector of signification. This positioning of the city and the protagonist becomes more clearly linked as Carlos's own transformation begins after these visits.

An Archaeology of History and *mexicanidad*

Highlighting urban spaces to evoke a parallel between transitions to maturity and transitions to modernity, the narrator maps his younger self's wanderings after falling prey to Americanization at Mariana's apartment. The infatuated boy walks home in the evening shadows: "Caminé por Tabasco, di vuelta en Córdoba para llegar a mi casa en Zacatecas. Los faroles plateados daban muy poca luz. Ciudad en penumbra, misteriosa colonia Roma de entonces. Átomo del inmenso mundo, dispuesto muchos años antes de mi nacimiento como una escenografía para mi representación" (27).[48] The adult Carlos highlights a spatialized relationship to

---

47 "There were no Jews or Arabs, no poor kids on scholarships, no battles in the desert, although there was, as usual, mandatory English" (109).

48 "I walked down Tabasco Street, turned onto Córdoba to get to my house on Zacatecas. The silvery streetlamps only dimly illuminated the streets. A city immersed in semidarkness: the mysterious Roman Quarter of those days. An atom in the immense world, prepared many years before my birth like a stage set for my performance" (93).

personal history by mapping the walk onto a precise street and moment in time. As the boy emerges onto Colonia Roma's central avenue, Avenida Álvaro Obregón, he fixes the place in his memory: "Miré la avenida Álvaro Obregón y me dije: Voy a guardar intacto el recuerdo de este instante porque todo lo que existe ahora mismo nunca volverá a ser igual. Un día lo veré como *la más remota prehistoria*. Voy a conservarlo entero porque hoy me enamoré de Mariana" (28; emphasis added).[49] Past, present, and future once again overlap on a street that originally led to a colonial hacienda, later renamed Avenida Jalisco when Colonia Roma was established, and finally renamed again in honour of the revolutionary caudillo General Álvaro Obregón, who lived on the street until his assassination in 1928. In Pacheco's hands, the site becomes a threshold through which Carlos passes as he leaves behind "el mundo antiguo" of a traditional Mexico in order to embrace modernization and an impossible love for Americanization.[50] Hovering between boyhood and manhood, between the post-revolution and the *milagro mexicano*, Carlos returns to his childhood haunt, the Porfiriato's Plaza Ajusco. There he glimpses Mexico's past, symbolized by the widow of the assassinated revolutionary war hero Francisco Madero, as she disappears into an old crumbling building. Together she and the decaying plaza represent a national process of forgetting and disappearance, which are linked to his own upbringing. Carlos's father even links his son's scandalous behaviour to a head injury incurred when the baby boy was dropped in Plaza Ajusco. The plaza, as a site of memory, triggers recollections of earlier traumas in his own childhood, his father's life, and even farther back into the past.

Concrete places are geographies of ongoing socio-historical processes, a layering of space and history that is both exposed and covered over, a process that continued into the turn of the century in this very plaza. After it was destroyed in the 1985 earthquake and left in ruins for years, the government rebuilt and renamed it Plaza Luis Cabrera, commemorating a post-revolution bureaucrat whose protectionist policies for peasants influenced President Carranza's Ley Agraria (1915). Cabrera also published works that deeply racialized Mexico's Indigenous populations, treating them as a social problem to be solved by education and assimilation.[51]

---

49   "I looked down Álvaro Obregón Avenue and said to myself: I'm going to keep my memory of this moment intact because everything that exists now will never be the same again. One day it will all seem to have been part of *the most remote prehistoric era*. I'm going to preserve it because today I fell in love with Mariana" (94; emphasis added).

50   "The ancient world" (81).

51   See, for example, Cabrera, "The Mexican Situation."

Elsewhere in the novel Carlos continues to map the logics by which the biopolitical stratification of populations is embedded in the city's colonias. When Carlos's father successfully climbs the social ladder, his mother not only owns her own car but now goes to a salon in the elegant Colonia Polanco. When his sister's boyfriend commits suicide because, as a non-English-speaking actor, he cannot compete with Hollywood, his body is found amidst the degradation of the working-class Colonia Tacubaya. When Carlos's abusive older brother commits crimes, the narrator carefully maps the sites of delinquency, all marginalized areas on the outskirts of Colonia Roma: prostitutes along Meave and 2 de abril; gangs along the border Río de la Piedad; and drugs in Parque Urueta.

Later that year the protagonist returns to Avenida Álvaro Obregón, the street fixed in his memory after his meeting with Mariana. Once again he maps his personal transformation by naming streets. At the intersection with Avenida Insurgentes, a street that Alemán had developed and later named after heroes of the War of Independence (1821), Carlos comes to understand his own transformation into a certain foreignness. He unexpectedly meets Rosales, his former classmate, who is now peddling Adams chewing gum. This product, as Jiménez-Sandoval notes, originated with the pre-Hispanic Maya and was introduced to the United States by Antonio López de Santa Anna during his exile there; it was then reintroduced to Mexico by US transnational companies as a modern commodity (443). In stark contrast to Rosales's tattered appearance as a street vendor, Carlos now sports the attire of the Americanized Mexican elite. As he registers the material markers of their respective social classes, the protagonist notes a social tension and projection: "Quiso vengarse de que lo encontré muerto de hambre con su cajita de chicles y yo con mi raqueta de tenis, mi traje blanco, mi Perry Mason en inglés, mis reservaciones en el Plaza."[52] Yet, he insists that Rosales acknowledge his family's upcoming trip to the iconic Plaza Hotel in New York City, asking, "¿Sabes qué es el Plaza?" (55).[53] Jiménez-Sandoval observes: "Este es el momento decisivo para Carlos: darles al sistema de explotación que destruye vidas ... y sufrir una condenación eterna de ser territorializado ... por el capitalismo" (445).[54] Later

---

52   "He wanted to get his revenge because I saw him starving to death with his little box of chewing gum and me with my tennis racket, my white suit, my Perry Mason in English, my reservations at the Plaza" (114–15).

53   "Do you know what the Plaza is?" (112).

54   "This is the decisive moment for Carlos: give into the exploitation system that destroys lives ... and suffer the eternal damnation of being territorialized ... by capitalism."

we find out that Carlos attends an American university, and his family spent years working for transnational companies. Their geographical racialization of *blanqueamiento* is complete.

When Carlos offers Rosales food in exchange for information about his old school – and Mariana – Rosales recounts Mariana's violent death, attributed to her suicide following a denouncement of Alemán's administration at a party in the elite Colonia Las Lomas. Later Carlos attempts to prove Rosales wrong and goes to her apartment, only to find evidence of a state cover-up. No neighbour confirms ever knowing Mariana, and even the reliable doorman, an ex-colonel of the Zapatistas during the revolution, has disappeared. In subsequent years, Mariana's building is demolished. Sites of personal memory and forgetting become symbols of state-organized disappearances, demolitions, and concealment. The spatialization of modern infrastructure and its role in social production combine with a deeper commentary on historical processes of erasure and death. Mariana's death, in fact, foretells the death of a national culture and the death of "marcas mexicanas": "Vi la muerte por todas partes: en los pedazos de animales a punto de convertirse en tortas y tacos entre la cebolla, los tomates, la lechuga, el queso, la crema, los frijoles, el guacamole, los chiles jalapeños ... Vi la muerte en los refrescos: Mission Orange, Spur, Ferroquina. En los cigarros: Belmont, Gratos, Elegantes, Casinos" (57).[55]

Carlos's emerging foreignness is juxtaposed to the heightened poverty of Rosales's family under PRI state repression. Rosales now works the streets of Mexico City because his mother was fired for attempting to unionize at the state hospital. Cultural and political production from this period often employed the figure of the *indio* as a collective conscience for Mexico, depicting characters who highlighted a divide between the promises of the revolution and modernity and an ongoing racialized class system in which Mexico's original colonized populations still occupied the most vulnerable positions of society's biopolitical stratification. Yet in Pacheco's hands, there is a subtle difference. Rosales seems to be categorized as *indio* because of economic class; he may have the phenotype that marks him as of either Indigenous or mestizo heritage, but it is his poverty that makes him an *indio* in the eyes of the novel's middle-class characters. In the new urban modernity

---

55 "I saw death everywhere: in the little pieces of animal about to become sandwiches and tacos, along with the onions, tomatoes, lettuce, cheese, cream, beans, guacamole, jalapeño peppers ... I saw death in the soft drinks: Mission Orange, Spur, Ferroquina; in the cigarettes: Belmont, Gratos, Elegantes, Casinos" (114).

Rosales occupies a corner on the iconic streets that represent heroes of the War of Independence and the revolution and is called *indio* as a derogatory term that connotes class more than ethnolinguistic markers or phenotypes.

At first Rosales appears to be a background character who only serves to contextualize Carlos's memories of the main event (the disappearance of Mariana), but in fact he is central to the story and a stubborn reminder of the cyclical nature of race and class inequalities. Notably, what really makes Rosales *pobre* is not simply lack of wealth but where he lives, what he eats, and how he eats it. Class is written in material and spatial practices. Carlos's family, meanwhile, evolves from eating traditional Mexican foods – "pozole, la birria, las tostadas de pata, el chicharrón en salsa verde" – to "rosbif" (roast beef). They also all slowly move on from Colonia Roma in order to occupy new sites in the emerging cosmopolitan world (26). Childhood acquaintances (Rosales, Jim, and Mariana) are displaced or simply disappear. As Rosales tells Carlos about Mariana, he interrupts himself to reveal the hardship that he and his mother have endured lately. Carlos responds by refusing responsibility: "No es asunto mío y no tengo por qué meterme" (55).[56] As Rosales's story unfolds, the reality – as Carlos's father states – that urban poverty is equated with the racialized category of *indio* undermines the liberal promise of equality within the nation, the ideal espoused by the teacher and by the ideological state project of mestizaje and *mexicanidad*.

Social Forgetting and the City as Memory

This second transformation on Avenida Álvaro Obregón appears to last a lifetime for Carlos. In the final paragraph of the novel the narrator reflects on his reluctance to acknowledge this story, closing with a verdict on the role of place, history, and memory. Like a record, a memory can be replayed again and again, but with a price – it degrades and distorts over time. And yet, he insists for a second time:

> Qué antigua, qué remota, qué imposible esta historia. Pero existió Mariana, existió Jim, existió cuanto me he repetido después de tanto tiempo de rehusarme a enfrentarlo … Demolieron la escuela, demolieron el edificio de Mariana, demolieron mi casa, demolieron la colonia Roma. Se acabó esa ciudad. Terminó aquel país. No hay memoria del México de aquellos

---

56 "It's none of my business and I have no reason to get involved" (112).

años. Y a nadie le importa: de ese horror quién puede tener nostalgia. Todo pasó como pasan los discos en la sinfonola.[57] (59–60)

The repetition of the opening line to the novel, "me acuerdo, no me acuerdo," in the penultimate paragraph further highlights ambivalence and a process of forgetting and remembering as his memories of Roma, Mariana, and modernization under Alemanismo do not remain fixed in the past. And the narrator's repetition of the sentence "Y a nadie le importa: de ese horror quién puede tener nostalgia" signals again that nostalgia here might play a recuperative process for uncovering the past. As readers we begin to participate in an excavation of the complex layering and trajectory of a past-present-future of coloniality. The spaces that established the *mundo antiguo*, as well as the revolution's fight against the Porfiriato and foreign influence, are radically and permanently changed by the *milagro mexicano*, which Pacheco expresses in terms of completed actions with the repeated use of the preterite tense. Still, the imperfect past continues to bubble up through a haze of memory and forgetting. The narrative voice layers past actions, present narration, and hindsight, which creates a chaotic fluctuation between present pasts and possible futures (subjunctive), demanding that the reader stake an uncertain interpretation of the events. To emphasize this collective role, Pacheco mixes individual with collective narrative voices, employing both the first person singular and the first person plural (*yo, nosotros*). Moreover, there is slippage between Carlos's commentary as narrator and his use of "direct" dialogue for Carlos and other characters. No quotation marks signal the distinction between speaker and narrator as everything is channelled through the haze of memory. The fluidity of voices, the verb tenses, and other narrative techniques characteristic of many post-1968 novels underscore a questioning of historical narrative. These narrative strategies also underscore a certain ambivalence in confronting why social forgetting takes place: is it a reaction to personal trauma? To the continued oppression of the state? Or to our own complicity with the process as we seek to maintain our privileged status?

---

57 "How ancient! How remote! What an impossible story! But Mariana existed; Jim existed; everything I went over in my head existed even after such a long time of refusing to confront it … They demolished the school; they demolished Mariana's building; they demolished my house; they demolished the Roman Quarter. That city came to an end. That country was finished. There is no memory of the Mexico of those years. And nobody cares: who could feel nostalgic for that horror? Everything came to an end just like the records on the jukebox" (116–17).

The reader participates in sorting out the story and its overlapping characters, time periods, and spaces. In a self-reflective moment after going to Jim's house, the narrator provides a key: "Nadie escoge cómo nace, en dónde nace, cuándo nace, de quiénes nace."[58] He further suggests that upon meeting Jim, he understood that "no soy su juez"; the reader is left to interpret its meaning (18; order modified). As a middle-aged man living in 1980 and reflecting on the past, Carlos searches for an understanding of how Mexico's class system exchanged the *blanqueamiento* of colonial European infrastructure for another whitening project under the guise of modernization and Americanization once the ideals of the revolution had come up short. Pacheco implicates the reader in this collective chronicle, using the first person plural: "todos somos hipócritas" (37).[59]

The author foregrounds place and the infrastructure of class under Alemanismo to excavate an archaeology of the relationship between space, class, and coloniality that ignores a strict application to a single point in time or a linear chronology, and, in doing so, implicates the reader as well. As Pacheco weaves together a complex temporal spatialization, he unearths layers of history that have been covered up and repressed. His narrative spatial practice points to a dialectic of remembering and forgetting that serves as a subterranean current throughout the novel, but he notes that no one cares to remember this period in which the ideals of the revolution are abandoned as an archaic, foreign "vestigio de épocas prehistóricas" (15).[60] In this metaphorical reading, Colonia Roma is both a childhood place and a national space that has been violated and then renamed. By presenting the official story in a literary form, the novel uses *escenografía* to highlight the gaps in meaning. The author invites readers to uncover through an archaeological dig the ongoing coloniality of socio-economic spaces, the enduring effects of a coloniality-modernity that haunt the present.

Guy Beiner studies the process of social forgetting, which he defines as not a collective amnesia but rather private practices of remembrance that endure outside of official historiography. Private remembrances, argues Beiner, continually resurface around historical events that have been suppressed and subtly shape new narratives. Significantly, it is the anxiety of a possible forgetting of these histories that fuels the continuation of storytelling (4–9). In *Las batallas en el desierto* the protagonist-narrator casts doubt

---

58 "Nobody chooses how, when, where, or to whom one is born"; "I do not judge him" (88; order modified).
59 "We are all hypocrites" (100).
60 "Vestige of some prehistoric era" (85).

on his own memory of the past precisely because it goes against the state narrative of modernization as success. The interior dialogue between his current self and his pubescent self evokes an unresolved attempt to find truth. In one paradigmatic moment doubt is cast on the very existence of Mariana and the nation she represents; when Carlos enquires about her, the doorman replies that no such person ever lived there: "Cosas que te imaginas, niño" (59).[61] Although Beiner studies social forgetting in Ireland, he mentions other cases, including post-Franco Spain and what he calls the "Mexican stand-off" at the turn of the twenty-first century. Public silencing, he argues, ensures "muted remembrances" and "their continued remediation" through the persistence of vernacular stories (523). Even though these private remembrances/stories at times are exhibited in public, they soon return to social forgetting and the "inconspicuous contestations that are found in everyday social and cultural activities" (613).

Beiner's theory of social forgetting provides a lens for reading how two other historical periods could be implicated in Pacheco's critique of modernity. Carlos dismisses generations of warfare as "prehistory," but he also notes that no one remembers the thousands of dead peasants, teachers, reformers, and soldiers who remain as a "subterranean vestige" of Mexico. Instead, people bought into PRI propaganda and building projects: "Pero aquel año, *al parecer*, las cosas andaban muy bien: a cada rato suspendían las clases para llevarnos a la inauguración de carreteras, avenidas, presas, parques deportivos, hospitales, ministerios, edificios inmensos" (15; italics in original).[62] Yet, official memory and attempts to reconfigure space do not obliterate how space holds memories; on the contrary, they rely on it. The use of *al parecer* casts doubt on modernity's ability to cast off the fundamental biopolitical structures upon which it is built.

Accordingly, the novel closes with images of the city that reveal the outcome of these infrastructural practices. Carlos recounts an almost apocalyptic disintegration of Roma, a microcosm of Mexico City, as a dystopia caused by modernization: "Demolieron la colonia Roma. Se acabó esa ciudad. Terminó aquel país" (60).[63] The post-revolutionary ideal is literally in ruins as the competing ideal of Americanization, the *blanquemiento de los gustos*, triumphs.

---

61 "You're imagining things, kid" (116).

62 "But things seemed to be going well that year. Classes were constantly being called off so they could take us to the inaugurations of highways, avenues, sports arenas, dams, hospitals, ministries, enormous buildings" (85).

63 "They demolished the Roman Quarter. That city came to an end. That country was finished" (116).

Layered Histories of Coloniality and Violence

Pacheco's portrait of Alemanismo – symbolically signed by the opening juxtaposition of the president's smiling political posters and the "misery of most of Mexico"[64] – uses concrete places and more generalized concepts of spatialization to evoke parallels between historical periods dating from colonialization, independence, the Porfiriato, and revolution. As Mbembe notes, biopolitics, racism, and colonialism made way for state violence, which was "legitimized" by its bringing of "civilization" (*On the Postcolony* 15). Mariana's/Mexico's violent death, along with the continued impoverishment of the *indio* Rosales in *Las batallas en el desierto*, points a guilty finger at PRI's *milagro mexicano* as a realignment of classes that continued a process of territorialization of colonial space, race, and violence. The actor boyfriend commits suicide as his profession becomes Americanized; Mariana is said to have committed suicide after revealing a PRI scandal; and Rosales's family is destitute after the state shut down a workers' strike. This violence escalated later into full-fledged disappearances and massacres by the late 1960s. Pacheco's archaeological layering of space and history, and his emphasis on both violent erasure and cycles of dispossession that rewrite relations of race and class, however, also dialogue in a significant way with his other works on conquest, coloniality, and PRI state violence.

As Edith Negrín notes in her important article "Huellas del 68," Pacheco's first publications linked the Spanish conquest and colonization with violence in his own era. But it was a series of works from 1968 to 1972 that increasingly made direct connections between the conquest and PRI state violence. For example, in the wake of the Tlatelolco massacre, perpetrated at the symbolic site of Cuauhtémoc's surrender to Cortés, Pacheco rewrote his own "Cantares mexicanos" (1959), publishing it under the pointed new title "Lectura de los 'Cantares mexicanos': Manuscrito de Tlatelolco (octubre 1968)." Through a complex weave of intertexts, historical events, and points of view Pacheco's new work drew parallels between the Spanish conquest and the 1968 massacre. Several years later, in his short story "Señas de identidad: Historia de un muchacho mexicano (La Generación del 68 y Tlatelolco)" published just a month after a second state massacre in 1971 (the Halconazo massacre), Pacheco

---

64 "La cara del Señor presidente en dondequiera: dibujos inmensos, retratos idealizados, fotos ubicuas, alegorías del progreso con Miguel Alemán como Dios Padre, caricaturas laudatorias, monumentos" (Pacheco 10).

extended his critique of modernity and the "dirty war." His student protagonist, Fernando, whose *transnacional* family has moved to an elite colonia, becomes aware of his *desmexicanización* and the rising state injustices, and thus decides to join the student movement. Soon afterwards, he witnesses the Halconazo massacre. The traumatic event leaves Fernando with a "wound" that can't heal until justice is done, even as he recognizes "que la investigación sobre los 'halcones' no llegará a ningún resultado concreto."[65] A year later, in "Fiesta Brava," Pacheco wrote about an American Vietnam War veteran who kidnaps a disillusioned Mexican translator of English. As the translator disappears into the depths of the metro, he mentions seeing an advertisement for Raleigh cigarettes that has been defaced with a message of resistance: "ASESINOS, NO OLVIDAMOS TLATELOLCO Y SAN COSME" (cited in Negrín 183).[66] Avenida San Cosme was the concrete setting of the 1971 massacre, and nearly forty years later it would also serve as the site for Alfonso Cuarón's restaging of the massacre for his film *Roma* (2018) in order to expose what he, too, calls this national wound.

Pacheco's description of a sign for American cigarettes that has been defaced by protest graffiti underscores the relationship between the site of a state massacre, the politics of capitalism and the Cold War, and a new colonization under Luis Echeverría Álvarez, the alleged mastermind of the 1968 and 1971 student massacres, who has been popularly implicated in engaging the US military to help train Mexican paramilitary groups. Ten years later, in the wake of the rapid devaluation of the peso under Echeverría Álvarez's presidency and on the eve of the 1982 declaration of Mexico's bankruptcy, *Las batallas en el desierto* not only returned to the theme of state violence but also provided an origin story of the economic restructuring of Mexico and a new coloniality linked increasingly to US capitalism and culture.

Indeed, the continued editorial success of the brief novel as well as the author's own comments about it thirty years later make clear its continued relevance today. In 2011, when José Emilio Pacheco received the prestigious Alfonso Reyes award for lifetime literary achievement, he delivered a lecture entitled "A 30 años de la publicación de *Las batallas en el desierto*." Rather than focus on his highly acclaimed poetry or

---

65   "That the 'halcones' investigation will never arrive at any concrete result."
66   "ASSASSINS, WE WILL NOT FORGET TLATELOLCO AND SAN COSME." For more on the effect of the massacre on many Mexican authors see Merrell, "Uncommonplace Happenings."

novel *Morirás lejos* (1967), Pacheco traced the feeble beginnings of *Las batallas*. Reflecting upon the unexpected – and continued – popularity of his novel, Pacheco observed: "[P]ensé que iba a interesar tan solo al muy reducido número de personas que vivieron esa época y esa Colonia Roma. Sucedió todo lo contrario. Quienes han leído y hecho suyo este libro son aquellos y aquellas para quienes la historia y sus personajes son tan remotos como la Roma de los Césares" (205).[67] Evoking Rome as a place and an empire, Pacheco links the novel with a globalized and centuries-old process. As he finished his speech, the author asked: "¿Qué puede esperar un humilde escritor de lo que era el tercer mundo y ahora es el octavo o décimo? Sólo una cosa: que dentro de muchos años una abuela o un abuelo, ya no digan un día a sus nietos el libro que para entonces ya no existirá, sino les cuente la historia y les diga: 'Esto es algo que leí cuando tenía los mismos años que ahora tienen ustedes" (207).[68] Storytelling is integral to keeping the lessons of history alive. We will see a similar impulse in the next chapter, wherein we study how Juan José Arreola's narrators reveal deeply ingrained rural infrastructures of race, memory, and history.

In this same 2011 speech Pacheco also asserted that his historical novel was founded on "[un] transfondo y los escenarios ... absolutamente reales" ("A 30 años" 202).[69] Through a fiction based on real places, the author exposes the social forgetting and negative impact of a continued coloniality-modernity in Colonia Roma and beyond. In fact, in the intervening years between the first edition and the 2011 edition, the author continued to make this central theme more explicit and contemporary. Among other revisions to the novel, he updated the year from 1980 to 2000, adding the key verb *modernizar* and conjugating it in the first person plural.[70] That these revisions are simple makes them no less significant: they implicate the reader in a contemporary society and

---

67 "I only thought it would interest that very small number of people who lived the Colonia Roma during that time. What happened was quite the contrary. Those who have read the book and made it their own are those for whom the story and its characters are as remote as the Caesars' Rome."

68 "What can a humble author expect of what was once the third world, and what is now the eighth or tenth? Just one thing: that within many years' time a grandmother or grandfather will not read to their grandchildren the book that by that time will no longer exist, but that they tell them the story and say, 'This is something that I read when I was the same age as you are now.'"

69 "A background and scenes that are absolutely real."

70 For a more detailed study of these changes see Sobrit, "Metamorfosis de *Las batallas en el desierto*."

a globalized culture based on Americanized consumerism. Indeed, the relative ease with which the dates are updated *denies* the possibility that we perform a historicist reading of the novel. Pacheco links coloniality / modernity to a violence that persists through form and structure and which resists a singular truth.

As we have seen, at the time of the events in Pacheco's story, Colonia Roma was a middle-class neighbourhood struggling to maintain its social status. Pacheco depicts a protagonist who struggles through the haze of memory to recall his transformation from an adolescent in Colonia Roma to the Americanized person he has become. Notably, an exact year is never given; rather, the era is evoked as a set of shared temporally and socially delimited experiences. As the narrator shifts verb tenses, subjects, and historical eras, he creates a kaleidoscope within a radical transformation in the post-revolutionary period and builds upon colonial categories of space/race to project a future of neocolonialism.

The opening references to Orwellian images of President Alemán and the presence of the PRI state in Pacheco's novel point to state practices that mediate biopolitical processes of the regulation of Mexico's population in an era of rapid modernization. But the author also evokes the historical layers of these practices of racialization and classism, antagonisms that point beyond the form of the state. Drawing out these points of structural invisibility – points that are no less structuring despite their invisibility – the author performs an archaeological dig that uncovers glimpses of a coloniality set in motion by Spanish colonization and later modified by state practices throughout the Porfiriato and late twentieth century. As we will explore in later chapters in this volume, such excavations reveal ongoing attempts to cover over past historical eras, actors, and ideological projects. Yet Pacheco's vernacular story also acts as a catalyst for us as readers to confront social forgetting. His story counters the forces of social amnesia after a period of repression and censorship, enticing us to consider not only the past, the *milagro mexicano,* and what would later become the dirty war under PRI depicted by Cuarón but also an enduring coloniality, with relevance to Mexico – and the United States – today. The author immerses us in a personal story that allegorizes a larger collective, past and present. This process is especially visible in the effects of globalization, decolonization, and efforts to promote social justice, which come to the fore in new transnational contexts. Pacheco's work thus contributes to a broader understanding of the coloniality of modernity as he excavates places, class structures, and colonial histories that, forty years later, Cuarón develops in his film.

Colonial Inheritance and the Racialization of Space in Alfonso Cuarón's *Roma*

The novelized *escenografía* of the Colonia Roma reveals the infrastructures of class and coloniality that inflect the development of Pacheco's protagonist, and it is also the set, two decades later, for *Roma* – and the historical site of Cuarón's boyhood home as well as the place where the thirteen-year-old Liboria Rodríguez (the film's Cleo) landed when she migrated to Mexico City to become his family's live-in nanny. In the film, we watch as the Mixteca domestic worker, played by Yalitza Aparicio, performs her daily routine within the family's domestic space. But just as Pacheco's character Carlos ventures into other colonias, Cleo ventures far beyond both the family home and the Colonia Roma. We follow her downtown to the cinema, to an old hacienda, to the infamous Nezahualcoyotl shantytown, as well as to what becomes the site of the 1971 Halconazo massacre, and even to Veracruz. The violence that plays out in the public sphere is accompanied by private anguish when she sees her former lover participate in the massacre and when her unexpected pregnancy by him results in a stillborn child. As Cleo moves through these different spaces, a once-tacit social unrest gradually builds until it finally erupts into the foreground action, where it implicates the PRI state and US neocolonialist practices as well as classist practices based on racialization.

By situating Cleo's story in a broader geography of social class and place within and around Mexico City, and by framing scenes with a common element – political posters – Cuarón opens the sites up for comparison with each other. In the first half of the film, PRI propaganda appears in the opening shot of each scene that involves Cleo visiting a new place. As the posters become more prominent with each such scene, we become increasingly aware of the ubiquitous presence of the PRI during the campaign year of President Díaz Ordaz's hand-picked successor, Luis Echeverría Álvarez. This visual strategy culminates in the film's climactic portrayal of the Halconazo massacre, thus symbolically framing the man who many believe helped mastermind the state massacres of 1968 and 1971. Notably, these posters disappear from scenes after the massacre. As we will see, posters ultimately function as a metonymy for the PRI regime and its Big Brother surveillance – also seen in Pacheco's novel – that orchestrated daily life, reconfigured by the modern state and its citizens through the discourses of class and race inherited from colonialism. The director's use of PRI political posters as signature elements in the spatial elaboration of the cinematic representation of moments of historical tension addresses a wider

Figure 1.2. Film still from *Roma* (2018). Director Alfonso Cuarón employs political posters from Mexico's 1970 presidential elections to frame scenes and suggest a Big Brother surveillance by the ruling Partido Revolucionario Institucional (PRI).

phenomenon of social forgetting, as the posters themselves implicate a new coloniality of power (see fig. 1.2.).

Cuarón explains that in his film "places dictate what was going to happen" (Solórzano), and while "time can't be brought back, our perception of space lingers longer than time itself" (*Road to Roma*). He meticulously recreated entire city blocks and went so far as to replicate storefronts, cars, and posters, and even the minutia of the contents of kitchen drawers that are never opened in the film, in order to immerse viewers in this specific historical place. The use of long takes with panning and lateral tracking shots, of wide angles that take in more space, and of Dolby Atmos technology that only records ambient sounds, evidences an intentional use of cinematic technique, strengthening a sense that our experience of place is key to interpreting *Roma*. As wide-angle filming records broad socio-historical scenes through which his characters move, Cuarón elaborates a complex interplay between foreground and background in which the characters exist both in and in relation to the spaces they inhabit. He performs an archaeological process of unearthing and reconstructing 1970–1 Mexico City and his boyhood home but chooses to tell the story through Cleo, whose look skewers the presentation of the middle-class family for which she works.

In what follows I argue that as we witness the unravelling of family life, Cuarón uses a purposeful spatialization both to unearth the story of social trauma and to reveal sites of ongoing coloniality. He references classism and the dirty war under President Luis Echeverría Álvarez

(1971–6) and points to a new coloniality of power borne out of modernization and globalization. The role of lived space is paramount to the film's exploration of class, race, and modernity. Although critics frequently point to the key role of place and social history in *Roma*, I contend that Cuarón's meticulous attention to spatialization encourages us to see not just one period in history but rather multiple historical pasts and their relevance to the world today.[71] I develop this argument by first exploring two narrative and spatial strategies used in the film: the revealing of Cleo's domestic sphere within the household in Colonia Roma and then the sequencing of her movement around and outside of Mexico City – places all signed with political propaganda and imbued with a crescendo of violence. Following this, I touch on broader questions about the making of the film and its implications for the telling of cultural stories to combat social forgetting.

Domestic Space and Coloniality

Taking full advantage of the ways in which film can highlight spatiality and its ability to reveal racial constructions, Cuarón's *Roma* underscores a complex interplay between daily life and historical backgrounds of social unrest. As Anthony Giddens argues in *The Constitution of Society* (1984), to study the routine of daily life enables us not only to understand spatialization as lived spaces of social production in an abstract sense but also to conceptualize how everyday habits produce and structure place. Within the interior spaces and private scale of the house Cleo's routines reveal her social status. Although the family depends on her to maintain their middle-class lifestyle – and especially after the father abandons his wife and four children – their unpredictable behaviour further accents her precarious position. She is alternately embraced and yelled at, taunted for using Mixtec and then accused of being "mute," expected to wait on them but being told it is a vacation. The set emphasizes this pull between affection and abuse as Cleo is intimately integrated into the family space, yet is always outside of it.[72]

---

71 See, for example, O'Brien, "Remembrances as Reconstruction"; Neumann, "Why Is Alfonso Cuarón's 'Roma' Important?"; and Sánchez Prado, "Special Dossier."

72 Within these spaces, as O'Brien notes, the camera also plays with perspective, using windows to mark both separation and spectatorship. A stationary camera often "watches Cleo at work from behind a window: she is visually compartmentalized, sectioned off, removed, yet she is also often the only one doing the active looking" (O'Brien 13).

The camera allows us into the closet-like space that Cleo shares with the family's live-in Mixteca cook, Adela. It is above the utility washroom, just off the interior patio, a space barely large enough for the two to do nightly stretches by candlelight because their employer limits their use of electricity. These static shots of bare-bone material scenes contrast sharply with the long takes and camera panning of the children's rooms in the main house, revealing shelves filled with modern Mexican and US commodities: Mickey Mouse, Daisy Duck, footballs, and stereos. The colonial legacy of spatial production continues as this family of the urbanized upper-middle class depends on migration from rural, and largely Indigenous, Mexico to take care of its household and children. As was the case in many such families, the domestic workers are kept in separate, impoverished quarters within the hacienda's replacement: the urban city house in colonias like Roma.

In fact, it is only on the rooftop above the main house, where in an early scene Cleo did laundry as other maids tended to laundry on other rooftops, that she makes one of her rare but telling statements. After singing along to a popular song about poverty and love and intervening in a dispute among her charges, who play at being dead, Cleo finally takes a rest and confesses to no one in particular: "I like being dead." Notably, after a year of personal and national upheaval she returns to this space as the film ends. In the liminal rooftop space where maids escape temporarily from the eyes of employers, Cleo pauses. The rooftop, although marginal with respect to the interior dwellings, is the building's highest vantage point and thus provides a positional space for this paradoxically privileged perspective of the domestic worker. The panning shot from Cleo's rooftop vantage point takes in a cityscape that emphasizes a sense of infinite embeddedness in the spatialized networks of social life.

Sites, Signs, and Social Conflict

The filmmaker marks this interplay between place, social production, and modernity – between Cleo's daily life, the broader social unrest, and the surveillance state – with an increasing directness as the film progresses. Beginning with the subtle and strategic placement of political posters for the upcoming elections, along with a few subtler signs of resistance (e.g., peace signs), Cuarón carefully marks the arenas of conflict. The signs frame the places visited, and like in Pacheco's novel, they reflect class conflict as a legacy of colonialism and thirty years of PRI land reform, industrialization, and repression. Understanding the placement and sequencing of these sites and posters is key to seeing how the film projects a tension between official history and vernacular stories about a continuing coloniality of power. The narrative crescendo marked by political signs in the first half of the film both guides viewers and suggests ironic juxtapositions – reminiscent of the wry observations made by Pacheco's narrator – between the reality of daily life and a political propaganda that connects modernity and *mexicanidad*.

Our initial glimpse of PRI propaganda occurs during the first scene filmed outside of Cleo's domestic space. As she picks up the children from school, we see a lopsided poster of Echeverría, but it goes largely undetected as the camera focuses instead on the school courtyard swarming with children; the poster appears only as though it has been stuck onto the scene at the last minute. In the next scene, amid a chaotic family lunch, the middle son, Paco, recounts a story about the army shooting a young boy at play in the city's iconic Chapultepec Park, a place that maintains its original Nahua name and served as home to rulers and presidents until 1940. Only Cleo reacts with a look of surprise as the rest of the family simply continues in their routine.

This politicized background, largely ignored by the middle class, continues to be signed with posters as the plot unfolds, but it moves closer to the foreground in Cleo's next outing, this time to the movies. The scene change depicts a public space where social mixing takes place and also serves as a leitmotif for transitions throughout *Roma*. Moving through the streets of downtown Mexico City, which are brimming with vendors and pedestrians, Cleo and her friend Adela, the other Mixteca domestic worker who lives with the family, meet their boyfriends at La Casa del Pavo. The exterior walls are plastered with large, slightly skewed signs for the upcoming elections: "Vote Así PRI," and a poster for the opposition, the Partido Popular Socialista (PPS).[73] Outside the popular Teatro Metropolitano in the city centre hangs another PRI poster. Telling details of this exquisite mise-en-scène – the skewed posters next to hanging skeletons – produce a subtle foreboding.[74]

---

73 The PPS, however, was accused of being a puppet party for the PRI to create the appearance of democratic elections.

74 Notably, in *Road to Roma* Cuarón reveals that ethnicity was integral to this scene; he created ethnic profiles based on extras' phenotypes: "we had to do a demographic analysis. Not just how many men and how many women, but also how many from each social class. And for each social class, how many from each ethnicity. There will be indigenous, there will be mestizos, and these will be white Mexicans." We even briefly see how he organized photographs by ethnicity into a document that is reminiscent of the famous colonial *cuadros de casta*, which depicted phenotypes. "We had huge pieces of paper with all the different faces arranged according to those demographics. That's how I chose them. Not by seeing the actors in person but I chose each one from the photographs."

In fact, the scene segues into latent PRI-inspired violence when Fermín takes Cleo into the intimate space of a hotel room, where he demonstrates (in the nude) his prowess in martial arts. Fermín then recounts his rogue personal story. Growing up in the slums, he was orphaned at an early age and became a petty thief and drug user, until the state offered to train him for paramilitary manoeuvres to quell social unrest. Significantly, this lumpenproletariat character is the sole character in the movie who directly narrates his own story.[75] For all other characters, spectators must piece together partial scenes, interactions, and overheard conversations in order to understand motives and social backgrounds.[76] As the film continues, we see how modernity and the authoritarian regime brand Fermín's life: he is both a victim of the PRI's paramilitary recruitment efforts among Mexico's lowest classes and later a perpetrator of state-sponsored violence.[77] After Cleo witnesses Fermín's demonstration of his kendo stick (the weapon later used by paramilitary in the massacre), she returns to her daily domestic routine. Moving into the children's room, however, the camera pans the bedroom and its contents. Tucked into a cognate private space, near the closet, a peace poster ("Make Love Not War") quietly comments on the underlying social unrest.

Moving beyond Mexico City to a rural town and hacienda, the film explores other sites of ongoing coloniality and class conflict, pointing back to the revolution and to the current influx of anglophones/Europeans into Mexico. As the camera follows Cleo, now pregnant and abandoned by her boyfriend, and Sofía, now abandoned by her husband, it highlights a town marked with traditional symbols of death as well as more posters, which once again underscore social tension. Iconic symbols of rural Mexico (and death) greet them as they enter the town

---

75 I employ Marx's term *lumpenproletariat* because Fermín is from the class that was both needed for the revolution to succeed and used to suppress any further revolution once the PRI was established.

76 In our first view of the family patriarch, for example, telling material detail establishes him as an Americanized part of the state bureaucracy: without showing his face, the camera records him parking a Ford Galaxy in which there is a state hospital file folder on the front seat.

77 Foucault notes: "[That t]he sovereign has a right of life and death means that he can, basically, either have people put to death or let them live, or in any case that life and death are not natural or immediate phenomena which are primal or radical, and which fall outside the field of power" (240). He continues: "To be more specific, I would say that discipline tries to rule a multiplicity of men to the extent that their multiplicity can and must be dissolved into individual bodies that can be kept under surveillance, trained, used, and, if need be, punished" (242).

to celebrate New Year's Eve: dried fields of maize, crosses, remnants of Día de los Muertos, a donkey pulling a cart, and a tamale vendor. In the background two signs at the village's only crossroads foreshadow social conflict. Although the elections are now over, a wind-blown PRI poster still insists "México vota así," while a hand-painted banner stretches across the dirt street proclaiming the ideals of the revolution: "Por la Defensa de Nuestros Derechos, Unidos la Tierra."[78]

The conflict over land rights is silently presented through the posters and is developed further as Cleo and Sofía enter the hacienda. The camera lingers on taxidermy of the owner's prized hunting dogs and in particular the monument to the first dog, which carries the date 1911, the beginning of the revolution, implying that the acquisition of the hacienda was linked to that time of upheaval and land reform. Next, the camera focuses on a recently deceased dog, allegedly poisoned, as the hacienda's housekeeper confirms, "I'm sure it was the villagers angry with Don José over the land." Elaborate mises-en-scène highlight the division between villagers/laborers and the hacienda elite. The "upstairs" elite are depicted at a target-practice picnic and New Year's Eve party, where heaping piles of cigarettes, whisky, and empty bottles of Coca-Cola litter tables, and American pop music, such as "Jesus Christ Superstar," combines with traditional Mexican music. The "downstairs" employees celebrate the New Year wearing traditional ranchero white straw hats, drinking pulque from ceramic jugs, and dancing to corrido music. Before a fire breaks out that interrupts these scenes, we overhear about unrest again from the housekeeper informant, as she talks about the tragedy of one of the campesinos: "They killed his son last August over the land dispute."

Asides such as these fill celebratory scenes, revealing a multilayered socio-economic conflict that goes beyond a simple post-revolutionary portrait of class conflict between elite criollo hacendados and Indigenous and mestizo peasants. American culture infiltrates the scenes of the upstairs party, suggesting that we see both continuities and fissures in colonialism's legacy of racism and place as a new coloniality emerges. This background of class and neocolonialism becomes clearer during the hacienda target-practice picnic. A Mexican woman picks up a pistol and joins the American women to shoot, as one of the men says in Spanish: "Watch out, Pepe! Your wife is going to join the guerillas?!

---

78   "In Defense of Our Rights, United the Land." Elections were held on 5 July 1970, when Luis Echeverría Álvarez won and replaced Díaz Ordaz. He took office in January 1971.

She's going to expropriate your hacienda!" The criollo hacendado's European and American guests challenge traditional Mexican social hierarchies and cultural norms by insisting on speaking only English, allowing women to participate in traditionally male practices, and by speaking of their acquisition of large tracts of land in Mexico. A shift in cultural norms and labels among some hacienda workers is hinted at with a single comment when the housekeeper does not tell everyone about the downstairs party, but comments: "We don't want those city nannies here. They feel fancier than their bosses." The larger post-revolution, national struggle over land rights, signalled in the film by the opening rural scene's juxtaposition of PRI propaganda and a resistance banner, becomes more complex through these scenes and seems to ask viewers to consider the implications of new socio- economic processes and actors as they relate to spatial production, including the arrival of transnational companies, foreign land ownership, imported Anglo-gender and -language norms, and urbanized domestic workers no longer tied to traditional Indigenous rural society. Rather than consigning it to the past, these factors reconfigure colonial power as an enduring coloniality in the present.

Whereas the housekeeper's comment suggests that changes are occurring in the traditional social constructs of domestic service at the hacienda, a later scene set in the countryside prompts Cleo's own comment that reveals a rural-urban tension. In the *falda* of the nearby volcano, geographical areas in which Indigenous communities had often resided since colonial times, the camera and ambient sound track evoke a sensuous tranquillity. In this familiar landscape Cleo smiles and mentions for the first and last time her origins: "This feels like my village. It's drier there. But it feels like it … It sounds like this. And smells the same." In this brief moment we perceive the radical difference between her home village and the congested modernity of Mexico City, where, as we learn later, Cleo has to remain because the government has seized her mother's land in Oaxaca, and she has no place to go. With these two brief evocations of place by Cleo, the film invites viewers to consider the radical change experienced by millions of Indigenous peasants and rural mestizos who were forced to migrate to urban areas when land reform and modernization policies displaced them.

The fallout from these policies is signed and witnessed at its height in two subsequent exterior scenes. In search of Fermín, Cleo goes to his settlement. Cuarón marks the destination as the camera lingers on the bus sign "Ciudad Nezahualcoyotl." Like the spatial dimensions of coloniality and class/race in Colonia Roma, Nezahualcoyotl's foundations speak to the role of space in neocolonial social relations.

As the town lies on a lake-bed drained in the 1930s, access to basic services and utilities, as well as rights of land tenure, would continue to be points of contention for much of the twentieth century. Amid open sewage and muddy streets Cleo steps into a political rally in progress. Although PRI propaganda begins to proliferate here, it seems to lie in wait, still largely in the background, as a Fellini-like scene that includes a band and a voice projected over a loudspeaker plays out. The voice announces PRI's promise to build infrastructure in this "ciudad perdida": "[F]ollowing our illustrious governor's instructions to improve the infrastructure, I've come here today to respond to your demand for water! This can only happen by uniting the will of the people with the leadership of our illustrious President Luis Echeverría Álvarez." This booming yet faint voice recalls Cuarón's earlier use of a disembodied voice-over in *Y tu mamá también*, which Sánchez-Prado suggests takes shape as the mediation of "the impossibility of political articulation itself as a formal resource" (186).[79] In *Roma* this device remains the same, but more explicitly disclosing its obscenity and its artifice. As Cleo walks away from the centre of the frame, our attention is suddenly pulled to the background, where a man is shot from a bulky cannon. The extravagance is nothing if not out of place amidst this forgotten urban periphery. Redirecting us, just as the zealous politician redirects his audience members in the distance, this compensatory gimmick further highlights the impossibility of narrating fully the relationship between class, politics, and modernity.

The staging of propaganda juxtaposed with the sensorial experience of the lack of modern infrastructure, in order to comment on the PRI state, moves to new ground when Cleo finds Fermín's cousin Ramón.[80] Moving through filth and sinking into mud, Cleo goes to his one-room shanty built within a chicken coop, where he and his band play rock music, which was censored by the PRI after 1968.[81] The band members are clearly marked as part of the resistance movement as Ramón wears his hair long and another student-like member drives a car (in a place largely devoid of cars) that has a bullet hole in the windshield. Barely

---

79   See also Acevedo-Munoz, "Sex, Class, and Mexico."

80   Sánchez Prado calls *Roma* "an archaeology of Mexico's class trouble" and notes: "The concurrence of urban development and rural failure became the infrastructure that led to the new ways in which social class was constructed through race, pigmentocracy and labor regimes ... modernity here is not narrated ... but sensorially conveyed ("Special Dossier" n.p.).

81   First banned from public airwaves in 1968 for a period of time, it was banned again for several other periods of time under Echeverría (1971, 1975).

visible through the shadowed entrance to the shack hangs a peace sign similar to the one in the boys' room in Colonia Roma. Although the cousins come from the same poverty-stricken place, Cuarón breaks easy class stereotypes again and reveals difference as one man opts for the counterculture movement and the other is co-opted by the system to escalate violence. Characters like Fermín and Ramón, we might suggest, following Stacey Balkan's study of rogues in the post-colony, enable us to see a different side of the city and its material culture, a part of the city that is made invisible in the lettered neoliberal city (35). The details of place absorb our senses, while strategically placed signs guide our understanding of the role of ideological constructs behind infrastructures of race and class in this modern urbanization (and urban modernization) process controlled by a neocolonial state.

As the foregrounding of place in *Roma* projects viewers into a sensorial experience of the story, these background political signs continue to index a historical referent, asking us to perceive the gaps between the vernacular story of a domestic worker and a mestizo paramilitary, and the official history of this period. As the film continues to follow Cleo, still in pursuit of Fermín, it moves even further beyond the city to the higher, drier grounds in the state of Mexico where Fermín's paramilitary group is being trained. Here PRI signs are no longer sidelined and lopsided; their proliferation dominates the landscape. As a group of Indigenous women and old men wearing L.E.A. (Luis Echeverría Álvarez) T-shirts watch the military manoeuvres, the camera pans across an entire hillside inscribed with the large, white initials L.E.A. The Echeverría propaganda evokes a panoptic state control that unites the army officer, an American CIA look-alike wearing a "Wes Pont" [*sic*] sweatshirt, the Asian martial arts instructor, and a celebrity stunt and escape artist named Zovek, as they (at times comically) direct the Halcones, the group who initiated the Corpus Christi massacre.[82] By becoming an Halcón, Fermín became both a victim and a perpetrator of state biopolitical stratification. The violent consequences play out first at a personal level. As the scene closes, Fermín verbally abuses and threatens Cleo, calling her a *pinche gata* (a classist, misogynist slur for domestic workers in Mexico City).

---

82   Kate Doyle published selections from US government correspondence about paramilitary manoeuvres in Mexico, noting its link with US support of authoritarian regimes in Latin America during the Cold War. Significantly, the name of the paramilitary group also references an infamous gang from the poverty-stricken area of Romita that had been protected by the PRI; see Doyle, "The Corpus Christi Massacre."

This socio-political violence and the resistance movement that calls it out climax in a tense visual dialogue before the Halconazo massacre erupts. When Cleo and her employer go to a furniture store in Mexico City, they pass a handmade protest sign depicting a hammer and sickle and another, Che Guevara. The camera then lingers on protesters painting a banner, which we can only partially make out, but it clearly refers to "Revolution." As they pass truckloads of police and soldiers standing down – idly smoking, talking, reading the paper, or sleeping – and as the Halcones lie in wait with their kendo sticks in hand, the black-clad matriarch, depicted largely as an incompetent figure from a bygone era, voices her opinion for the first and only time in the film: "I hope this time they don't beat them." Moments later, first from the window of the furniture store and then from within the store, we witness the massacre through Cleo's eyes. Wearing the same T-shirt he wore in the initial scene with Cleo (one bearing an American Precious Moments figure and the words "Amor es … recordar tu primer beso"), Fermín points a gun, ready to kill or be killed. As a rogue turned paramilitary, Fermín illustrates a phenomenon that Mbembe elucidates in his work on necropolitics: it is amongst the lowest classes of the neocolony that the violence of colonial rule most often continues to play out ("Necropolitics"). As the film continually refers us back to Cleo's eyes, we alternatively see her shock and the complexity of her position.

This climactic scene in Cleo's personal story is embedded in a historical recreation of the site in which Mexico's "dirty war" took on new dimensions. Under Echeverría, the PRI unleashed new tactics to quell resistance, and the violence increasingly spilled over into the domestic sphere. The furniture store itself – whose filming site was an actual furniture store in 1971 – is portrayed in the film as a site for the consumption of domestic comfort, yet this promise is broken as violence erupts inside it.[83] Beyond the store itself, the filmmaker also replicated cars, signs, and even a Pietà-like scene based on an archival photograph of an anguished woman holding her wounded partner. Cuarón's meticulous historical research and recreation included interviewing survivors

---

83 Several critics read this scene differently. The sudden eruption of state violence that had been latent since the first mention of soldiers killing a boy thus becomes a "sensorial jolt of buried memory … the material transference of a personal, national, and even cinematic history," and it casts "cinema as a living, breathing, sensing memory" (O'Brien 12). They witness a personal and collective loss, as Cuarón notes: "a period that scarred me … the social events that were portrayed are one of the most important and deep scars in the Mexican psyche, in the collective consciousness" (quoted in Utichi).

of the massacre, as he wanted to document in some measure their unrecorded stories. Immersing the viewer in this recreation, the film foregrounds a personal story within a historical reference to combat official history and processes of social forgetting. As viewers we are invited to witness an event that was suppressed in national and international news at the time. He brings to the foreground the memory of this massacre and the lives destroyed by it.

The post-revolutionary promise of a national modernity that would integrate Mexico's most impoverished and displaced lower classes is violently squashed. This failure of the state plays out at the level of the vernacular story as well. When Cleo views the violence, she goes into early labour, and her and Fermín's child is stillborn. The film invites a possible metaphorical reading of this scene: the "product" of a biological union of Mexico's lowest classes – the *ladino* from the *ciudades perdidas* and the migrant Indigenous domestic worker – dies, and with it the promise of change. Notably, no further scenes are framed by political posters. It is as though even the appearance of democracy and civil protest is now completely silenced.

This central scene was seared into the collective memory at a time when many Mexicans were still grappling with the 1968 massacre. Yet increased state repression in subsequent years meant that no official histories or stories would surface about it. Cuarón recaptures the place and experience of the ten-year-old boy who was deserted by his father and who saw footage of the massacre on television, but more significantly he underscores a nearly fifty-year process of forgetting and remembering.[84] As spectators we witness his historic recreations of the same street, parked cars, furniture store, and even the doubles of people in historic photographs. This historical grounding of the visual scene helps a sense of witnessing that is key to Cuarón's technique. Through an elaborate spatialization of a moment in the historical event the film offers millions of global viewers a glimpse of the social dynamics behind the massacre, a state repression fed by US involvement and built upon colonial spaces and class systems.

A final set of strategically placed signs points to a parallel process unfolding alongside PRI repression: the burgeoning urban modernity of Mexico City. As we saw in Pacheco's story, when Carlos lingers at the central artery of Avenida Insurgentes in Colonia Roma, he glimpses

---

84 Cuarón notes that as he explored this through Cleo's life, he "realized these were wounds that I shared with many people in Mexico. And then I came to the conclusion that they are wounds shared by humanity" (Hattenstone).

for the first time the beginning of his own transformation to a new era in the 1950s. It is on this same avenue lined with signs of modernization (the national Aeronaves de México, and Banco Serfín, a Mexican bank later taken over by a London-based entity) that Cuarón places Cleo and the children on their way to the movies in downtown Roma. The scene evokes both a palpable excitement and a sense of the fear of disappearing into the crowd of this new modernity when Cleo cannot find one of the boys. During a later scene in which Sofía and Cleo drive to the medical clinic to confirm Cleo's pregnancy, the distraught pair passes more commercial signs of progress. Among them are advertisements for Corona beer, signalling the rise of a transnational beer company that would largely replace the popular, local pulquerias, and a sign for Cruz Azul cement and its promise to build "El México moderno."[85] The same Cruz Azul advertisements appear again later in the film, this time set against the poverty and lack of modern infrastructure in Nezahualcoyotl. This commercialized web of national and transnational processes further resignifies space and material culture in conjunction with the racial and class axises of coloniality-modernity. *Roma*'s cinematic layering of signs, places, and material culture produces a nuanced social history of spatialization in the form of a personal story.

Coloniality and Cultural Spatialization: Questions for Further Reflection

While critics generally agree that Cuarón accurately depicts a larger national narrative of state violence, they debate the nature of his portrayal of his Indigenous character Cleo. With these ongoing discussions in mind, I close by posing a number of questions for continued reflection as developed in and by *Roma*. First, I touch on the portrayal of Cleo and then I move on to suggest that while Cuarón seeks to depict an awareness of racial politics and of their cultural significance, his use of spatialization as technique evidences the impossibility of gaining full access to an Indigenous perspective. It is apparent, as many critics have shown, that in the very process of filmmaking, Cuarón repeats some of the same colonizing gestures he sought to expose, yet in doing so, he opens up avenues for further consideration.

---

85 One perspective on Cruz Azul reveals a positive alternative to Americanized industry. The cement company is a workers' cooperative and sponsored a popular and highly successful soccer team that won six championships in the 1970s. In one scene in the film *Roma* the older Cuarón son jokes about the team, and one of them wears a Cruz Azul jersey.

To begin, critics have discussed widely whether the film only further recolonizes Indigenous domestic workers. Díaz de la Vega, for example, argues: "podría hacer más visible los problemas de clase a los que alude y que resuelve con un abrazo. Después de todo, querer a la sirvienta no es liberarla."[86] Other critics focus on Cleo's relative silence in the film, for indeed, one familiar archetype that *Roma* inherits from the colonial era is that of the silent *indio* in need of white patriarchal guidance, whether by the church, by the state, or by individual employers.[87] This portrayal flourished in mid-century Mexico as part of the inheritance of *indigenismo* and in such influential authors as Octavio Paz.[88] Yet, still other critics see a more complex subtlety in Cuarón's portrayal of Cleo within the middle-class family and how it reveals the domestic social spaces inherited from colonialism that exacerbated classism during Mexico's modernization process.[89] The camera, as we have seen in the scenes described earlier, records society's dysfunction, a panoptic *imperfection* made visible in the middle- and upper-classes' dependence on maintaining class and racial boundaries through the new domestic economy.

The camera focuses on Cleo's daily routines in a way that highlights one thing in particular about the relationships of which she is a part and those spaces in which they develop: they are not the kind of social spaces in which an Indigenous domestic worker, much less one who is a woman, can engage in long speeches. As a liminal figure in the film's middle-class household – both a physical space and a relationship of employment – Cleo silently registers everything around her. Her look serves as a strong counterpoint to her reticence to speak, and the realities of the life of a female Indigenous domestic worker and the film's script deny Cleo a *discurso* like the one we hear from Fermín; she has no opportunity to relate her origins and poverty. In this respect, the spaces

---

86   "He could give greater visibility to the class problems he alludes to and solves with a hug. After all, loving the maid does not liberate her."

87   See Brody, "There's a Voice Missing"; and Zatarain, "How Criticisms of Roma Have Revealed American Biases."

88   Some have argued, however, that a number of Mexican artists have worked actively to subvert these tropes. Notably, Lund argues that Elena Garro, among others, inverts the archetype of the *indio callado* in order to highlight a subtle resistance to systematic racial discrimination (*The Mestizo State* 118).

89   See, for example, Sánchez Prado: "Detractors of the film have noted that Cleo's submission and silence reproduce longstanding stereotypes. They also wish there was more of her voice . . . . These critiques are fair, but also somewhat simplistic ... A film in which Cleo 'had a voice,' whatever that could have meant, would altogether miss the point of her constant dehumanization" ("Special Dossier").

through which she moves become just as telling as her "muted" but highly visual interactions with others in the film.

Notably, however, as the camera moves into rooms that are out of earshot of the family, we begin to hear more of Cleo's voice and learn something of her origins. Through short exchanges between Cleo and her more talkative Mixteca friend Adela, we find out that the government has confiscated Cleo's family land in Oaxaca. These two elements – land and language – have been the official "markers" of indigeneity for centuries. Although infrastructures of race began in the colonial period, land reform was also at the heart of the revolution, promising fair redistribution of land. The PRI altered land-reform policies multiple times over decades, but these policies were largely unsuccessful in creating equality. Instead, the reforms, together with modernization in general, stimulated huge migrations of Indigenous communities to urban centres. By the twenty-first century, however, laws that had often linked indigeneity with spatial practices had been recodified and had increasingly linked indigeneity along historical and ethnolinguistic traits.[90] Like many others, the state's confiscation of land, as well as its changing of the laws defining indigeneity and its accompanying rights, has disenfranchised Cleo. With no *pueblo* to return to, she has no choice but to move to the city as a domestic worker, her connection to the public space now defined by her employment in the private sphere.

The film adds another suggestive dimension to Cleo's voice and story within her domestic space and Indigenous language. After the scenes of a stillbirth and a near-drowning in Veracruz, Cleo returns to Roma and her domestic duties. As she carries the laundry up to the rooftop, however, she uncharacteristically initiates conversation and animatedly calls out in Mixtec to Adela: "But I have so much to tell you." The film suggests that her full story can only be told off-screen – away from the eye of the camera and that of the spectator – in the privacy of their closet-like quarters and in Mixtec. In so doing, the filmmaker seems to acknowledge that as an outsider – and his own position as a transnational filmmaker living in the United States – he cannot tell the whole

---

90 See, for example, changes in the ejido system before the signing of NAFTA (1992) and the 2001 and 2003 constitutional amendments. Cuarón notes that he not only wanted his actor to look like his Mixteca nanny but was pleased when he found one who also spoke enough Mixtec and could add the linguistic and personal "mystery" he experienced as a child; his family did not understand Mixtec. Cuarón observes: "[I]f we're looking at the disparity that exists in our country between class and ethnic group, the effect is even more pronounced when an ethnic group speaks several indigenous languages other than Spanish" (*Road to Roma*).

story, a story built upon, as he notes, "a solid power dynamic cultivated over centuries and rooted in colonial hierarchies of power" (quoted in Shaw 2018).

Cuarón's awareness of these limits to the story that he tells about Mexico and his impulse to explore those very limits emerged much earlier in his career. Sánchez Prado glosses Cuarón's repositioning of Mexico's cinematic portrayal at the turn of the millennium as "the construction of a national cinema thoroughly uninterested in engaging with the nation as such." Much as we have observed in *Roma*, "[t]his is due, in part, to the collapse of Mexicanism as an apparatus of the construction of overarching identitary narratives" amidst the rising importance of "race, class, [and] gender ... in the ideological economy" of global cinema (*Screening Neoliberalism* 192). Here, the filmmaker further complicates this dialogue among different social classes and even seems to suggest that the truth can only ever be that which remains just out of earshot. Although Cuarón breaks with the traditional representations of Indigenous characters, argues Sánchez Prado, his transnational films require familiarity with their national origins if only to "fully deterritorialize and undermine the codes of the national." Moreover, he posits that the director himself intentionally exploits "the ability of film to reflect on its own ideological and identitary limits ... [opening] the door for a properly post-national cinema" (195; order modified). In this respect, then, the clear impasses of Cuarón's *Roma* seem to constitute more an ongoing and unsettling engagement with the limits of the modern Mexican nation than either a collective disavowal of it or a personal alibi for its violence.

This absence of a single narrative interpretation poses a dilemma for audiences because understanding Cleo presupposes that we accept the filmmaker's projection of his own interpretations onto her. In this respect, the critic who chides Cuarón because "querer la sirvienta no es liberarla" (Díaz de la Vega) creates an impossible situation. If he had liberated Cleo, giving her autonomy and a voice, then it would have only further conferred power on the filmmaker, now seen as capable not only of representing history but also of liberating oppressed subjects and even giving them voice. Cuarón's refusal to do this appears to be an ethical move, even if it is not without problems of its own.

Moving beyond issues of equivalence between fictional representation and Indigenous agency, there emerge further questions about how in the very process of filmmaking Cuarón repeats some of the same colonizing gestures he sought to expose – and in so doing, he brings a larger polemic to light. *Roma* is largely a tribute to Cuarón's real-life Mixteca nanny, Liboria Rodríguez, whose bit part in *Y tu mamá también* – in which Rodríguez herself plays a domestic worker for a self-absorbed middle-class character – has since transformed into a full-fledged portrait, now acted by the Mixteca actress Yalitza Aparicio. Cuarón's methods for researching Rodríguez's life in order to make the film nevertheless call into question his ability to escape the more subtle recolonization practices that one might have associated with her flat role in *Y tu mamá también*. In detailed interviews of Rodríguez, the filmmaker did not explicitly tell her why he was digging into her past, initially gathering information without her knowledge or her consent. She notes in an interview, "He was getting all this information without me knowing what it was for," and she continues: "'How do you remember this, Libo?' he said. 'Help me remember and understand.' Then it started to become weird. 'Libo, what did you used to wear? How did you dress?' Things like that." (Tapley).[91] Like anthropologists, historians, and documentary filmmakers who have mined Indigenous knowledge and practices for public consumption and to advance their own careers, Cuarón mined Rodríguez's memory and experiences to supplement his own for the film. Without Rodríguez's insights into her life in social spaces separated from those of a ten-year-old, middle-class boy – her domestic "closet," the servants' quarters at the hacienda, or the places where suitors came from – the film would not carry such social weight about classism and racism.

Roma certainly moves towards a deeper study of an Indigenous domestic-worker experience than in his 2001 film. In this way, it could be seen as indexing a broader trend towards decolonial projects that endeavour to tell the story of modernity from the standpoint of oppressed peoples, but it remains a middle-class cultural project. In fact, telling the story in this way relies on Cleo (Libo) continuing to occupy the same position within the social hierarchies of Mexico City in the early 1970s. Nevertheless, this contradictory thought put forth for us by the film prompts a larger question still: perhaps the recording of this past-present exposes a colonizing process more than Cuarón had first intended, but in doing so, it projects a possible space for a different future.

---

91 Notably, Cuarón does not mention this key input from Rodríguez in his documentary about the making of *Roma*. Instead, he mentions how he asked his creative crew, including Eugenio Caballero, who also grew up in Colonia Roma, to participate in group writing sessions about their memories of Mexico: "They used their own particular memories to create an interpretation of what I had asked for" (*Road to Roma*).

In a similar vein the question of Indigenous representation in global cultural spaces has also come to the fore in discussion about the actor who played Rodríguez. Reactions to Yalitza Aparicio's performance as Cleo span the spectrum. *Vogue México*, for example, featured Aparicio on its cover. For the first time in its twenty-year history of marketing Americanized culture to Mexicans, an Indigenous woman occupied this media space that has reinforced the ethnic privileging of white appearances and culture (Tillman). The move reflects, once again, a broader decolonizing gesture, as well as the changing dynamics of the cultural wars within the market system. Both the bilingual (Spanish and Mixtec) headline and Aparicio's folkloric dress proclaim her ethnicity. This process reveals how Americanization has reached into Indigenous communities, and Cuarón has played a part in this by bringing Aparicio to Hollywood. The actress herself notes the shift in media representations and cultural production with respect to race: "I never watched too much TV myself as a kid, because no one else looked like me on the screen" (Cabral).

The responses to this decolonization of the fashion industry – or, alternatively, the use of decolonization as an opportunity for capital gain – revealed a deep, ongoing racism. Anonymous readers, for example, posted comments such as "fea," "mantente en tu lugar," and a popular soap opera star was caught on tape denigrating Aparicio with racial slurs. Aparicio's hometown, Tlaxiaco, Oaxaca, however, commissioned a sixteen-foot mural of the actor for the town plaza, where residents gathered to watch the 2018 Oscars. One inhabitant observed that Aparicio was "like an emblem for us … she is a strong spirit" (Kahn). As Aparicio's image occupies cultural spaces, whether they be the Mexicanized *Vogue* or the central plaza in an Indigenous town, it provides new venues in which ethnicity and identity are debated and centuries-old social history is worked out. Film critic Carla Marcantonio observes the popular reception of *Roma* and the key role that Aparicio plays in challenging aesthetic and ideological standards: "In fact, global cinema can resonate only when the language it speaks exceeds the need for translation. It may be the case that Netflix and its distributor, Participant Media, leveraged Aparicio's image for marketing purposes, but it is also unmistakably the case that in giving her such a high-profile and global platform, they have also given her a place where her voice may be amplified" (43–4). Whether or not people agree with Cuarón's working methods and the film industry, *Roma* has reached a far more diverse, international audience than would have been possible through traditional distribution channels, and it became a phenomenon in 2019, possibly even influencing recent attempts at new legislation to protect Mexico's more than two million domestic workers.[92]

This broad spectrum of reactions that focus on Indigenous characters, domestic workers, and actors raises a final question: As viewers how do we navigate our own responses to the relationship between the director, the film, the actor, and the industry? What else might this tell us about continuing sites of coloniality? Cuarón can only partially tell the story of an Indigenous domestic worker, unlike the well-documented story of PRI violence, and his choice of working methods and actors showcases the impossibility of his effort to tell a story based on an Indigenous character steeped in the racialized spaces of the domestic sphere, the urban core, and the rural hinterlands. Such representations, he notes, draw on "some aspects of the colonia [colonial period]," yet one cannot blame Cuarón alone for what, as he puts it, "is true for the rest of the world … for developed countries that … nunca se pone el saco … they never own their own guilt" (Utichi). In this respect we need not marvel that the story of an Indigenous woman forced from her community and living with a middle-class family as a domestic worker in the Mexico City of the 1970s has hit home around the world today. *Roma*'s cinematic *escenografía* forwards a contradiction so intimate that it should resonate with viewers without their fully recognizing it.

Contemporary Social Forgetting

Roma's visual detail recreates sites of colonial encounters that point to the coloniality of political and class formation in modern Mexico. While political posters frame for us the PRI's strategy of governance, as well as the failure of the projects of the revolution and *mexicanidad*, they also insist on this history's contemporary relevance. In fact, Cuarón first began to conceptualize *Roma* in 2000, around the filming of *Y tu mamá también*, and the year in which decades of PRI secessionism ended with the election of PAN's Vicente Fox. Upon taking office, Fox initiated an investigation of the massacres that had taken place when Echeverría was minister of the interior (1968) and president (1971). Although he was formally charged, the judiciary branch concluded that there was insufficient evidence to link him to either massacre. Popular calls for justice occasionally resurface, one even demanding that Echeverría be charged with genocide.[93]

---

92   There are new measures for Mexico's 2.5 million domestic workers, 85 per cent of whom are women; see Villegas, "Mexico's Congress Votes."

93   See "Mexico Ex-President May Avoid Massacre Trial."

Since Fox's presidency the office has bounced back and forth between parties, first with Felipe Calderón (2006–12) and the war on drugs, which escalated violence to an official death toll of approximately sixty thousand people, and later, Enrique Peña Nieto, under whom forty-three university students disappeared in the Ayotzinapa incident. These state practices are a reminder that the "dirty war" and necropolitics continue. Cuarón's film looks back on 1971, aware of the modifications and repetitions that have marked the intervening decades of Mexican history. Echeverrían propaganda in a variety of spatialized sites of colonial encounters serves as a motif to evoke the human face of a hidden, controlling biopolitical power. In this case Cuarón stresses how an authoritarian regime has taken over the ideals of the post-revolutionary state. He recalls placing one sign in particular, reading "L.E.A. [Luis Echeverría Álvarez] for the greatness of Mexico," at the site of the Halconazo massacre to highlight "the context of the Mexico I grew up in, and to weave in this perverse relationship that exists in Mexico … between class and race" (2020). *Roma* does not purport to solve problems registered in terms of class and race but to show such solutions for what they are: "perverse," as Cuarón notes.

Cuarón's local and personal story reveals sites of social forgetting, of stories that go underground and are surrounded by "a cloud of socially produced silence" (Beiner 15). But his mission goes deeper, seemingly to highlight something more akin to Achille Mbembe's conceptualization of the post-colony as an entanglement and displacement of peoples, places, and stories – an enduring biopolitical stratification and the legacies of coloniality in modernity.[94] Through the narrative and cinematic depiction of his childhood home, of Colonia Roma's modern boulevards, and of the social landscapes of wealth (the hacienda) and poverty (Nezahualcoyotl) surrounding Mexico City, the filmmaker reveals layers of coloniality-modernity amidst urbanized geographies, and in doing so, he connects multiple historical eras by way of an enduring classism and racism exercised through spatial practices. The film both implicates state practices and suggests individual complicities in the racialized creations of space. This overlaying of past and present, of narrative points of view, and of formal elements immerses us in the sensory, material space of the modern capital, prodding us to awaken to awareness of our own processes and places of social forgetting and colonization.

---

94   See Mbembe, *On the Postcolony*.

In subsequent chapters we study further this contemporary coloniality as explored in a wide range of cultural production and spaces. In a similar manner to the works of Pacheco and Cuarón considered here, chapter 2 studies the works by novelist José Arreola and filmmaker Carlos Reygadas and asks us to re-evaluate the success of the Mexican Revolution. Chapter 3 moves into discussions about the resurgence of popular religion as a contemporary form of resistance, and chapter 4 examines the US-Mexico borderlands as ongoing sites of colonialism in relation to a new imperial power. All three of these chapters continue to pull on threads established here. Our final chapter brings us back full circle to contemporary Spain and to the subtle – and not so subtle – ways that an ongoing struggle to maintain colonial hegemony over Mexico finds itself mediated in the cultural sphere.

Both Pacheco's and Cuarón's local and personal stories reveal sites of social forgetting in Mexico City's Colonia Roma and beyond. Pacheco's story of the colonia in 1950 and Cuarón's cinematic vision of the same place twenty years later reveal sedimented layers of racialization through the elaboration of evolving colonial, post-colonial, and neocolonial power structures. We witness the failure of the revolution – a point studied further in the study of Arreola and Reygadas in chapter 2 – and its ideological *mexicanidad*, alongside the emergence of PRI repression and modernization. Taken together, the two works just studied point to an assemblage of coloniality-modernity some fifty years after the revolution and the promotion of a mestizo state. Their stories call up the inherent multiplicity of history and bring into view our own processes of social forgetting, which in turn raises questions about "the potential geographies of our social responsibility" (Massey 10) and asks for "a fuller recognition of the simultaneous co-existence of others with their own trajectory and their own stories to tell" (Beiner 10–11). They show us how cultural objects and space can be mobilized in storytelling to reveal suppressed histories retroactively from the present.

WORKS CITED

Acevedo-Munoz, Ernesto R. "Sex, Class, and Mexico in Alfonso Cuaron's *Y tu mamá también*." *Film & History: An Interdisciplinary Journal of Film and Television Studies*, vol. 34, no. 1, 2004, pp. 39–48.

Balkan, Stacey. "Rogues in the Postcolony: Chris Abani's *GraceLand* and the Petro-Picaresque." *The Global South*, vol. 9, no. 2, 2015, pp. 18–37.

Barrantes, Beatriz. "Transformaciones seculares en la Ciudad de México: *Las batallas en el desierto* de José Emilio Pacheco." *Taller de Letras*, vol. 34, 2004, pp. 25–37.

Beiner, Guy. *Forgetful Remembrance: Social Forgetting and Vernacular Historiography of a Rebellion in Ulster*. Oxford UP, 2018.

Brody, Richard. "There's a Voice Missing in Alfonso Cuarón's *Roma*." *The New Yorker*, 18 Dec. 2018,

Buscaglia-Salgado, José F. "Race and the Constitutive Inequality of the Modern/Colonial Condition." *Critical Terms in Caribbean and Latin American Thought: Historical and Institutional and Trajectories*, edited by Yolanda Martínez-San Miguel, Ben Sifuentes-Jauregui, and Marisa Belausteguigoitia, Palgrave Press, 2016, pp. 109–24.

Cabral, Javier. "Roma Made Yalitza Aparicio a Star. Now She's Giving a Voice to Her Indigenous Fans." *Washington Post*, 21 Feb. 2019, https://www .washingtonpost.com/entertainment/roma-made-yalitza-aparicio-a-star -now-shes-giving-a-voice-to-her-indigenous-fans/2019/02/21/d003f3da -2ef8-11e9-813a-0ab2f17e305b_story.html.

Cabrera, Luis. "The Mexican Situation from a Mexican Point of View." *The Journal of Race Development*, vol. 4, no. 3, 1914, pp. 245–61.

Cárdenas, Lázaro. "El problema indígena de México." Primero congreso Indigenistas Interamericano. Departamento de Asuntos Indígenas, 1940.

Contreras, Joseph. *In the Shadow of the Giant: The Americanization of Modern Mexico*. Rutgers UP, 2009.

Cuarón, Alfonso. "Alfonso Cuarón on *Y Tu Mamá También*." YouTube, uploaded by Film at Lincoln Center, 11 Jan. 2019, https://youtu.be/Auvz7kBw1Hk.

– *Road to Roma*. Netflix, 2020. https://www.netflix.com/title/81085934.

– "ROMA Press Conference | Alfonso Cuarón, Yalitza Aparicio & Marina de Tavira | NYFF56." YouTube, uploaded by Film at Lincoln Center, 8 Oct. 2018, https://youtu.be/_ngzNMD_bvg.

Díaz de la Vega, Alonso. "Roma, o las dicotomías de la forma." *El Universal*, 28 Nov. 2018, http://www.eluniversal.com.mx/alonso-diaz-de-la-vega /roma-o-las-dicotomias-de-la-forma.

Doyle, Kate. 2003. "The Corpus Christi Massacre: Mexico's Attack on Its Student Movement, June 10, 1971." *The National Security Archive*, 3 June 2003, https://nsarchive2.gwu.edu/NSAEBB/NSAEBB91/.

Epple, Juan Armando. "De Santa a Mariana: La Ciudad de México como utopía traicionada." *Revista chilena de literatura*, vol. 54, 1999, pp. 31–42.

Foucault, Michel. *Society Must Be Defended: Lectures at the Collège de France, 1975–76*. Translated by David Macey, Picador, 2003.

Franco, Jean. *Cruel Modernity*. Duke UP, 2013.

García Canclini, Néstor. *Consumidores y ciudadanos: Conflictos multiculturales de la globalización*. Grijalbo, 1995.

– "Narrar la multiculturalidad." *Revista de crítica literaria Latinoamericana*, año XXI, no. 42, 1995, pp. 9–20.

Giddens, Anthony. *The Constitution of Society: Outline of the Theory of Structuration*. Polity, 1984.

Hattenstone, Simon. "Alfonso Cuarón on *Roma*." *The Guardian*, 21 Dec. 2018, https://www.theguardian.com/film/2018/dec/21/alfonso-cuaron-on-roma-we-cast-for-almost-a-year-i-couldnt-find-the-right-person.

Hill, Ruth. *Hierarchy, Commerce, and Fraud in Bourbon Spanish America: A Postal Inspector's Exposé*. Vanderbilt UP, 2005.

Jiménez-Sandoval, Saúl. "Capitalismo, deseo, y el anti-Edipo en *Las batallas en el desierto*." *Mexican Studies/Estudios Mexicanos*, vol. 27, no. 2, 2011, pp. 431–48.

Kahn, Carrie. "Roma Actress Brings Attention to Indigenous Roots in Hometown." *NPR Morning Edition*, 22 Feb. 2019, https://www.npr.org/2019/02/22/696944227/roma-actress-brings-attention-to-indigenous-roots-in-hometown.

Lefebvre, Henri. *The Production of Space*. Translated by Donald Nicholson-Smith, Blackwell, 1991.

Lomnitz-Adler, Claudio. *Exits from the Labyrinth: Culture and Ideology in the Mexican National Space*. U of California P, 1992.

Lund, Joshua. "The Mestizo State: Colonization and Indianization in Liberal Mexico." *PMLA*, vol. 123, no. 5, 2008, pp. 1418–33.

– *The Mestizo State: Reading Race in Modern Mexico*. U of Minnesota P, 2012.

Maldonado-Torres, Nelson. "Colonialism, Neocolonial, Internal Colonialism, the Postcolonial, Coloniality, and Decoloniality." *Critical Terms in Caribbean and Latin American Thought: Historical and Institutional and Trajectories*, edited by Yolanda Martínez-San Miguel, Ben Sifuentes-Jauregui, and Marisa Belausteguigoitia, Palgrave Press, 2016, pp. 67–78.

Marcantonio, Carla. "Roma: Silence, Language, and the Ambiguous Power of Affect." *Film Quarterly*, vol. 72, no. 4, 2019, pp. 38–45. https://doi.org/10.1525/fq.2019.72.4.38.

Martínez, María Elena. *Genealogical Fictions: Limpieza de Sangre, Religion, and Gender in Colonial Mexico*. Stanford UP, 2008.

Massey, Doreen. *For Space*. Sage, 2005.

Mbembe, Achille. "Necropolitics." Translated by Libby Meintjes, *Public Culture*, vol. 15, no. 1, 2003, pp. 11–40.

– *On the Postcolony*. U of California P, 2001.

Merrell, Floyd. "Uncommonplace Happenings: Post-Tlatelolco Mexican Narrative." *Latin American Research Review*, vol. 23, no. 3, 1988, pp. 180–7.

Mexico. Constitución política de los Estados Unidos Mexicanos. https://www.diputados.gob.mx/LeyesBiblio/pdf/CPEUM.pdf.

"Mexico Ex-President May Avoid Massacre Trial." *Reuters*, 12 July 2007. https://www.reuters.com/article/us-mexico-echeverria/mexico-ex-president-may-avoid-massacre-trial-idUSN1237142520070712.

Mignolo, Walter. *The Darker Side of Western Modernity: Global Futures, Decolonial Options*. Duke UP, 2011.

Moorhead-Rosenberg, Florence. "Message in a Bottle: Tricks of Time in *Las batallas en el desierto*, by José Emilio Pacheco." *Rocky Mountain Review of Language and Literature*, vol. 53, no. 1, 1999, pp. 11–28.

Myers, Kathleen Ann. "An Archeology of Mexican Modernity: Social Forgetting and the Coloniality of Space in José Emilio Pacheco's Colonia Roma." *Estudios Mexicanos*, vol. 37, no. 2, 2021, pp. 232–62.

Negrín, Edith. "Huellas del 68 en textos de José Emilio Pacheco." *José Emilio Pacheco: Reescritura en movimiento*, edited by Yvette Jiménez de Báez, Colegio de México, 2014, pp. 171–92.

Nemser, Daniel. *Infrastructures of Race: Concentration and Biopolitics in Colonial Mexico*. U of Texas P, 2017.

Neumann, Emiliano Bautista. "¿Por qué 'Roma' de Alfonso Cuarón es importante para construir la memoria colectiva de la Ciudad de México?" ["Why Is Alfonso Cuarón's 'Roma' Important for Building the Collective Memory of Mexico City?"]. *ArchDaily*, 3 Mar. 2019, https://www.archdaily.mx/mx/910816/por-que-roma-de-alfonso-cuaron-es-importante-para-construir-la-memoria-colectiva-de-la-ciudad-de-mexico.

O'Brien, Gabrielle. 2019. "Remembrances as Reconstruction: Excavating Memory in Roma." *Screen Education*, vol. 96, 2019, pp. 8–15.

Ouweneel, Arij, and Rik Hoekstra. "Las tierras de los pueblos de indios en el altiplano de México, 1560–1920: Una aportación teórica interpretativa." CEDLA, 1998, https://www.researchgate.net/publication/237825118.

Pacheco, José Emilio. "A 30 años de la publicación de *Las batallas del desierto*." *José Emilio Pacheco: Reescritura en movimiento*, edited by Yvette Jiménez de Báez, Colegio de México, 2014, pp. 195–207.

– *Las batallas en el desierto*. Mexico: Ediciones Era, 1981.

– *Battles in the Desert*. Trans. Katherine Silver. New Directions Publishing, 2021.

Puar, Jasbir K. *The Right to Maim: Debility, Capacity, Disability*. Duke UP, 2017.

– *Terrorist Assemblages: Homonationalism in Queer Times*. Duke UP, 2017.

Quijano, Aníbal. 2000. "Coloniality of Power and Eurocentrism in Latin America." *International Sociology*, vol. 15, no. 2, pp. 215–32. https://doi.org/10.1177/026858090001500200.

Road to Roma. Directed by Gabriel Nuncio and Andres Clariond, Netflix, 2020.

Ruiz, Eduardo. "El reverso del 'milagro mexicano': La crítica de la nación en *Las batallas en el desierto* y *El vampiro de la Colonia Roma*." *Ciberletras*, vol. 26, 2011.

Saldaña-Portillo, María Josefina. *Indian Given: Racial Geographies across Mexico and the United States*. Duke UP, 2016.

Sánchez Prado, Ignacio M. *Screening Neoliberalism: Transforming Mexican Cinema, 1988–2012*. Vanderbilt UP, 2014.

– "Special Dossier on Alfonso Cuarón's *Roma*: Class Trouble." *Mediático*, 24 Dec. 2018, https://reframe.sussex.ac.uk/mediatico/2018/12/24/special-dossier-on-alfonso-cuarons-roma-class-trouble/.

Shaw, Deborah. "Special Dossier on *Roma*: Children of Women? Alfonso Cuarón's Love Letter to His Nana." *Mediático*, 24 Dec. 2018, https:// reframe.sussex.ac.uk/mediatico/2018/12/24/special-dossier-on-roma -alfonso-cuarons-love-letter-to-his-nana/.

Sobrit, Antonio. "Metamorfosis de *Las batallas en el desierto*." *Nexos*, vol. 34, no. 408, 2011, pp. 93–4.

Soja, Edward W. "Taking Space Personally." *The Spatial Turn: Interdisciplinary Perspectives*, edited by Barney Warf and Santa Arias, Routledge, 2009, pp. 11–36.

Solórzano, Fernanda. "Entrevista a Alfonso Cuarón 'Con Roma quería honrar el tiempo y el espacio; que los lugares dictaran lo que iba a pasar'" ["Interview with Alfonso Cuarón"]. *Letras Libres*, 2 Dec. 2018, https:// letraslibres.com/revista/entrevista-a-alfonso-cuaron-con-roma-queria -honrar-el-tiempo-y-el-espacio-que-los-lugares-dictaran-lo-que-iba-a-pasar/.

Tapley, Kristopher. "Alfonso Cuarón on the Painful and Poetic Backstory Behind *Roma*." *Variety*, 23 Oct 2018, http://www.variety.com/2018/film /news/roma-alfonso-Cuar%C3%B3n-%20netflix-libo-rodriguez-1202988695/.

Tavares López, Edgar. *Colonia Roma*. Clío, 1996.

Tillman, Laura. "Yalitza Aparicio of Roma and the Politics of Stardom in Mexico." *New York Times*, 17 Jan. 2019, https://www.nytimes.com/2019/01/17/movies /yalitza-aparicio-roma.html.

Utichi, Joseph. "'Roma' Director Alfonso Cuarón on How His Most Personal Film Became His Biggest Career Challenge – Venice Q&A." *Deadline*, 31 Aug. 2018, https://deadline.com/2018/08/roma-alfonso -cuaron-venice-film-festival-netflix-interview-1202455061/.

Vasconcelos, José. *La raza cósmica: Misión de la raza iberoamericana; Argentina y Brasil*. Espasa-Calpe, 1948.

Villegas, Paulina. "Mexico's Congress Votes to Expand Domestic Workers' Labor Rights." *New York Times*, 14 May 2019, https://www.nytimes. com/2019/05/14/world/americas/mexico-domestic-workers-law.html.

Warf, Barney, and Santa Arias. *The Spatial Turn: Interdisciplinary Perspectives*. Routledge, 2009.

Wolfenzon, Carolyn. "*Las batallas en el desierto*: La inversión del melodrama cinematográfico como estrategia crítica sobre la revolución mexicana." *Confluencia: Revista hispánica de cultura y literatura*, vol. 27, no. 2, 2012, pp. 46–60.

Zatarain, Ana Karina. "How Criticisms of *Roma* have Revealed American Biases." *Hyperallergic*, 4 Feb. 2019, https://hyperallergic.com/482505 /how-criticisms-of-roma-have-revealed-american-biases/.

2 Pocket-Sized Apocalypses: Coloniality in Juan José Arreola's *La feria* and Carlos Reygadas's "Este es mi reino"

PABLO GARCÍA LOAEZA

While *Las batallas en el desierto* and *Roma* focus on Mexico's urban centre through their respective protagonists' point of view, Juan José Arreola's *La feria* (*The Fair*) (1963) portrays Mexico's rural periphery – including its marginal spaces and groups – through myriad perspectives going back to pre-Hispanic times. However, like Pacheco and Cuarón, Arreola overlays different historical periods, eschewing strict chronology to uncover conflicted histories and reveal enduring legacies and practices built on centuries of discriminatory racialization and supported by colonial, post-colonial, and neocolonial power structures.

La feria begins with an act of historical recollection by Juan Tepano. His seemingly timeless voice ties the present and the past as he lays out the two issues, religious devotion and land ownership, that run through the text:

> Somos más o menos treinta mil. Unos dicen que más, otros que menos. Somos treinta mil desde siempre. Desde que Fray Juan de Padilla vino a enseñarnos el catecismo, cuando Don Alonso de Ávalos dejó temblando estas tierras. Fray Juan era buena gente y andaba de aquí para allá vestido de franciscano, con la ropa hecha garras, levantando cruces y capillitas … Pero le fue mal y dizque lo matamos. Dicen que aquí, dicen que allá. Si fue en Tuxpan, lo hicieron cuachala. Si fue aquí, nos lo comimos en pozole. Mentiras. Lo mataron en Cíbola a flechazos. Sea por Dios.

> Antes la tierra era de nosotros los naturales. Ahora es de las gentes de razón. La cosa viene de lejos … Lo cierto es que la tierra ya no es de nosotros y allá cada y cuando nos acordamos. Sacamos los papeles antiguos y seguimos dale y dale. "Señor Oidor, Señor Gobernador del Estado, Señor Obispo, Señor Capitán General, Señor Virrey de la Nueva

España, Señor Presidente de la República ... Soy Juan Tepano, el más viejo de los tlayacanques, para servir a usted: nos lo quitaron todo." (Arreola 7–8)[1]

According to Arreola, these two paragraphs condense the spirit of a work that he characterized as an *apocalipsis de bolsillo*, a pocket-sized apocalypse (Carballo 406; Albala 680). The central plot follows the efforts by the local Indigenous authorities, the Tlayacanques, to reclaim the sponsorship of Señor San José, the town's patron saint, as well as their ancestral property rights, against the will, wealth, and clout of Zapotlán's ruling class, represented mainly by Don Abigail. However, instead of there being a single, sequentially ordered narrative, the reader must reconstruct several stories from 288 short fragments that offer a semi-fictionalized social and historical panorama, from ancient times to 22 October 1957, of Zapotlán el Grande, Arreola's birthplace.[2] Most fragments are statements that reflect the various characters' individual views in their own voices. Some characters speak more than others, some belong to the past, and some even come from heaven. *La feria*'s intentionally fragmentary and non-coherent nature is a structural manifestation of its apocalyptic sense.

A more recent example of a pocket-sized apocalypse is the short film "Este es mi reino" ("This Is My Kingdom") (2010) by internationally acclaimed director Carlos Reygadas. Though its production design and running time (twelve minutes) preclude *La feria*'s level of

---

1 "We are thirty thousand, more or less. Some say more, some less. We've been thirty thousand since forever. Since Friar Juan de Padilla came to teach us the catechism when Don Alonso de Ávalos made these lands shudder. Friar Juan was good people and went to and fro in Franciscan garb, with his clothes in tatters, erecting crosses and little chapels. ... But he came to a bad end, and they say we killed him. Here, they say; there, they say. If it was in Tuxpan, he was made into *cuachala* stew. If it was here, we ate him in *pozole* soup. Lies. He was killed by arrows in Cíbola. God's will be done.

   "The land used to belong to us, the natives. Now it belongs to 'right-reasoning' people. It's been so since way back. ... The fact is that the land no longer belongs to us and, every now and then, we think about it. We take out the old papers and keep trying, over and over. 'Señor Judge, Señor State Governor, Señor Bishop, Señor Captain General, Señor Viceroy of New Spain, Señor President ... I'm Juan Tepano, the oldest of the Tlayacanques, at your service: they took everything from us.'" All translations are my own.

2 In 1856, Zapotlán el Grande was officially renamed Ciudad Guzmán in honour of General Gordiano Guzmán, who fought in the Mexican war of independence and the

depth and substance, the film presents similar issues in analogous ways. Its analysis confirms that the apocalyptic genre is well suited to revealing Mexico's enduring coloniality. The opening scene shows a donkey standing by a stone wall; it is a timeless evocation of rural Mexico. Next, a fashionably dressed man, speaking to a woman sitting next to him, says: "Todas las montañas que están aquí, que ves, son las mismas, bueno, el paisaje es el mismo que pudo haber visto Hernán Cortés cuando conquistó la zona. Se ha de haber quedado de a cuatro con el Tepozteco."[3] The historical reference sets the stage for the stark social contrasts – ultimately stemming from the conquest and its colonial aftermath – exposed through a rapid succession of images and snippets of conversations held during a ten-hour-long outdoor party held in Tepoztlán, Morelos, a small rural town that has long been a weekend destination for a certain "counterculture" set of Mexico City's upper-middle class, and which Reygadas calls home. The three hundred guests include people of all ages and walks of life, from the affluent to the homeless. Food, drink, and music fuel the revelry that eventually descends into chaos and fiery destruction. Everything is unscripted. Events seem to progress chronologically, but the film does not follow a linear narrative from a singular point of view.

Arreola and Reygadas focus on enduring problems and complex social landscapes generated by Mexico's colonial past. Both highlight the ethnic and economic divide that is historically linked to the systematic expropriation of Indigenous land by European settlers and the caste system that made Indigenous labour available to be exploited. Both manifest the real precariousness of the status quo and the possibility of revolution. The questions they seem to ask are: How much longer can such imbalance persist? And how will it end? They offer the hopeful yet fearsome revelation that upheaval is imminent and inevitable. For this and other reasons detailed below, *La feria* and "Este es mi reino" may be called apocalyptic works, and as such, they lay bare and challenge Mexico's coloniality.

US-Mexican war and against the infamous dictator Antonio López de Santa Anna. However, the city never ceased to be known as Zapotlán el Grande. It is located in the state of Jalisco, in a seismically active region ("Zapotlán el Grande").

3 "All the mountains you see here are the same, well, the landscape is the same that Hernán Cortés may have seen when he conquered the region. He must have been blown away by the Tepozteco." El Tepozteco is one of the peaks of the Tepoztlán sierra.

La feria and "Este es mi reino" resonate strongly, even if particular production contexts and media result in different emphases. For instance, Reygadas does not address directly the issue of land ownership, but it is implicit in the purposeful display of socio-economic disparity set in a rural community that is progressively transformed by the influx of weekenders from Mexico City and immigrants from the United States and Europe.[4] Also in contrast with *La feria*, "Este es mi reino" does not engage with religion overtly. However, the title may be interpreted as a biblical reference. In the Gospel of John, Jesus tells Pontius Pilate: "My kingdom is not of this world: if my kingdom were of this world, then would my servants fight" (*American Standard Bible*, John 18:36). Reygadas's film stages an earthly kingdom where chaotic violence may be not only an unavoidable consequence of coloniality but also the vehicle for improbable change – though not necessarily significant or positive.[5]

"Este es mi reino" offers a dour commentary on the failure of the Mexican Revolution (1910–29) to bring about change. Reygadas created it for *Revolución*, a collection of ten short films that was produced and released to coincide with the commemorations of the centenary of the revolution in 2010. According to the producers, the goal of the collection was to generate a contemporary vision of the revolution, not by revisiting the historical event but by treating it as a concept (*Revolución* 9). The long and bloody civil war that started with a call for democracy but quickly descended into widespread chaos was, as Thomas Benjamin asserts, woven into the master narrative of Mexico as a nation. Popular notions about the revolution owe much to the synthetic narrative that was first proposed in the 1930s, when Mexico's mainstream political culture embraced a story that melded raging factionalism into a single social struggle. In 1951 the state-sponsored *Historia de la revolución mexicana* presented it as a continuation of the struggle against reactionary forces that had begun with the War of Independence (1810–21) and the War of Reform (1857–60), and whose primary goal

---

4   Agriculture continues to be important in Tepoztlán's economy, but it has been steadily losing ground to tourism. In the 1990s many weekend houses were built on plots of land that had been sold fraudulently or even illegally in the case of communal lands (*ejidos*). However, in the same decade Tepoztlán defeated efforts to build a golf-club resort in the Tepozteco national park (Velázquez García and Clausen 136, 138, 145).

5   I thank Beth Boyd for this reference and insight. Two other films directed by Reygadas also have titles with religious connotations: *Batalla en el cielo* (2005) and *Post Tenebras Lux* (2012).

was agrarian reform.[6] The book was endorsed by the Secretaría de Educación Pública in 1959, which ensured its dissemination through the public school system. By that time, however, historians had begun to challenge the official narrative by underscoring not only the partisan in-fighting that exacerbated the conflict but also its apparent pointlessness. Poverty was still widespread, land redistribution remained an unfulfilled promise, and violence served to stifle dissent.[7] Though it continues to be produced, official history is generally discredited among academics and artists (Benjamin 14, 142, 148–50, 158–9).[8] Most of the short films that make up *Revolución* reveal as much, in spite of the fact that the production benefited from government funding.[9] At the same time, the film's limited visibility beyond the international film circuit reflects the Mexican government's failure to find a credible celebratory narrative.[10]

Just as the anniversary of the Mexican Revolution inspired Reygadas's portrait of contemporary Mexican society, the political debates

---

6   The beginning of the Mexican War of Independence is traditionally associated with the call for a commoner uprising issued by the priest Miguel Hidalgo y Costilla; independence from Spain was declared by former royalist officials who were disenchanted by political developments in Spain. The War of Reform pitted liberals against conservatives over a set of laws that undermined the status of the Church in Mexico. The triumph of the liberal faction led to the French intervention and the Second Mexican Empire under Maximilian of Hapsburg (1862–7).

7   The best-known case is the Tlatelolco massacre in 1968. Other examples include the repression of a rail workers' strike in 1959, the murder of agrarian activist Rubén Jaramillo in 1962, and the Halconazo massacre in 1971.

8   Contrasting attitudes towards the legacy of the revolution made news in December 2019 when a display of Fabián Cháirez's portrait of revolutionary leader and icon Emiliano Zapata, in the nude, wearing high heels and a pink hat, provoked a brawl between protesters from the farmers' union Frente Auténtico Campesino and supporters from the LGBTQ community in front of the Palacio de Bellas Artes museum (see Romo).

9   The short films that make up *Revolución*, individually or as a set, have received very little scholarly consideration. According to Maricruz Castro Ricalde, the failure of the uprising is the main premise of Mariana Chenillo's "La tienda de raya," which "postulates that the power structures are still the same: a dominant group exploits a majority that is powerless against the authoritarian decisions that affect it." In his sparse comments about the collection, Ignacio Sánchez Prado praises Amat Escalante's "El cura Nicolás Colgado" for artfully conveying a powerful message: "Mexico has not changed much since revolutionary times" (225).

10   The regime of President Felipe Calderón (2006–12), of the Partido Acción Nacional (PAN), faced the challenge of dealing with a deeply ingrained historical narrative that had served for decades to justify the dominance of the Partido de la Revolución Institucional (PRI). Moreover, Calderón sought misguidedly to associate the struggle of the revolution with his highly unpopular war on drugs (Perochena 165, 169).

of the 1950s may have heightened Arreola's interest in agrarian issues. As Mexico sought to become a modern industrialized nation, support for agriculture in general waned, even though the promises of the revolution regarding land reform remained unfulfilled. The policies of the regimes of Manuel Ávila Camacho (1940–6) and Miguel Alemán (1946–52), which tended to favour the private property of large landowners, had already caused concern in the country's rural sector. In the presidential contest of 1952 the political platform of Vicente Lombardo Toledano, candidate for the Partido Popular, centred on agrarian issues. Besides underscoring the misery, inequality, and exploitation prevalent in rural Mexico, Lombardo Toledano's campaign called for a progressive stand against big landownership, insisting that land redistribution was unfinished business and that the ejido – a state-allotted, collectively managed tract of land – should be the basis of rural development (Moguel 107, 115).

Meanwhile the official discourse, espoused by the PRI's candidate, Adolfo Ruiz Cortines, promoted the idea that the real problem of Mexico's rural sector stemmed not from uneven land distribution but from insufficient technology and productivity, and proposed private landownership and modernization as the best solutions. In 1955 the Ruiz Cortines administration (1952–8) modified the Ley de Crédito Agrícola (Agricultural Credit Law) and made it impossible for local credit unions to obtain bank loans, thereby hindering the operation of collective ejidos. The frustration of the rural sector manifested itself more strongly towards the end of the decade when a number of new rural organizations called attention to long-standing issues. In 1957 the workers and peasant farmers' union, Unión General de Obreros y Campesinos de México (UGOCM), made a strong push for the break-up of *latifundios* ("large land tracts") especially in northwestern Mexico. The government failed to do so. The following year thousands of campesinos (peasant farmers) occupied various *latifundios*, which did lead to some expropriations. However, rather than promote a change in governmental policies, the mobilization brought about a methodical undercutting of rural organizations. This in turn made it easier for capitalist landowners to take over Indigenous lands and curtail communal efforts, including the establishment and maintenance of ejidos (Moguel 121–2, 125, 126–7).

During the electoral campaign of 1958 the agrarian situation appeared as a full-blown economic, social, and political crisis. Nonetheless, the administration of Adolfo López Mateos (1958–64) continued to promote a capitalist model of development and to push for the modernization of ejidos as a way to increase productivity. The only significant difference with the previous regime was more direct intervention on the part of the government. In his 1960 State of the Union address, López Mateos declared that the age of land redistribution was over, even as new rural movements were brewing. In that year, former president Lázaro Cárdenas (1934–40), who still had significant political standing, noted the social unrest created by government policies and warned that a revolution was still possible in Mexico. Cárdenas also participated in the Conferencia Latinoamericana por la Soberanía Nacional, la Emancipación Económica y la Paz (Latin American Conference for National Sovereignty, Economic Emancipation, and Peace), which, among other things, called for the end of all forms of production based on the *latifundio* and for turning over the land to those who laboured on it.[11] The Movimiento de Liberación Nacional (National Liberation Movement, MLN) was founded two months later. Cárdenas, who spoke at its inaugural ceremony, decried the unprecedented degree of collusion among the dominant oligarchy, the dogmatic clergy, and US imperialists. The MLN's program explicitly called for agrarian reform and full legal equality for the Indigenous masses. Stemming from the efforts of the MLN, a new organization was founded specifically to address rural issues, the Central Campesina Independiente (Independent Peasant-Farmers Central, CCI). One of its stated objectives was to return the lands unlawfully taken from Indigenous communities and ejidos. Such notions alarmed the conservative camp, and the government responded with further harassment and more active repression. By 1962, radical agrarianism seemed all but defeated (Moguel). Yet, as a result, the frustration over the government's blatant disregard for the revolution's agrarian aims, which lent credence to revisionist historiography, would have been at a high point among class-conscious academics and artists when Arreola published his pocket-sized apocalypse in 1963.[12]

Pocket-Sized Apocalypses

Very few critics have addressed the characterization of *La feria* as an apocalypse. Carmen de Mora Valcárcel believes that it refers to its biblical intertextuality, added to its heterogeneous style and fatalism (111).

---

11 The conference also supported the aims of the Cuban Revolution and criticized the colonialist attitude of the United States. When mainstream media deliberately failed to report on the conference's resolutions, Cárdenas headed a delegation that visited several Mexican states, including Jalisco (Moguel 145).

12 Elena Garro's *Los recuerdos del porvenir*, which presents a dismal assessment of the revolution's final stage, was also published in 1963. An earlier example of the same disenchantment is Juan Rulfo's *Pedro Páramo* (1955).

There are in fact numerous references to the Bible throughout the text, starting with two epigraphs (slightly modified verses from the book of Isaiah) that serve as keys for interpreting Arreola's effort: "he hath made my mouth [tongue] like a sharp sword; in the shadow of his hand hath he hid me: and he hath made me a polished shaft; in his quiver hath he kept me close" (49:2), and "I will preserve [made] thee, and give [gave] thee for a covenant of the people, to restore the land/earth, to cause them to inherit the desolate heritages" (49:8).[13] Many fragments quote or paraphrase biblical passages, drawn mainly from the books of Isaiah, Jeremiah, and Zachariah, with some from the New Testament, including Revelation. There are also several near citations of apocryphal Christian literature.[14] Sara Poot Herrera, who has carefully tallied most of them, finds that quoting the Bible serves to legitimate the struggle of the dispossessed, while quoting the Apocrypha lends a light heretical tone that undermines the overarching religiosity of *La feria* (146, 151). Poot Herrera, however, does not address directly the apocalyptic nature of the text.

According to Raúl Chávarri, Arreola's text is an apocalypse insofar as it ends in confusion, marking the dizzying end of an era and of a constellation of hope (421). Most critics interpret negatively the conflagration at the end of *La feria*. For Luis Leal, it was the final letdown of a text whose central theme, and what ties all the fragments together, is societal failure (42). *La feria*'s last fragment can be precisely dated to 22 October 1957, the day of the canonical coronation of Señor San José, Zapotlán's sworn patron against earthquakes and natural disasters.[15] It describes how the grand fireworks display that was meant to close the

---

13   American Standard Version. The words in brackets are those found in *La feria*. In Spanish *tierra* may refer to soil, land, or the earth. The third epigraph is a verse from the poem "Calendau," written in Occitan by Frederic Mistral: "Amo de moun pais, tu que dardais manifesto E dins sa lengo e dins sa gesto" (Soul of my country, you that gleams, manifestly, in its language and in its history).

14   The Proto-Gospel of St James is just such an example. A fragment in *La feria* describes how Joseph saw time standing still: "los que simulaban masticar, en realidad no masticaban, y los que parecían en actitud de tomar la comida, tampoco la sacaban del plato, y finalmente, los que parecían introducir los manjares en su boca, no lo hacían, sino que tenían sus rostros mirando hacia arriba" (Arreola 88–9). The Proto-Gospel reads: "those who were chewing were not chewing; and those who were taking something from the bowl were not lifting it up; and those who were bringing their hands to their mouths were not bringing them to their mouths. Everyone was looking up" (Ehrman 33).

15   In the Roman Catholic Church a canonical coronation is a special honour granted to a specific image of Jesus, Mary, or Joseph through a papal bull or decree.

celebrations surrounding the event – the *feria* of the book's title – was sabotaged:

> Justamente en el momento en que iba a darse la orden para que fuera encendido irrumpió una pequeña banda de desalmados. Nadie pudo darse cuenta de quiénes eran, ni cuántos. Iban vestidos de Viejos de la danza, con máscaras de diablo. Unos llevaban teas encendidas, otros baldes y machetes, otros más, pistolas que disparaban al aire. En cosa de instantes, bañaron de petróleo la base de las cuatro torres que sostenían la plataforma desde donde se alzaba el castillo principal, y les prendieron fuego.[16]

As a result, instead of the grand spectacle everyone was expecting, the rockets went off haphazardly and fiery chaos ensued (Arreola 198). Since it frustrates general expectations, the cataclysm at the end of *La feria* may be interpreted as a failure. However, shifting the focus from the catastrophe to the fact that it was the result of arson allows for a very different reading. In contrast with the general view, Pedro Trigo sees the destruction of the fireworks display as a sign of revolt, a fall into chaos that may allow order to be rebuilt on a more solid basis. From this perspective Juan Tepano's opening statement about the centuries-long effort to recover the land does not necessarily reflect resignation in the face of an inescapable cycle, but hopeful tenacity in a righteous struggle (Trigo 1: 94–5).

Something comparable happens in "Este es mi reino," in which the nearly static, seemingly timeless image that opens the film contrasts violently with the final conflagration scene. Ignacio Sánchez Prado comments briefly on the "decadent crescendo" that turns a fancy party into a "drunken carnival." However, the film does more than just put the "utter selfishness of the rich" on display (Sánchez Prado 224). In a review of *Revolución* published in *Slant Magazine*, Andrew Schenker posits that "Este es mi reino" creates an apocalyptic vision and comments on how "Reygadas brilliantly uses sounds and images devoid of specific context to generate an ineluctable feeling of mounting hysteria" and "imagines revolution as the coming together of people with diverse

---

16 "Just when the order to light it was about to be given, a small band of scoundrels burst onto the scene. No one was able to tell who they were or how many. They were dressed as Old Men [*Viejos*] from the dance, wearing devil's masks. Some carried torches; others, pails and machetes; others fired guns into the air. In an instant they drenched with oil the bases of the four columns that held up the platform on which the main display stood and set them on fire."

interests in the pursuit of a giddy destruction." In fact, the movie's context is Mexico's coloniality, and within it the heterogeneous gathering, the mounting chaos, and the fiery end take on their truly apocalyptic meaning.

More than just the biblical intertextuality and the cataclysmic endings per se, *La feria* and "Este es mi reino" may be justly called apocalypses because of the oppressive disorder they reveal and the revolutionary expectations they manifest. The word *apocalypse* comes from *apokalyptein*, which means "to reveal" or "to discover" in ancient Greek. Apocalyptic texts tend to be associated with some sort of catastrophic ending, but of equal or greater importance is the revelation of the circumstances that lead to such an outcome (Riedl and Murphy 6, 8). The earliest Jewish apocalypses sought to transmit a political message associated with imperial domination. Specifically, they rationalized the predominance of God's enemies over the true believers. Confronting a situation in which the enemy was so powerful that any act of rebellion seemed pointless, apocalyptic works such as the apocryphal Fourth Ezra anticipated a radical transformation of reality to console the faithful (Riedl and Marno xvi–xvii).

Apocalypses can also be considered a literature of resistance, as in the case of the first Hebrew examples produced in the third century BCE, when king Antiochus IV Epiphanes proscribed Judaism and its traditions. The empire promoted drastic restructuring not just through force but also through the manipulation of social institutions, with the intent to reinforce imperial vision and values. Under these circumstances apocalypses defied both material and epistemological impositions. As Anathea E. Portier-Young asserts, "the apocalyptic worldview envisioned a radical relocation of power and in this way redefined the possible and the real, thus clarifying the context for action and empowering the work of resistance." Those who resist do not always do it openly or with the explicit goal of toppling government structures; rather, they fight to preserve their world-view, their traditions, and their identity. Such struggles may be over material things but also over symbols, history, and accountability. Moreover, the lack of an armed uprising or formal obedience to dominant institutions does not mean that the discourses of the oppressors have been fully accepted by the oppressed, who may have their own discourse and may persist, without scandal, in affirming its validity. Apocalyptic literature may serve as a formal and conceptual instrument of that struggle. Apocalypses' formal strategies include employing alternative cosmologies, examining the past to lay bare the contingency of present circumstance, and using particular syntax that subverts the logic of hegemonic structures and generates a perspective that, while being substantially different, may still take advantage of traditional discourses. Apocalypses encourage resistance by unmasking and condemning the control structures that imperial power would rather keep hidden, and, at the same time, validate the existence of a superior power that is no less effective for being invisible (Portier-Young xxi–ii, 4–6, 13–14, 35, 37).

All these elements are present in *La feria*. Given the accuracy of Arreola's definition of his work, however, what is to be made of the adjectival qualifier *pocket-sized*? It may be an acknowledgment of its limited scope because it does not claim to have universal implications, like Saint John's book of Revelation, dealing instead with a more localized reality – even if Zapotlán may be read as a synecdoche of Mexico and many of the issues it addresses are simply human. In any case, the qualification points to the ironic humour that is prevalent in Arreola's writing in general and of *La feria* in particular. This trait, which distinguishes it from the biblical and apocryphal apocalypses, links it instead to postmodern apocalyptic texts, which generally seek to reveal the ills of present-day society without promising a definitive resolution. Instead postmodern apocalypses tend to discredit such finality and question the possibility of issuing an indisputable judgment (Rosen xx–xxi, xxv). Revelation is in itself an act of criticism; satire only adds bite. Moreover, the fact that the situation brought to light remains unresolved may be seen as a call to action. In the case of *La feria*, the call could be for violent action against structures that the colonial regime put in place and that neither independence nor the revolution managed to dismantle. Thus, Arreola's pocket-sized apocalypse also has a decolonial impetus in that it reveals the woes of a materially and ideologically oppressed community, examines its history, and proposes an alternative perspective in a way that challenges hegemonic paradigms. Though the historical background is more implicit and the signs of resistance are less evident, "Este es mi reino" does the same in a different medium: it exposes wide disparities and multiplies the points of view to undermine standard discourses.

A possible challenge to characterizing *La feria* and "Este es mi reino" as works of resistance comes from the fact that both Reygadas, an internationally acclaimed auteur, and Arreola, a highly celebrated author, dwell within the *ciudad letrada*, or lettered city.[17] The lettered city, as identified by Ángel Rama, was the cohort of intellectual workers

---

17   Reygadas is the recipient of several international film awards, including best director at the Cannes Film Festival. Arreola is regarded as a major Mexican author, along with such renowned figures as Octavio Paz, Elena Garro, and Juan Rulfo; all of them were born in the 1910s.

that managed the cultural dimension of the colonial power structure (17–18). As Martin Lienhard explains, in postcolonial times the lettered city continued operating not only from within the halls of power but also through universities, publishers, and the press, generally by following metropolitan trends. Even when scholars began in the 1960s to seek out subaltern expressions, such as oral testimonies of marginalized economic or ethnic groups, their editorial interventions resulted in texts that tended to reflect the lettered city's interests and standards, positing a monological "truth" from a position of discursive authority. A possible remedy to this general trend is to acknowledge and represent dialogical multiplicity. Lienhard maintains that effective testimonials are those that make popular discourse tangible, which calls for strategies beyond those of traditional documental narrative. Fiction may be better suited to recreate the richness of the discursive realms that exist beyond – and sometimes resist – the jurisdiction of the lettered city by simulating the existence of radically alternative voices (Lienhard 787, 789, 793–5).[18] *La feria* and "Este es mi reino" intentionally stage popular discourse through a wide assortment of voices in order to reflect fragmented realities that stimulate response to an ongoing crisis, one with deep historical roots. Thus, both works may be regarded as works of resistance.

The Past

Apocalyptic literature is concerned, first and foremost, with the present. An apocalypse aims to expose particular dysfunctionalities (social, political, religious, etc.) that exist at the time of its writing (Schedtler and Murphy 10–11). A series of fragments in *La feria* reflect the renewed impetus for land reform in Mexico in the late 1950s and the hegemony's reactions. In one fragment two men are seen measuring land parcels; one is identified as a Tlayacanque, the other as an outsider, likely an engineer. In a later fragment a dialogue stakes out the two positions. One concerned speaker says: "Todo el valle de Zapotlán es de ellos, según les están metiendo en la cabeza los historiadores y tinterillos que los azuzan contra nosotros."[19] Parroting actual official arguments, his interlocutor argues that returning the lands would ruin

---

18   Lienhard identifies José María Arguedas, Juan Rulfo, João Guimarães Rosa, Augusto Roa Bastos, and Jesús Morales Bermúdez as writers who managed to successfully recreate alternative oralities (795).

19   "The whole valley of Zapotlán belongs to them, according to what the historians and shyster lawyers who goad them against us are putting in their heads."

the region's agriculture because the Indigenous peasants do not have enough money to put clothes on their backs, let alone to plant and harvest crops; the few sharecroppers left cannot afford the most basic tools. Were the peasants to start using wooden ploughs again? Beyond such arguments, *La feria* also captures the repressive measures against land-reform agitators. A man tells how two strangers came up to him, showed him a badge, and told him to take them to the house of Don Muncio, one of the Tlayacanques. When he refused, they locked him up in the city hall, incommunicado. He was falsely accused at his hearing and sent to jail despite the lack of evidence:

> Quise que me sacaran con fianza, pero no se pudo. Mandé por un amparo a Guadalajara y me lo negaron. Pero mi defensor obtuvo que los tres individuos rectificaran sus declaraciones, y entonces dijeron la pura verdad: a punta de pistola los hicieron firmar la acusación contra don Mucio y yo, a deshoras de la noche. Que no se echaran para atrás porque los mataban, y que luego que estuviéramos presos nosotros, ellos saldrían libres y con dinero ganado. (Arreola 147–8)[20]

All of them remained stuck in prison nonetheless (Arreola 158–9).

While it is very much about the present, apocalypse is also a myth-historical genre that engages with both an otherworldly realm and actual historical events (Parkinson Zamora 18). Juan Tepano's opening statement speaks to the early history of Zapotlán. Alonso de Ávalos led a violent campaign in the region in 1524. In 1532 the Franciscan missionary Juan de Padilla began preaching the Christian gospel to the Indigenous community of Tlayolan-Tzapotlan, where the town of Santa María de la Asunción de Zapotlán was founded in the following year.[21] Starting in the sixteenth century, the Spanish expansion across the territory

---

20   "I wanted them to let me out on bail, but that didn't work. I sent to Guadalajara for an *amparo*, but it was denied. However, my lawyer got the three individuals to change their statements, and then they told the whole truth: they made them sign the accusation against Don Muncio and me in the middle of the night at gunpoint; they would kill them if they backed out; and as soon as we were jailed, they would go free with money in their pockets." Exclusive to Mexican law, an *amparo* is a writ intended to guarantee an individual's constitutional rights against any kind of infringement.

21   Padilla went on to accompany the expedition of Juan Vázquez de Coronado to the fabled Seven Cities of Cibola – a North American El Dorado – in 1540. Coronado desisted from the enterprise in 1542, but Padilla went on to preach in the region known as Quivira, in present-day Kansas, where he was killed in that same year.

of New Spain was accompanied by the expropriation of Indigenous communities' productive lands. The systematic amassing of such lands by a wealthy minority eventually resulted in the consolidation of the great Mexican haciendas.[22] According to historian James Lockhart, the Spanish city and the great estate were two complementary "master institutions" at the root of the changes wrought by colonization (411).[23] The third master institution that must be added to the list is the Church, which not only had an impact on social organization but was at the core of new identity formations. In the very first fragment of *La feria*, Juan Tepano's comments on early evangelization efforts speak to the multi-faceted relationship between the Church and the Indigenous community. Padilla's use of music and dance as part of his conversion efforts underscores the presence of a pre-Hispanic culture with its own rituals. Early on, Spanish missionaries co-opted traditional song and dance as a way to encourage Christian devotion and, as Robert Ricard points out, the missionaries' efforts in this regard have very much withstood the test of time. However, the fact that this syncretic form of worship persisted in spite of Church efforts to curtail it – for fear it could be a subterfuge for the preservation of pagan beliefs – shows that the power of the clergy over Indigenous neophytes was not absolute (Ricard 239–40, 242).

Juan Tepano mentions another evangelical instrument that Indigenous groups quickly transformed into a means of self-affirmation, the *cofradía*, or religious confraternity. Originally established by missionaries to instruct Indigenous neophytes in Catholic tenets and rituals, *cofradías* allowed Indigenous communities to maintain a separate collective identity (Gibson 127). Religious celebrations, such as the *fiesta patronal* held in honour of a particular saint, were often sponsored by *cofradías*, which could, to the dismay of colonial authorities, spend lavishly on fireworks, food, drink, music, and bull fights to enhance the festivities (Martínez Domínguez 63–4).[24] While the modern-day

---

22 James Lockhart notes that from the time of the conquest and up to the twentieth century the consistent trend was for the Spanish properties to grow, while the Indigenous villages and their lands and production shrank (426).

23 While technically different, the *encomienda* and the hacienda were directly linked because "the organization and social composition of those who owned and managed the estate" hardly changed over the course of two centuries (Lockhart 427).

24 The issue is addressed in several fragments of *La feria* but most pointedly in one that instructs against spending money on "las exterioridades de fuegos, que sirven más a la vanidad y pompa, ni a las comedias y toros, que antes destruyen la devoción y ceban los vicios" (Arreola 196; "the flamboyance of fireworks, that mostly serve vanity and pomp, or in plays and bullfights, which mainly destroy devotion and fuel vice").

celebration that gives *La feria* its name is not explicitly linked to a *cofradía*, the spirit behind the Indigenous community's efforts to take it back from the city's civil and religious establishment is the same. The latter is represented in Juan Tepano's statement by the Holy Inquisition, which allegedly prosecuted Francisco de Sayavedra, a heterodox priest, for arguing against the expropriation of Indigenous lands. This is a case where myth meets history. In 1539, New Spain's first inquisitor, Bishop Juan de Zumárraga, presided over Francisco de Sayavedra's trial for suspicion of heresy. He was found to be misguided and was punished with penance, prayer, and a fine ("Proceso"). There is nothing to indicate his attitude towards his Indigenous charges. Thus, his stance in favour of the Tlayacanques appears to be fictional. Nevertheless, it serves to set up a contrast between a solidary ministry and a repressive ministry that will also come to the fore in the modern conflict surrounding the climactic celebration of *La feria*.

The canonical coronation of Señor San José did in fact take place on 22 October 1957 – footage of the ceremony can be found on YouTube (*Coronación Pontificia del Señor San José de Zapotlán*). The description found in *La feria*, along with the account of the way it came about, was deemed accurate enough to be cited in a series of articles about the history of the coronation written in 2007 by Fernando G. Castolo, official chronicler of Ciudad Guzmán, for the regional newspaper *El sur*. Castolo's account blurs the line between history and literature by using Arreola's work of fiction as a primary historical source when, for example, he applies the description of the coronation's main promoter, called Farías in *La feria*, to Antonio Arias Pedroza, the real person behind the pious effort (part 1, n.p.). However, set out of context, certain quoted passages lose their ironic potential. Castolo draws from a fragment that celebrates the papal approval of Señor San José's coronation: "Este octubre Zapotlán ha obtenido, pues, la más alta recompensa por su acendrado catolicismo" (part 3, n.p.; Arreola 157).[25] But Zapotlán's faith is far from unblemished in *La feria*.

Early on, the reader learns about the priest who likes to climb a hill to see the city from above when he gets tired from seeing it, as he puts it, from below: "¡Qué iniquidad, Dios mío, qué iniquidad! Un río de estulticia me ha entrado por las orejas, incesante como las aguas que bajan de las Peñas en las crecidas de julio y agosto. Aguas limpias que la

---

25 "This October, Zapotlán has obtained, therefore, the highest reward for its untarnished Catholicism."

gente ensucia con la basura de sus culpas."[26] The flow of sinful rubbish is the subject of *La feria*'s central and longest fragment. It is a breathless, multitudinous confession that takes place after a series of earthquakes identified in the previous fragment as a rehearsal (orchestrated by Señor San José) of Judgment Day. Most of the statements are from a first-person-singular perspective, but every "I" is a different confessant. "Me acuso Padre de Todo. ¿Cómo que de Todo? Sí, de Todo, de todo ... Yo no puedo absolverte así nomás de todo ... Barájamela más despacio ... Pues ái le va."[27] A long list of transgressions follows. Some are relatively minor, like being disrespectful or having evil thoughts. Others are more serious, like theft or murder. Some, spread throughout the fragment, relate directly to the land issue: "Me quedé con las tierras por menos de la mitad de lo que valían"; "fui de la Junta Repartidora de Tierras"; "sabíamos que eran mal habidas pero de todos modos las compramos, los indios no sabían qué hacer con ellas"; "por mi culpa, por mi grandísima culpa se quedaron todos esos indios sin tierras."[28] The first sin – "me robé una peseta" ("I stole a coin") – and the last confession are the same, which hints at a never-ending cycle (Arreola 14–15, 90–3).

Such privileged access to the confessional secrets of Zapotlán's inhabitants is part of *La feria*'s apocalyptic perspective. The reader can see and listen without being seen or heard, easily travelling instantaneously not only from place to place but also back and forth through time. This totalizing vision of Zapotlán also reveals otherworldly actors. The short fragment that follows the city's panicked confession is a brief conversation. "Uno de por allí" ("Someone from over yonder") – who will turn out to be a fallen angel – complains that despite their reputation, they are not as bad as the people of Zapotlán, whom God keeps punishing with earthquakes. Then the interlocutors' nature is revealed with a statement from Revelation (14:8): "Y otro ángel le siguió, diciendo: 'Ha caído, ha caído Babilonia, aquella grande ciudad, porque ella ha dado

---

26 "Such wickedness, my God, such wickedness! A river of rubbish penetrates through my ears, as ceaseless as the swollen waters that come down from Las Peñas in July and August – clean waters that people pollute with the filth of their sins."

27 "Bless me, Father, for I'm guilty of Everything. What do you mean, everything? Yes, Everything, everything ... I can't absolve you of everything just like that ... You'll have to go slowly ... Then here goes."

28 "I got the lands for less than half their worth; I was a member of the Land Redistribution Commission; we knew they were ill-gotten, but we still bought them; the *indios* didn't know what to do with them; through my fault, through my most grievous fault all those *indios* became landless."

a beber a todas las naciones del vino del furor de su fornicación.'"[29] The heavenly voices that can be heard in *La feria* include those of Jesus, whose account of his human father's first marriage is taken directly from the apocryphal *History of Joseph the Carpenter*, and of Señor San José, who humbly summarizes the short history of his official cult.[30] At one point he also issues a warning and perhaps a call to arms. The statement is addressed to the Indigenes carrying the heavy platform on which Señor San José is being paraded on the day of his canonical coronation:

> "Yo no soy Dios, yo soy un hombre como todos ustedes, un artesano, un carpintero de obra blanca … No se los digo por asustarlos, pero no carguen sobre el suelo todo el peso de su cuerpo. Este pueblo está fincado sobre un valle de aluvión y sus tierras fértiles son puramente superficiales: ocultan una colosal falla geológica y ustedes están parados sobre una cáscara de huevo … Hagan otra vez la feria del año que viene, pero sean un poco más angelicales, y no gasten toda la pólvora en infiernitos."[31] (Arreola 94, 196)

Perhaps Señor San José is implying that the Indigenous community has wasted enough time pleading their case through institutional or supernatural channels, that there is no more time to lose, that the time for action has come.

The reader of *La feria* may infer as much because, as the text flips through the whole history of Zapotlán, all manner of truth is revealed. The secrets of the town are peppered throughout *La feria*, notably in various fragments that address the long history of dispossession of Indigenous lands. At first, this happens unequivocally when a phlegmatic historian who has been invited by the local Athenaeum delivers a lecture titled "La traición y los traidores en Zapotlán el Grande, durante las guerras de Conquista, de Independencia y de Reforma" ("Treason

---

29 "And there followed another angel, saying, 'Babylon is fallen, fallen, that great city, because she has made all nations drink of the wine of the wrath of her fornication.'" In John Steinbeck's famous novel, the grapes of wrath also symbolize that the time of justice over unbearable social situations has come.

30 Arreola drew the details from Ernesto Giménez Caballero's essay "San José, contribución para una simbología hispánica," which was originally published in 1930.

31 "I am not God. I am a man like you all, a craftsman, a humble carpenter … I don't say it to scare you, but don't let the ground carry the full weight of your body. This town is built on a floodplain and its fertile soil is only superficial: it hides a colossal geological fault and you are standing on an eggshell … Have the *feria* again next year, but be a little more angelic, and don't spend all the powder on fireworks."

and Traitors in Zapotlán el Grande during the Wars of Conquest, Independence, and Reform"). The surprised and increasingly dismayed audience learns that "Zapotlán no había sido en toda su historia más que un semillero de cobardes y de traidores."[32] The enlightening presentation is cut short by a sudden blackout; by the time the event's host has lit a match, all the listeners have left without further enquiry. Later a fragment that mimics a colonial-period petition denounces the corruption that allows land speculation and accumulation; another indicts a priest for selling the lands of a *cofradía* as if he were the owner in 1846; another decries the land redistribution of 1902 as "el fraude más grande y vergonzoso que registra la historia de este pueblo";[33] another exposes the systematic removal of old boundary markers that prove that most of the agricultural land actually belongs to the Indigenes (Arreola 122–3, 10, 25, 35, 146).

The Indigenous perspective on that history of expropriation is provided by Juan Tepano, who seems to have lived through its entirety. When he tells it, he speaks "lentamente, usando los términos, como quien lleva mucho tiempo de hablar con abogados y huizacheros."[34] Tepano expresses his disagreement with the unlawful expropriation of Indigenous lands and his frustration with the legal system, which acknowledges the Indigenous community's legal rights but does not return the expropriated lands. Tepano laments that agrarianism has not benefited the Indigenous community and that everyone has forgotten that the Tlayacanques still hold some authority, which is represented by his *vara*, or staff of office.[35] It is the very same one that was granted by the king of Spain in 1583, to Agustín Hernández, *indio principal*, along with the right to ride a saddled and bridled horse, wear European clothes, and go where he pleased. "Y fue hasta a México a pelear su derecho,

---

32 "Throughout its history Zapotlán had been nothing but a breeding ground for cowards and traitors."

33 "The greatest and most shameful fraud registered in this town's history."

34 "Slowly, using the proper terms, as one who has been talking to lawyers and shysters for a long time."

35 Indigenous communities throughout Mexico have commonly appealed to the colonial past to assert their land rights. One way of doing so was by acquiring or creating *títulos primordiales*, apocryphal historical documents intended to demonstrate their antiquity. Such documents were still being presented as evidence in legal proceedings in the early twentieth century. For Ethelia Ruiz Medrano, this strategy evidences the "notable ideological flexibility" that allowed many Indigenous groups to claim a place in the national society by adopting new political systems without sacrificing traditional practices (27, 122).

porque lo que pasa ahora ha pasado siempre. Las autoridades de arriba nos dan la razón y las de abajo nos la quitan" (Arreola 26, 28).[36]

The result of Zapotlán's history of inequity is allegorically represented on the day of Señor San José's canonical coronation in 1957. Someone explains to an unidentified audience – standing in for the reader – that, in fact, people attend Zapotlán's *feria* to see the parade floats. They represent biblical scenes: Judith holding Holoferne's bloody head; Pharaoh's daughter finding baby Moses; Abraham about to sacrifice his son Isaac; Saint Joseph's workshop, where a child Jesus plays with two blocks of wood. The most important float comes last, the only one that is not on wheels. The large and extremely heavy platform is full of flowers and children dressed as a host of angels. They surround the figures of Mary and Señor San José, who holds baby Jesus. "Ahora asómense para abajo. ¿Qué es lo que ven? Sí, son ellos, los miembros de la Comunidad Indígena que han alcanzado el honor de cargar con el santo y con su gloria. Son cien o doscientos aplastados bajo el peso de tantas galas, cien o doscientos agachados que pujan por debajo, atenuando con la cobija sobre el hombro los filos de la madera, y que circulan en la sombra sus botellas de tequila para darse ánimos y fuerzas."[37] The speaker goes on to say: "¡Adelante con la superestructura, pueblo de Zapotlán! ¡Animo, cansados cireneos, que el anda se bambolea peligrosamente como una barcaza en el mar agitado de la borrachera y el descontento!" (Arreola 194–5).[38] These expressions of encouragement are also a warning about the consequences of keeping to the centuries-old course because what might otherwise indicate submissiveness may be in fact an expression of resistance.

---

36 "And he went all the way to Mexico City to fight for his rights, because what's happening now has happened always. The high authorities grant us our rights and the lower ones take them away."

37 "Now look underneath. What do you see? Yes, it's them, the members of the Indigenous community who have gained the honour of carrying the saint in his glory. One or two hundred of them, crushed under the weight of much finery, one or two hundred drudges straining below, a blanket mitigating the wooden edges on their shoulders, and passing around bottles of tequila in the shadows to give themselves courage and strength."

38 "Onward with the superstructure, people of Zapotlán! Courage, tired Cyreneans, for the frame wobbles dangerously like a barge on the rough sea of drunkenness and discontent." *Cyreneans* refers to Simon of Cyrene, who was compelled by Roman soldiers to bear Jesus's cross, as told in the gospels of Matthew, Mark, and Luke.

Resistance

At every turn Juan Tepano underscores the Tlayacanques' centuries-long efforts to reclaim their land from the *gente de razón*, which can be loosely translated as "right-reasoning people." Originally this notion referred to Christians in general, including Christianized Indigenes. However, owing to the *sistema de castas*, the colonial stratification of people based on phenotype, the phrase became a common, blatantly racist expression to distinguish Indigenes from non-Indigenes.[39] *La feria* reveals it as nothing but a fallacy by playing on the various connotations of the term *razón*, which in Spanish include "reasoning" and "rightness." Zapotlán's non-Indigenous landowners lack both, as exemplified in the tale of the shoemaker who wanted to be an agriculturalist. The reader learns of the shoemaker's efforts through the fragments excerpted from his notebook. In the first entry he acknowledges that no one in his family has ever worked the land and he hopes that next year he will be able to fend for himself without constantly asking "las gentes que saben" ("the people who know"). He also expresses unease about all the paperwork related to the acquisition of his plot of land, which has apparently passed through many hands (Arreola 9). The outcome of the undertaking confirms that the uneasiness was well warranted.

The shoemaker's notes describe systematically, like a manual, the farming of his fields. The actual work is done by peons hired to prepare the soil, to sow it – which he describes as "una danza lenta y antigua" ("a slow and ancient dance") – and to tend the crops. The single time he goes to help, he realizes that the work is backbreaking. At one point he comments on the Indigenes's alarming attitude – a reference to the renewed controversy over land rights. In the end the shoemaker fails to harvest the maize he planted. His notebook's last entry explains that he decided to sell his land, wary "del peligro que hay por lo de la Comunidad Indígena" ("of the danger posed by what's going on with the

---

39 Tepano states: "Antes la tierra era de nosotros los naturales. Ahora es de las gentes de razón" ("Previously, the land belonged to us, the natives. Now it belongs to the *gentes de razón*"). Another fragment highlights the contrast between the two groups: "¿No ha oído usted hablar de los repartos de indios? Si era usted hacendado en aquel entonces, por el simple hecho de tener tierras y ser gente de razón, usted podía solicitar que le dieran indios, como ahora se les dan bueyes a los medieros." (Arreola 7, 36; "You've never heard about the allotment of *indios*? If you were a hacienda-owner back then, just for owning land and being *gente de razón*, you could request to be given *indios*, like sharecroppers get oxen nowadays.")

Indigenous Community") and to avoid litigation, because he had unknowingly bought his plot from someone who did not have full ownership. The shoemaker scarcely comes out even and he returns to his trade, bearing out the popular saying "Zapatero, a tus zapatos" ("let the cobbler stick to his last") (Arreola 67, 37, 179). When it came to working the land, the shoemaker was *gente de razón* in name only. In fact, *no tenía razón* – that is, he was in the wrong and had no right to work the land.

Those who know, the ones who have the right to the land but do not have the land itself, are the peons who work in the fields of others. They include Juan Tepano, first among the Tlayacanques, who appears happy and hopeful, as if the lands had already been reclaimed. He sings bits of a hymn, recites poetry, repeats old sayings, and dances a few steps from a traditional dance. He also recalls an age-old story about how they got their maize back. Long ago, when their territory was still called Tlayolan, neighbouring peoples banded together and stole every single grain because they were jealous of how well it grew there. "Pero tuvimos un rey y su nahual era cuervo. Se hacía cuervo cuando quería, con los poderes antiguos de Topiltzin y Ometecutli."[40] The Tlayolan king taught his people how to turn into crows, and one year, after cleaning and ploughing their fields, they flew to their enemies' lands and pecked out their maize. They were to carry it back in their beaks without eating it because those who did would remain crows forever. "Y muchos de nosotros," Juan Tepano explains, "no se aguantaron las ganas y se tragaron el grano en vez de sembrarlo en nuestra tierra." And that is why he asks Layo, one of the peons, not to shoot the crows, and when one passes overhead, he says, "Mira Layo, allí va volando un cristiano" (Arreola 69–70).[41] The story manifests the resilience of Indigenous memory, embodied by Tepano, and expresses a distinct Indigenous identity that resisted wholesale incorporation into the colonizer's paradigm by absorbing imported notions into autochthonous cosmologies, as in the case of Zapotlán's Christian crows, or by appropriating its symbols, as in the case of Christian saints.

The Indigenous Peoples' original response to the missionizing efforts that began in New Spain in the sixteenth century – the so-called spiritual conquest – was generally not the acceptance or addition of a

---

40 "But we had a king, and his spirit animal was a crow. He became a crow whenever he wanted, the ancient powers of Topiltzin and Ometecutli."

41 "And many of us could not resist the urge and swallowed the grain instead of sowing it in our land ... Look, Layo, there goes a Christian flying by."

new set of symbols but rather a reinterpretation consistent with pre-existing models. The result was an idiosyncratic Christianity belonging to them. Thus appropriated, Christian observances granted Indigenous Peoples a viable character within colonial society, as well as a communal identity, generally focused on devotion to a local saint, that "promoted social cohesion in the face of Spanish racism and exploitation" (Burkhart 6, 44, 190).[42] These notions hold true in the twenty-first century. Interviewed in 2006, Gilberto Galicia Muñoz, the *mayordomo*, or caretaker, of Cholula's Sanctuary of the Virgin of Remedios, stated: "I believe it's like we've already put aside the Spanish influence. This is ours ... definitely ours ... We firmly believe in our Catholic religion ... We follow our ancestors' path but with the real faith, the Catholic faith" (Myers 174). A survey of modern popular devotions in Indigenous communities from across Mexico finds that the cult of patron saints, which seldom aligns with the official liturgy, allows particular ethnic identities to coalesce and assert themselves against political and religious hegemonies (Báez-Jorge 39, 92). In general, the image of the patron saint is regarded as a living being who participates in the life of the community, using supernatural powers to reward or punish its members (Gómez-Arzapalo). The centrepiece of a saint's cult has always been the fiesta, an event whose many dimensions include faith, feasting, emotional attachments, and creative expression, as well as identity affirmation and resistance (Lastra et al. 125). It can also be connected to agriculture. In a 2006 interview Rolando Torres Hernández, who was working with Indigenous communities through the Instituto Veracruzano de la Cultura (Cultural Institute of Veracruz) at the time, emphasized that "traditional festivals have to do with the relationship with the land, with what's produced on the land" (Myers 91). The devotion for Señor San José, the fiesta in his honour, and the struggle to reclaim the land are closely linked in *La feria*.

Juan Tepano's happiness and hope come not only from apparent progress in the land rights case – as the surveying that is taking place suggests – but also from the opportunity to assert the standing of the Indigenous community through its sponsorship of the *feria* for Señor San José. After the sudden death of the city's nameless usurer, who

---

42 Nevertheless, colonial forms of Indigenous devotion were infinitely varied and changing. David Tavárez argues that hybridization, or any such concept, is inappropriate to discuss what is in fact "a colonial archipelago of faith composed by hundreds of local cosmologies that incorporated insights and theories drawn from Mesoamerican and European beliefs following autonomous and historically contingent criteria" (271).

was to be the *feria*'s steward, the Tlayacanques propose to assume the responsibility: "En una palabra, ellos querían encargarse de todo, en nombre de sus viejas cofradías."[43] Someone belonging to the so-called *gente de razón* complains to the priest about the prospect:

> Con todo respeto, señor Cura, esto me parece ¿cómo le diré?, un poco revolucionario. Apenas si se está calmando tantito la gente, y con esto les pueden perder otra vez el respeto a los patrones. El Mayordomo es un símbolo, señor Cura, es un símbolo, no lo olvide usted. Y ahora se están sintiendo mayordomos, como si no hubiera arriba y abajo ni clases sociales ni nada. ¿Sabe lo que le oí decir el otro día a una mujer que estaba vendiendo tortillas en la plaza? "Le vamos a hacer a Señor San José una Función como no se la han hecho nunca toda esta bola de ricos muertos de hambre ..." ¡Imagínese nomás![44]

The stakes are high even for Señor San José. In an exchange that exposes the connection between the land issue and religious devotion, one speaker contends that it is time for Señor San José to demonstrate once and for all whether he is truly Zapotlán's patron saint and whether his allegiance is to the rich or to the poor. The question is, how? The *feria* is set to become a vehicle for the expression of the community's will and power to rise in dignity (Trigo 1:97). "Pues si está con nosotros, que se arregle lo de las tierras. Y si no, nosotros para qué nos metemos ya en lo de la Función."[45] The interlocutor proposes that the best thing to do would be to save some of the money they plan to collect for the *feria* and use it to pay legal fees. "Necesitamos," he says, "ayudarle a Señor San José a que nos haga el milagro" (Arreola 63, 64–5, 148).[46]

---

43 "In a word, they wanted to take care of everything, in the name of their old confraternities." The usurer is only ever called Licenciado, a title for someone with a bachelor's degree; it implies a relative degree of authority.

44 "With all due respect, Father, this seems to me ... How can I put it? Somewhat revolutionary. The people are just beginning to calm down a bit and this may cause them to lose respect for the owners again. Don't forget the Stewardship is a symbol, Father, a symbol. And now they're making themselves out to be stewards, as if there was neither up nor down, or social classes, or anything. Do you know what I heard a woman selling tortillas on the square say the other day? 'We're going to celebrate Señor San José better than this bunch of miserable well-to-dos ever have ...' Imagine that!"

45 "If he is with us, let the land issues be sorted out. And if not, there's no point in us getting involved with the Feast."

46 "We need to help Señor San José grant us the miracle."

The controversy generated by the Tlayacanques' decision to sponsor the *feria* exposes different attitudes within the institutional church. While the secular priest supports the Tlayacanques' disruptive efforts, the letters penned by a Jesuit priest to his superiors unmask the higher clergy's complicity in maintaining the status quo.[47] The Jesuit expresses concern about the increasingly loud rumours that the secular priest or, rather, the leaders of the Indigenous community, who are also senior members of the old sodalities, have been using the money they are collecting not for the religious festivities but for helping defray the costs of the litigation that the *naturales*, or natives, are pursuing against the *señores hacendados*, or owners of large estates. The Jesuit worries that the secular priest has taken the side of the Indigenes "y les está dando mucha beligerancia en los asuntos de la Función, cosa que afecta los intereses y el prestigio de las otras clases sociales, injustamente postergadas y puestas a un lado, por decirlo así."[48] However, a group of distinguished gentlemen, most of them Knights of Columbus or members of the Honour Guard of Our Lady of Guadalupe, has approached him to offer funds for the construction of a new seminary, a project that according to the Jesuit is being sabotaged by the general unwillingness of the middle and lower classes to contribute any funds for it. But the reader knows that the upper classes' support of the project is less about piety than about undermining the Indigenous community's efforts to collect money for the *feria*. In a previous fragment the scheming Don Abigail, who is the voice of the oligarchy, says: "Lo único que nosotros debemos hacer, es no soltar dinero para la feria, y para no quedar mal con Dios Nuestro Señor, podemos dar todo lo que se pueda para el Seminario que quieren hacer aquí los padres jesuitas" (Arreola 150, 64).[49]

---

47   The Jesuits played an important role in New Spain as missionaries and educators from the time of their arrival in 1572 to their expulsion from the Spanish Empire in 1767. The Society of Jesus returned to Mexico in 1816, but its status remained contested until the twentieth century (see Zermeño Padilla). According to historian Jean Meyer, from the 1930s to the 1950s, fear of communism led the order to abandon social causes in favour of proselytizing Catholicism through elite education. Many captains of industry and high-ranking government officials were alumni of Jesuit institutions. However, starting in 1958, and spurred by the encyclical *Mater et Magistra* (1961) and the Second Vatican Council (1962–5), social justice became fundamental to the order's apostolic mission (Meyer 461–2). Arreola's Jesuit obviously represents the earlier stance.

48   "And is emboldening them in matters concerning the Feast, which affects the interests and prestige of the other social classes, unfairly overlooked and sidelined, so to speak."

49   "All we need to do is not give any money for the *feria* and, to avoid disappointing our Lord God, we can give as much as possible to the Seminary that the Jesuit priests want to build here."

The Jesuit's letter may be read as an ironic survey of colonial history. The archaic style renders it timeless rather than anachronistic; it suggests that institutional attitudes have not changed much over the centuries. The reference to the old sodalities conjures up the fraught relationship between the Church and organizations that often resisted its control (Gruzinsky 211). The reference to *naturales* and *señores*, or lords, evokes the feudal relationship imposed in the sixteenth century under the guise of the *encomienda*, later preserved in the hacienda system. In light of the historical treatment of Indigenous Peoples, the alleged marginalization of the "other social classes" seems absurd. No less ironic is the fact that the men who represent the upper class belong to the Knights of Columbus, a religious organization that originated in the United States and in the 1920s fuelled fears about the rise of communism in Mexico (Horn 35).[50] The connivance between the institutional church and the oligarchy is made explicit in another letter fragment, in which the Jesuit remarks that "un movimiento conjunto del alto clero y de la banca, con la colaboración de las autoridades del Estado, daría los mejores resultados" in thwarting Farías, the businessman who promoted Señor San José's coronation and appears to be supportive of the Tlayacanques.[51] Moreover, the Jesuit recommends replacing his secular colleague with a priest who would threaten to excommunicate recalcitrant members of the Indigenous community (Arreola 170).

The short fragment that follows the Jesuit's machinations is bitterly prophetic: "Todo el año parecemos coheteros, nomás pensando en la feria y llenándonos de pólvora la cabeza, para que a la hora de la hora, todas las ilusiones se nos seben."[52] And on the day of the coronation, things go awry. A speaker in one fragment remarks that, for the first time in history, entrance to the parish church is by invitation only. Significantly, the doors are guarded by individuals dressed like soldiers of old. Only two of the Tlayacanques have been invited, but they are barred from entering, allegedly because they are wearing their traditional gala attire instead of black tie, until Farías intervenes. In a different fragment, a witness of the lavish ceremony comments on the sermon

---

50 The campaign was intended to undermine the anticlerical regime of Plutarco Elías Calles (1924–8).

51 "A joint movement of the upper clergy and the banks, with the cooperation of state authorities, would yield the best results."

52 "All year long it's like we're making fireworks, just thinking about the *feria* and filling our heads with gunpowder, just so that when it comes right down to it, all our illusions misfire."

delivered by "un Monseñor muy viejito" ("a very old monsignor") well versed in Zapotlán's history, who mentions the Tlayacanques and says something about the land, but then, as if coming to his senses, changes the topic. Juan Tepano, whose eyes have shined for a moment, lowers his head. Contrarily, Don Abigail, who is very near him, "[a]lzó los ojos como dándole gracias a Dios y María Santísima de que a Monseñor no se le hubieran ido los bueyes" (Arreola 171, 186, 190).[53]

A discontented voice expresses what may be a widespread sentiment among those excluded from the coronation: "Yo estoy indignado. Esa fiesta tan lujosa es un verdadero insulto a la población. No se hizo más que para los ricos, que a la hora de la hora y como siempre, se colgaron los galones."[54] Thus, in the end, as always, history repeats itself: without regard for the community in general and the Indigenes in particular, the wealthy minority takes over Señor San José's celebration as a symbol of prestige. Arreola does not recount the precise history of the feast's sponsorship. However, it is evident that at some point the patronage, which had initially distinguished the Indigenous *cofradía*, was usurped by the town's ruling class. It is the spiritual correlate of the material expropriation of the land. Even as the reclaiming of the sponsorship and the arrival of the government's surveyors raise the Tlayacanques' hopes, the oligarchy schemes against their efforts on both fronts. And, again, as always, the *gente de razón* manage to preserve the oppressive status quo. Adding insult to the injurious exclusion of the Tlayacanques from the coronation ceremony, later, a chorus of oligarchs offers answers to the question of when the lands will be returned to the Indigenes:

– El año de la hebra y el mes del cordón ...

– Primero me cuelgan del palo más alto.

– Para eso hay arriba y abajo.

– Dios Nuestro Señor dispuso que nosotros fuéramos arriba y que los indios cargaran con las andas ...

– Al fin y al cabo que ellos también se divierten mucho por debajo ...

– Ahora les hemos parado todos los pleitos y juicios ...

---

53 "Raised his eyes as if thanking God and most holy Mary that the monsignor hadn't let his thoughts run away from him."

54 "I'm outraged. That lavish celebration is a real insult to the population. It was made exclusively for the rich, who, when the time came, claimed the credit for themselves, as always."

– ¿Y el Día del Juicio Final?
– Ya tenemos todos nuestros papeles arreglados, con la debida antici-
pación." (Arreola 193, 197)[55]

Soon afterwards *La feria*'s final fragment, which describes the destruction of the fireworks display, begins by stating: "Nadie podía
haber previsto lo que sucedió esta noche, última de la feria, a las doce
en punto."[56] The statement is likely tongue in cheek, however. Given
the accumulation of grievances, the attack on the firework display is
not surprising. Although there are no casualties, the last scene conjures
up the incident's meaning. The narrator is all alone on the square: "Solo,
porque los demás estaban tirados en el suelo, dormidos y borrachos,
aquí y allá, como los muertos de un falso campo de batalla" (Arreola
198–9).[57] The conclusion of the feria seemingly supports Leal's reading
of *La feria* as a representation of societal failure. According to Leal, individual and societal failure is due to trying to do things without knowing how, as in the case of the shoemaker who became a landowner (45).
But the shoemaker's example is symptomatic of a much larger problem. The world represented in *La feria* is topsy turvy: the so-called *gente
de razón* lack reason, and those who are in the right lack rights.

Numerous fragments indicate that the primary culprit is coloniality,
the persistence of the social, political, and economic structures imposed
by colonialism that sustain a system founded on inequality. Chávarri,
who commented on *La feria*'s apocalyptic ending, found that Zapotlán's
lower classes accepted the status quo without protest or hope of vindica-
tion (421). However, the deliberate destruction of the fireworks display
can be seen both as an act of defiance and as prophetic forewarning. *La
feria* as a whole is an apocalypse for revealing a reality in disarray. Guided
by the voices of Zapotlán, the reader travels unseen and unhindered
through space and time to see how it came to be this way and to witness
the iniquity of those in power and the resilience of those who lack it. In

---

55 "It'll be a cold day in hell; they'll have to hang me from the tallest pole first; that's
the point of having up and down; our Lord God decreed that we should ride up top
and that the *indios* carry the load …; after all, they also have a lot of fun underfoot …;
we put a stop to all their lawsuits and court cases now …; and Judgment Day?; we
already have all our paperwork in order, well ahead of time."

56 "No one could have foreseen what happened that night, the last of the *feria*, at exactly midnight."

57 "Alone because everyone else was on the ground, drunk or asleep, here and there,
like the dead on a pretend battlefield."

the end, when everything seems hopeless, *La feria* imagines a revolution. Nonetheless, Arreola appreciated that the inherent irony of the apocalyptic genre was that the promised end was always yet to come. Hence the satirism that suffuses *La feria*, as well as the melancholy tone of the last voice heard in the text: "Ya para venirme, me volví por última vez y vi desde lejos el escenario. En el lugar donde estaba el castillo, vi subir al cielo la última columna de humo, recta y delgada. / Dejé de mirar en el momento en que se desprendió de su base de ceniza, donde ya no quedaba nada por arder" (Arreola 199).[58] As the speaker turns back, what could possibly come after the upheaval remains an open question.

Voices

La feria is also an apocalypse because it does not conform to standard literary forms. Chávarri answered in the affirmative the question of whether *La feria* could be considered a novel, acknowledging the adoption of felicitous narrative innovations (425). Mauricio Ostria argued that *La feria* was a novel because the relationships among sets of fragments created a functional system and a unitary atmosphere (196, 199). Arreola, however, maintained that it was not a novel but rather a series of notes or sketches (M.A. Campos 134). Numerous critics – most of whom insist on calling it a novel – have commented on the fragmentary structure and the orality of the text. But as Edgar Campos accurately points out in his survey of the critical literature, the simple mention of a handful of literary-theory concepts developed by Mikhail Bakhtin has generally served to define *La feria* as a polyphonic narrative with traces of carnivalization produced by the contrapuntal dialogue among the different voices. Without contradicting this definition, Campos adds the notion that the overlapping dialogue keeps reconfiguring Zapotlán's social reality through the simultaneous expression of diverse world-views (E. Campos 242, 258). The full implications of this insight become clear when *La feria* is read as an apocalypse – which is the only way to adequately relate its content to its peculiar form.

Even silent spaces "speak" in *La feria*. Adding to the text's formal peculiarities, the fragments are separated by asterisks designed by the

---

58 "As I started heading back, I looked back one last time and saw the scene from afar. Where the display formerly stood, I saw the last column of smoke rising straight and thin to heaven. / I only stopped looking the moment that it detached from its base of ashes, where there was nothing left to burn."

Figure 2.1. Sample asterisks based on the set included in the first edition of *La feria*. Drawings by Pablo García Loaeza.

artist Vicente Rojo especially for the book (fig. 2.1). The drawings have not garnered much attention because the full set of eighty in their original layout only appears in the earliest editions. But as Fernando Castro Chávez points out, they were designed and purposefully placed to complement or underscore the content of a fragment and thus they are integral to the text (46). For example, a biretta – a type of bonnet worn by Catholic clergy – often appears before fragments in which a priest plays a role, such as the town's general confession. A pair of eyeglasses precedes fragments that feature learned individuals, such as the doctor, the historian, and the Jesuit. The asterisks that accompany the descriptions of the shoemaker's agricultural efforts include a plough, a donkey, a set of maize stalks, and an ear of maize, but also a shoe after the fragment in which he gives up and decides to go back to his trade. Prostitution is associated with a pair of lips, high heels, and a leg, and it is not by chance that the leg also precedes the fragment that deals with the candlemaker's dismay at discovering that his daughter has been defiled (Arreola 90, 179, 168).

Adding to the asterisks' meaningfulness, Castro Chávez finds that they tend to appear in multiples of three and calculates that the total number of drawings in the original edition, including the five that appear on the cover, is 294, or ninety-eight times three (47–9). Castro Chávez's numerological deductions further suggest *La feria*'s apocalyptic bent. Numerical symbolism was commonly used in Jewish and

Christian apocalyptic literature to create "the impression of order in the physical world and in human experience." In the Book of Revelation, numbers play particularly important formal and conceptual roles that include exposing meaningful patterns in time and a divine cosmic order, as well as conveying coded messages (Yarbro Collins 135, 114–16).[59] Their possible numerical symbolism aside, the asterisks recall *milagros*, small charms commonly found in Mexican churches as votive offerings in recognition of a fulfilled vow or prayer. The charms symbolize the favour obtained; a leg, for instance, might indicate the miraculous healing of that limb. This religious connotation reinforces the irony present throughout Arreola's text, in which the image of a leg, for example, is usually associated with sinful behaviour. Thus, *La feria*'s asterisks as originally conceived echo, enhance, and add meaning to its words.

La feria, and indeed Zapotlán, is the sum of an assortment of voices, some recurring and some unique, talking to, at, or over one another, in a way that cuts not only across class but also across time and even across existential planes. The Tlayacanque Juan Tepano and the oligarch Don Abigail speak from the two extremes of the social spectrum. A nameless king of Spain who in one fragment orders that the mistreatment of his Indigenous subjects be punishable and prevented is rebuked in the next fragment for paying lip service to justice, out of self-interest. Don Isaías regularly makes scathing comments, using statements from his biblical namesake, which creates an odd doubling effect. The homeless and mentally ill Juan Vites, so called because of the only sentence he ever says, becomes a prophet when, after a major earthquake, he asks, as he always does, "¿Vites cómo salió cierto?" ("You see how it came true?") One speaker, who claims a special affinity with ghosts, never manages to benefit from the hidden treasures they reveal (Arreola 97, 162–3). Not to mention the many small stories of love, hope, pride, greed, lust, loss, regret, infidelity, jealousy, and vengeance that express life's minutiae as manifested in a small provincial city.

A series of fragments about Zapotlán's red-light district pits morality policies against practical realities The controversy also involves three of the four socio-historical domains in which, according to Walter Mignolo, the logic of coloniality operates: control of the economy, control

---

59 The number of the beast, 666, is a famous cryptogram to which "a staggering variety of solutions has been proposed." Angela Yarbro Collins attributes the prominence of numerical symbolism in Revelation to the author's neo-Pythagorean convictions about the power of numbers to reveal the basic order in all reality (117, 136).

of authority, and control of gender and sexuality (15).[60] Someone celebrates the decision to cleanse the town by putting all the houses of ill repute in the same zone, because "más vale tener un lugar de a tiro echado a la perdición, que no todas esas lacras desparramadas por el cuerpo de Zapotlán."[61] Someone named or nicknamed Marqués argues, on the contrary, that the red-light district is a bad idea because what were formerly *espinillas* ("pimples") on the city's face have been gathered into a serious and growing tumour. Someone replies that such comparisons are irrelevant; the truth is that Marqués is unhappy that regular escapades cannot be as convenient and inconspicuous as they were before. Another voice: "A mí me da lo mismo: con tal de que las haya, no me importa dónde estén."[62] María la Matraca, however, is happy to increase her income by improving the houses she rents in the newly established district: "Al cabo de todos modos da igual, si hacen lo que hacen, más vale que lo hagan con comodidad. El pecado es el mismo."[63] One girl is unhappy about having received a medical certificate to be able to work because it turned her from an amateur without a title into a licensed professional. Another girl, who for anatomical reasons has remained a virgin, complains instead about not getting certified. When a big earthquake hits, alleged differences are shown to be superficial: the working women "están muertas de miedo y no son peores que otras con familia y que también tienen miedo y se les revuelven los rezos."[64] Later, during the *feria*, a comment about the influx of prostitutes from the neighbouring town of Tamazula leads to a lecture about how the women there are not as phony as those of Zapotlán, who are all "unas moscas muertas, unas viejas troyas" ("hypocrites, old whores") (Arreola 78–9, 81, 87, 182). The multiplication of perspectives exposes the hypocrisy and the inefficacy of efforts to exert control over basic human drives.

Through myriad voices Zapotlán appears an infinitely varied and unstable entity in *La feria*. Arreola stated that his aims were to slice

---

60   The fourth domain is control of knowledge and subjectivity (Mignolo 15).
61   "It's better to have one place fully given to hell that all those cankers spread through the body of Zapotlán." The idea echoes Matthew 5:30: "It is better for you to lose one part of your body than for your whole body to go into hell."
62   "It's all the same to me: provided there are some, I don't care where they are."
63   "In the end it makes no difference, if they do what they do, they might as well do it in comfort. The sin is the same."
64   "Are dead afraid and are no worse than those with families, who are also afraid and mix up their prayers."

through the city's consciousness to reveal a capriciously fragmented reality and to capture the local language (Carballo 405). These two features render the task of summarizing or translating *La feria* practically impossible; it is an eminently regional text that nevertheless reflects realities common throughout Spain's former empire in the Americas. In that sense, *La feria* provincializes metropolitan centres at various levels: Spain, Mexico City, and even Guadalajara, the state capital of Jalisco. To paraphrase Dipesh Chakrabarty, the citizens of Zapotlán maintain a tense dialogue between the totalizing narrative of capital – of imperial, national, and state capitals – with its always yet-to-be-realized promise of prosperity, and the "infinite incommensurabilities" of real human struggles that keep disrupting that narrative (254). Predicated on coloniality, the narrative of capital privileges a single overarching point of view to postulate established hierarchies, "universal" values, and a developmental model of history. In *La feria*, however, competing individual voices, including marginal ones, underscore deep economic, social, and moral disparities. The dissonant chorus undermines the possibility of producing an all-encompassing historic narrative because the story is constantly being disrupted by contradicting arguments and new connections. In response to Fernando del Paso's historical novel *Noticias del imperio* (*News from the Empire*, 1987), Katherine Ibsen proposes that its fragments foreground instability "not only in radicalizing the narrative form ... but, ultimately, by questioning the power relations behind history." In its particular way, *La feria*'s multitudinous form also disrupts "the scripts of official discourse and the pretense of progress," mobilizing the past as a source for active engagement with the present as well as an eye to the future (Ibsen 148, 151).

The penultimate fragment of *La feria* seems directed at its author as a judgment from a superior entity: "Y tú ya vete a dormir, contador impuntual y fraudulento. Pero como tu castillo de mentiras sostiene una sola verdad, yo te consiento, absuelvo y perdono. Y como creíste te sea hecho" (Arreola 197).[65] In a 1985 interview Arreola stressed that the fragment's second sentence was the one that mattered most to him in a book whose one sustaining truth was the betrayal of the original population and the taking away of their land. However, two decades after the publication of *La feria*, Arreola had no hope left. "I know," he

---

65 "And now to bed, you inaccurate and deceitful storyteller. But since your castle of lies supports a single truth, I allow, absolve, and pardon you. And as thou hast believed, so be it done unto thee." The last sentence is a statement from Matthew 8:13.

said, "that now it's too late, because everything has changed and those who own the land and the heirs of the landowners are different and a restitution is no longer possible" (M.A. Campos 136).

Even so, the apocalyptic genre is still suitable for exposing – more bitterly perhaps – an ongoing predicament, as reflected in "Este es mi reino," a contemporary pocket-sized apocalypse similarly constructed from a multitude of voices. Reygadas employs all the conceptual aspects of an apocalypse: the revelation of a state of crisis, a historical reflection, and the notion of impending radical change; he gives them a suitably apocalyptic form by challenging film narrative conventions. The only apocalyptic element missing from the film would be literal otherworldly entities. Their witnessing role, however, is taken by the twelve videographers – a couple of them are shown – who allow the spectator to wander among the partygoers and listen to what they say to one another or directly to the camera.

The fragments that make up "Este es mi reino" cannot be adequately summarized or translated. The first voice belongs to a fashionably dressed man, who tells his female companion that the mountains, the landscape they can see, are the same as Hernán Cortés may have seen when he conquered the region, and that he must have been blown away by Mexico's landscape. A woman, who later identifies herself as preppy but happy, talks about the importance of getting to know one's own country first. A local drunkard introduces himself to two light-skinned women – who may or may not be foreign – as Juanito: "ya sabe que … en inglés, Johnny, ¿no?" ("you know … in English, Johnny, right?") (Reygadas 3:16). One scene shows the luxury cars of some of the guests. In another, a local man arrives on horseback. A man argues that the legalization of marijuana entails legalizing different types of murder and would eventually lead to social chaos. His immediate audience seems dismissive of such assertions. Two men discuss a murder that the police did nothing about. An indigent old man, who claims to have worked for the national press, touches his genitals as he talks; later he unapologetically pees in full view of the attendees. A man dedicates a poem "a nuestras ancestrales tradiciones" and "también a todo lo nuevo, todo lo que tiene que surgir y a todo lo que a nivel de imagen, la inteligencia, la conciencia y nuestra raíz" (6:18–6:33).[66] The next cut shows several people throwing a bench onto the windshield of an old

---

66 "To our ancestral traditions … to everything new, everything that must come, and to everything in terms of image, intelligence, consciousness, and our roots."

car. Two people in wrestler masks appear to engage in a mock fight, and a random guest jumps in as well; later the masked couple shares a kiss. A very drunken local person hearteningly declares that "aquí no entra ni la policía y nunca va entrar la policía" (6:55).[67] Children hurl rocks at the old car; a grown woman does the same; someone shouts, "¡Esto no es Canadá!" ("This isn't Canada!") (7:38). Speaking in her native English, a woman says: "Oh, come on, let's see, I can throw it farther than you and … They don't need this disorder. They need order. They need you to tell them" (8:13–8:19). A man wearing Indigenous clothing eats ice cream. A local man takes up a drink and says, "Como dicen allá en el gabo: 'Cheers!'" ("As they say in the US: 'Cheers!'") (9:03). Spectators sometimes appear in the background, standing behind a low stone wall. In one particularly long and expressive scene, a small group of people stand or sit quietly, unmoved by, or perhaps resigned to, all that is going on near their house. As evening grows, there is dancing and a bonfire of benches piled around the old car; people throw lit alcohol bottles at it. The final scene shows nothing but orange flames and smoke over which the words *Este es mi reino* appear one letter at a time, each a different colour.

The first speaker's survey of the landscape echoes one that the (in) famous Hernán Cortés might have conducted – even if his own awe at the Tepozteco is tinged with nationalist pride. The speaker's statement underscores the persistence of the past. The reference to the Spanish conquest, an event that is widely regarded as Mexico's foundational moment, sets the stage for the scenes that follow and demonstrates both the great diversity and the crushing disparity that resulted from Spanish imperialism. The film also evokes connections to a more recent brand of imperialism when Juanito, a man unlikely to have travelled much, finds that using the English version of his name is more fitting than the Spanish one, or when another who has seemingly crossed the border to work in the United States makes a toast in English.[68] The complicated

---

67 "The police don't dare come in here and the police will never come in here."

68 Of course, the name Juan also points to Mexico's colonial history as a sign of both Christianization and the progressive imposition of Spanish over numerous Indigenous languages – more than half of the sixty-eight that are still spoken today are endangered. Notwithstanding recent efforts to acknowledge and revitalize Indigenous languages, many Mexicans consider them inferior because Spanish or English afford greater social mobility within their communities (Terborg and García Landa 466). On language shift and the language situation in Mexico, see Terborg and García Landa. Some signs of revitalization on this front include Instagram and Facebook accounts that promote acquisition of Nahuatl, as well as a surge in popular music in Maya.

relationship between Mexico and its neighbour to the north is also conveyed by the foreigner who criticizes the growing disorder and stresses the need to impose control. These three voices point to a tense history, which includes instances of cooperation – such as in the Bracero Program (1942–64) and the North American Free Trade Agreement (1994) – and of forceful intervention, as in the Mexican-American War (1846–8) or the seizure of the port of Veracruz in 1914. Mexicans generally place relations with the United States along an imperialist continuum that connects to the Spanish conquest (Myers 269–70). More immediately, it underscores the influx of foreigners to the town of Tepoztlán and the disruptions it entails – including the increasingly chaotic party being filmed.

Against this historical background, "Este es mi reino" exposes deep contrasts among a variety of Mexicos. In the late 1980s, Mexican anthropologist Guillermo Bonfil Batalla proposed the notion of two Mexicos fundamentally at odds with each other. One, which he dubbed "imaginary Mexico," is the realm of a powerful minority intent on following the Western developmental model. The other is the "deep Mexico" of an oppressed majority whose way of life remains rooted in Mesoamerican civilization. The contrast between them is the unavoidable result of a colonial history still unfolding within Mexican society (Bonfil Batalla 9–11). More recently, Claudio Lomnitz-Adler has criticized Bonfil Batalla's dichotomy as "merely a refashioned inversion of the modernist trope of tradition versus modernity." Through a historical analysis of the role of intellectuals and the public sphere in the municipality of Tepoztlán, Lomnitz argues that the expression "silent Mexico" is more useful and precise because, rather than claiming historical priority or appealing to nationality, "it simply comprises the various populations that live beyond the fractured fault line of Mexico's national public sphere" and thus lack a public voice (264, 286). Albeit on a very limited and relative scale, "Este es mi reino" allows populations on both sides of the fault-line to speak, and in doing so, the filmmaker offers a more multilayered, accurate, and striking portrait than that allowed by either critic's categories.

At the party in Tepoztlán, where pre-Hispanic ruins, corn fields, and posh weekend homes share the landscape, many kinds of imaginary Mexico converge. For instance, when the preppy woman remarks on the importance of getting to know one's own country, the knowledge she is referencing – visited places, pinned on a map – celebrates touristic Mexico, a set of iconic places promoted in glossy brochures. Perhaps the man who warns about the dangers of legalizing marijuana believes in institutional Mexico. The man who dedicates a poem to "our ancestral traditions" and envisions the revival of an idealized past is probably imagining a neo-Aztec Mexico. He represents a growing movement of people, urbanites generally, who, without direct ties to an Indigenous heritage, consciously seek to reconnect with an ethnic identity through practices unlikely to have actual pre-Hispanic precedents (Myers 71). Interrupted by images of indigence, drunken mayhem, and wanton destruction, such visions seem far removed from the unvarnished reality manifested at the party. There are voices, however, that express suspicion or hostility towards official authority; the poignant silence of the man wearing traditional Indigenous clothes, who is not seen interacting with anyone; and the silence of a group of four local residents patiently waiting for the revel to be over so they can get on with their lives.

Obviously, as the intentional product of selective editing, Reygadas's short film also constitutes a particular vision of Mexico, but that does not invalidate its apocalyptic message. The last image of "Este es mi reino" suggests that everything has gone up in flames, all the different Mexicos have turned to smoke. In contrast with the sabotage that takes place at the end of *La feria*, the fiery conflagration in "Este es mi reino" seems aleatory. Nevertheless, it does insinuate that the disparities laid bare in the short film are unsustainable and will ultimately lead to ruin. On the one hand, there is some room for hope: the appearance of the different-coloured letters of the film's title, which reiterate its widely assorted cast of characters, may portend resurgence, a rising from the ashes. On the other hand, the contrast between images of a raging fire and the festive music and colourful letters is disconcerting. Along with the fact that the title appears as fast as it disappears, the film's final sequence hints at the absurd irony of this or any revolution: in the end, the more things change, the more they stay the same.

The documentary nature of "Este es mi reino" does not lend itself to the sort of historic survey that *La feria* offers, yet there is a clear historical awareness as attested by internal references. Moreover, it was purposely created as a critical commentary on a major historical event, the Mexican Revolution, which in spite of much rhetoric did not bring about substantive change – a point that several of the short films included in *Revolución* also make. Unlike the Tlayacanque-sponsored feast in *La feria*, "Este es mi reino" does not contemplate deliberate acts of defiance against the status quo. However, some voices do call authority into question. And to the extent that it calls attention to a lasting, ongoing, and deepening crisis, the film is also a work of resistance. In the collection's companion volume Reygadas is quoted as saying that "Mexico is a country full of life and strength, but now it's lost and sick," and that the centenary of the revolution should generate thought, remembrance, and compassion against omnipresent demagoguery. "I am a realist," he explains. "Everything eventually turns around and transforms after a long time in the hole" (*Revolución* 56). Finally, very much like *La feria*, "Este es mi reino" disrupts formal conventions by eschewing a linear narrative presented from a single perspective in favour of a multitude of voices that speak for themselves. Aside from any religious connotation, this justifies the film's title. "This is my kingdom" is a personal statement that not only Reygadas but any Mexican who is likely to be a guest at the party can utter truthfully.

La feria and "Este es mi reino" share the hallmarks of the apocalyptic genre. Both works reveal a present state of crisis, considering it in light of the past and with an eye towards a future that forebodes devastation; these works additionally expose the long-standing structures of social inequality that are rooted in colonialism – the source of the crisis – and both challenge coloniality by subverting the narrative and perspective that support it. Through the accumulation of discrete experiences conveyed by individual voices, they decentralize the loci of enunciation and redistribute narrative authority, challenging the colonial/modern notion of history as a single, shared, and steady flow towards ever greater prosperity. The text and the film highlight colonialism's grievous faultlines, but they use different temporal layouts. On the one hand, Arreola distributes polyvocality diachronically, sweeping through history to show how hierarchies are constructed and contested within persistent colonial frameworks, namely land ownership and religious devotion. On the other hand, Reygadas presents polyvocality synchronically, juxtaposing disparate realities at a single event to expose the resonances of colonialism in contemporary Mexico.[69] *La feria* is unambiguous in its position regarding the dispossession of the Indigenous Peoples' lands, with the text's ironic barbs exclusively reserved for the so-called *gente de razón*. The lines of contestation are evident, the point of the struggle is clear, and the solution seems obvious. Thus, there is room for hope – humour, even. Hope is less palpable in "Este es mi reino," in which no particular group is explicitly vindicated and a sour irony undermines every position. Yet, in contrast with ancient apocalypses, neither *La feria* nor "Este es mi reino" proposes a definite post-apocalyptic outcome. The apparent absence of a higher power directing the course of history, and therefore the uncertainty of salvation for the just and of punishment for the wicked, mark these works as postmodern apocalypses.

---

69   I owe this valuable insight to Justin Knight.

The texts lay the responsibility for the crises they reveal, and for their resolution, squarely on us humans with all our virtues and vices. Nonetheless, the narrative foundation is biblical and thus fundamentally tied to the colonial past. In light of those ties, the next chapter examines how the manipulation of religious images on social media can help contest or reinforce contemporary coloniality in Mexico.

WORKS CITED

Albala, Eliana. "Juan José Arreola: Fragmentos para el rompecabezas de un mundo que se perdió como las piedras." *Revista Iberoamericana*, vol. 55, nos. 148–149, 1989, pp. 675–83. *Liverpool UP*, https://doi.org/10.5195/reviberoamer.1989.4619.

Arreola, Juan José. *La feria*. Joaquín Mortiz, 1963.

Báez-Jorge, Félix. *Entre los naguales y los santos*. Universidad Veracruzana, 1998.

Benjamin, Thomas. *La Revolución: Mexico's Great Revolution as Memory, Myth and History*. U of Texas P, 2000.

Bonfil Batalla, Guillermo. *México profundo: Una civilización negada*. Grijalbo, 1990.

Burkhart, Louise M. *The Slippery Earth: Nahua-Christian Moral Dialogue in Sixteenth-Century Mexico*. U of Arizona P, 1989.

Campos, Edgar. "El aplazamiento de la voz: Dialogismo y simultaneidad en *La feria* de Juan José Arreola." *Literatura Mexicana*, vol. 21, no. 2, 2010, pp. 235–61.

Campos, Marco Antonio. "Con Juan José Arreola." *De viva voz (entrevistas con escritores)*. Premià, 1986, pp. 127–37.

Carballo, Emmanuel. *Diecinueve protagonistas de la literatura mexicana del siglo XX*. Empresas editoriales, 1965.

Castolo, Fernando G. "Historia de la Coronación 'Pontificia' de San José de Zapotlán." *El sur*, 17 Sept.–8 Nov. 2007. https://web.archive.org/web/20190421093851/http://www.periodicoelsur.com/noticia.aspx?idnoticia=12998. Accessed 26 June 2019.

Castro Chávez, Fernando. *Otra lectura de "La feria" de Arreola: Las viñetas de Vicente Rojo; Presentada en el 2018 en los "XI Coloquios arreolinos" del Centenario de Arreola*. Self-published, 2018.

Castro Ricalde, Maricruz. "Revolución y neocolonialismo en 'La tienda de raya' de Mariana Chenillo." *Cinémas d'Amérique latine*, no. 22, 2014. *OpenEdition Journals*, https://doi.org/10.4000/cinelatino.861.

Chakrabarty, Dipesh. *Provincializing Europe: Postcolonial Thought and Historical Difference*. Princeton UP, 2000.

Chávarri, Raúl. "Arreola en su varia creación." *Cuadernos Hispanoamericanos,* 242, 1970, pp. 418–25.

Coronación Pontificia del Señor San José de Zapotlán. YouTube video, uploaded by Pastoral de la Cultura Gdl, 5 Aug. 2014. https://youtu.be/QkdIyxR3qDU.

Ehrman, Bart D. *The Other Gospels: Accounts of Jesus from Outside the New Testament.* Edited by Zlatko Plese. Oxford UP, 2013.

"Este es mi reino." Directed by Carlos Reygadas, *Revolución,* Canana, 2010.

Garro, Elena. *Los recuerdos del porvenir.* Joaquín Mortiz, 1963.

Gibson, Charles. *The Aztecs under Spanish Rule: A History of the Indians of the Valley of Mexico, 1519–1810.* Stanford UP, 1964.

Giménez Caballero, Ernesto. "San José, contribución a la simbología hispánica." *Revista de Occidente,* vol. 83, 1930, pp. 169–227.

Gómez-Arzapalo Dorantes, Ramiro Alfonso. "Consideraciones antropológicas frente al fenómeno de la religiosidad popular en comunidades campesinas de origen indígena en México." *Gazeta de antropología,* no. 24, 2008, https://hdl .handle.net/10481/6994.

Gruzinsky, Serge. "Indian Confraternities, Brotherhoods and *Mayordomías* in Central New Spain: A List of Questions for the Historian and the Anthropologist." *The Indian Community of Colonial Mexico: Fifteen Essays on Land Tenure, Corporate Organizations, Ideology and Village Politics,* edited by Arij Ouweneel, CEDLA, 1990, pp. 205–23.

Horn, Lames J. "U.S. Diplomacy and 'The Specter of Bolshevism' in Mexico (1924–1927)." *The Americas,* vol. 32, no. 1, 1975, pp. 31–45. *Cambridge Core,* https://doi.org/10.2307/980401.

Ibsen, Kristine. *Maximilian, Mexico, and the Invention of Empire.* Vanderbilt UP, 2010.

Lastra, Yolanda, Dina Sherzer, and Joel Sherzer. *Adoring the Saints: Fiestas in Central Mexico.* U of Texas P, 2009.

Leal, Luis. "*La feria* de Juan José Arreóla: Tema y estructura." *Nueva narrativa hispanoamericana,* vol. 1, no. 1, 1971, pp. 41–8.

Lienhard, Martín. "Voces marginadas y poder discursivo en América Latina." *Revista iberoamericana,* vol. 66, no. 193, 2000, pp. 785–98. *Liverpool UP,* https://doi.org/10.5195/reviberoamer.2000.5816.

Lockhart, James. "Encomienda and Hacienda: The Evolution of the Great Estate in the Spanish Indies." *Hispanic American Historical Review,* vol. 49, no. 3, 1969, pp. 411–29. *Duke UP,* https://doi.org/10.1215/00182168-49.3.411.

Lomnitz-Adler, Claudio. *Deep Mexico, Silent Mexico: An Anthropology of Nationalism.* U of Minnesota P, 2001.

Martínez Domínguez, Héctor. "Las cofradías en la Nueva España." *Primer Anuario,* 1975, pp. 45–71.

Meyer, Jean. "Los jesuitas mexicanos en el siglo XX: Historia de la disidencia." *Los intelectuales y el poder en México: Memorias de la VI Conferencia de*

Historiadores Mexicanos y Estadounidenses [*Intellectuals and Power in Mexico*], edited by Roderic A. Camp, Charles A. Hale, and Josefina Zoraida Vázquez, Colegio de México, 1991, pp. 455–77.

Mignolo, Walter D. "Preamble: The Historical Foundation of Modernity /Coloniality and the Emergence of Decolonial Thinking." *A Companion to Latin American Literature and Culture*, edited by Sara Castro-Klaren, John Wiley & Sons, 2013, pp. 12–32. *Wiley Online Library*, https://doi.org/10.1002 /9780470696446.cha.

Moguel, Julio. "La cuestión agraria en el período 1950–1970." *Política estatal y conflictos agrarios, 1950–1970*, vol. 8 of *Historia de la cuestión agraria mexicana*, Siglo Veintiuno, 1989, pp. 103–221.

Mora Valcárcel, Carmen de. "Juan José Arreola: *La feria* o 'Un apocalipsis de bolsillo.'" *Revista Iberoamericana*, vol. 56, no. 150, 1990, pp. 99–115. *Liverpool UP*, https://doi.org/10.5195/reviberoamer.1990.4672.

Myers, Kathleen A. *In the Shadow of Cortés: Conversations along the Route of Conquest*. U of Arizona P, 2015.

Ostria, Mauricio. "Valor estructural del fragmento en *La feria*, de Juan José Arreola." *Estudios filológicos*, no. 6, 1970, pp. 177–225.

Parkinson Zamora, Lois. *Writing the Apocalypse: Historical Vision in Contemporary U.S. and Latin American Fiction*. Cambridge UP, 1993.

Paso, Fernando del. *Noticias del imperio*. Mondadori, 1987.

Perochena, Camila. "¿Qué recordar de 1910? Los centenarios en las celebraciones bicentenarias en Argentina y México." *Cuadernos del Sur – Historia*, nos. 43–44, 2014–15, pp. 157–82.

Poot Herrera, Sara. *Un giro en espiral: El proyecto literario de Juan José Arreola y otros ensayos sobre su obra*. Universidad Nacional Autónoma de México, 2009.

Portier-Young, Anathea. *Apocalypse against Empire: Theologies of Resistance in Early Judaism*. William B. Eerdmans, 2011.

"Proceso contra Francisco de Sayavedra, por erasmista, 1539." *Boletín del archivo general de la nación*, vol. 18, no. 1, 1947, pp. 7–15.

Rama, Ángel. *The Lettered City*. Translated by John Charles Chasteen, Duke UP, 1996.

Revolución 10.10. Random House Mondadori, 2010.

Ricard, Robert. *La conquista espiritual de México: Ensayo sobre el apostolado y los métodos misioneros de las órdenes mendicantes en la Nueva España de 1523–1524 a 1572*. Fondo de Cultura Económica, 1986.

Riedl, Matthias, and David Marno. "Introduction: The Resilience of the Apocalyptic." *Apocalyptic Complex: Perspectives, Histories, Persistence*, edited by Nadia Al-Bagdadi, David Marno, and Matthias Riedl, Central European UP, 2018, pp. vii–xxi. *Project MUSE*, https://muse.jhu.edu/book/62788.

Romo, Vanessa. "Nude, Pin-Up-Style Portrait of Emiliano Zapata Sparks Protests in Mexico City." *NPR*, 11 Dec. 2019. https://www.npr.org/2019

/12/11/787244533/nude-pin-up-style-portrait-of-emiliano-zapata-sparks
-protests-in-mexico-city.

Rosen, Elizabeth K. *Apocalyptic Transformation: Apocalypse and the Postmodern Imagination*. Lexington Books, 2008.

Ruiz Medrano, Ethelia, Claudio Barrera Gutiérrez, and Florencio Barrera Gutiérrez. *La lucha por la tierra: Los títulos primordiales y los pueblos indios en México, siglos XIX y XX*. Fondo de Cultura Económica, 2012.

Rulfo, Juan. *Pedro Páramo*. RM, 2005.

Sánchez Prado, Ignacio M. *Screening Neoliberalism: Transforming Mexican Cinema, 1988–2012*. Vanderbilt UP, 2014.

Schedtler, Justin J., and Kelly J. Murphy. "Introduction – From Before the Bible to Beyond the Bible: Apocalypses throughout History." *Apocalypses in Context: Apocalyptic Currents through History*, edited by Justin J. Schedtler and Kelly J. Murphy, Augsburg Fortress, 2016, pp. 3–18. *JSTOR*, https://doi.org/10.2307/j.ctt1b3t7n8.

Schenker, Andrew. "Review: *Revolución*." *Slant Magazine*, 9 Oct. 2010. https://www.slantmagazine.com/film/revolucion/.

Steinbeck, John. *The Grapes of Wrath*. Penguin Books, 2002.

Tavárez, David E. *The Invisible War: Indigenous Devotions, Discipline, and Dissent in Colonial Mexico*. Stanford UP, 2011.

Terborg, Roland, and Laura García Landa. "The Language Situation in Mexico." *Current Issues in Language Planning*, vol. 7, no. 4, 2006, pp. 415–518.

Trigo, Pedro. *La institución eclesiástica en la nueva novela latinoamericana*, 2 vols. Universidad Católica Andrés Bello, 1999.

Velázquez García, Mario Alberto, and Helene Balslev Clausen. "Tepoztlán, una economía de la experiencia íntima." *Latin American Research Review*, vol. 47, no. 3, 2012, pp. 134–54.

Yarbro Collins, Adela. *Cosmology and Eschatology in Jewish and Christian Apocalypticism*. Brill, 1996.

"Zapotlán el Grande." *Jalisco*, Gobierno del Estado de Jalisco, https://www.jalisco.gob.mx/es/jalisco/municipios/zapotlan-el-grande. Accessed 26 June 2019.

Zermeño Padilla, Guillermo. "El retorno de los jesuitas a México en el siglo XIX: Algunas paradojas." *Historia mexicana*, vol. 64, no. 4, 2015, pp. 1463–1540. https://doi.org/10.24201/HM.V64I4.3116.

3 Colonial Foundations, Digital Futures: Recasting the Spanish Conquest in Social Media

BETH T. BOYD

Colonialism depends upon the subjugation of peoples to create a unified narrative. As Pablo García Loaeza makes clear, Juan José Arreola's *La feria* and Carlos Reygadas's "Este es mi reino" demonstrate the ways in which the plurality of voices can decentralize hegemonic perspectives. "Pocket-sized apocalypses" become explosive methods of exposing colonial inheritances – even if they provide no clear solutions to a world outside these oppressive systems. Social media platforms welcome this same plurivocality in Mexico today. Yet how might digital technologies move us closer to decolonial initiatives in the twenty-first century?

"Secularism has become in many ways the religion of the modern world." Nelson Maldonado-Torres's opening to his 2008 essay on the interchangeability of religion and secularism presents an uneasy prospect: far from replacing the underpinnings of conquest and control when confronting Latin America's foundations, we have simply renamed them (360). As Maldonado-Torres suggests, the Spanish Crown's theological approach to empire leaves an indelible mark on thinking about what comes afterwards. Whether postcoloniality, decoloniality, or any of its replicants, Latin America's transition to secularized republics has often wrestled with the religious remnant of its colonial frameworks. In Mexico alone, secularist movements of the nineteenth century and the subsequent rise of the Cristero War suggest a complex relationship between the Catholic Church and the power structures that once underwrote practices of domination (Reich 3). Their interplay proposes perhaps, as the Mexican Conference of Catholic Bishops posited in the late twentieth century, the unique tensions of Mexico's postcolonial inheritances. Politically free from Catholicism on paper, daily practice suggests a varied narrative (Loaeza 119).

But just what can be considered "daily practice"? As a part of a larger project on how to think about the re-articulations of colonization in

Mexico's twentieth and twenty-first centuries, the concept of coloniality today must also turn towards the elements of daily life that emerged under colonial frameworks. As Ignacio Sánchez Prado observes in the Latin American Keywords Project (2015), routines resist critical scholarship because they are often considered under the umbrella of *lo popular*, or popular culture (261). New information technologies have redefined popular culture; digital networks mediate "between the national and the global in a see-sawing climate" of social, cultural, and political change in the twenty-first century (Kantaris and O'Bryen 1–2). As Geoffrey Kantaris and Rory O'Bryen observe, incorporating products of popular culture may be touted as proof of multiculturalism and attention to the avant-garde, but the tendency of *lo popular* to inhabit heterogeneous spaces has equally created spaces of aperture and debate. Such practices thrive between "the country and the city, between the folk and the street, between the 'masses' and the elite national/political structures," as part of Latin America's colonial foundations (1, 3).[1]

In this vein, I suggest that a turn to popular culture and its relationship to colonial frameworks demands an approach to outlets that foment cultural transmission in the twenty-first century. Specifically, I argue that the manipulation of religious images by way of digital technologies such as memes and viral videos reveals a continuing, fervent engagement with debates on piety and control that have been active on Mexican soil since the foundation of Spain's colonizing project. I turn to the viral video "Todos bailan el Pasito perrón, hasta él," uploaded by late-night, talk-show host Rolando Ávila (2015), as well as the meme "¿Somos o no somos?" created by the Querétaro-based social-media account Tlacaélel, as two timely examples. I ultimately suggest that memes contribute more to conversations on postcolonialism than previously considered, operating as a varied "collection of texts" that bring diverse voices on decolonial initiatives into public discourse (Shifman 56).

The field of memetics is broad. As such, I want to clarify what we mean by *memes* before discussing how Ávila's and Tlacaélel's posts reflect conversations on postcolonial inheritances in Mexico today. The evolution of internet memetics has previously corresponded with scientific discourses made popular by Richard Dawkins (*The Selfish Gene*) and Susan Blackmore (*The Meme Machine*) in the last decades of the twentieth century. The unique social sphere that internet communities provide, however, expands biological theories on the replication

---

1 See also García Canclini, *Hybrid Cultures*, xxx. With regard to Beezley and Curcio-Nagy's interventions, consult their introduction to *Latin American Popular Culture*, xii.

of ideas themselves – moving on to how these bits of text and image can encourage, challenge, and even dismantle social movements in the twenty-first century.

"Networked Publics": Memetics, Social Media, and Definitions of the Popular

The disjuncture between the content we expect on social media platforms versus traditional archival sources can make scholarship on memes an uneasy project. A picture, some text, or a message shared between phones – the commonplace and satirical nature of memes suggests a disregard for serious commentary, let alone critical scholarship. Digital scholar danah boyd notes that an understanding of social media emerges in part from fervent debates on how concepts such as community, the public sphere, and social engagement have changed over time, as well as how technological advancements continue to shape these conversations ("Social Network Sites" 40–1). Social media is often "used to describe the collection of software that enables individuals and communities to gather, communicate, share, and in some cases, collaborate or play." It incorporates "social network sites, video sharing sites, blogging and microblogging platforms, and related tools that allow participants to create and share their own content" as originally developed in the early 2000s (*It's Complicated* 6). Boyd affirms that the underpinnings of social media are in many ways similar to other types of public spaces. They allow people to gather "for social, cultural, and civic purposes, and they help people connect with a world beyond their close friends and family." Unlike other types of public spaces, however, social media platforms are distinct in their affordances. Their ability to amplify, record, and spread information "can destabilize core assumptions people make when engaging in social life." Blending of private and public spheres, lack of distinct social cues, and a largely invisible audience contribute additional factors that users must consider when engaging with these technologies ("Social Network Sites" 50–2).

Despite the intersection of memetics with digital technologies, interest in memetics has existed for more than a century. In 1904, Richard Semon published on the term *mneme* (taken from the Greek *mimema*) to describe the glue for human experience as "memory" broadly defined.[2]

---

2   Semon mentions that the idea for *mneme* was not entirely his own. It was rather taken from German physiologist Ewald Hering and his paper "Memory, a Universal Function of Organic Matter," presented some forty years earlier (30 May 1870). "In

Memes were the human ability to pass on facts and figures, traditions and customs, but also the biological processes of heredity and reproduction that linked "the past and present in a living bond" (300). By the late 1970s, biologist Richard Dawkins had reinvigorated conversations on memes by comparing information transmission to the reproduction of genetic codes. Dawkins argued in *The Selfish Gene* (1976) that the mechanisms that drove evolutionary change could be used to explain variations in human behaviours over time (174). Now rhyming with *genes*, memes were "small cultural units of transmission" that could spread from person to person "by copying or imitation" (Shifman 10).

Scholars have since encouraged Dawkins's idea as a productive way to understand how and why cultural information survives across generations.[3] "Everything that is passed from person to person in this way is a meme," psychologist Susan Blackmore affirms. "This includes all the words in your vocabulary, the stories you know, the skills and habits you have picked up from others and the games you like to play" (7). Today memetics has a wide interdisciplinary value. Memes can be any unit that can be transferred from one person to another, "a heterogenous class of entities, primarily including behaviors and artefacts – the observable things that permit empirical work" (Aunger 6).

Media scholar Limor Shifman asserts that internet memetics presents its own particularities when placed within social networks. In *Memes in Digital Culture* (2014), Shifman states that in a digital age, memes are exceptional in that "they have become highly valued pillars of a so-called participatory culture" (4). Memes have traditionally been considered singular cultural units (behaviours, tools, etc.) passed from one entity to another. Shifman argues, however, that internet memes are rather "a *group* of digital items sharing common characteristics … created in awareness of each other … circulated, imitated, and/or transformed via the Internet by many users" (7–8).[4] While the format of these groups may vary,

---

this short paper of only twenty pages Hering, with admirable insight and clearness, summed up the chief points of resemblance between the reproductive powers of heredity, of practice and habit, and of conscious memory. Satisfied, however, with combining these in a harmonious scheme ... Hering refrained from analytically demonstrating that the resemblances between the different reproductive processes were more than accidental, and left behind him the task of proving that all these reproductive processes – whether of heredity, habit, or memory – owe their resemblance to their common origin in one and the same faculty of organic matter" (9). See also Shifman's introduction, p. 10.

3 See also Dennett's *Darwin's Dangerous Idea*, pp.17–34.

4 For a complete definition of memetics in light of digital technologies, consult Shifman's chapter 4, "Defining Internet Memes," pp. 37–54.

memes emerge when a user makes changes to pre-existing content and subsequently reinserts it into social media networks. Memes in this way have the ability to function as "socially-constructed public discourses" where variations speak to a multiplicity of interacting voices (8). They thrive as a "collection of texts" that are always dependent upon a larger corpus to be fully intelligible while demanding pre-existing knowledge on the part of the user (56).

The quantity of public institutions on social media has only grown with interest in sharing platforms, increasing exponentially the digital visibility of the Mexican state and the Catholic Church in the last ten years. Incumbent president Andrés Manuel López Obrador (2018–) has notably cultivated accounts on Twitter, Facebook, Instagram, and YouTube in line with the presidencies of Enrique Peña-Nieto and Felipe Calderón. They join La Conferencia del Episcopado Mexicano (CEM; 52,000 followers on Twitter) and heads of church such as Carlos Aguiar Retes (36,000 followers) and Father José de Jesús Aguilar (200,000 followers) as recurring commenters on national events. In Mexico specifically, initiatives such as Misioneros EnRedados (inaugurated by the Vatican's Pontifical Council for Social Communications) remain popular projects in which "e-priests" promote the value of social media in evangelization projects.[5] Mario Maraboto affirms that organizations such as the Episcopal Conference of Mexico recognize blogs, social media, and podcasts as those that "constituyen una posibilidad de llegar cada día a más fieles."[6] These digital tools can be used "no sólo para llamar la atención o fijar una postura sobre situaciones específicas que le afectan a [la Iglesia] o a la sociedad, sino también para comunicar mensajes de esperanza e inclusive para incidir en la formación de sus fieles" (Maraboto).[7]

In this way social media platforms have been able to extend objectives that have defined the Catholic Church since its inception. Evangelization, continuing education, and social reform can be facilitated through online initiatives irrespective of in-person constraints. Responses from users have additionally become more accessible as "likes," comments, and posts or reposts offer unprecedented opportunities for public

---

5 Consult "Comienza 'Misioneros en'red'dados'" and "Misioneros Enredados."

6 "Make it possible to reach new faithfuls each day." All translations are my own unless otherwise noted.

7 "Not only to call attention to, or to focus on, a position on certain situations that affect [the Church] or society, but also to communicate messages of hope and even to influence the faith formation of their followers."

engagement. And as Rolando Ávila's "Todos bailan el Pasito perrón, hasta él" suggests, the popular may still provide strategic methods of rethinking the impact of social networks and their products in the twenty-first century.

Image and the Popular in Rolando Ávila's "Todos bailan el Pasito perrón, hasta él"

In 2011 Rolando Ávila's *Ah pa' Nochecita* was a novel show, a late-night newcomer as part of TV Azteca's regional programming. Skits, musical interludes, and cheeky pranks garnered early appeal from audiences throughout central Mexico. The show's regional success took a turn in December 2015, however, when Ávila posted a small video clip online (fig. 3.1). Dance competitions were a regular part of Ávila's programming, and his recent feature of El Grupo Dinastía Mendoza's song "El Pasito perrón" entertained audiences with guests frantically keeping time to the song's catchy rhythm.[8] Ávila later saw an opportunity to recreate the dance when he found a group of nativity figurines for sale in a local market (*tianguis*). "Nos encontramos con la figura del Niño Dios ... [entonces] agarré el celular y otro chavo puso la canción en el suyo, y ya, lo demás es historia" ("¿Te puedes ir a la cárcel?").[9] The video quickly garnered over three million views through YouTube and shares across multiple social media platforms (Lopez). Ávila ultimately attributed the national success of *Ah' pa' Nochecita* to the video's viralization. ("Ah Pa' Nochecita").[10]

The same renown that promoted *Ah' pa' Nochecita*'s national success, however, grabbed the attention of ecclesiastical officials throughout central Mexico, albeit two years after the video's initial release. Father José de Jesús Aguilar, current director of Sacred Art and previous subdirector of media through the Sistema Informativo de la Arquidiócesis de México (SIAME), commented as an aside on TV Azteca that "el riesgo de hacer bailar a una imagen religiosa es que se puede confundir con un juguete" (Aguilar).[11] The extraneous comment quickly inspired

---

8   Consult YouTube video "Pasito perron – ha pa nochesita," uploaded by Dinastía Mendoza.

9   "We found ourselves with this Baby Jesus figurine ... so I grabbed my phone and the other guy put the song on his, and there you have it, the rest is history."

10   A copy of the video is also available on Ávila's official YouTube account. Consult "Pasito perrón."

11   "The risk of making a religious image dance is that it can be confused with a toy."

Figure 3.1. Still from Rolando Ávila's original Facebook post "Todos bailan el Pasito perrón, hasta él."

reports that the archdiocesan officials had demanded Ávila's imprisonment and excommunication.[12] Aguilar took to Twitter to clarify that the response was tangential to the topic of decorum in private home and church spaces. Digital spaces, however, could also be a part of the discussion for Mexican Catholics as long as the treatment of religious images was involved. "Creo que cada persona está en su derecho de hacer lo que quiera con sus imágenes," Aguilar affirmed. "Solamente invitamos a quién es creyente: respeta a sus imágenes … Si alguien toma una imagen como juguete, [y] lo quiere hacer, y la quiere bailar, lo que sea, está en su total derecho. Pero, sobre todo, con una información clara y correcta."[13]

Aguilar's Twitter exchange over the Niño Jesús resonates with the "likes" and replies that are now representative of public engagement. But as art historians Elizabeth Hill Boone and Thomas B.F. Cummins make clear, religious images (and discourse about them) have long served as agents that "shaped the cultural climate and visual discourse" in navigating imperial relations between the Spanish Crown and its subjects (13). Edicts issued during much of the first half of the seventeenth century (1626–65) identified a repeated concern with Christian iconography and how colonial subjects bought, sold, and incorporated them into their daily lives.[14] This included abolishing any

---

12 Aguilar was originally interviewed by TV Azteca regarding appropriate celebrations for Candlemas.

13 "I believe that everybody has the right to do what they want with their [religious] images. We only say to believers: respect your images. If someone treats an image like a toy, and makes it do this and that, and wants to make it dance, or whatever, they're completely within their rights. But, above all else, as well informed."

14 Edicts throughout Mexico's colonial period marked a centuries-long debate over sacred images and their use by the general population. For concerns over image

use of religious art that was intended to cultivate traditions outside the auspices of the New Spanish Church ("Edicto … que no se porten ciertas medallas"). As late as 1768, Inquisitors such as Dr. Cristóbal Fierro y Torres noted that misuse of images posed a consistent problem in public markets, their design and circulation threatening to "ocasionar [a los fieles] que se vayan deslizando, y apartando de la integridad, y pureza con que deben vivir, y estar en nuestra santa Fe" ("Edicto en el cual se prohíbe el uso de imágenes").[15] Placement of images in unsuitable spaces such as public forums and less affluent neighbourhoods could further encourage indecorous treatment if not watched carefully ("Edicto … sobre la prohibición de esculpir, pintar, vaciar").

The bobbing Niño featured in Ávila's video would have been a familiar sight in Mexican *tianguis* as well as a staple for Christmastime celebrations. The late-night host mentions that, much like the Inquisitors commented in the seventeenth century, he chose the statue because it was readily available in a public space. The criticisms he received included those from a variety of users who condemned his content as having an impact beyond social media platforms: "Me decían, 'se van a ir al infierno.' Se viralizó. Se hicieron memes, luego el 'Pasito Perrón Challenge.' El tema es que el Día de la Candelaria del siguiente año el Padre José de Jesús Aguilar recomendó no utilizar las figuras del niño Dios como juguete … Recibí muchas críticas e incluso insultos de personas religiosas" ("¿Te puedes ir a la cárcel?").[16]

To mention Ávila's viral sensation (or similar memes) in tandem with New Spanish approaches to religious imagery does not necessarily aim to explore the colonial inheritances of religious imagery through establishing a one-to-one correspondence over time. In terms of reiterations of coloniality in the twenty-first century, however, the presence of Mexico's Catholic Church in public forums works to reinvigorate

---

design broadly, see "Edicto que ordena que no se ponen ciertas medallas," "Edicto de la Inquisición," "Edicto en el cual se prohíbe el uso de imágenes," and "Edicto del Tribunal del Santo Oficio." For an example of specific governance over the characteristics of specific images of Christ, see "Edicto que prohíbe las imágenes desnudas" and "Edicto de la Inquisición … imágenes de Jesús Nazareno."

15   "Cause the faithful to stray and to fall away from the integrity, and purity, with which they should live and be within our holy Faith."

16   "They told me, 'You're going to hell.' It went viral. They made memes, and then the 'Pasito Perrón Challenge.' The thing is that for next year's Candlemas Father José de Jesús Aguilar recommended not to use the Holy Infant figurines as a toy. I received a lot of criticism and even insults from clergy."

debates on the role of colonial-era institutions in postcolonial countries where, despite governmental changes, the afterlives of these systems continue to thrive. This is not a question of whether Catholicism and its iconography continue to be relevant in Mexico today. This is especially so when the Virgen de Guadalupe thrives as an internationally recognized symbol of Mexican Catholic identity, *fiestas patronales* remain central to local civic identity, and nearly 78 per cent of Mexicans still identified as active Catholics in 2020, even if the rate has continued to decline over the last century.[17] The question appears more broadly where the influence of Mexico's Catholic Church operates in a secular state that once rested upon Catholicism as integral to political rule, and where digital technologies now circulate on an increasingly postnational level.

Imperialism, Secularism, and the Rise of the Digital Popular

Social media, like other forms of collective organization, comprises those bits of popular culture that not only represent new possibilities for long-theorized ideas such as *lo popular* but also rearticulate concepts such as nationalism and globalization, at unprecedented speed. This comes at a time when articulations of mass culture have been considered too fragmented to be considered in any unified assemblage (Antebi 274). As Ignacio Sánchez Prado and Susan Antebi observe in the Latin American Keywords Project (2015),[18] products of *lo popular* often resist critical scholarship in that they are simultaneously defined, yet obscured by, their own ambiguity (Sánchez Prado 261–2). Social media platforms are a prime example of the pluralistic and postnational interactions that characterize global power structures in the twenty-first century where "a notion of the popular … is no longer operative to encompass productions that circulate regionally and transnationally with unprecedented speed" (270).

In her essay "Globalization and the Crisis of the Popular," Jean Franco suggests that we are at such a point of global interconnectivity that to reflect upon the popular is primarily an act of nostalgia. Firm national boundaries are no longer viable except in memory (208). For

---

17 See "Población de 5 años" for data, as well as "Religion in Mexico Declining" and Olvera y Armando Martínez for media coverage.

18 This concept is part of the collection *Critical Terms in Caribbean and Latin American Thought: Historical and Institutional Trajectories*, edited by Yolanda Martínez-San Miguel, Ben. Sifuentes Jáuregui, and Marisa Belausteguigoitia.

communities not incorporated into globalized processes, the popular may become a site of disruptive potential when official discourses fail to represent those who do not experience modernity "as democracy or change or progress" (208, 215). Antebi further notes in "Globalized Digital Cultures" that digital platforms that incorporate high volumes of anonymous participation not only minimize the role of "national, racial, or gendered subjectivities" but also may eliminate their detectability on social networks entirely (275). The cacophonous aspects that made popular culture difficult to conceptualize have incidentally become its strength – especially when such conversations are confronted with the decentralization of political entities in the previous decades. "The explicit deactivation of prior identity categories, such as the citizen or the people," Antebi observes, "works toward the project of an alternative political imaginary" (273).

This is not to say that the disruption of systems of power through popular technologies is entirely new. Digital social media platforms may be novel creations, but the formation of globalized networks remains coterminous with colonial systems of control (Antebi 276; Quijano 533, 537). In New Spain, circulation of Catholic iconography through print culture and the plastic arts thrived in public and private spaces as an integral component of social and political belonging. Images placed in homes, revered in churches, carried through city streets, and sold in marketplaces created a continuous conversation on the role of the holy visual as a conduit of popular taste and as crucial to "an enterprise of domination" through which Western epistemologies could take hold (Gruzinski 41).

Yet as global trade to the Americas and new technologies increased, clergy were less able to control the design and distribution of religious images and, with them, the messages these images communicated to viceregal subjects about the institutions that governed them. As New Spanish Inquisitors remarked throughout the long seventeenth century, consumers (*gente ordinaria*) sought "muy bastas y disonantes figuras" that could speak to their interests and were in line with the latest trends ("Edicto en el cual se prohíbe el uso de imágenes").[19] Saints who were painted on dinner plates and pocket watches were popular ways in which holy persons could accompany their users during their daily

---

19 "Very rough and unseemly figures." While the Inquisitors in this document mention the vast networks of producers and merchants that made this economy possible, there is no specific mention of the populations that make up *"gente ordinaria."* These everyday people differ from Indigenous neophyte populations, on whom

routine. Adding astrological signs to Catholic symbolism could further increase the luck of its owner ("Edicto ... que no se porten ciertas medallas"). Merchants who sold images of uncanonized folk saints or images with extra-biblical details that appealed to local *gustos* presented yet another challenge to Inquisitional authorities ("Edicto de la Inquisición ... imágenes de Jesús Nazareno"). While Inquisitors were able to identify these images by way of their ubiquity, the large and fragmented network that produced them made it nearly impossible to control their circulation. "Casi a toda clase de personas y gremios," remarked one Inquisitor, "como son comerciantes y mercaderes, tenderos con trapaleros, pintores, escultores, plateros, impresores, vaciadores," contributed to an unruly economy that found church officials "divirtiéndole y ocupándole" solely in identifying networks of distribution ("Edicto en el cual se prohíbe el uso de imágenes").[20]

Where multivalent sources infiltrated New Spain's devotional economy, interest in Rolando Ávila's video presented a similar challenge for Aguilar and Mexican bishops seeking to quell negative media attention from rapidly multiplying parodies. Users on Facebook, YouTube, Twitter, and Instagram were quick to create copycat versions of Ávila's popular video, while media coverage from *El Universal* and *El País* spread attention beyond social media platforms.[21] In Mexico City the proposal of a flash mob in La Plaza de la Constitución "con colaboración por parte del Niño" (in conjunction with the Infant Jesus) in 2017 garnered over 30,000 Facebook users interested in the event (Watson,

---

clergy received special instructions. Clergy were asked to individually enquire and remove images from their homes, if possible: "que siendo como es notorio, y manifiesto a todos, que los Indios tienen comunmente en sus casas un quarto ... en que conservan multitud de Efigies de Christo nuestro Señor, de su Santissima Madre, y Santos; muchas, o las mas de ellas de construccion, y escultura muy extraña, y ridícula ... donde fuere necesario, que usando del estilo, y modos, y medios mas suaves ... les persuadan que no es agradable a Dios, ni corresponde a su Culto, el tener, y venerar, tales Imagenes." ("Edicto en el cual se prohíbe el uso de imágenes" 4; "Being that it is well known, and widely apparent, that the *Indios* commonly have in their homes a room ... in which they keep many effigies of Christ our Lord, of his Holiest Mother, and the Saints; many of them, or at least the majority of them, of make and model very odd and ridiculous ... where if it might be necessary, using the style, means, and gentlest ways possible ... you could persuade them that it is not pleasing to God, nor corresponding to his cult, to have and to venerate such images.")

20 "From almost all types of people and guilds, from merchants and market sellers, to grocers and shop keepers, to painters, sculptors, silversmiths, printers, and carvers."

21 See Cruz, "No nadie irá a la cárcel."

"Baile Masivo"). Rumours even suggested that Aguilar had demanded Ávila's imprisonment and excommunication. News sources such as Vanguardia MX affirmed that "hace unos días fue [que] se hizo viral un video donde se ve a la figura de un niño dios bailando … sin embargo, la iglesia católica no lo tomo de buena manera y pidió que se castigue con cárcel al responsable" ("Piden cárcel").[22] On his YouTube show *El pulso de la República* (with 2.5 million subscribers), Mexican comedian Chumel Torres notably reported in the episode "El Pasito perrón de la corrupción" (1.3 million views as of 2021) that "hasta cárcel pidió [Aguilar] para los responsables" (Aguilar even demanded imprisonment for those responsible). "El padre Aguilar dice que al hacer bailar 'El Pasito perrón' al Niño Dios, se corre el riesgo de que la imagen religiosa sea identificada como un muñeco," the host reported. "Y no como lo que es: una imagen religiosa. En forma, pues … de muñeco."[23]

Media attention to Aguilar's comments sparked formal responses from both Aguilar and SIAME. Aguilar responded on Twitter that Chumel Torres's segment was "totalmente falso y absurdo, sin ningún fundamento" (completely untrue and absurd, baseless). In his Twitter post "El problema de la desinformación y la invención de cosas no dichas!" ("The Problem with Misinformation and Making Things Up!"], Aguilar affirmed that his comments were tangential to the original interview in that "[tan sólo] en los últimos segundos me preguntaron qué opinaba del Niño Dios bailando el Pasito perrón" (only in the final seconds did they ask me what I thought about Baby Jesus dancing "El Pasito perrón"]. When it came to Ávila's video, "No sé de qué se trata. Me dijeron que existía un video, y yo contesté: 'No conozco el video, no conozco "El Pasito perrón"'" (Aguilar).[24] The director also refuted claims that he condemned a Facebook event to which attendees would bring their own statues for a group dance in Mexico City's *zócalo*. "Este joven [Torres], sin la información correcta," Aguilar asserted, "dice que se está prohibiendo que se vaya a un baile determinado. Creo que cada

____

22   "A few days ago a viral video was made in which one can see the figure of a Baby Jesus dancing … however, this was not well received by the Catholic Church and they requested that the guilty be imprisoned."

23   "Father Aguilar says that to make Baby Jesus dance 'El Pasito perron' is to run the risk that a religious image be mistaken for a doll. And not for what it really is: a religious image. In the form of, well … a doll."

24   "I don't know what it's about. They told me there was this video, and I told them: 'I don't know about any video, I'm not familiar with "El Pasito perrón."'"

persona está en su derecho de hacer lo que quiera con sus imágenes."[25] The Archdiocese of Monterrey (La Arquidiócesis de Monterrey) and SI-AME released a video days later, supporting Aguilar's statement and requesting a definitive stop to the Pasito Perrón Challenge. "Lejos de que la Iglesia está molesta," the two organizations affirmed, "la mayor preocupación es la falta de atención a temas importantes para México, como la relación diplomática con E.U.A. o el aumento de la gasolina. ¿Hacía donde ponemos nuestra atención?" (Arquidiócesis Primada de México).[26]

This multiplicity of voices, as Celeste Olalquiaga notes in her work *Megalopolis*, is both the hallmark of popular culture and its most potent tool. "What is so threatening about popular culture is not, as has been often affirmed, its supposed mechanical or passive traits, but rather ... the enjoyment with which it is integrated into daily practice" (xiii). Falling into a world of polyvocality and kitsch, "it gathers its motifs randomly and eclectically, fragmenting the cohesion and continuity ... an irreverent recycling, a taste for iconography and the artificial" (xvi). This recycling, as Ávila's video demonstrates, can be an effective way to challenge hegemonic systems, even as they manage to reproduce themselves over time (coloniality).[27] For SIAME and the Archdiocese of Monterrey, attention on the #pasitoperronchallenge and its reproductions emerged as "algo muy lamentable para toda la comunidad cristiana católica Mexicana" (Arquidiócesis Primada de México; "something regrettable for all of the Mexican Catholic community"). Yet at the same time, Ávila affirmed that the video operated as a space for productive dialogue on Mexico's relationship with Catholicism today. "Creo que [el video] cambió la manera de pensar de muchos," Ávila affirmed, "sin intentar ofender a toda una religion ... creó una disyuntiva sobre sonreír o no" ("¿Te puedes ir a la cárcel?").[28] He even joked that his use of the Niño Dios should not be held responsible for "las pandemias,

-----

25 "This young man, without the correct information, says that it's being prohibited that anyone go to a certain dance. I believe everyone has the right to do what they want with their images."
26 "It isn't that the Church is upset, but rather that the biggest concern is the lack of attention to other topics that are important for Mexico, like our diplomatic relationship with the United States or the recent increases in gas prices. Where should we really put our attention?" (Arquidiócesis Primada de México). Additionally consult "La reflexión de la Iglesia en México."
27 See García Loaeza's chapter 2 in this work regarding these types of works as apocalyptic.
28 "I believe that [the video] changed the way that a lot of people think without trying to offend a whole religion ... it created a dilemma about whether to laugh or not."

terremotos y demás castigos divinos" ("pandemics, earthquakes, and other divine punishments") in the wake of COVID-19 ("Pasito perrón"). Ávila's use of religious iconography may not have been specifically intended as a statement on Mexico's imperial histories, but viral interest suggests an identifiable element in his content that allowed users to reconsider religious objects and their institutions in Mexico today. On these platforms historically powerful institutions that once controlled popular behaviour are now only one of many users with equal access to social networks. And where social media challenges spatial and temporal boundaries, digital technologies entertain the multivalent capacities of *lo popular* at unprecedented speeds.

At the same time, digital networks cannot be heralded as completely novel popular technologies. As Ávila's case uniquely exemplifies, global systems and the popular discourse that fills social media platforms are not without their own foundations in early modern globalization and colonization narratives. As these patterns emerge, such technologies are inseparable from the conversations of conquest and colonization that made global networks possible in the first place. Whether it is Ávila's repurposing of religious iconography on social media or the debates surrounding New Spanish images and the tastes of *gente ordinaria* in New Spanish markets, the role of the Catholic Church as a hegemonic institution, the place of Catholic iconography in Mexico's social, cultural, and political life, and just who constitutes the ordinary people subsumed under *lo popular* – these are a few of the common threads that become part of conversations on coloniality as it rearticulates itself over time. It also reflects, as comments surrounding Ávila's video make clear, whether or not the achievement of secularization projects has completely affected the achievement of decolonial initiatives. This is a question especially when the Catholic Church continues to survive as a postcolonial institution that shapes Mexico's cultural landscape today.

In this section I have aimed to establish that the rise of social networks has encouraged a reconsideration of Mexico's relationship with the Catholic Church in the twenty-first century. These new products of visual culture continue a trajectory in which the Catholic Church has shaped centuries of social and political influence through religious iconography. But as the viralization of Rolando Ávila's video became a chance conversation surrounding the intersection of popular culture and Mexico's Catholic tradition, social media accounts dedicated to more intentional conversations on the persistence of colonial inheritances in the twenty-first century have increasingly grown. This includes accounts such as Tlacaélel, whose presence on Facebook, YouTube, Instagram, and Twitter has gained more than one million followers who are exploring educational media on Mexico's historical foundations and its Indigenous legacies.

Content Creators, Historical Mediators: Tlacaélel's "¿Somos o no somos?"

"El pasado más presente que nunca" ("The past more present than ever before"), Tlacaélel was started in 2012 by content creator Oscar Ramírez in order to "devolver a los mexicanos según poética expresión nahuatl 'in ixtli in yolotl'; un rostro y un corazón para que sepan representar y defender con pasión y orgullo la cultura" (Tlacaélel, "About").[29] With over a million followers on four platforms, Ramírez (who now more commonly goes by Xiu Blogger) seeks to facilitate conversations on Mexico's present as current events intersect with Indigenous and colonial inheritances.[30] Tlacaélel wrestles with the colonial as something that actively operates in its present and that without educational initiatives will continue well into Mexico's future. The account promotes historical sources (archaeological sites, museums, archives) as one way of claiming Mexican heritage. Just what objects, persons, and narratives are part of this identity comes into conversation along the way.

In March 2019, Xiu Blogger turned to social media networks when incumbent president Andrés Manuel López Obrador (2018–) acknowledged in an official statement Mexico's colonial past and its continued effects on the country's Indigenous communities ("*pueblos originarios*"). The president's announcement included the culpability of Spain and the Catholic Church in fomenting the country's systemic inequalities. López Obrador affirmed that he had sent letters to both the king of Spain and Pope Francis requesting their formal apologies as "un paso obligado": "la llamada 'Conquista' se hizo con la espada y con la cruz" (López Obrador; "a necessary step: the so-called 'conquest' was made by both the sword and the cross"). "Se edificaron las iglesias arriba de los templos … se excomulgó a nuestros héroes patrias, los padres de nuestra patria, a Hidalgo y a Morelos."[31] The president later uploaded a

---

29 "Return what belongs to Mexicans according to the poetic expression 'in ixtli in yolol'; in countenance and heart, so that they know how to represent and passionately, proudly defend their culture."

30 As of January 2021, this included Facebook with 899,116 followers; YouTube with 30,300; Twitter (@TlacaelelTwit) with 2,046; and Instagram with 85,900.

31 "They built churches on top of the temples … they excommunicated our national heroes, the forefathers of this country, Hidalgo and Morelos."

video to Twitter in which he stated that his administration would focus on the role of the Mexican government in the historical subjugation of various marginalized groups:

> Yo lo voy a hacer [una disculpa] también porque después de la colonia, hubo mucha represión a los pueblos originarios: el exterminio de los Yaquis, de los mayas, incluso el exterminio [de] los chinos en plena Revolución Mexicana, desde el Porfiriato, y luego, en la Revolución. Y que el año 2021 sea el año de la reconciliación histórica.[32]

Xiu himself noted through Tlacaélel's Facebook page "que la ignorancia es estúpidamente atrevida si creemos que los pueblos nativos no merecen una disculpa por los últimos 500 años de marginación, discriminación y saqueos" (Tlacaélel, "¿Qué es una estupidez?").[33] "Pues si los españoles llevan tanto tiempo haciendo negocios en este país," Xiu affirmed, "lo mínimo que pueden hacer es hasta por hipocresía ofrecer una disculpa."[34] In general, users on López Obrador's official social media accounts questioned the president's fervent statement on *pueblos originarios* given the repeated political action to the contrary during his incumbency. *El País*, *El Universal*, the BBC, and the *New York Times* generated global coverage, while memes incorporating *The Simpsons*, stock photos of Felipe VI, and even New Spanish archival documents further lampooned the president for his lack of self-awareness.[35]

Ramírez eventually sought to capture these sentiments in his own account, turning to the inconsistencies of López Obrador's administration towards Indigenous communities. In a post from 27 March, one day after AMLO's Facebook statement, Tlacaélel uploaded a single

---

32 "I'm going to apologize as well because after the colony, there was a lot of repression of the First Peoples: the extermination of the Yaquis, the Maya, even including the extermination of the Chinese during the Mexican Revolution, beginning in the Porfiriato, and then, in the Revolution. Let 2021 be the year of historic reconciliation."

33 "That our ignorance is stupefyingly daring if we believe that the First Peoples don't deserve an apology for the last five hundred years of marginalization, discrimination, and plundering."

34 "Well if the Spaniards have been here so many years doing business in this country, the least they can do is offer a half-hearted apology."

35 See @chagorock, "AMLO antes de mandar la carta"; Vásquez, "¿Quién se disculpará…?"; and Carmona, "Ha respondido el rey de españa!..." for a few examples. For periodical coverage, consult "AMLO solicita por carta"; Lafuente and Abellán, "España rechaza con firmeza"; Castañeda, "Disculpas y retribuciones"; and Zavala and Morales, "AMLO exige disculpas."

Figure 3.2. Instagram post "¿Somos o no somos?" from social media account Tlacaélel Oficial (27 March 2019) reflects on Andrés Manuel López Obrador's demands to both the Spanish Crown and the Catholic Church on the 500th anniversary of the conquest of Mexico.

meme titled "¿Somos o no somos?" ("Are we, or are we not?"), created in the popular memetic template "Ah, pero anoche" (fig. 3.2).[36] Divided into two panels to be read as a top-down narrative, the image starts with an Aztec jaguar warrior, or *cuauhocelotl*, as he battles a Spanish soldier in an illustration of La Noche Triste. He draws blood as the image is representative of the words "You, demanding apologies from the Spanish Crown." The viewer is then greeted from below with a much different scene. The battle between two men has suddenly changed to a photograph of a man in the heart of La Calzada, walking along a large pedway leading up to the famous basilica dedicated to the Virgin of Guadalupe in Mexico City. He totes a large statue of the Mexican madonna on his knees, and a child dressed as St Juan Diego, the first Indigenous (Chichimec) saint of the Americas, accompanies him to the main chapel. The text refers to the celebratory feast day of the Marian image, while asking the viewer to consider: "Ah pero el 12 de diciembre" ("Oh but on 12 December").

The intersection of colonial histories with digital culture has produced a growing collection of memetic content in recent years. In their work on Aboriginal activism on social media Ryan Frazer and Bronwyn

---

36 Consult "Jean Claude Van Damme recreó el baile" for more information on this genre.

Carlson argue that memes can be "entangled in the achievement of an anti-colonial politics," tracking "the shifting ideological justifications and material practices of colonialism" (1–2). Memes are a powerful tool in revising narratives that have systematically erased Indigenous histories in the creation of a palatable foundational narrative for colonial projects. Frazer and Carlson emphasize that chronological disparity between digital technology and colonial topics particularly demonstrates "how colonialism has been both varied over time but ultimately persist[s] in its being" (1–2). Briana Nichols similarly acknowledges that social media users engage in "meaning making and contestation" when they use memes to explore colonial histories (and neocolonial presents) between Mexico and the United States. "Despite their nature as ephemeral cultural products," Nichols finds that "memes become meaningful tools for contesting dominant narratives around immigration, the border, and histories of interaction between Mexico and the United States." Meme creators today particularly wield "a power to challenge privileged representations of Mexicanness and contest the naturalization of dominant historical discourses" when confronted with racial stereotyping and historical forgetting (83).

For Ramírez, posting "¿Somos o no somos?" draws attention to the problematic nature of López Obrador's statements as a democratically elected official dedicated to the welfare of all Mexican citizens. Regarding the welfare of Indigenous communities, the meme may evoke the inconsistencies between the president's recent comments and the political policies that have actively endangered *pueblos originarios* under AMLO's administration. This includes politically backed projects such as El Tren Maya – a 948-mile, sixteen-billion-dollar intercity railway that threatens the migratory routes of endangered species, the urban planning of Indigenous communities, and the integrity of Mayan archaeological sites.[37] That López Obrador identifies Spain's spiritual conquest as inherent to the erasure of *pueblos originarios* ("iglesias arriba de los templos") similarly appears problematic when the Mexican government has indirectly supported the continuation of Catholic initiatives, even after the beginning of nineteenth-century independence projects.

---

37   For general information see "Supervisa AMLO avances"; for debates on the relationship between the project and national government, consult Chan Caamal's "Tren Maya no soluciona."

As Xiu Blogger makes clear, Mexico's development of secularization legislation and of divestiture from colonial-era institutions, as well as policies surrounding its *pueblos originarios*, has been at the centre of national conversations since the nineteenth century. What to do with the Catholic Church vis-à-vis secular projects has particularly occupied these debates. Ana Carolina Ibarra affirms that during Mexico's independence period, survival of the Catholic Church did not depend upon the creation of a postcolonial, Mexican institution, but rather upon the avoidance of disagreements with political movements that would lead to its dissolution (186). Historian Peter Reich similarly observes that throughout the nineteenth and twentieth centuries this pattern of evasion became part of a "conciliation policy," one in which bishops supported secular projects with the hopes of economic and ideological support for Catholic social agendas (11).[38] As of 2019, politicians such as Senator Soledad Luévano Cantú have suggested even greater liberties where religious groups could pursue more freedom of speech and economic gain.[39] Although such movements have failed, their discussions have reflected growing conversations on the role of the Catholic Church in Mexico today, even if they were rejected officially by AMLO himself: "Considero que este tema no debe tocarse ... ya se resolvió este tema hace 150 años" (Excélsior TV).[40]

Xiu Blogger's post garnered forty-one thousand reposts and over thirteen thousand reactions ("like," "dislike," etc.) when it was shared across Facebook and Instagram. Some users pointed out the historical inconsistencies of AMLO's request in that Spanish conquest and colonization was not an exclusively European project. Others spoke to the futility of the president's reactions as a productive move, citing more pressing issues such as national poverty.[41] Most users debated AMLO's letters as reflecting a greater conversation on whether decolonial initiatives could be contrary to what it means to be Mexican today. Out

---

38 Although the decades following the Cristero War were marked by a series of pro-clerical and anticlerical waves, more substantive policies of reconciliation by the 1980s emerged under the administration of Carlos Salinas de Gortari (1988–94). Amendments to the anticlerical elements of the Constitution of 1917, including legislation such as the Ley de Asociaciones Religiosas y Culto Público (1992), further facilitated reconciliation between the Mexican government and the Catholic Church.

39 For the complete list of initiatives consult Luévano Cantú, "Iniciativa con proyecto de decreto." See also the thread posted by Luévano, "Sobre las modificaciones."

40 "I consider this topic off limits ... it was already resolved 150 years ago."

41 "Mejor deberíamos de afrontar la inseguridad que vivimos día a día ... y no estar pidiendo pendejadas" (Sergio.jaime.180).

of the more than one thousand direct comments, users such as Mario Rodriguez affirmed that "[s]omos herederos del imperio Azteca y del imperio español, negar a España es negar el mexicanismo. Que si hubo saqueo y matanzas, claro que las hubo; pero no podemos negar qui[é] nes somos y de d[ó]nde venimos" (Rodriguez).[42] Other respondents, such as Maria Cabanne, countered that holding previous colonial powers responsible does not negate socio-political or cultural heritage; it only reinforces Western narratives, "minimizando el #genocidio que se perpetuó en toda la América, y no sólo por los españoles, sino por los portugueses e ingleses" (Cabanne).[43] Ultimately, a nation founded on hybridity through colonization had little sense for users such as Armando Figueroa, who identified the cultural importance of Mexican Catholicism (and the Spanish language) as proof that independence efforts do not necessarily guarantee decolonization. "[¿]Y c[ó]mo celebran independencia si siguen hablando español y son católicos?" (Figueroa).[44]

Whether you see the aftermaths of colonialism as a spectrum or a trajectory, leaving colonialism behind consistently turns to the epistemological work that is dismantling its underpinnings.[45] While many similar bloggers decide to incorporate contemporary images of López Obrador as part of their rhetorical strategy, Xiu's use of images that hearken to the Spanish conquest, colonization, and evangelization of Indigenous Peoples calls our attention to a pattern of relationality that extends beyond López Obrador's administration. Where López Obrador himself acknowledged his participation in a centuries-long cycle of native discrimination, the visual comparison Ramírez makes in "¿Somos o no somos?" suggests that Mexico's *estado de derecho* is not one that is automatically decolonial in nature merely by the acknowledgment of crimes against Indigenous communities. This is especially the case as colonial-era institutions such as Mexico's Catholic Church continue to be representative aspects of Mexican cultural identity today. Tlacaélel's use of internet memes suggests that when it comes to

---

42 "We are inheritors of the Aztec Empire and the Spanish Empire, to deny Spain is to deny being Mexican. Yes, there was pillaging and killing, of course there was; but we can't deny who we are and where we came from."

43 "Minimizing the #genocide that was perpetuated through all of the Americas, not only by the Spaniards, but also by the Portuguese and the English."

44 "And how is it you celebrate independence if you still speak Spanish and are Catholic?"

45 Yet as Frazer and Carlson observe, processing colonial topics through social media gives space to expose colonialism not as an antiquated notion eradicated by democratization and secularization but as an active framework "that ultimately persist[s] in its being" (1–2).

confronting colonial histories, we may be too quick to equate democracy/secularism with the achievement of postcolonial and/or decolonial initiatives. As "logic, metaphysics, ontology, and a matrix of power that can continue existing after formal independence and desegregation," colonial power structures may continue far beyond formal divestitures of imperial forces (Quijano 533). For many, apologies from Spain and the Catholic Church cannot, and will not, be effective methods of post-colonization or decolonization as long as European configurations of sovereignty dictate the conditions under which these initiatives operate. And as Tlacaélel's post suggests, strong cultural affiliation for colonial-era institutions such as the Catholic Church appears discordant when one considers the government's commitment to historic reconciliation. A call to reconciliation may give visibility to *pueblos originarios*, but it does little to actively address systemic changes to the coloniality of power under which they exist.

As Marisa Elena Duarte affirms in *Network Sovereignty*, future generations "who are increasingly comfortable living through the cybersphere face the challenge of finding out the dimensions of power and struggle that emanate from digital technologies" (140). A critical element of this task is the way in which younger generations "relate to the colonial present and also evoke a range of possibilities for decolonial futures" (140). While Mexico-based social media accounts such as Tlacaélel Oficial (86,300 followers), Resistencia Tenochtitlán (102,000 followers), and NeoMexicanismos (163,000 followers) do not identify with particular *pueblos originarios*, their content encourages critical inspection of Mexico's pre-Hispanic and colonial foundations as integral to addressing the country's systemic inequalities. These conversations ultimately shed light on what it means to think about Mexico as an entity that has experienced centuries of cultural and political change, altered by centuries of colonial rule, and that still negotiates what it means to leave colonization behind, if possible. For Xiu Blogger, coloniality as a transhistorical process has the capacity to exist as "un lastre que [han arrastrado] desde hace 5 siglos y que tal vez nunca se puedan quitar" (Tlacaélel, "¿Somos o no somos?").

Media scholar Limor Shifman asserts that in a digital age, memes and viral videos are exceptional networks of participatory culture (4). Users who make changes to pre-existing content and reinsert it into these digital channels create "socially-constructed public discourses" in which variations speak to a multiplicity of interacting voices (8). But while Hispanists such as Jean Franco acknowledge that articulations of the popular have the potential to call attention to hegemonic systems, Ignacio Sánchez Prado asserts that popular culture is in no way obligated to align with destabilizing narratives. They can just as easily be complicit in the systems of "power, capital, and distinction," even if only in a partial capacity (264). As Xiu Blogger's post suggests, these cultural items generate multiple, and at times contradictory, readings that do not always reflect decolonial initiatives simply by the virtue of their users or their medium.

Memes and viral videos are no trendy solution in a world where postcolonial and decolonial dialogues are just two conversations on how to imagine the "after" of colonial frameworks. Like similar contributors to conversations on postcoloniality and decoloniality, content creators demonstrate the difficulties of imagining responses that adequately confront centuries of hegemonic practices. Their association with the complex notion of popular culture further makes them more challenging contributors to these conversations. And in terms of medium, access to digital technologies can be self-limiting in its economic and geographical prerequisites. Those marginalized groups that have traditionally been pushed to the bottom, or excluded from hegemonic formulations of power, frequently remain omitted by questions of accessibility to these digital spaces.[46]

Social media is an attractive medium precisely because it allows possibilities that may be largely untenable off-screen. Providing a shift in angle, time period, or place, these platforms combine with digital innovation to imagine our social circumstances as something slightly – or radically – different. The ways in which social media users are engaging with digital technologies bring new considerations on how these networks can be used to think about colonial power dynamics in the twenty-first century. Twenty-first-century technologies are not immune as vehicles that can perpetuate colonial systems of oppression. As Rolando Ávila's and Tlacaélel Oficial's examples have shown, however, memes can make significant interventions on how these systems may be re-evaluated over time. Messy and cacophonous, their disregard for regulation and linear narratives speaks to the complex relationship that has defined Mexico's connection to colonial histories from the country's inception. And as chapter 4 will demonstrate, such socially constructed technologies ultimately demonstrate how their borders – or lack thereof – destabilize cycles of coloniality over time.

---

46   For Indigenous content creators looking to promote decolonial initiatives through social media in particular, installing the physical elements of internet connectivity (cables, poles) on sacred lands is yet another difficulty that such communities undertake. See Duarte, *Network Sovereignty*, p. 51.

WORKS CITED

Aguilar, José de Jesús [@PadreJosedejesu]. "El problema de la desinformación y la invención de cosas no dichas!" *Twitter*, 9 Feb. 2017, 4:03 p.m., https://twitter.com/PadreJosedejesu/status/829797928105447424. Accessed 3 Mar. 2019.

"'Ah Pa' Nochecita' de Rolando Ávila se va a nivel nacional." *Trend Topic World*, 23 Nov. 2017, https://trendtopicworld.com/2017/11/23/ah-pa-nochecita-se-va-por-tv-azteca-nacional/.

"AMLO solicita por carta al rey de España y al Papa que pidan perdón por la Conquista de México." *BBC News Mundo*, 25 Mar. 2019, https://www.bbc.com/mundo/noticias-america-latina-47701387.

Antebi, Susan. "Globalized Digital Popular Cultures: A Response to Ignacio M. Sánchez Prado." *Critical Terms in Caribbean and Latin American Thought: Historical and Institutional Trajectories*, edited by Yolanda Martínez-San Miguel, Ben. Sifuentes Jáuregui, and Marisa Belausteguigoitia. Palgrave Macmillan, 2016, pp. 273–8.

Arquidiócesis Primada de México. "Ocho de cada diez mexicanos son católicos." *Facebook*, 15 Feb. 2017, https://www.facebook.com/arquidiocesismx/videos/1237064159717393/.

Aunger, Robert. Introduction. *Darwinizing Culture: The Status of Memetics as a Science*, by Aunger, Oxford UP, 2001, pp. 1–24.

Ávila, Rolando. "Pasito perrón – Baila el Niño Dios (el único y original)." *YouTube*, uploaded by Fables of Real Life, 28 Dec. 2015, https://youtu.be/jMrBJoG3zZg.

– "Todos bailan el pasito Perrón, hasta él." *Facebook*, 27 Dec. 2015, https://www.facebook.com/Ahpanochecita/videos/todos-bailan-el-pasito-perrón-hasta-él/10153726628456083/.

Beezley, William H., and Linda A. Curcio-Nagy. Introduction. *Latin American Popular Culture: An Introduction*, by Beezley and Curcio-Nagy, SR Books, 2000, pp. xi–xxiii.

Blackmore, Susan. *The Meme Machine*. Oxford UP, 1999.

Boone, Elizabeth Hill, and Thomas B.F. Cummins. "Colonial Foundations: Points of Contact and Compatibility." *The Arts in Latin America*, edited by J. Rishel and S. Stratton, Yale UP, 2006.

boyd, danah. *It's Complicated: The Social Lives of Networked Teens*. Yale UP, 2014.

– "Social Network Sites as Networked Publics: Affordances, Dynamics, and Implications." *A Networked Self: Identity, Community, and Culture in Social Network Sites*, edited by Zizi Papacharissi, Routledge, 2010, pp. 39–58.

Cabanne, Maria [maria_cabanne]. Comment on "¿Somos o no somos?" *Facebook*, 26 Mar. 2019, https://www.facebook.com/Tlacaeleloficial/photos/2605600419512286.

Carmona, Alan [@alanhzcarmona]. "Ha respondido el rey de españa!..." *Twitter*, 26 Mar. 2019, 1:29 a.m., https://twitter.com/alanhzcarmona/status/1110428432914178048.

Castañeda, Jorge G. "Disculpas y retribuciones: Una conversación pendiente." *The New York Times*, 12 Apr. 2019, https://www.nytimes.com/es/2019/04/12/espanol/opinion/amlo-disculpa-mexico-espana.html.

@chagorock. "*AMLO antes de mandar la carta al Rey de España.*" *Twitter*, 25 Mar. 2019, 4:19 p.m. https://twitter.com/chagorock/status/1110290131469193216.

Chan Caamal, Joaquín. "Tren Maya no soluciona lo que falta al Estado." *Diario de Yucatán*, 27 Mar. 2022, https://www.yucatan.com.mx/merida/2022/3/27/tren-maya-no-soluciona-lo-que-le-falta-al-estado-309846.html.

"Comienza 'Misioneros en'red'dados' I Congreso de Evangelización en Internet." *Ecclesia*, 4 Apr. 2014, https://www.revistaecclesia.com/comienza-misioneros-enreddados-congreso-de-evangelizacion-en-internet/.

Cruz, Mónica. "No, nadie irá a la cárcel por hacer bailar al niño Dios el 'Pasito Perrón.'" *El País*, 7 Feb. 2017, https://verne.elpais.com/verne/2017/02/07/mexico/1486429544_383982.html.

Dawkins, Richard. *The Selfish Gene*. Oxford UP, 1989.

Dennett, Daniel. *Darwin's Dangerous Idea: Evolution and the Meanings of Life*. Simon and Schuster, 1996.

Duarte, Marisa Elena. *Network Sovereignty: Building the Internet across Indian Country*. U of Washington P, 2017.

"Edicto de la Inquisición de que todas las imágenes de Jesús Nazareno aparezca vestido con túnica morada" (1665). *AGN*, Indiferente Virreinal, Caja 2625, Exp. 009 (Edictos de la Inquisición).

"Edicto de la Inquisición que prohíbe el levantar altar a imágenes y mártires que no sean reconocidos y canonizados por la iglesia" (n.d.). *AGN*, Indiferente Virreinal, Caja 2625, Exp. 010 (Edictos de la Inquisición).

"Edicto del Tribunal del Santo Oficio, sobre la prohibición de esculpir, pintar, vaciar o imprimir imágenes de Cristo, los santos, la historia sagrada o los misterios de la religión en alhajas u otros sitios en que puedan servir de irrisión, escarnio o menosprecio de la religión católica" (1781). *AGN*, Indiferente Virreinal, Caja 2020, Exp. 025 (Edictos de la Inquisición).

"Edicto en el cual se prohíbe el uso de imágenes de pinturas en las que se muestra a Jesucristo, su Santísima Madre, y Santos, distorsionados o en esculturas extrañas, pues lejos de invitar a la devoción y reverencia, provocan risa y son ridículas." *AGN*, Indiferente Virreinal, Caja 1137, Exp. 003 (Edictos de la Inquisición).

"Edicto que ordena que no se porten ciertas medallas, imágenes, láminas que llaman sigilos o anillos esculpidos o grabados en oro, plata u otro cualquier metal, escritos, pintados en pergamino, tabla o cartón con letras y números, nombres, y caracteres debajo de la constelación e influencia de alguno de los planetas, como de los astros o movimientos de las estrellas" (1622). *AGN*, Indiferente Virreinal, Caja 5226, Exp. 011 (Edictos de la Inquisición).

"Edicto que prohíbe las imágenes desnudas de costado hacia arriba y de
    rodillas hacia debajo de Jesús de Nasareno." *AGN*, Indiferente Virreinal,
    Caja 2226, Exp. 029 (Inquisición).
Excélsior TV. "Conferencia de prensa de Andrés Manuel López Obrador
    (11 de diciembre de 2019)." *YouTube*, uploaded by Excélsior TV, 11 Dec. 2019,
    https://youtu.be/hc7asUuXixE.
Figueroa, Armando. Comment on "¿Somos o no somos?" *Facebook*, 26 Mar. 2019,
    https://www.facebook.com/Tlacaeleloficial/photos/2605600419512286.
Franco, Jean. "Globalization and the Crisis of the Popular." *Critical Passions:
    Selected Essays*, by Marie Louise Pratt and Kathleen Newman, Duke UP,
    1999, pp. 208–20.
Frazer, Ryan, and Bronwyn Carlson. "Indigenous Memes and the Invention of
    a People." *Social Media + Society*, 2017, pp. 1–12.
García Canclini, Néstor. *Hybrid Cultures: Strategies for Entering and Leaving
    Modernity*. U of Minnesota P, 2005.
Gruzinski, Serge. *Images at War: Mexico from Columbus to Blade Runner
    (1492–2019)*. Translated by Heather MacLean, Duke UP, 2001.
Hernández, Ester. "Misioneros Enredados – Paola Pablo y Ester Hernández."
    YouTube, uploaded by Ester Hernández, 28 Oct. 2019, https://youtu.be
    /11dCDh6nki8.
Ibarra, Ana Carolina. "Los problemas de la iglesia en una época crítica:
    Obispos, cabildos y catedrales ante la Guerra de Independencia
    (Hispanoamérica, 1808–1824)." *El historiador frente a la historia: Religión
    y vida cotidiana*, edited by Alicia Mayer, UNAM, 2008, pp. 167–88.
"Jean Claude Van Damme recreó el baile que lo convirtió en meme (Video)."
    SinEmbargo, 5 Dec. 2015, https://www.sinembargo.mx/12-05-2015/1343222.
Kantaris, Geoffrey, and Rory O'Bryen. Introduction. *Latin American Popular
    Culture: Politics, Media, Affect*, by Kantaris and O'Bryen, Tamesis, 2013, pp. 1–42.
Lafuente, Javier, and Lucía Abellán. "España rechaza con firmeza la exigencia de
    México de pedir perdón por los abusos de la conquista." *El País*, 26 Mar. 2019,
    https://elpais.com/internacional/2019/03/25/mexico/1553539019_249884
    .html.
Loaeza, Soledad. *La restauración de la Iglesia católica en la transición mexicana*.
    El colegio de México, 2013.
Lopez, Karina. "El 'Niño Dios' y el 'Pasito Perrón,' una polémica entre la
    Gloria y el infierno." *Yahoo! Noticias*, 7 Feb. 2017, https://es-us.noticias.
    yahoo.com/el-nino-dios-y-el-pasito-perron-una-polemica-entre-la-gloria
    -y-el-infierno-171601132.html.
López Obrador, Andrés Manuel. "Estamos en Comalcalco, vamos a Centla a
    conmemorar 500 años de la batalla de los españoles contra la resistencia de
    los mayas-chontales." *Facebook*, 25 Mar. 2019, https://www.facebook.com
    /lopezobrador.org.mx/videos/comalcalco-tabasco/432289494241807.

Luevano, Soledad [@SoledadLuevano]. "Sobre las modificaciones a la Ley de Asociaciones Religiosas." *Twitter*, 17 Dec. 2019, 7:20 p.m., https://twitter .com/SoledadLuevano/status/1207093123349958661.

Luévano Cantú, María Soledad. "Iniciativa con proyecto de decreto por el que se reforman, adicionan y derogan diversas disposiciones de la Ley de Asociaciones Religiosas y Culto Público." *Gaceta del Senado*, 11 Dec. 2019, https://www.senado.gob.mx/64/gaceta_del_senado/documento/103131.

Maldonado-Torres, Nelson. "Secularism and Religion in the Modern/ Colonial World-System: From Secular Postcoloniality to Postsecular Transmodernity." *Coloniality at Large*, edited by Mabel Moraña, Enrique Dussel, and Carlos A. Jáuregui, Duke UP, 2008, pp. 360–84.

Maraboto, Mario. "Las redes sociales y la iglesia." *Forbes*, 21 Apr. 2014, https://www.forbes.com.mx/las-redes-sociales-y-la-iglesia/.

Mendoza, Dinastía. "Pasito perron – ha pa nochesita (Dinastía Mendoza)." *YouTube*, uploaded by Grupo Dinastía Mendoza Oficial, 19 July 2016, https://youtu.be/wqH-uEohzY4.

Nichols, Brianna. "Mexicans Be Like." *Working Papers in Educational Linguistics*, vol. 31, no. 1, 2016, pp. 68–86.

Olalquiaga, Celeste. *Megalopolis: Contemporary Cultural Sensibilities*. U of Minnesota P, 1992.

Olvera y Armando Martínez, Graciela. "Catolicismo y otras religiones pierden creyentes en México." *Milenio*, 25 Jan. 2021, https://www.milenio.com /politica/comunidad/catolicismo-pierde-creyentes-censo-inegi-2021.

"Piden cárcel para el responsable del video del 'pasito perrón' del Niño Dios." *Vanguardia MX*, 7 Feb. 2017, https://vanguardia.com.mx/noticias /nacional/piden-carcel-para-el-responsable-del-video-del-pasito-perron -del-nino-dios-EBVG3285076.

"Población de 5 años y más que profesa religión católica por entidad federativa según sexo y grupo quinquenal de edad, serie de años censales de 1990 a 2020." *Instituto Nacional de Estadística, Geografía, e Informática (INEGI)*, https://www.inegi.org.mx/app/tabulados/interactivos/?pxq=Religion _Religion_01_a7ac48a2-4339-47d4-841e-f34d0d2b3382&idrt=135&opc=t. Accessed 10 Mar. 2022.

El Pulso de la República, "El Pasito perrón de la corrupción – El pulso de la República." *YouTube*, uploaded by El Pulso De La República, 9 Feb. 2017, https://youtu.be/nOTLq7vOPL8.

Quijano, Aníbal. "Coloniality and Power, Eurocentrism and Latin America." *Nepantla: Views from the South*, no. 1, vol. 3, 2000, pp. 533–80.

"La reflexión de la Iglesia en México sobre el Niño Dios y el 'Pasito perrón.'" *ACI Prensa*, 16 Feb. 2017, https://www.aciprensa.com/noticias/video -la-reflexion-de-la-iglesia-en-mexico-sobre-el-nino-dios-y-el-pasito -perron-95553.

Reich, Peter. *Mexico's Hidden Revolution: The Catholic Church in Law and Politics since 1929.* U of Notre Dame P, 1995.

"Religion in Mexico Declining." *Yucatan Times*, 26 Jan. 2021, https://www.theyucatantimes.com/2021/01/religion-in-mexico-declining-inegi/.

Rodriguez, Mario [Mariorodriguez_j]. Comment on "¿Somos o no somos?" *Facebook,* 26 Mar. 2019, https://www.facebook.com/Tlacaeleloficial/photos/2605600419512286.

Sánchez Prado, Ignacio M. "'Lo popular'/Popular Culture: Performing the Borders of Power and Resistance." *Critical Terms in Caribbean and Latin American Thought: Historical and Institutional Trajectories*, edited by Yolanda Martínez-San Miguel, Ben. Sifuentes Jáuregui, and Marisa Belausteguigoitia, Palgrave Macmillan, 2016, pp. 261–72.

Semon, Richard. *The Mneme*. MacMillan, 1921.

Sergio.jaime.180. Comment on "¿Somos o no somos?" *Facebook*, 26 Mar. 2019, https://www.facebook.com/Tlacaeleloficial/photos/2605600419512286.

Shifman, Limor. *Memes in Digital Culture*. MIT Press, 2014.

"Supervisa AMLO avances del Tren Maya en Yucatán." *El Universal*, 3 Mar. 2022, https://www.eluniversal.com.mx/nacion/supervisa-amlo-avances-del-tren-maya-en-yucatan/.

"¿Te puedes ir a la cárcel por crear 'memes' y burlarte de imágenes religiosas?" *Cultura Colectiva*, 29 Mar. 2018, https://web.archive.org/web/20190815220349/https://news.culturacolectiva.com/mexico/carcel-por-hacer-memes-de-figuras-religiosas/. Accessed 8 May 2018.

Tlacaélel. "About: Details about Tlacaélel." *Facebook*, https://www.facebook.com/Tlacaeleloficial/about_details. Accessed 19 Feb. 2020.

– "¿Que es una estupidez la solicitud de AMLO al rey de España?" *Facebook*, 26 Mar. 2019, https://www.facebook.com/Tlacaeleloficial/posts/2603395876399407.

– "¿Somos o no somos?" *Facebook,* 11 Nov. 2019, https://www.facebook.com/Tlacaeleloficial/posts/somos-o-no-somos/32075782242647831/.

Vásquez, Toño [@Tono_VazquezA]. "¿Quién se disculpará por quien haber elegido a Andrés Manuel, los que votaron por él?" *Twitter*, 26 Mar. 2019, 12:14 a.m., https://twitter.com/Tono_VazquezA/status/1110409544419762176.

Watson, Alex. "Baile masivo del Pasito Perron CDMX (evento original)." *Facebook*, 16 Feb. 2017. https://www.facebook.com/events/distrito-federal-mexico/baile-masivodel-pasito-perron-cdmxevento-original/215202922283756/. Accessed 10 Oct. 2019.

Zavala, Misael, and Alberto Morales. "AMLO exige disculpas al rey de España por matanzas en la conquista." *El Universal*, 25 Mar. 2019, https://www.eluniversal.com.mx/nacion/amlo-exige-disculpa-al-rey-de-espana-por-matanzas-en-la-conquista/.

4 Travel, Migration, and the Making of Borderlands: Life and Death in the Neocolony

CARA ANNE KINNALLY

The previous chapter examined some of the ways in which memetics and social media exemplify the messy and complex relationship between popular culture and coloniality as well as decoloniality in Mexico. As Boyd suggests, various forms of visual popular culture have, since the colonial era, served as platforms through which the Mexican community can debate, both literally and figuratively, how it sees and defines itself, especially in its relationship with colonialist institutions, such as the Catholic Church. This chapter similarly examines the shifting conceptualizations and definitions of Mexican identity and its representation in both elite culture and popular culture. Moving from the centre of the nation in the previous chapters to the fringes of the nation, this chapter examines how Mexicans come to recognize more profoundly their own coloniality through travel and migration across national borders.

This chapter starts by examining a photograph that went viral in June of 2019 (although for very different reasons than those of the viral videos and memes discussed in the previous chapter), as I began researching and writing this study. Serving as a metonym of Central American migration – its perils and hardships, but also the increasingly desperate methods that refugees and migrants are willing to take in order to make it across the border to the United States – the photograph shows the bodies of Salvadoran migrants Óscar Alberto Martínez Ramírez and his twenty-three-month-old daughter, Angie Valeria, who both drowned while trying to cross the Río Grande after they had been turned away at the US border and instructed to wait for their chance to apply for asylum – which, two months after their arrival at the US-Mexico border, had still not happened (Leduc). Face down in the water, their bodies lie side by side, wrapped up together in his black T-shirt, her small arm encircling the back of his neck as if continuing to hold on.

Although Óscar's and Angie's deaths are unequivocally tragic, their fates are not unique. Indeed, between 1997 and 2018, the United States Border Patrol recorded 7,505 migrant deaths along the United States' southwestern border ("One of the Deadliest Places"). Most humanitarian organizations estimate that figure to be much higher as it only accounts for officially reported cases and cannot take into account those who are never found ("Stopping"). Most of these deaths, however, did not even make regional, much less international, news. So why did the deaths of Angie Valeria and her father provoke such outrage? Why did their story spread so quickly and so far? I believe that in order for US audiences to understand the deaths of Latin American refugees as tragic, they needed the face of a young child, someone who was unequivocally innocent. The news coverage and public outrage surrounding Angie's death, I suggest, actually highlight how the deaths of other migrants and refugees – those who are not unmistakably innocent like Angie – can come to be understood as less than tragedy, and in fact as so mundane that they deserve hardly any public attention at all.[1] How did we arrive to this point, where a migrant or refugee must literally be a baby in order for her life – and death – to be seen as worthy of grief? As I will explore in this chapter, this process of othering, racializing, and criminalizing border crossers, migrants, and undocumented immigrants has deep roots.[2]

While the majority of criticism on narratives of Latin American border crossings examines the place of the immigrant within the host country (the United States), I argue in this chapter that border crossings, like other forms of travel, also bring to light and provoke a deeper contemplation of the neocolonial position of the home country, as well as the internal forms of coloniality that have long permeated that home

---

1 The figures regarding the violence against transmigrants in Mexico are staggering. By some estimates, for example, 80 per cent of Central American women and girls are raped during their journey through Mexico towards the United States (Bonello and McIntyre). Other sources show that abductions, disappearances, and kidnappings of transmigrants in Mexico regularly number in the thousands every month (Rosagel).

2 Throughout this chapter, the term *im/migrants* (and *im/migration*) is used to refer to both migrants and immigrants. *Migrants* refers to internal movement (within a nation state or between regions) and/or movement between or among countries. The process of immigration, although it is also a form of migration, is framed by the nation state and its geopolitical borders. The term *transmigrants* (and *transmigration*) is used here, as is often used in the social sciences, to refer to those who are in transit to another country. The term *transmigration* emphasizes the process of travelling *through* other countries, such as Guatemala and Mexico, that are not the ultimate intended destination of the migrant.

country and that spring up anew in an age of heightened mobility. Indeed, this is what borders do: they provoke reflection on the limits of the nation on each side of a national dividing line. Borders become spaces of contention particularly when a national community is fractured and concerned about the slipperiness of defining themselves in opposition to an "other." They are sites that express anxieties about the permeability of the nation and the weaknesses or strengths of the nation state. They are physical and social locations where inequality and inequity become hyper-visible; in other words, they reveal the presence and permanence of coloniality.

In this chapter I examine how travel and border crossing bring into focus the overlapping structures of colonialism and coloniality that have permeated Mexican culture and society from the nineteenth century to our present. Although the works examined are quite different in terms of their content, style, and form, together they highlight both the deep histories of migration and movement that are in tension with the attempted immovability of geopolitical national borders, and the multiplicity of ethnicities, languages, and cultures within the Mexican nation that are often in conflict with totalizing notions of nationhood and national culture.

I start with a discussion of the importance of movement and the travel narrative as a key genre through which identity was explored and articulated in the eighteenth and nineteenth centuries, especially in relation to colonial and imperial formations during this foundational period of nation building. Through an analysis of the earliest-known Mexican narrative about travel to the United States and one of the earliest works that might be considered an example of a "border crossing" of sorts, Lorenzo de Zavala's *Viage a los Estados Unidos del Norte de América* (1834), I explore how travel narratives have long provoked reflections on identity, especially in relation to colonialism and empire. In his narrative Zavala discusses supposed differences in Mexico in contrast with the United States, and he does so through increasingly racialized discourses of historical and cultural underdevelopment, in particular through the racialization of Indigenous communities in Mexico, which Zavala sees as foreclosing Mexico's entry into "modernity."

I will then examine how im/migration narratives and specifically narratives of border crossings from Mexico to the United States, as a permutation of the travel narrative, take on new dimensions in the early twentieth century. While engaging with the history of the criminalization of the US border and border crossers, I discuss Daniel Venegas's *Las aventuras de don Chipote, o Cuando los pericos mamen* (*The Adventures of Don Chipote; or, When Parrots Breastfeed*, 1928), one of the earliest Mexican-American im/migration narratives. Travel once again provides a means to reflect on identity and especially coloniality in the novel, but this early-twentieth-century novel emphasizes the ways in which Mexican border crossers come to be understood as racial others within the United States, and how this affects their sense of identity within multiple, overlapping colonialist contexts – both in Mexico and in the United States. Venegas's novel, like the writings of Zavala, indicates the ways in which Mexican national identity remains tied to notions of underdevelopment, and travel across an increasingly controlled and patrolled border triggers a newfound recognition of the marginalized status of both the Mexican im/migrant and Mexico itself in relation to the United States.

Lastly, I will turn to Diego Quemada-Diez's critically acclaimed film *La jaula de oro* (*The Golden Dream*, 2013) to consider how the film dialogues with and builds upon the tradition of the travel narrative. In my analysis I highlight how narratives of travel and border crossing take on new dimensions in the twenty-first century with the intensified criminalization of borders and border crossers; the increased building, maintenance, and surveillance of geopolitical borders; and the expansion of US immigration policies to much of Mexico, which has become a *frontera vertical*, a massive vertical border, for Central American transmigrants en route to the United States. My exploration of the film builds upon the analyses of the previous two works by considering once again a transformation in how borders are imagined and constructed in the twenty-first century, as Central American transmigrants are criminalized, racialized, and brutalized in both Mexico and the United States.

What do migration and mobility mean in the twenty-first century? How are they expressed and how are they enmeshed within both old and new forms of coloniality? What does it mean to be a border crosser, in the past and in our present, and how was or is that process portrayed and understood? How does a migrant or a refugee, such as Angie or Oscar, generate compassion or, the opposite, hatred and antagonism? In this chapter, in order to understand these questions, I look back at early representations of travel, migration, mobility, and border crossing in Mexican and Mexican-American literature, while also paying attention to how they are changing in our globalized present.

Travel, Border Crossing, and the Neocolony

While Mexican and other Latin American im/migrants are often perceived as "new arrivals" in the United States, this is not accurate. Many Mexicans of course had already been living for generations in what would become the US Southwest when the United States seized these territories from Mexico at the end of the Mexican-American War in 1848. Mexicans living in these territories were granted US citizenship after the war, but it would be strange indeed to think of them as immigrants or migrants. However, they might be considered border crossers in the same sense that immigrant rights advocates and Chicanx activists have long insisted, "We didn't cross the border; the border crossed us."[3] This popular saying affirms that "borders move, migrate, and cross individuals and groups for good or ill, that borders are more than territorial boundaries but rather constitute a rhetorical process of demarcating and defining identity and social space" (Cisneros 3).

Mary Louise Pratt, among others, has written extensively on the pivotal role of travel and travel narratives in the development of Latin American identities. In her landmark work, *Imperial Eyes: Travel Writing and Transculturation*, she develops the ideas of transculturation and autoethnography to describe the processes by which writers on the "receiving" end of empire appropriated metropolitan modes of representation, such as the travel narrative, and used them to represent themselves in ways that engaged with but also contested the colonizer's views on, and ways of representing, the colonized. It is in what Pratt calls "contact zones" that such transculturation takes place. Contact zones, she explains, are "the space of colonial encounters, the space in which peoples geographically and historically separated come into contact with each other and establish ongoing relations, usually involving conditions of coercion, radical inequality, and intractable conflict" (*Imperial Eyes* 6). For Pratt, both colonizers and the colonized explore and grapple with their identities in the contact zone, and the travel narrative is a popular and ubiquitous literary form that is particularly well suited for delving into these tensions.

In more recent writings Pratt builds upon these ideas to develop more fully her concept of the "neocolony," which, according to Pratt, is perpetually relegated to a lesser status in comparison to the metropole (principally Europe and the United States). Latin America, as a neocolony, is both perceived and portrayed as being on the receiving – rather than

---

3   Josue David Cisneros explores how this saying "inverts the common notion of borders as static and natural entities that humans must encounter and cross ... [and foregrounds] that borders and citizenship are dynamic, mobile, and sources of rhetorical enactment and contestation that have crossed over and constituted the identities and social space of Mexican Americans, Chicana/os, Puerto Ricans, and Latina/os throughout U.S. history" (12). For more on the history of this popular saying see pp.11–12 in Cisneros.

the producing – end of knowledge and goods ("In the Neocolony" 465). The neocolony, she further explains, "tends to produce split subjectivities: one's lived reality lacks significance; the *'real' real* is elsewhere, and it owns you much more than you own it" ("In the Neocolony" 465; italics in original). Like Quijano, Mignolo, and others who discuss the coloniality of power, Pratt is referencing the allure of modernity for neocolonial subjects, as well as their perpetual exclusion from that modernity.[4] In fact, this is the essence of the neocolonial relationship: the neocolonial nation state seeks to be "modern," subscribes to the values of the metropole, and seeks to fulfil those values; however, neocolonial relationships of control and dependence constantly frustrate that nation state's ability to develop itself, yet also do not permit that nation state to "exit the system" or seek an alternative path to development (*Imperial Eyes* 226). As Pratt explains, the cultural predicament of the neocolony and the neocolonial subject is this: "norms generated elsewhere cannot be implemented where one is, but cannot be refused either. One is forced to be a second-class member of a club in which membership is not optional" (*Imperial Eyes* 226).

Yet Pratt also points out that this space/place of cultural unease is also an "engine of self-invention" (*Imperial Eyes* 227). Writers use the neocolonial position of both destination (or terminus) and receptor as a continuous point of reference for the negotiation of identity and representation of self.[5] This is strikingly similar to Gloria Anzaldúa's description of the borderlands as a site of tension, ambivalence, and unrest – but also creativity and innovation (26). As Anzaldúa explains, living "in a state of psychic unrest, in a Borderland, is what makes poets write and artists create" (95). She describes the creative process and its connection to life in the borderlands: "My soul makes itself through the

---

4   Quijano's description of the coloniality of power, although from a Marxist perspective, is strikingly similar: "The market is the foundation but also the limit of possible social equality among people. For those exploited by capital, and in general those dominated by the model of power, modernity generates a horizon of liberation for people of every relation, structure, or institution linked to domination and exploitation, but also the social conditions in order to advance toward the direction of that horizon. Modernity is, then, also a question of conflicting social interests" (548).

5   Literary critics, historians, and even philosophers have long recognized the importance of travel as a way of exploring the identity of the traveller – on a personal or communal level – and not necessarily that of the culture, people, or place being visited. For example, in his now classic *Orientalism* (1978), Edward Said shows how depictions of the "Orient" or "the East" by Western writers was often more a reinforcement of their own beliefs in their own cultural and racial superiority and a self-justification of their colonial endeavours rather than an actual exploration or accurate description of the places about which they were supposedly writing.

creative act. It is constantly remaking and giving birth to itself through my body. It is this learning to live with *la Coatlicue* [duality, a synthesis of duality, and also that which exceeds duality] that transforms living in the Borderlands from a nightmare into a numinous experience" (95). For Anzaldúa, living and creating in the borderlands is "always a path/state to something else" (95), once again emphasizing the liminality of the border dweller, always in transit, and also reaffirming the metaphor of travel as a means of creating and learning.

Pratt argues that the neocolonial "crisis of belonging" – the uncomfortableness or unrest that Anzaldúa describes as an essential part of the borderlands and the border dweller – is often expressed and explored in literature through travel. Anzaldúa similarly explores travel *across* and *through* physical, social, metaphorical, and psychological borders as a means of knowing oneself and one's community. Reflecting on her own journey of self-discovery, for example, she acknowledges, "I had to leave home so I could find myself" (38). For Anzaldúa, the border dweller – who is also a perpetual border crosser – dwells in discomfort, unease, and ambivalence, in a constant process of migration and movement. But it is also through travel that Latin Americans, according to Pratt, come to recognize their own colonial or neocolonial status – their position of subordination in relation to the metropole(s). Travel, to put it succinctly, "is the code that expresses the neocolonial relationship" (Pratt, *Imperial* 229). As Pratt, Anzaldúa, and other critics have pointed out, travel, or living outside the home, can serve as a method for learning about the explicit destination, but also for learning about the traveller's home/homeland and identity (whether personal or communal).

For Mexicans, who share a physical border with the United States, the relationship with the United States (the so-called metropole) has been one of constant contradiction and paradox: the border is a space of opportunity and vulnerability, of contact and conflict, of collaboration and competition, of ambiguity and rigidity, and of violence and productivity. As Anzaldúa explains, Mexico and the United States cannot be understood without one another. "Admit that Mexico is your double," she writes, "that she exists in the shadow of this country [the United States], that we are irrevocably tied to her. Gringo, accept the doppelganger in your psyche" (108). Her wording here conveys the conflicted subjectivity of Chicanas/os: she simultaneously distances herself from the United States ("Gringo," a group to which she does not belong) and includes herself in the United States ("*we* are irrevocably tied to her [Mexico]"; emphasis added). As Anzaldúa indicates, narratives about travel across the US-Mexico border and life within the borderlands are inevitably tied up with reflections on identity – not just about the place of Mexicans (or Mexican-Americans) within the United States but also about the relationship between border dwellers/crossers and Mexico. The literary works and film explored in this chapter speak to the importance of travel and border crossing for the construction of Mexican identity. While more traditional readings of narratives of border crossing frequently focus on the destination – the United States – my readings of these works instead focus on what such border crossings reveal about Mexico (and, perhaps more broadly, Latin America). The works studied in this chapter about different sorts of travel and border crossing explore the limits of Mexico and *mexicanidad*, its neocoloniality, and the ways in which various forms of coloniality continue to permeate Mexican culture and society. Indeed, borders are important precisely because they expose the contradictions of modernity/coloniality and how coloniality continues to shape nation states (and their boundaries) just as much in the present as in the past.

Coloniality Revisited: Nineteenth-Century Journeys

Looking back to nineteenth-century travel narratives, travel diaries, and writings about exile reveals that travel, particularly *from* Mexico and *to* the supposedly more modern metropole of the United States, often produces anxiety for Mexican writers about their past colonial status. In addition, this travel also activates an augmented awareness that past colonization marks them as once again marginal within new imperial or neocolonial relations. To explore one example, I will briefly examine the first known published travel narrative about travel to the United States by a Mexican writer, Lorenzo de Zavala's 1834 *Viage a los Estados-Unidos del Norte de América*.[6] Zavala (1788–1836) was a Yucatecan-born statesman, writer, and editor. He was a strident liberal and a principal architect of the Mexican constitution of 1824, and, later in his life, he was a key figure in the Texas Revolution, serving as the first vice-president of the Republic of Texas and helping to draft its first constitution. In *Viage*, Zavala reflects upon his time spent in the United States as an exile. Through his text he remarks on the cultural

---

6 All quotations of *Viage a los Estados-Unidos del Norte de América* are from the original 1834 edition (hereafter referred to as *Viage*), which is accessible in the *Sabin Americana, 1500–1926*, digital archive. I have maintained antiquated spellings, accentuations, etc., as they appear in the original text. All English translations of *Viage* are from Wallace Woolsey's translation, in the Arte Público Press bilingual edition.

practices, social organizations, and political institutions in the United States, and also compares these – often unfavourably – with those in Mexico. As I will discuss, it is through travel, and the constant comparisons to his home country that travel draws out for him, that Zavala comes to recognize the neocolonial status of Mexicans in relation to the United States. His work is significant because it highlights both the ways in which Spanish colonialism continues to influence Mexican culture and the ways in which he sees future US neocolonialism emerging in Mexico. In other words, even this very early work of travel and border crossing assessed how overlapping colonialities – Spanish, US, and internal forms of coloniality – shaped and shape Mexican culture and identity, preventing the country and its people, according to Zavala, from escaping an eternal position of inferiority and underdevelopment.

In one chapter of *Viage*, Zavala discusses at length the textile mills and the female millworkers in Lowell, Massachusetts, which had garnered international attention for being a novel social and economic experiment[7] – a radical departure from similar textile mills in England, for example, which were largely understood as profiting from the poorest classes (including child labour) while perpetuating an inescapable cycle of poverty.[8] Indeed, it is significant that he chose to write about Lowell because it "set the pace for, and was representative of, the most rapidly growing and innovative sector of the industry" (Dublin 9). Historian Thomas Dublin notes that "the basic technology, organization of production, and systems of housing, wage payment, and work discipline adopted by the Lowell firms became the standards for much of New England" (9). The original goals of this company town were to pay young women decent wages, while also serving as a sort of social uplift for the community as a whole by providing educational opportunities for the young women. The intention was also that the mills

---

7   In *Women at Work*, historian Thomas Dublin explores how textile mills in New England were part of a radical economic, social, and demographic transformation of the United States in the first half of the nineteenth century (5–6). Textile mills like the ones in Lowell were also novel in that they offered "one of the first opportunities for large numbers of American women to work outside of the domestic context," thus transforming women's work and their social positions within their communities and families (7).

8   Dublin explains that the mills in New England, in contrast, "offered individual self-support, enabled women to enjoy urban amenities not available in their rural communities, and gave them a measure of economic and social independence from their families" (40).

would be temporary or transitional employers; this would prevent the stagnation of the lowest classes in a vicious poverty trap, as had largely been the case for millworkers in Europe.

Zavala's descriptions of Lowell, "aquel pueblo prodigioso, levantado de entre bosques en el corto espacio de siete años,"[9] are glowing with admiration and awe bordering on disbelief at the types of mechanical innovation, development, and social improvement he sees there (284). "¿Quién no se maravillará á la vista del pueblo de Lowell," he asks, "lugar silvestre hace diez años, y hoy una poblacion de siete mil almas, con establecimientos manufactureros que compiten con los de Europa?" (287)[10] Zavala is amazed by the good wages, the living conditions of the workers, and the virtue and industriousness of the young women themselves, which have all combined to make Lowell a place of "admirable progreso" (284; "amazing progress," 153). The factories in Lowell are a model of capitalist democracy in action, both economically and socially beneficial to the workers and the communities. "En las sociedades modernas," he pontificates, "los progresos de la mecánica han producido las manufacturas que prometen ser para el género humano, una fuente inagotable de prosperidad y bienestar" (286).[11]

He then draws several parallels between the all-female factories and what he sees as the equivalent in Mexico, the Catholic convent or monastery, noting that Lowell, as a company town in which everyone is subjected to and follows the rules of the company, "es como un vasto monasterio, en donde poco tiene que hacer la autoridad civil" (292).[12] He continues measuring the two side by side, stating:

Los reglamentos de las compañías se observan religiosamente en Lowell. En las fábricas, que son edificios de una grande estension, hay campanarios para llamar las gentes al trabajo, de manera que parecen conventos de una de nuestras ciudades. Pero en Lowell no hay demandantes con santos, no hay limosneros, no hay andrajosos y gentes miserables: en vez de ocuparse estas monjas del siglo diez y nueve en hacer relicarios,

---

9   "The remarkable town which had sprung up among the trees in the short space of seven years" (153).

10   "Who is not amazed at the sight of Lowell," he asks, "a forest village ten years ago, and today a town of seven thousand people with factories that are competing with those of Europe?" (155)

11   "In modern societies, mechanical progress has produced factories that promise to be for the human race an inexhaustible source of prosperity and well-being" (155).

12   "Is like a vast monastery where civil authority is little concerned" (157).

escapularios y sudarios, se emplean en hilar algodon y hacer tejidos de
todas calidades. (293–4)[13]

Zavala describes Lowell as a modern version of a convent, with nineteenth-century (i.e., modern) nuns (the millworkers), convent-like
boarding houses in which the young women lived and worked under
supervision from older matrons (similar to a Mother Superior),[14] and
even bell towers tolling the work hours in a fashion strikingly similar
to the way in which bell towers would call nuns to prayers in a convent.
The paternalistic company rules dictate and enforce the moral behaviours of the young women. And the physical structures of the mill – its
boarding houses, bell towers, modern technologies, and machinery –
announce, create, contain, and regulate this modern world for the
workers.[15]

While his descriptions of Lowell by themselves are fascinating, what
he implies about Mexican culture and identity, through these comparisons, is equally important, particularly because the topic of public morality and whether it was possible to maintain it without the aid of the
Catholic Church was a source of division in Mexico at the time, where
they were ardently debating (and sometimes waging battle over) the
role and rights ("*fueros*") that the Catholic Church should have in the
newly established independent Mexican nation. For example, it is significant that he describes the millworkers as "nineteenth-century nuns"
because they appear to have taken the nuns' places in modern society

---

13   "The company rules are religiously observed in Lowell. In the factories which
are buildings of great extent there are bells to call the people to work so that they
resemble the convents of one of our cities. But in Lowell there are no supplicants with
saints, there are no beggars, there are no ragged and poverty stricken people. These
nineteenth-century nuns, instead of keeping busy making relicaries [*sic*], scapularies and
shrouds, are employed in spinning cotton and weaving textiles of all qualities." (158)

14   Such companies, Zavala explains, paternalistically "velan sobre las costumbres de
estas jóvenes obreras ... Allí están bajo la proteccion y patrocinio de las matronas,
que cuidan de la pension ... Las matronas responden á la compañía de las costumbres
de las jóvenes confiadas á su cuidado, y se manejan por reglamentos que les dan al
efecto" (291; "watch over the habits of these young working women ... There they
are under the protection and sponsorship of the landladies who run the places ...
The landladies keep the company informed of the conduct of the young women in
their care, and they live by the rules that are laid down for them," 157). For more
on the boarding house as a paternalistic instrument of social control, see pp. 77–9 in
Dublin.

15   Dublin explains, for example, that the bell towers in the massive textile mills "stood
as a visible and audible symbol of the new time-discipline ushered in by the Lowell
factory system" (61).

as virtuous young women who work to improve themselves and their communities, while also producing valuable goods. Zavala here seems to be expressing anxiety about two interconnected endeavours: capitalist production and modernity. The female millworkers are always producing some type of capital, but the factory itself produces perhaps the most modern good of all: the young women themselves, who will, in turn through their own offspring, produce future generations of modern white citizens and workers. The Mexican Catholic nuns, however, produce little if any tangible capital, merely reproducing symbols of death and stagnation – reliquaries, scapulars, and shrouds. Moreover, while the millworkers are part of the public sphere, the Catholic nuns, conversely, maintain and reinforce symbolic colonial structures of power (the Catholic Church) and often literally inhabit physical colonial structures (their convents) that are distant if not completely removed from the modern public sphere (in cloistered convents, for example).[16] The nuns, it should be obvious, will produce no future offspring and thus no future citizens, just as they themselves are also removed from "circulation." Read through this lens, Zavala's comparisons between the nuns and the millworkers convey profound trepidation about the role of the Catholic Church in the development of a modern nation state in Mexico.

In fact, Zavala explicitly connects Mexican Catholicism with Spain and its colonial legacies in Mexico. It becomes, in Zavala's writings, a metonymy of Spanish imperialism and a symbol of Mexico's continued coloniality and lack of modernity. At one point, for example, he describes the Catholic mass and the influence that Catholic religious holidays and celebrations have on the people in Mexico, noting: "El resto del dia, despues de estas ceremonias, el pueblo bajo bebe y come; la gente de categoría juega y baila" (60).[17] He further comments on the influences of Catholicism on Indigenous communities in Mexico:

¿Y qué diremos de las [fiestas religiosas] de los Indios en Chalma, en Guadalupe y en los otros santuarios? ¡Ah! la pluma cae de la mano para no esponer á la vista del mundo civilizado, una turba de idólatras que vienen

---

16 While the female millworkers in places like Lowell were similarly "isolated from the larger world while on the job . . . [as] outside influences were not allowed to 'intrude' and disturb the work," there was a general assumption that their work in the mills was temporary – a stepping stone for a young woman before getting married, for example – and that they would eventually leave the mill (Dublin 61).

17 "The rest of the day, after the ceremonies, the lower classes eat and drink; those of the upper class play and dance" (35).

á entregar en manos de frailes holgazanes, el fruto de sus trabajos anuales para enriquecerlos, mientras ellos, sus hijos y sus mugeres no tienen un vestido, ni una cama. ¡Y á esto han osado llamar religion los Españoles nuestros padres!!! (60)[18]

According to Zavala, Spanish Catholicism has created a populace that prefers festivity over industry, games and gluttony over piety, and subservience over self-determination. Like with his comparison of the mill-workers and the nuns, a concern emerges once again over a supposed lack of capitalist productivity, particularly for the lowest classes and Indigenous communities. According to Zavala, such Mexicans consume (food and drink) but do not produce. And when Mexican Indians do actually produce something, it is not put into circulation but taken by the "lazy friars." For Zavala, this relationship epitomizes the decadence of the Catholic Church and Mexican culture as a whole, its apparent incompatibility with modern capitalist production, and the dependence of Mexicans upon such antiquated systems of power and control – remnants of Spain's colonial legacies in Mexico. In other words, Zavala indicates that Spain, through the religious practices it brought to and enshrined within Mexican culture, has created communities – especially of the lower classes and Indigenous Peoples – that are supposedly unprepared to be productive, modern citizens. Even if these masses do produce or re-produce (offspring), Zavala suggests that they are unsuitable for helping to build a modern nation. Importantly, this "turba de idólatras," which Zavala depicts as unprepared for the modern world and unable to produce modern goods or future modern citizens, would also have been composed predominantly of darker-skinned and non-Spanish-speaking communities within Mexico. Zavala thus articulates the ways in which modernity and religion were becoming increasingly racialized in the nineteenth century, with Protestantism tied to whiteness and modernity, and Catholicism tied to off-whiteness, indigeneity, and decadence.

While Catholicism continues to impede Mexico's emergence as a "modern" nation, according to Zavala, Protestant culture, in contrast, has supposedly enshrined the values of industriousness, productivity, and individualism at the centre of white Anglo-American identity,

---

18 "And what shall we say of the Indians in Chalma, in Guadalupe and in other shrines. Ah! The pen falls from the hand in order not to expose to the civilized world a horde of idolaters who come to deliver into the hands of lazy friars the fruits of their year's work to enrich them, while they, their women and children have no clothing, not even a bed. And the Spaniards, our fathers, have dared call this religion!" (35)

resulting in the growth of capitalist progress in the United States.[19] In Zavala's descriptions of Lowell he repeatedly emphasizes the ways in which virtue and accumulation of capital are connected, stating that the women leave the factories "después de algunos años, con el capital que han hecho en numerario, fruto de las economías, y ademas con los hábitos de amor al trabajo, respeto á la virtud, y horror al vicio" (292).[20] He then once again contrasts this with Mexican culture: "El domingo, que entre nosotros es un dia de placer y de fiesta, en estos lugares se dedica á la oracion, al recogimiento y al descanso" (292).[21] In essence, he argues that the factories in Lowell are "manufacturing" more virtuous and more economically productive young women (who also acquire the habits of "good" workers in the factories) than are the convents in Mexico.

When Zavala describes the young women working in the textile factories as "nineteenth-century nuns," he is suggesting that they are more modern versions of nuns, serving a communal, nearly altruistic purpose. But he also positions these women as agents of a new type of modern colonization that works through economic, social, and cultural methods to achieve power and dominance in the hemisphere. The purportedly industrious and virtuous women of Lowell are not only the product of Protestant culture but also the producers of that culture through their future white children. Thus, Zavala foreshadows the introduction of new, more indirect, but nonetheless incredibly powerful, methods of expansion, domination, and colonization that will take root more deeply in the decades to follow.

Zavala's discussions of Lowell and, by comparison, of Catholicism in Mexico are significant because although Lowell serves as a model for modern society, that model also brings to light Mexico's own supposed lack of modernity and its continued coloniality, especially in comparison to a new metropole, the United States. His travels to the United States bring this perceived lack to the forefront. According to Zavala's reasoning, this deficiency is both the *result* of colonial Spanish legacies

---

19 In *Faithful Bodies*, Heather Miyano Kopelson explores the connection between Puritanism, race, and nationality. Puritanism, she argues, became a way of drawing dividing lines between insider and outsider, starting in the seventeenth century, and helped to shape ideologies of race and gender.

20 "After some years with the monetary capital which is the fruit of their savings, and furthermore with the habits of love of work, respect for virtue, and horror towards vice" (157–8).

21 "Sunday, which among us [in Mexico] is a day of pleasure and fiesta, in these places is dedicated to prayer, meditation and rest" (158).

(here, for example, Spanish Catholicism as practised in Mexico) and, he hints, the *cause* of Mexico's future position as a neocolony. Zavala thus creates parallels between the mills and their female workers and the Catholic convents and their nuns in order to critique past Spanish colonialism, which has supposedly created masses, particularly Indigenous masses, who are unfit for the demands of modern democratic citizenship. Marissa K. López similarly points out that Zavala's depiction and sustained references to the "liberal state's necessary construction of a racial other that it is unable to incorporate" in both Mexico and the United States is evidence of the failure of a trans-American ideal grounded in liberal democracy (43). *Viage* thus highlights "the impossibility of reconciling democratic praxis with liberal theory, an impossibility that cuts to the heart of modern liberal democratic rule" (Mexal 99). Zavala also infers, however, that Mexico's history of colonization has primed Mexico for its *future* dependency on and inferiority to the United States. In other words, his travels generate not just comparisons with the United States but also recognition of the ways in which Mexico has existed and will continue to exist on the margins of modernity as a neocolony. In essence, then, travel to the United States spurs Zavala to reflect on what his nation allegedly lacks and on what is supposedly preventing Mexicans from being "truly" modern; it simultaneously generates a more profound recognition of Mexico's position both as a product of past Spanish colonialism and as a subject of new forms of coloniality, such as US economic and cultural imperialism. Indirectly his recognition of the failure of the Mexican nation-building project to incorporate Indigenous communities – in fact, he blames Indigenous, non-Spanish-speaking communities for Mexico's presumed lack of modernity and for their own supposed backwardness – also reveals the ways in which racialized colonial hierarchies persist in his present and how they are intertwined with neocolonial manoeuvres.[22] Colonial hierarchies denigrating Indigenous Peoples, such as the *casta* system, are reproduced but also transformed within nineteenth-century republican nation-building and modernization projects. Interestingly, in his comparison of Mexican nuns and the "secular nuns" of Lowell, he also seems to predict some of the ways in which religion (particularly Catholic versus Protestant) would become tied to racialized categories of belonging, and he anticipates the spread of racial hierarchies that

---

22 Historian Stephen J. Mexal similarly concludes that *Viage* is interested in showing "the impossibility of reconciling democratic praxis with liberal theory, an impossibility that cuts to the heart of modern liberal democratic rule" (99).

would place those of Northern European descent above those of Southern European (or mixed European and Indigenous) descent.

Zavala's travelling across geopolitical national borders brings him to question the limits of his own national community, provokes him to question ideas about modernity in Mexico, and causes him to re-examine the ways in which coloniality continues to permeate his home country. His travels bring to light, in other words, the ways in which modernity and coloniality are intertwined and dependent upon one another. His travels also prompt him to consider how internal colonial legacies – such as the influence of Catholicism on Indigenous communities – have left Mexicans yet again newly excluded, "in the neocolony," as Pratt describes it, perpetually behind the metropole, which in this case is the newly emerging capitalist empire of the United States. Perhaps unwittingly, he replicates and reinforces colonial hierarchies in his paternalistic and demeaning view of Indigenous communities, even as he laments the ways in which these colonial legacies perpetuate Mexico's position as a neocolony. He also reinforces newly emerging racial categories that denigrate Mexicans and feed into fears in both Mexico and the United States about racial and cultural impurity.

Twentieth-Century Border Crossings

Mexico's northern border with the United States has changed in significant legal, political, social, cultural, and physical ways over the last two hundred years. These changes have, in turn, altered the significance of travel across the border and how that border is experienced for those who cross it and live alongside it. Border crossing is inevitably shaped by the side of the border on which one happens to be born or live at any given time. The way in which governmental agencies define this dividing line, and what it means to cross it, has a huge impact on the ways in which Mexicans and Mexican-Americans understand their own identity and are understood by others.

First, it is important to recognize that prior to 1848 almost all of the present-day southwestern United States was part of Mexico. With the signing of the Treaty of Guadalupe Hidalgo in 1848 at the close of the Mexican-American War, Mexicans living on the northern side of the newly redefined border found themselves transformed, seemingly overnight, into US citizens, border dwellers, and part of a new ethnic minority within the United States, without having travelled a single step. Although it is not the central focus of this chapter, it is important to note the profound transformation that this redrawing of national borders had for the Mexican national community as well as those of Mexican descent now living within US territory. Writings by Mexicanos/as[23] living in the borderlands from the late nineteenth century, such as the novels of María Amparo Ruiz de Burton, a nineteenth-century writer originally from Baja California, call attention to the increasing marginalization and racialization of Mexicanos/as in the United States. Nonetheless, nineteenth-century narratives also show that travel across the border remained fairly unregulated, and many people of Mexican descent living in the United States during this time were legally US citizens, even if in name only. In the decades following the Mexican-American War, in parts of what is today the US Southwest, many elites of Mexican descent intermarried with Anglo-Americans and worked together to maintain their positions of power. Of course, the darkest and poorest Mexicanos/as were largely excluded from this negotiation of power, as they also had been when these territories were part of Mexico. Mexicanos/as in these territories, which had been sparsely populated before the Mexican-American War, were quickly outnumbered when waves of land-hungry Anglo-Americans began to arrive and settle there in the late nineteenth century, using various means – marriage, coercion, fraud, purchase, debt payment, and outright violence – to dispossess Mexicanos/as of their land.

The first big waves of im/migrants from Mexico did not arrive in the United States until the early decades of the twentieth century. These waves of im/migration were driven at least in part by the Mexican Revolution, which started in 1910. After ten long years of war the Mexican infrastructure and economy were in shambles, and by conservative estimates, more than one million Mexicans were dead or missing as a result of violence, famine, disease, disappearance, and emigration.[24] The majority of Mexicans crossing the border in the early twentieth century were working-class or poor laborers, migrating initially for the purpose of finding temporary work and with the goal of returning to their homeland.

In the first two decades of the twentieth century, interest in policing the racial and geopolitical borders of the United States intensified, not just in the US Southwest but among nativist eugenicists across the United States. The Immigration Act of 1917, for example, increased entry and visa fees, required literacy tests, and prohibited "entry into the United States at any point other than an official port of entry" (K.L. Hernández, *Migra!* 27). The Emergency Quota Act of 1921

---

23   Here and throughout the chapter I use the term *Mexicanos/as* to refer to people of
　　Mexican descent on both sides of the US-Mexico border regardless of citizenship.
24   See Ventura, "The Real Cost of Mexico's Violent Revolution."

introduced numerical limits on immigration and a nationality-based quota system, and the National Origins Act of 1924, or Johnson-Reed Act, placed broader limitations on legal immigration, permanently established and further restricted the quota system, confirmed the exclusion of Asians from entry, and reinforced a dedication to the creation of a white, able-bodied community in the United States.[25] As a gesture of appeasement to southwestern agribusiness, which depended heavily on a Mexican migrant workforce, however, the National Origins Act included a Western Hemisphere exemption.[26] As historian Natalia Molina discusses, agribusiness and industry leaders, constantly in need of cheap labour, fought against increased immigration restrictions for Mexicans, arguing that "Mexicans were not a threat to US society in any way because they were 'birds of passage' who would work hard for low wages and then return to Mexico" (163). This portrayal of Mexican immigrants as "birds of passage" highlighted not only their temporary status within the US but also their disposability; they could always be deported because they were not citizens (166).

Although southwestern agribusinesses had initially argued that they could control the influx of Mexican migrant workers and that Mexican workers would not settle permanently in the United States, communities of Mexican descent continued to grow in the United States in the 1920s. Inevitably some Mexican migrant workers decided to stay and make permanent or semi-permanent homes in the country, buying property, opening businesses, and raising families in which the children, born in the United States, would now be US citizens. Thus, it is not surprising that in the 1920s the US government and public started to think about ways to restrict movement across the US-Mexico border, with the specific goal of restraining the growth of permanent enclaves of "racially suspect" Mexicans and Mexican-Americans. Accordingly, the United States Border Patrol was formed in 1924. As historian Kelly Lytle Hernández shows in her brilliant work on the history of the United States Border Patrol and the mass incarceration predominantly of communities of colour, the Border Patrol quickly came to focus almost exclusively on stemming the unlawful entry of Mexicans into the United States and, more broadly, on policing Mexican im/migrants in

---

25 For further discussion of the 1924 National Origins Act, its use of quotas, and how it helped to established a new category of racialized non-citizens, see pp. 21–55 in Mae Ngai's *Impossible Subjects* and pp. 26–32 in Kelly Hernández's *Migra!* For a discussion of the eugenicist origins of the Act, see pp.16–28 in Stern's *Eugenic Nation*.

26 See K.L. Hernández, *Migra!* 28–32; and Molina, pp. 162–3.

the borderlands, often with the complicity of the Mexican government on the Mexican side of the border (*Migra!* 83–97). Thus, the 1920s – what Molina calls the "long immigration debate era" (158) – was a key period in the transformation of the US-Mexico border, the process of border crossing for Mexicans, and the ways in which Mexicans and Mexican-Americans would come to be racially and legally defined in the United States. Over this period of time Mexican immigration became increasingly restricted, and by 1930, "repatriations, voluntary and involuntary, and restrictions on visas severely curtailed Mexican immigration" (Molina 158).

Las aventuras de don Chipote, o Cuando los pericos mamen,[27] first published in 1928 in the Spanish-language, Los Angeles newspaper *El Heraldo* by the locally known humorist and satirist Daniel Venegas, attempts to give voice to the experiences of working-class Mexican im/migrants in the United States during this transformative period for Mexican immigration. His novel reflects on the common experiences of crossing the border both with and without registering at official ports of entry; it also focuses on the experiences of Mexican im/migrants within the United States and, for men travelling alone, the impact on their wives and families back in Mexico. *Don Chipote* is in many ways a travel narrative. Like earlier travel narratives such as Zavala's, *Don Chipote* shows how travel – specifically in this case, crossing the border between the United States and Mexico – prompts a recognition of the border crosser's neocolonial position in relation to the metropole (the United States). However, unlike earlier travel narratives, such as Zavala's, which were predominately written by elites, Venegas's novel represents a fundamental difference: it is written from a working-class perspective and is much more openly pessimistic and critical of both Mexico and the United States, as it emphasizes the inability of working-class and poor Mexicans to escape poverty in either country. The novel in fact underscores the neocolonial position of Mexico and Mexicanos/as on both sides of the border.

Whereas earlier travel narratives, such as Zavala's, explore Mexican identity (especially in political and cultural terms at a national level) through their writers' travels and comparisons between the destination country and the home country (something *Don Chipote* also does), later narratives of Mexican immigration and border crossing additionally

---

27   Hereafter referred to as *Don Chipote*. All English translations of *Don Chipote* are from Ethriam Cash Brammer's translation, *The Adventures of Don Chipote*, edited by Nicolás Kanellos.

explore the limits and transformations of *mexicanidad* once individuals have crossed over and settled permanently or semi-permanently in another country. In other words, they explore the cultural limits of an extra-national *mexicanidad*. In *Don Chipote* there is an exploration of personal (internal, psychological, and cultural) as well as communal identity, and an exploration of the very limits of who can continue to claim *mexicanidad* – a theme that will reverberate in narratives of border crossing and immigration and in Chicano/a literature and film throughout the twentieth and even into the twenty-first century.

In the novel Venegas probes the borders of *mexicanidad* through an exploration of modern culture and its place in Mexico and the United States. Like Zavala before him, Venegas largely portrays Mexico as a place lacking in modernity. For example, we see very little of Mexico besides the small rural farm on which Don Chipote de Jesús María Domínguez, the eponymous protagonist, lives and which offers little more than subsistence. In contrast, the narrator repeatedly emphasizes the modernity of the United States, as well as Chipote's lack of understanding of modern life and inventions. When he first crosses the border and arrives in El Paso, Texas, for example, he gets a ride on an electric trolley car, which he thinks is a "carreta que se movía sin bueyes y que según él pensaba, la movía el demonio" (35).[28] The narrator further explains that "por aquello de las dudas hizo la señal de la cruz y esperó a que aquella carreta lo jalara a donde Dios quisiera" (35).[29] Chipote's initial reaction to such modern technologies is one of superstitious fear: that which he does not understand must be evil. And, of course, it is also a moment of humour for Venegas's presumedly more cosmopolitan, Los Angeles–based readers. The movie theatre, another space of modern technologies, emerges as a site that encapsulates the allure and the deceptions of modern life for Chipote. When Chipote enters the theatre for the first time, the narrator explains that since Chipote had never seen a "cinematographic projection," he of course did not know it would be in the dark, and "luego que se asomó y que no vio nada, le dieron ganas de echar a correr para atrás, pues pensó que aquello sería el infierno" (110).[30] Chipote hastens to leave, but he cannot see where he is going in the dark, and he smacks into a pillar, then clings to it, shaking

---

28 "Big cart which moved without oxen, and consequently made Don Chipote believe that it must be possessed by evil spirits" (44).

29 "In his trepidation he made the sign of the cross and prayed that the wagon would take him to wherever God wanted him to go" (44).

30 "When the house lights grew dim, and he couldn't see anything, he wanted to run out of the theater, for he thought that he had descended into Hell" (114).

with fear, uncertain about what to do next. On one level, this slapstick routine once again provides comic relief for readers; Venegas asks his readers to join in laughing at Chipote – and perhaps themselves, too – for his naïveté.[31] But on another, deeper level Chipote's lack of sophistication, while perhaps endearing him to readers, also demonstrates the vast differences between rural Mexico and Los Angeles.

There are certainly parallels between Zavala's descriptions of Indigenous masses who are supposedly unprepared for the demands of modern citizenship and Venegas's comic portrayal of the newly arrived "greenhorn" im/migrant who is oblivious to the ways of modern life. Unlike in Zavala's travel narrative, however, in *Don Chipote* the United States is not positively portrayed; it is represented as a space that corrupts the individual, the Mexican community, and the very concept of *mexicanidad*. The theatre where Chipote first trembles in terror, for example, quickly transforms into a space in which he quivers in anticipatory delight. Once he realizes that people are laughing at the films, he finally opens his eyes and realizes his own ignorance because he reasons that "para ir a los infernos no hubiera tenido que pagar" (111).[32] He soon joins in, laughing louder than anyone else in the audience. Once the movie ends, the variety show starts with live performers, and a female dancer appears "casi en cueros menores, lo que hizo que don Chipote se tapara la cara que se le puso color de vergüenza de ver a aquella mujer con tales vestiduras" (111).[33] The narrator speaks directly to his readers, explaining Chipote's reaction:

> [Y] esto no vayan a pensar que era falso pudor de nuestro paisano, pues como deben comprender, en su terreno nunca había visto a mujer alguna, vamos ni a su mujer, más allá del tobillo; por lo que ya pueden imaginarse lo que pasó por él al ver aquella hembra enseñarle al público las piernas, que más parecían chorros de atole que piernas. (111–12)[34]

---

31   See pp.19–22 in Urquijo-Ruiz's *Wild Tongues* for a reading of the significance of the physical humour in *Don Chipote* and for an exploration of Don Chipote as an iteration of the *peladito* stock character.

32   "If he were being dragged down into Hell, they wouldn't have made him pay first" (115).

33   "Wearing almost nothing at all, making Don Chipote cover his face, which turned red from the embarrassment of seeing a woman in such regalia" (115).

34   "And don't go thinking this was false modesty on the part of our compatriot, for as you well know, in his homeland, he had never seen the body of any woman – dare we say, not even his wife – higher up than the ankle. So you can just imagine what happened to him when seeing that doll-face showing off her legs to the crowd, looking more like streams of *atole* than legs" (115–16).

Although initially embarrassed by the spectacle of female flesh, little by little he uncovers his face, and by the end of the performance he finds himself hollering for an encore and drooling with delight (112). Here, we witness the vast changes that Chipote undergoes in just a few hours. He moves from terror of the film and discomfort at the sight of the female body to raucous enjoyment and consumption of both. This is significant because the movies and the female dancer represent modern innovations, in terms of technology and social/gender norms. Although he is initially unprepared to "consume" them, he quickly adjusts and immerses himself within this new environment.

Chipote's discovery of the theatre is a turning point in the novel and in his development. Shortly after this first experience in the theatre the narrator explains quite simply that "[h]an pasado unos meses" (121),[35] making use of ellipses to catapult readers forward in time to see how Chipote has been changed into a "modern" man living in the United States. It is not a positive transformation. The narrator makes it clear that Chipote has lost sight of his original goals – to work, make money, and support his family back in Mexico. Chipote has a steady job, but instead of sending the money home to his family, he has bought himself fancy – but vulgar and impractical, according to the narrator – clothes: "un traje de color azul marino con muchos botones, zapatos amarillos and sombrero texano ... [y] pantalones de campana y el saco rajado" (121).[36] Chipote has not completely forgotten Doña Chipota and his "chipotitos," but he only sends them a tiny bit of his weekly cheque – "alguna piquita" (121) – knowing that it will still seem like a lot to them back in Mexico. He also spends money frivolously at his new daily pastime, the theatre, "en donde lo tienen embobado las vistas y las que cantan y enseñan las piernas" (122).[37] Doña Chipota wants to join him in the United States and tells him so in her letters, but Chipote "no piensa traerlos por lo pronto, porque anda detrás de una pelona" (122).[38]

The figure of the *pelona*, or flapper, like the theatre, represents the allure of the modern United States as well as its corrupting influence on Mexicanos/as. With their bobbed haircuts and short dresses, flappers were the personification of modern femininity. They were viewed by many at this time as outrageous, immoral, materialistic, foolish, and

---

35 "A few months passed" (124).
36 "An aquamarine suit with lots of buttons, yellow shoes and a cowboy hat ... [and] bell-shaped slacks and tail-coats" (124).
37 "Where the shows and the girls who sing and show off their legs keep him ga-ga" (125).
38 "Isn't thinking about bringing them over any time soon, because he is now after a flapper" (125).

dangerous, even as they were also seen and portrayed as sex symbols, temptresses, and figures of female empowerment and independence – which, of course, can be horrifying or inspiring, depending on one's perspective.[39] In *Don Chipote* the *pelona* is a woman with loose moral standards who exploits Chipote for his money and strings him along, while also distracting him from his responsibilities to his wife and family. Chipote tries to win his flapper's affection by buying her presents and even by purchasing an expensive love potion from a scam *curandero*. But the semi-omniscient narrator explains that this will ultimately not give any results because the *pelona* is not really interested in Chipote, even though she feigns affection when he brings her presents. The implicit conclusion seems to be that the *pelona* – who presumably speaks Spanish (since Chipote does not speak English) – represents the influence of modern US culture on Mexican and Mexican-American women. In the novel, as in much US Hispanic literature and journalism of the time, she is portrayed as a sell-out to US material culture, a corruption of the ideal Mexicana (who, especially as an unmarried woman, should be meek and unassuming), and a cultural traitor who undermines sacrosanct Mexican values, such as the monogamous married couple and the nuclear family.[40] The *pelona* thus emerges in the novel as a symbol of the ultimate corruption not just of Chipote but of *mexicanidad* itself, which has frequently been embodied in women, particularly mothers.

In fact, it is through the female figures in the novel that the question over the differences between Mexico and the United States – and the limits of Mexican identity – is perhaps most clearly articulated. Mexico and Mexican values, for example, are represented through the figure of Doña Chipota, who is comically and constantly surrounded by her large, demanding brood of children, her *chipotitos*. Doña Chipota maintains the household back in Mexico, defends their marriage in her husband's absence (despite being sexually harassed by other men, including the local parish priest), and ultimately "rescues" Chipote from the United States when she decides to make the journey herself across the border – *chipotitos* in tow – and force Chipote to return to Mexico with her.

---

39 See Sagert, *Flappers*, and pp.121–35 in Kitch, *The Girl on the Magazine Cover*.

40 As María Montserrat Feu López explains, "U.S. Hispanic *pelonas* became symbols of undignified acculturation and ethnic disloyalty for conservative [Hispanic] authors. Although the Modern Girl was a global phenomenon, *flapperismo* (flapperdom) was perceived as an assimilation force … [F]*lapperismo* conflicted with the expected domesticity and modesty for [Hispanic] women. Journalistic humor represented *pelonas* as a danger to traditional Hispanic femininity" (193). She also reveals how Spanish-language newspapers "would sarcastically describe her [the *pelona*] as weird, frivolous, foolish, money-seeking, immature, and unreliable … [and] [o]pinion columnists lectured readers about the evils of *flapperismo*" (200).

Through these two opposing female figures, we see how women serve as symbols of Mexican cultural identity (or its degeneration), and we also see an exploration of the limits of *mexicanidad*. Is a *pelona* who does not follow the model of the self-sacrificing, modest, and devote woman, "really" Mexican? Venegas seems to tell us "no" and takes as a given that his readers – who, he seems to assume (probably rightly), are almost entirely men[41] – will be on his side, laughing along at his crass caricatures of the *pelona*.[42] The *pelona* represents the allure of modernity but also its superficiality and lack of substance. After all, the *pelona* is really just interested in Chipote's money, not Chipote himself, and her "modernity" is represented primarily through self-indulgent consumption.[43] Venegas was not unique but rather representative of the US-based, Spanish-language press's "conservative, antimodernist reaction to *flapperismo*, mordantly represented as morally outrageous and as a monstrous transgression of traditional Hispanic femininity" (Feu López 212). As María Montserrat Feu López discusses, while US Hispanic "journalists lauded dutiful domesticity as a model of ethnic loyalty, they caricatured the flapper as an unnatural aberration … [thus revealing] their own anxiety in the 1920s about the social changes enticing U.S. Hispanic women, who were crossing ethnic borders and questioning male prerogatives" (Feu López 212).

Doña Chipota, however, is neither alluring nor sexualized but instead a maternal figure, associated with traditional, conservative Mexican values, such as the home, family, marriage, and conventional gender roles. As Nicolás Kanellos affirms, it is her "express task to represent the nuclear family and religious and patriotic values in her rescue of Don Chipote from perdition in the United States" (10). Even her name, Doña Chipota, is an extension of her husband. Her name is comic for its ridiculousness, certainly, but also serves to underscore that her primary role in the novel is to remind Chipote of his commitments to her and their family – and, metaphorically, also to his country.[44]

---

41 Kanellos affirms that Venegas was most likely writing primarily for Chicano men (10).

42 Feu López, in fact, argues that mocking "*pelonas* helped male authors and their readers to acquire a sense of control at home, at work, and in their social life" (196).

43 Feu López similarly notes how the *pelona* became a stock character commonly associated with consumption, self-indulgence, and immodesty in US Spanish-language press of this era (194).

44 Venegas is representative of tendencies of the time, given that most intellectual refugees of the Mexican Revolution were similarly promoting an "ideology of exile … [that] called for the protection and preservation of the mother culture and the mother tongue in anticipation of an ultimate return to Mexico" (Kanellos 7).

Although this is a very conservative representation and affirmation of traditional monogamous heterosexual relationships and gender norms,[45] what is key here is that the novel is interested in exploring the limits and transformations of *mexicanidad* when Mexicans leave the geopolitical space of the Mexican nation state, thus anticipating later writings on the topic, like Octavio Paz's discussion of the *pocho* and what he termed "other extremes" in his now canonical *El laberinto de la soledad* (1950). It is also significant that, once again, travel is what allows Chipote – and the readers of the novel – to question these limits, to explore what it means to be Mexican, and to consider how this identity shifts – or not – upon crossing the border. The meditations on modernity and its supposed link with gender roles, for example, is brought to the forefront precisely because of the comparisons between Mexico and the United States that his travels permit. Similarly, Chipote also becomes aware of both his own and his country's neocolonial position of marginalization in new ways once he has crossed the border.

On his first attempt to cross the border, for example, Chipote passes through one of the official ports of entry. He is forced to strip, bathe, and be deloused, and his clothes are fumigated. When his clothes are returned to him, however, he finds they are rumpled and have shrunken in size, but since he has nothing else to wear, "tuvo que ponérselas y ser el hazmerreír de cuantos lo veían" (27).[46] After passing through what the narrator calls "la primera humillación que los gringos obligan a sufrir a los emigrantes mexicanos" (27),[47] he finally reaches the office where they review his papers, only to find that there is an eight-dollar fee and a literacy test. Chipote does not know how to read and write, and he does not have the money to pay the fee; he is therefore summarily turned away. Here, Venegas's novel dramatizes the very real and dehumanizing process that Mexican border crossers underwent during that time period. As historian Alexandra Minna Stern shows, in the early decades of the twentieth century "Mexican border crossers and their baggage were subjected to rigorous procedures of disinfection and fumigation" at ports of entry in the United States (59). Such procedures included forced stripping, chemical scouring of clothes, delousing, head shaving, kerosene and vinegar showers, and invasive medical inspections; these extreme methods were justified by the US government

---

45 Urquijo-Ruiz similarly notes that while Venegas criticizes "assimilation and the oppressive economic system, … [the] novel presents contradictory ideas that arise out of various discourses, including elitism, paternalism, and nationalism" (*Wild Tongues* 3).

46 "He had to put them on and become the laughingstock of all those who saw him" (36).

47 "The first humiliation that the *gringo* forces on Mexican immigrants" (35).

as a supposed means for stemming the spread of infectious diseases. At one point the United States Public Health Service even started to brand the arms of Mexican border crossers "in permanent ink, with the word *admitted* after they had been bathed and physically examined" at a port of entry in Laredo, Texas (Stern 57). Upon his first attempt to cross the border, we see how Chipote, like other Mexican border crossers, is marked as a second-class member of society and as someone who does not belong and who, potentially, is a threat to the health of the nation. In fact, as Rachel Conrad Bracken has shown, this "medicalization" of im/migrant bodies in the 1920s is significant because public health protocols, such as these, "gave rise to policies meant to limit transnational movement and exclude 'undesirable' populations," such as Mexicans (29).[48] Although Chipote is not branded with ink (because he is also not admitted), he is marked by the rumpled, shrunken clothes he wears as a result of the fumigation and forced bathing, and he is further marked symbolically as not belonging or not being desirable when he is turned back to Mexico for his illiteracy and poverty. In these first encounters with the United States, Chipote thus finds that he already does not belong, even before he is able to cross over.

He eventually does make it across the border but not through an official port of entry, because he cannot pay the fee or pass the literacy test. Once in the United States, however, he is paid subpar wages, preyed upon by con artists, and repeatedly taken advantage of by both Anglo-Americans and Mexicanos/as because he does not speak English, cannot read, and is undocumented. Throughout the novel, however, Don Chipote seems largely undeterred and continues to chase after his fantasy, the American dream of making quick and easy money. As a parody of *Don Quijote*, the novel obviously satirizes this idea. The American dream is as much an illusion as Don Quijote's quest to defeat the giants/windmills. Even if Chipote, who seems hopelessly dim-witted at times, does not seem to always fully comprehend the futility of his efforts or the ways in which he is being exploited, the narrator certainly does, repeatedly speaking directly to the readers and calling their attention to the racism, classism, and prejudice that Mexicanos/as face in the United States. For example, when Chipote is recruited to work on the railroad, the narrator explains that Mexican im/migrants should be

---

48 See Bracken, "Borderland Biopolitics," pp. 29–34, for an exploration of medical inspection as a technology of surveillance in the novel. Bracken shows how the racist medicalization of Mexican bodies led to the criminalization of the border and of Latinx bodies within the United States (32).

wary of this situation because, although it appears to be a good job at first, "son tratados como animales" (45).[49] "Estos negreros," the narrator continues, "viven de la desgracia del mexicano ... Como la mayoría de nosotros cruzamos la frontera sin cinco y solo con esperanzas" (45).[50] In his asides to his Spanish-speaking readers, the narrator thus encourages them to consider the ways in which poor, uneducated, and working-class Mexican im/migrants become even more disenfranchised – not less – once they cross the border.

Another key scene at the very end of the novel takes place once again in the theatre and further reinforces this idea that Mexicanos/as more fully recognize their position as neocolonial subjects upon travelling across borders. Doña Chipota travels to Los Angeles in search of her husband; overcoming countless obstacles and still unable to locate her husband, she decides one afternoon to rest with her children in the theatre for a few hours. As chance would have it, it is the very same theatre that Chipote frequents, and he is there that day to participate in a singing competition, hoping to win a five-dollar prize and his *pelona*'s affections with his performance. Unaware that his wife and children are in the audience, he begins his serenade, only to be attacked by his angry wife mid-song. At first the audience thinks it is a comedy routine, and they laugh and demand "que les dieran el premio a los que tan bien estaban representando la comedia de marido y mujer" (152).[51] But when the children come on stage, this moment of metafiction – a play within a novel – crumbles around the Chipote family, as the audience realizes that the "performance" is actually real. In reaction, the audience promptly demands they be arrested. The Chipotes are brought to jail, found guilty of violating immigration laws, and, shortly thereafter, deported.

This culminating scene in the theatre is significant in the way that it uses metafiction to expose Chipote's position of marginalization and, by extension, that of other Mexican im/migrants like him. The revelation for the theatre audience that the "comedy" of the fighting married couple is actually a real, physical altercation is a metafictional moment where theatre and real life bleed into one another for the theatregoers. As Paul Fallon explains, this "framework of a staged performance is interrupted in such a way that artifice and reality are brought into

---

49   "The workers are usually treated like animals" (53).
50   "Those slavedrivers ... make their living from Mexican disgrace ... Because the majority of us cross the border without a nickel and only dreams" (53).
51   "The prize be awarded to those who so brilliantly portrayed the comedy of husband and wife" (152).

question" (121). Although the theatregoers apparently find it hilarious to watch a comedy routine in which a wife wrings her husband's neck, they find it much less funny – and perhaps very disturbing – to watch someone strangle another person in real life. The breakdown of the distinction between "reality" and "fiction" that we see in the theatre scene is of course compounded for us as readers, because the "real" life for the theatregoers is part of a novel that we are reading. Thus, to confuse matters even more, the audience's "reality" is, for readers, actually fiction.

These layers of metafiction, however, not only make readers question the differences between fiction and reality but also compel readers to consider the parallels between the "comedic performance" of the Chipotes and the novel *Don Chipote*, and between the theatregoers and the readers of *Don Chipote*. Just as the theatre audience finds the fight comedic when it is a performance, but threatening when they realize it is real life, readers similarly find humour in *Don Chipote* – with its loads of eschatological humour and the seemingly absurd predicaments in which Chipote finds himself due to a combination of bodily urges, stupidity, and naïveté – but perhaps might find much less humour in these situations when they realize that real people are living through these hardships. As other critics have noted, the narrator uses numerous metafictional devices to remind readers that Chipote's travails are representative of the real-life struggles of many Mexican im/migrants.[52] Throughout the novel the narrator repeatedly speaks directly to the readers, discusses the process of writing *Don Chipote*, and interjects his own first-person, eye-witness testimony about his experiences crossing the border, working on the railroad, and being exploited and abused by employers. This recurring use of metafiction pushes readers to consider the fact that this might be not just a funny novel but also a forceful critique of the situation of the Mexican im/migrant in the United States. Although the theatre "performance" and the novel itself appear to be comedies, they both end on a more sombre note with the expulsion of Chipote and his family from the US community. The unmasking of Chipote in the theatre is doubled: not only is his "performance" as the bad husband revealed to be not a performance at all, but also it is made

---

52　Fallon, for example, explores the importance of the metafictional devices in the novel (122–3). And Urquijo-Ruiz similarly notes the narrator's repeated metafictional interventions in the narrative, which criticize "the exploitative nature of the economic, social, and political systems in place in the United States that allow the mistreatment of these workers" (*Wild Tongues* 6).

public that he does not belong in the United States. As undocumented Mexicans, the Chipotes were never full members in the community to start with, even if Chipote himself put on and embraced the outward trappings of modern US culture.

The literary genres with which Venegas is playing in the novel are also meaningful. As I mentioned briefly before, *Don Chipote* is most obviously a parody of *Don Quijote* – from the names of the protagonists and the use of metafictional devices, right down to the parallels between his trusty sidekick and mutt, Sufrelambre (a play on the phrase *sufre hambre*, meaning "to go hungry") and Quijote's old but faithful workhorse, Rocinante.[53] But it is also a picaresque parody of the travel narrative. In a more traditional travel narrative the traveller (who is usually an elite male, especially prior to the nineteenth century) generally learns, changes, grows as a person, and shares insights with his audience. Indeed, travel narratives are often as much about the traveller's inward journey of self-discovery and change as they are about the physical journey. *Don Chipote* parodies the traditional travel narrative at every turn. Chipote is, first of all, portrayed as an illiterate, poor, country bumpkin – the opposite of an elite cosmopolitan. He seems to have changed, according to the narrator, only in negative, vulgar, or superficial ways during his travels – for example, his outrageous and impractical clothes, his frivolous spending, his immoral pursuit of the flapper, and his embrace of the theatre (a stand-in for "modern culture," but a superficial, merely performative one) and its associated depravities. It is also significant that *Don Chipote* both begins and ends in rural Mexico, with Don Chipote hard at work on his little *rancho*. He is right back where he started and has gained nothing in material terms from his travels. Although socio-economic transformation was his primary reason for leaving Mexico, at the end of the novel he and his family are perhaps even poorer than they were at the beginning of it. Doña Chipota sells almost everything they own in order to finance her trip and is swindled out of her money at nearly every step of her journey. And because of his irresponsible spending on his flapper girlfriend, Chipote finds himself with only a few dollars when he is deported back to Mexico. Venegas uses a satiric mode to undermine the traditional travel narrative, thus turning the

---

53 Numerous critics have noted the parallels between *Don Quijote* and *Don Chipote* (see Kanellos's introduction to the novel, for example). Urquijo-Ruiz, "Estudio onomástico de los personajes," discusses parallels with names in both texts. And Fallon discusses the similar use of metafictional devices in *Don Chipote* as another parallel with and homage to *Don Quijote*.

travel narrative on its head and showing how this genre carries very different implications for Mexicans – particularly poor, working-class, and illiterate Mexicans who cannot afford to get a passport and who would not be approved for admission to the United States through official ports of entry. As the ending of the novel shows, Mexicans like Chipote, though they may travel to the metropole, will never be admitted as full members. However, it is only through travel that Chipote comes to recognize the full extent of his exclusion.

Indeed, perhaps the most significant change in the novel is that by the end Chipote seems to have a new and heightened level of discontentment with his life and, in particular, with his expulsion from the United States. Despite the somewhat idyllic description of his country life of "paz y calma" (159) when he returns to Mexico, the narrator notes that as Chipote toils away once again on his *rancho*, he daydreams:

> [Y] en sus sueños veía pasar como cinta peliculera las amargas aventuras de que fue protagonista, las que eran endulzadas por el recuerdo de sus amores pelonescos, recuerdo que no le hacía olvidar los fracasos que los chicanos se llevan por dejar a su patria, ilusionados por los cuentos de los que van a los Estados Unidos, dizque a barrer el dinero con la escoba. (159)[54]

Even his dreams themselves have been tainted by his brief foray into the United States, as they now "unwind like a movie reel," suggesting a profound transformation of the way in which he thinks and of the desires that his trip has inflamed: to be his own protagonist in his own "movie." Moreover, his memories do not appear entirely accurate: his flapper never really loved him at all. At the end of the novel the main lesson Chipote has learned is summed up in the very last line of the novel: "los mexicanos se harán ricos en Estados Unidos: CUANDO LOS PERICOS MAMEN" (159; emphasis in original)[55] – in other words, never. There is thus a satiric play on the journey of discovery in the

---

54 "And in his dreams he saw bitter adventures, in which he had played the protagonist, unwind like a movie reel, sweetened by the remembrance of his flapper's love. It was a memory that would now allow him to forget the troubles that Chicanos experience when leaving their fatherland, made starry-eyed by the yarns spun by those who go to the United States, as they say, to strike it rich." (160)
55 "Mexicans will make it big in the United States ... WHEN PARROTS BREAST-FEED" (160; emphasis in original).

traditional travel narrative. Chipote learns to put on the outward trappings of modernity (his outrageous aquamarine suit, for example) and to consume modern culture (the movies and the female dancers), but he has never truly belonged or been accepted into modern US culture. Or perhaps, more profoundly, Venegas suggests that there is no actual substance to modern culture because it is all merely performative consumption. Regardless, in the end Chipote is expelled from it, yet still desires it. Moreover, he never truly benefits from his brief and only superficial admittance into the modern metropole. In fact, because of his travel across borders, he is further impoverished and ostracized. His very existence within the national space of the United States is what makes him "illegal," yet there is no legal way for someone like him to cross the border. This is the same sort of neocolonial relationship that Pratt discusses, in which the norms of modernity are both compulsory and impossible to realize in the neocolony, constantly alluring and yet permanently out of reach (Pratt, *Imperial Eyes* 226). For Chipote and others, the American dream promises a life of economic stability and even prosperity, but upon crossing into the United States, poor Mexican im/migrants like Chipote find that they are pre-emptively barred from that community and from the chance to be full and equal participants in that society.

While *Don Chipote* is certainly about Mexican im/migrant experiences in the United States – and has even been called the first Chicano novel by critics[56] – the novel is also very much about Mexico and Mexican identity. Like in Zavala, travel (in this case specifically across the border with the United States) is what prompts an exploration of what it means to be Mexican. But while in Zavala and earlier travel narratives there may be a questioning of what *mexicanidad* is, especially in political and cultural terms, in border-crossing narratives of the early twentieth century, as we see in *Don Chipote*, an important distinction emerges in which Mexicans, especially poor, illiterate ones, are not only colonized but also deemed "illegal," perpetually relegated to life in the neocolony, wherever they may physically reside.

---

56   See Kanellos's introduction to the novel, and Cabrera, "Dialogismo." As Kanellos discusses, the narrator uses the term *Chicano* for self-referentiality and when speaking to his fellow Mexican immigrant laborers or *braceros* (2). But, as other critics have also pointed out, the term *Chicano* did not have the same meaning as it does today and was often used to refer to both Mexicans and Mexican-Americans during this time; indeed, Venegas's use of *Chicano* in the novel refers not only to Mexican-Americans but also Mexicans (Fallon 118).

Social Death and the Neocolony

In her book *Social Death: Racialized Rightlessness and the Criminalization of the Unprotected*, Lisa Marie Cacho examines the ways in which undocumented immigrants in the United States have been "prevented from being law-abiding" and, thus, have been "criminalized" (4). While so-called illegal aliens (among other groups such as gang members and terrorist suspects) are often treated as outcomes of law-breaking, Cacho argues that they should more accurately be understood as the "*effects* of the law,*" or "produced by the law" (4; italics in original). Cacho elaborates:

> [P]eople who occupy legally vulnerable and criminalized statuses are not just excluded from justice; criminalized populations and the places they live *form the foundation* of the U.S. legal system, imagined to be why a punitive (in)justice system exists. Although they are excluded from law's protection, they are not excluded from law's discipline, punishment, and regulation ... As targets of regulation and containment, they are deemed deserving of discipline and punishment but not worthy of protection. They are not merely excluded from legal protection but criminalized as always already the object and target of law, never its authors or addressees. (5; italics in original)

Cacho further elucidates that people "subjected to laws based on their (il)legal status ... are unable to comply with the 'rule of law' because U.S. law targets their being and their bodies, not their behavior. They are denied not only the illusion of authorship but even the possibility of compliance" (6). In other words, one of Cacho's main arguments here is that the law is "dependent upon the *permanence* of certain groups' criminalization" (6). Furthermore, these permanently criminalized people, such as undocumented im/migrants, are, as she says, "*ineligible for personhood* – as populations subjected to laws but refused the legal means to contest those laws as well as denied both the political legitimacy and moral credibility necessary to question them" (6; italics in original). Such groups of people "are excluded from the ostensibly democratic processes that legitimate U.S. law, yet they are expected to unambiguously accept and unequivocally uphold a legal and political system that depends on the unquestioned permanency of their rightlessness" (6). As Cacho eloquently concludes, to "be ineligible for personhood is a form of social death; it not only defines who does not matter, it also makes mattering meaningful" (6).

Cacho's application of the concept of social death[57] to undocumented im/migrants is enlightening because it highlights the ways in which travel across the US-Mexico border, which has been criminalized since the early twentieth century, works to redefine undocumented border crossers as "other" and deprives them of what the philosopher Hannah Arendt called "the right to have rights," effectively rendering their bodies and their very existence as ineligible for legal personhood within the United States.

Unlike the type of travel across borders that we see in the nineteenth century or even the type of crossing that we see in *Don Chipote*, travel across the US-Mexico border took on new meaning as a criminalized act starting in 1929. With the passing of the Immigration Act of 1929, the United States Congress outlawed undocumented border crossings from Mexico with the specific intent of criminalizing, prosecuting, and imprisoning undocumented Mexican immigrants (K.L. Hernández, *City of Inmates* 137–8).[58] Prior to this Act, as we saw in *Don Chipote*, there had been official ports of entry through which Mexicans could legally register, pay a fee, submit to required tests, and enter the United States. But many Mexicans, especially those of the working class migrating in search of work, chose other ways to cross the border and often did not register for legal entry due to the high entry fees, degrading delousing procedures, invasive medical tests, and biased literacy tests, all of which were required for entry.[59] With the passage of the Immigration Act of 1929, however, "unlawful entry" into the United States became classified as a misdemeanour, and "unlawful re-entry" became a felony. As both Hernández and Molina show, these changes to US immigration law were directly aimed at controlling the movements of Mexicans and preventing them from permanently settling in the southwest because they were seen as racially unfit to be US citizens.

These laws criminalizing undocumented border crossing have thus been in place in the United States since 1929, but actual "prosecutions for unlawful entry and reentry remained low until 2005" (K.L. Hernández, "How Crossing the U.S.-Mexico Border"). Under the George W. Bush and Obama administrations (2001–9 and 2009–17, respectively), however,

---

57 Orlando Patterson defined and explored the idea of social death in the context of slavery and emancipation in his ground-breaking work, *Slavery and Social Death: A Comparative Study* (1982).

58 For more on the politics surrounding the Immigration Act of 1929, and its effects on Mexican immigrants, see chapter 5 (pp. 131–57) of K.L. Hernández, *City of Inmates*.

59 See Stern, pp. 60–7, for more on the development and growth of "sanitation plants" or "disinfection plants" on the US side of the Mexican border.

prosecutions for unlawful entry and re-entry surged. Hernández notes that by 2015 in the United States "prosecutions for unlawful entry and reentry accounted for 49 percent of all federal prosecutions and the federal government had spent at least US$7 billion to lock up unlawful border crossers" ("How Crossing the U.S.-Mexico Border"). Thus, the Immigration Act of 1929 targeted the caging of undocumented im/migrants (primarily Mexican), with *removal* being a primary goal in order to discourage permanent residency and thereby simultaneously preclude the birth on US soil of future generations of Mexican-Americans with full citizenship. In the first two decades of the twenty-first century, however, the intensified governmental focus on the *prosecution* and *incarceration* of undocumented Mexican and Central American im/migrants has led to the increased criminalization of this community, making them progressively more illegible as lives – and deaths – that matter.

Diego Quemada-Diez's film *La jaula de oro* (2013) dramatizes and gives voice to the experiences of transmigrants in the twenty-first century. Like the other works I have examined in this chapter, this film uses travel and border crossing to uncover the multiple, overlapping structures of coloniality that continue to permeate Mexican society in the twenty-first century, while also questioning the limits – both literal and figurative – of Mexico and *mexicanidad*. However, the film also represents an important evolution of the travel narrative and border-crossing genres, as it focuses on the ways in which undocumented Central American migrants are being increasingly criminalized in both the United States and Mexico in the twenty-first century, making their journeys more and more difficult and dangerous.

La jaula de oro depicts the journey through Mexico of three Guatemalan teenagers – Juan (Brandon López), Sara (Karen Martínez), and Samuel (Carlos Chajón) – and a new acquaintance, Chauk (Rodolfo Domínguez), a Tzotzil Indian who does not speak Spanish and whom Sara befriends along the way. During their journey the group encounters numerous obstacles and tragedies, including their physical abuse, robbery, and deportation by Mexican border patrol agents; their exploitation as undocumented migrant agricultural laborers in southern Mexico; Sara's kidnapping, disappearance, and implied rape by a gang; the kidnapping and attempted ransoming of Juan and Chauk; and Chauk's murder on the US side of the border. While the protagonists seem to hope, just as Chipote did, that crossing national borders will bring positive transformations in their lives, the film emphasizes just the opposite. In crossing these borders, they confront the ways in which they have become even more marginalized: they are already marked as "other" and criminal within the geopolitical borders of both Mexico and the United States. They are effectively criminalized for merely existing – not for acting criminally – in these spaces.

In fact, I think the film emphasizes how the lives and bodies of the protagonists really were never fully valued, even before they undertook their journey and crossed these borders. If we go back to the very beginning of the film, we witness the extreme poverty and violence in which these young people are living, in spaces already abandoned and forgotten by their government and national community. In other words, the film once again emphasizes how the protagonists are already part of the neocolony. Their travels to the metropole (the United States) and their horrific experiences en route are revealing. Travel once again serves as a mode through which the viewers can come to understand the position of the neocolonial subject because we witness the great danger, trauma, violence, and exploitation that they are willing to face. We see, in other words, through the travels and hardships, the desperation and precarity that drive this migration.

As other critics have similarly pointed out, from the very opening of *La jaula de oro*, silence, absence, and a seeming lack of affect permeate the visual world created in the film.[60] In fact, there are no words spoken at all for the first seven minutes of the film. And yet the sense of place and the situation of the protagonists are immediately and urgently communicated to the audience. In the opening scenes Juan walks, eyes looking down at the ground, through a dirty and noisy shanty town of corrugated metal. In the background, stray dogs bark, babies cry, and a police siren wails. The shaky handheld camera further underscores the precarity and grittiness of the world in which Juan lives as it follows him through the shanty town. Two soldiers with large automatic weapons pass in the opposite direction; small children play with realistic-looking guns and pretend to shoot Juan as he walks by; Juan never breaks his stride or even lifts his eyes, indicating the mundaneness of such threatened violence in his life. In the second shot sequence we see Sara enter a bathroom made of mismatched planks of wood and scrawled with "damas" ("ladies"), handwritten in red paint. Looking at herself in a dirty mirror, she slowly but methodically cuts her hair and then binds her breasts. Lastly, she takes a birth control pill and emerges from the bathroom now dressed as a young man, with short hair and a flat chest, wearing baggy jeans, a faded T-shirt, and a baseball cap.

---

60 See pp. 48–9 in Curry, "The Migration Genre" for example, for further discussion of these "voids" in *La jaula de oro*.

Throughout this sequence she seems to have little affect – there are no tears, no long and dramatic pauses, and she does not utter a single word. In the next scene we see Juan once again, presumably in his home – corrugated metal walls, cardboard floors, and little else. He pauses only briefly before packing up his things in a small backpack and leaving. After another cut we see an extreme long shot of Juan walking towards a garbage dump; he is dwarfed by mountains of garbage. The long shot emphasizes the enormity of the garbage dump, the proximity of the homes to it, and Juan's smallness in comparison to it – he is just one of many similar stories. The camera then shows him walking towards Samuel, another young teenager who is scavenging through the trash along with many others. Juan and Samuel look at each other, once again seemingly devoid of emotion. Without a single word exchanged between them, they leave the dump and begin their journey north.

The feeling of silence, absence, violence, and danger in this space is further underscored by one of the few images in the film of the city from which they come: it shows a wall on a city street filled with black-and-white photographs of presumably the missing, disappeared, and dead. The photographs take up the entire wall and are eerily reminiscent of the photographs of the *desaparecidos* that were used in demonstrations and protests by their families and loved ones during and after the so-called dirty wars in Argentina and Chile, as well as in Guatemala following the military atrocities committed against civilians in its decades-long civil war. The camera focuses on this wall for only a few seconds and without commentary or explanation, but the message is clear: this is a place of violence, death, and disappearance.[61]

The image and feeling of where the protagonists live is one of complete social abandonment. They are literally living and working in the refuse, the remnants of modern Guatemala and the world. Astute viewers will also know that this is Guatemala City's Zone 3, a desperately poor neighbourhood commonly called simply Basurero by locals, since it is home to the city dump. Here several residents earn their living by picking garbage among the raw sewage that flows through the dump and the garbage fires that, according to many *guajeros* ("garbage pickers"), burn almost constantly below the surface.[62] Zone 3 lacks many

---

61 Pugibet interprets this scene similarly, stating: "Es sin lugar a dudas, una advertencia clara tanto para el espectador como para los muchachos" (25; "It is without a doubt a clear warning as much for the viewer as for the teenagers"; my translation).

62 See Pinzón for a description and discussion of the garbage fires and other extreme health dangers that *guajeros* face in their daily activities in the Guatemala City dump.

basic social services, is one of the most dangerous neighbourhoods in the city, and for many Guatemalans it is synonymous with criminality (Reeves).

These opening scenes effectively set the stage for the rest of the film, commenting on the absences left behind by these massive waves of migration and the dangers that transmigrants – especially women and girls – face in their journeys, not to mention the silencing and ostracization of them even before they begin their migration. Indeed, one of the major themes of the film revolves around how personal and tragic stories of criminalized, undocumented im/migrants are silenced, never told, or denied a public forum, thus rendering their suffering and deaths, in the words of Judith Butler, "ungrievable" because "they are cast as threats to human life as we know it rather than as living populations in need of protection from illegitimate state violence, famine, or pandemics" (31). As Butler explains, "when such lives are lost they are not grievable, since, in the twisted logic that rationalizes their death, the loss of such populations is deemed necessary to protect the lives of 'the living'" (31).

As each main character is impeded on the journey north or decides not to continue, they simply vanish from the film. For example, after he has been deported back to Guatemala, Samuel decides he does not want to continue on the journey. When Juan asks him why, he never responds; they simply hug and Samuel starts to cry. Samuel warns Sara, "Deberías regresarte conmigo."[63] She never verbally responds. She hugs Samuel, and the group continues without him. There is no further explanation or exploration of what happens to Samuel. Later in the film, when Sara, along with all the other migrant women on the train, is kidnapped by a gang, her screams for help grow fainter and fainter as the car she is in pulls away, until she, like Samuel, disappears from the camera's view and from the film's narrative. In this way the film fails to succumb "to the sometimes anesthetizing violence of the genre, … [instead leaving] a gap where the end of Sara's journey might be" (Curry 64). This gap, however, is perhaps just as unsettling for viewers. When Chauk is murdered by a vigilante sniper, the camera simply leaves his body in the field and follows Juan as he runs for safety. What happened to Samuel, Sara, and Chauk? They are part of the masses of migrants who never make it to the north – those who disappear, are kidnapped, forced into abusive and exploitative scenarios, or die on the journey. The film cannot show

---

63 "You should go back with me" (this and all further translations from *La jaula de oro* are my own).

the "end" of their stories, because, like the black-and-white photographs on the wall back in Guatemala City that the viewers – and protagonists – saw in those first few minutes of the film, they too have disappeared. This reinforces the lack of closure for those left behind. But even more so, it stresses once again the marginalization of these young adults in the system. In these three cases, no one seems to acknowledge that the young people have even left. There are (at least on film) no tearful goodbyes or even any other family or friends shown on screen. It seems unlikely that someone will even place their photograph on a public wall. At the end of the film the burden of loss is placed on Juan, but it is also placed on the viewer. The film strives to give a voice to the young people and asks its audience to stand witness to their disappearance, even as it also shows that their stories remain incomplete, haunting the other protagonists and the viewers. Knowing that Quemada-Diez wrote the storylines of the film based upon hundreds of testimonials that he had collected from real transmigrants travelling through Mexico adds a layer of urgency to the film's call for the audience to stand witness and to grieve, and to understand these lives – and deaths – as worthy of grief and as grievable.

The lack of affect in such scenes also shows the way in which migrants have almost come to expect these horrific cruelties. Sara, for example, seems to anticipate this possibility when she cuts her hair, binds her breasts, dresses like a man, and starts taking birth control pills before the start of her journey. Although the film is fictional, there is ample evidence that many female migrants do take birth control before embarking on their journeys precisely because many are raped or sexually assaulted at some point on their journey.[64] As the film vividly demonstrates, migration and border crossing are experienced in different ways for women, and sexism manifests in extreme ways in this context. Through Sara's experiences, the spectator is therefore also a witness to the violence of gender (Pugibet 26).

The film is also clearly engaging with the coming-of-age narrative, as it shows, through the character of Juan, the "psychological passage of an adolescent to a man" (Curry 62). In the conventional coming-of-age narrative or a *Bildungsroman*, young protagonists (traditionally men) go on a journey (metaphorical or physical) through which they learn about their identity, their place in society, how to be good citizens/subjects,

---

64 "A staggering 80 percent of Central American girls and women crossing Mexico en route to the United States are raped along the way, according to directors of migrant shelters" (Bonello and McIntyre). Even more conservative numbers by non-profit organizations estimate the number to be approximately 60 per cent, which is still stunningly high (Bonello and McIntyre).

and how to integrate themselves into their community. In the most schematic examples of the *Bildungsroman* "its primary function is to make integration into existing social order legitimate by channeling individual energy into socially useful purposes" (Bolaki 12). As numerous critics have made clear, it is traditionally a conservative genre that reaffirms or reconciles the individual's place within the established social order, serving as an official narrative of national integration (Lowe 99). What we see in *La jaula de oro* is an inversion of this, whereby the protagonists discover instead their lack of value, the way in which they do not and cannot fit into these societies as full human beings who are valued and allowed to flourish. Not only are they criminalized for merely existing in this space, but also they eventually must resort to illegal activities in order to get by – thus compounding the ways in which they are criminalized. For example, when federal police officers detain the detain the group in southern Mexico, officers steal Juan's and Chauk's boots, leaving them barefooted; so Juan steals a new pair. Later he steals a chicken so they can eat. Still much later Juan and Chauk decide to carry drugs over the US-Mexico border in exchange for passage with a coyote. As they cross national borders in both Mexico and the United States the protagonists become transformed into beings who exist outside the law and who simultaneously come to be understood as threats to the law. Here is the paradox of undocumented migrants and the protagonists in the film: they are subjected to laws that target them for merely existing, but because of their "illegal" status they are also unable to comply with the rule of law (Cacho 6). It is no coincidence that as the protagonists move further north throughout the film, images of fences, roadblocks, darkness/night, black tunnels, and grand vistas emphasize their isolation and lack of belonging within these hostile environments and reinforce the metaphor of the journey as a loss of their innocence and hope.

The protagonists' search for belonging, a "home," and a supposedly better place paradoxically transforms them into beings who can never achieve membership in that community. Travel across national borders does not bring a reprieve from colonial structures of exclusion but instead brings into greater relief the continued and even increased stigmatization of these already marginalized communities. For the protagonists their position of vulnerability increases upon crossing national borders – first in Mexico and then in the United States, where they are literally fair game to rapists, drug dealers, extortionists, and murderers. We witness the process by which this community of people comes to occupy a permanently rightless status according to Mexican and US law. Their lives and bodies are legally illegible, making them "ineligible for personhood" (Cacho 6).

These depictions of the experiences of transmigrants in Mexico highlight not just the marginalization of Central Americans but also the neocolonial position of Mexico itself. Indeed, while the film focuses on Guatemalans, the majority of the film takes place in Mexico and concentrates on the experiences of transmigrants *within* Mexico. It is relevant to note that in the first two decades of the twenty-first century the Mexican government increased its militarization of its southern border with Guatemala, while also drastically expanding its efforts at the surveillance, detention, and deportation of Central American transmigrants en route to the United States; this has been driven in part by political pressure from the United States.[65] The United States has made use of a phenomenon termed "externalization," which describes the ways in which nations in the Global North, or so-called developed countries, are able to extend their own border and migration controls and measures beyond the geopolitical borders of their nation, often by influencing migration policies in the "sending" nations or "nations of transit," such as Mexico for Central Americans, in order to prevent migrants and refugees from reaching their country.[66] Between 2000 and 2005, for example, the Mexican government built a significant number of "estaciones migratorias," or migrant detention centres, increasing them from twenty-five to fifty-two during that period (Torre-Cantalapiedra and Yee-Quintero 90). Equally important, they also began placing more of these centres not just at Mexico's southern border but throughout the country so that undocumented migrants could be detected and detained at any point during their journey in the entire nation (Torre-Cantalapiedra and Yee-Quintero 90). In this sense we can see how, through the processes of externalization, Mexico has become a neocolonial extension of US immigration and border control policies, effectively criminalizing border crossers even before they reach the militarized US border and continuously subjecting them to the threat of detection, detainment, and deportation during their journey through Mexico.

With the increased focus on stopping the flow of Central Americans through Mexico as a way of curtailing undocumented border crossings and applications for asylum in the United States, Mexico has become,

---

65   For example, in an article from 2017, Jeff Abbott discusses the "intensified border security that exists across Mexico" and how Mexico's southern border has become "the frontline in the United States' campaign against migration from the Northern Triangle of Central America."

66   For more on the phenomenon of externalization see Baggio, "Fronteras nacionales," pp. 62–7; and Stock et al., "Externalization at Work."

according to many political scientists, essentially an immense, dangerous, and legally ambivalent "vertical border" for Central American
transmigrants.[67] Mexico might also be considered a vertical border in the
sense that the immigration controls are particularly aimed at stopping
the poorest and most marginalized from migrating, thus further exac-
erbating economic disparities and accentuating the distance between
those at the "top" and those on the "bottom." *La jaula de oro* dramatizes
many of the ways in which Mexico has been turned into a vertical border for Central American migrants, who are constantly in danger of being deported, unable to make a living in the legitimate market, unable
to seek help from law enforcement, and thus easily exploited, abused,
and driven to illegal or extra-legal options because of this predicament.
In southern Mexico, for example, Sara, Juan, and Chauk work on what
appears to be a sugar-cane plantation, most likely making a pittance
for their back-breaking labour. This is one of the industries most well
known for exploiting undocumented Central American workers near
the border with Guatemala. To give another example, Juan and Chauk
never report Sara's kidnapping to the authorities or even talk about rescuing her; there really are no options for them to seek help. And when
they, along with other transmigrants, are held for ransom, they also do
not report this to authorities but simply continue on their journey after
escaping.

The film also shows, however, that this position of precarity – of living perpetually on the border – is not limited to Central Americans.
Through the character of Chauk, Quemada-Diez highlights the fact
that it is not just Central Americans who "do not belong" in Mexico.
Chauk is most likely a Mexican citizen, part of several large Tzotzil
communities in Chiapas, Mexico's southernmost state, but because he
has pronounced Indigenous features and does not speak or understand
Spanish, numerous people assume he is not Mexican. In fact, when
the group is detained in southern Mexico and deported across the border, Juan blames Chauk for marking their group as conspicuously not
Mexican because he does not speak Spanish – even though there are
nearly seventy Indigenous languages recognized as national languages
in Mexico and around seven million Mexicans who speak them.[68] The
Mexican police also assume he is not Mexican, and Chauk is deported

---

67   For further discussion of the concept of Mexico as a "vertical border," see, for exam-
     ple, Torre-Cantalapiedra and Yee-Quintero, "México ¿Una frontera vertical?"
68   According to the Instituto Nacional de Estadística, Geografía e Información (INEGI)
     and the Instituto Nacional de Lenguas Indígenas (INALI).

to Guatemala with the others. Chauk's early interactions with Juan, who initially rejects him as part of their group and disparages him with racially charged insults such as "indio ignorante," also bring to light the perception of Indigenous communities within Mexico and Central America as outsiders and inferiors, even if they have been formally included within the nation. Borders, of course, are not just geopolitical but also socio-cultural, and they permeate our societies, many remaining unspoken or largely invisible. Part of why Juan dislikes Chauk has to do with Chauk's transgression of these socio-cultural borders. Sara befriends Chauk, and Juan is jealous of him. There seems to be an unspoken assumption, at least initially by Juan, that Chauk cannot be part of their group because he is Indigenous. Chauk's transgression of these borders paradoxically reveals their persistence and the power they have.

The inclusion of Chauk in the film is important because it points to the ways in which colonial legacies, such as racism within Mexico, continue to define the limits of *mexicanidad* in the twenty-first century, while also serving as factors that drive im/migration on an international scale. Both Indigenous communities and Central American transmigrants are defined socially, culturally, and/or legally as not belonging within the Mexican nation. I am suggesting that travel across different sorts of borders in this film certainly prompts an acknowledgment of the vulnerable position of undocumented im/migrants within host communities, as well as a recognition of both the internal and the external neocolonial structures of power and domination that drive this migration in the first place, and a reconsideration of how certain communities are deemed unworthy of incorporation into a national community (formally or informally), whether that community be Guatemala, Mexico, or the United States.

La jaula de oro explores how vulnerable populations attempt to seek out the benefits of the supposedly civilized world through migration and how they are violently punished for doing so. Once again, this is the essence of the neocolonial predicament and what Latin American cultural studies critic Jean Franco calls the "cruelty of modernity." In her book *Cruel Modernity*, Franco shows how the nation state in much of Latin America has worked to establish its own modernity and cohesion only by simultaneously working to distinguish itself and its citizenry from the groups, communities, and individuals whom it does not consider part of the nation – those who do not belong because they are supposedly not modern or civilized enough. This quest for a cohesive and "modern" nation state, she explains, has authorized state-sponsored violence and the creation of communities that do not receive the social, political, and economic tools that will allow them to thrive as full human beings and full members of the national community. The modernity of the modern nation state is thus doubly cruel: it begins by marginalizing certain communities and initiates programs of violence that deprive those communities of the resources they need in order to be a contributing member of the nation. It then blames, criminalizes, and punishes those same communities, often in extremely violent ways, for not being a part of the "modern" nation. This process has its origins in nineteenth-century nation-building projects and is particularly aimed at Indigenous communities, as we saw in Zavala's discussion of how he understood Indigenous communities as simultaneously the cause as well as the result of Mexico's failed modernity.

La jaula de oro explicitly engages with this history of state-sponsored cruelty through the allusion in its title. The film takes its name from a corrido with the same title, written in the 1980s by Enrique Franco Aguilar and popularized by the California-based *norteño* band Los Tigres del Norte. In the original corrido, which has become almost an anthem for undocumented Mexican immigrants in the United States,[69] a first-person narrator tells about his experiences as an undocumented immigrant. In constant fear of being deported, he feels that even though he is making a good living and succeeding financially in the United States, he cannot return to his beloved Mexico as he pines to do, and he also cannot live fully in the United States. To make matters worse, his children have forgotten their culture: they only speak English, reject the idea of returning to Mexico, identify as American, and deny their Mexicanness (even though the narrator notes that they are the same colour as he is). In the chorus, the singer of the corrido thus laments that he is living in a "jaula de oro," a golden cage of his own making.

In its referencing this earlier corrido, Quemada-Diez's film harkens back to the long history of Mexican immigration to the United States and the constant cycles of migration in and through Mexico.[70] The story of the undocumented immigrant is one that has been told many times before, and at its core it is about the transformation of a person into a non-person, a citizen into a non-citizen, a free person into a prisoner, all

---

69   In her study of *norteño* music Cathy Ragland notes that Los Tigres del Norte "emerged as the undisputed voice of the undocumented" in large part because of the popularity of songs such as "Jaula de oro" (179). Fans came to expect songs and albums from the group that made social and political statements about the situation of undocumented immigrants (179).

70   Quemada-Diez acknowledges the allusion in his film to the corrido by Los Tigres del Norte in his interview for *Democracy Now!* ("Extended Interview").

through the crossing of national borders. In his film's title, Quemada-Diez thus indexes the ways in which the criminalization of im/migrants is not new but rather part of a much longer, deeper history of state-sponsored violence and cruelty.

Quemada-Diez's choice to engage with the corrido is also significant because the film itself mirrors many of the characteristics of the corrido genre. Traditionally the corrido is a lyrical-narrative genre that can be recited or sung. As Américo Paredes, the founding critical voice in the field, shows in his landmark work, *"With His Pistol in His Hand": A Border Ballad and Its Hero*, the corrido has a long history of production stretching back to the colonial period. It is a popular and still vibrant form of storytelling in Mexico, especially in northern Mexico and in the US-Mexico borderlands. It is an inherently hybrid genre, often straddling the line between history and fiction and between individual and collective representation. Historically the corrido has also been associated with and used by marginalized groups (Chamberlain 30).

La jaula de oro, as a sort of modern form of the corrido, strives to similarly speak, as a subversive and hybrid form, for the under-represented masses of im/migrants. For example, like in a corrido, the film straddles the line between collective and individual representation and between history and fiction, using the specific stories of Juan, Samuel, Sara, and Chauk to stand in for larger and very real collective experiences. In fact, in preparation for writing the film script Quemada-Diez conducted over six hundred interviews with real migrants travelling through Mexico and living in the United States and then wrote the individual stories of the characters in the film based upon those interviews ("Extended Interview").[71] Using a quasi-documentary style,[72] Quemada-Diez frequently employs handheld camera work and eschews more slick production techniques like cranes and camera dollies for moving shots; he also used Super 16 mm film, a classic documentary format

---

71   Numerous extreme long shots and wide shots in which large numbers of migrant bodies fill the frame also emphasize the sheer numbers of migrants, the vastness of the territory they are traversing, and the smallness of these characters as part of a more massive phenomenon. Curry similarly explains that in the film the migrants "are an anonymous mass because they all react and move as a single entity when the train stops, when the police arrive, when La Migra shows up, when they are stopped by the gang, when the priest offers food and shelter to all" (58). Even when individual migrants (besides the protagonists) do appear on screen, they almost always appear as part of larger groups, are often shown with their faces partially or fully covered, or are represented only with close-ups of their feet and legs hanging off the sides of the train, allowing them to "remain an anonymous synecdoche for the emigrating masses" (Curry 58).

72   Pugibet, for example, calls *La jaula de oro* a "docuficción" (22).

("A Conversation"). He sought out non-professional actors who were actually from Zone 3 in Guatemala City for his main protagonists (in the process reportedly auditioning over six thousand youngsters) and paid real transmigrants to work as extras in the film ("Extended Interview"). The frequent use of straight-on, medium close-up framing, a shot frequently employed in "talking head" documentaries, especially when the characters in the film ride the train, further heightens this sensation of blurring the lines between film (fiction) and documentary (history) for the audience.[73]

Historically corridos were often used to tell about current/historical events – for example, the Mexican Revolution – but from the perspective of marginalized individuals and groups who did not necessarily always have a voice in official, national histories (Chamberlain 30). The corrido thus long served as a subversive repository of community history that countered the official historical narratives of dominant groups. *La jaula de oro* continues and builds upon the corrido tradition, working to represent the experiences of transmigrants and, as I have shown, also subversively critiquing the role of US and Mexican governments in the criminalization of such communities.[74]

This contemplation of the criminalization of borders and transmigrants in the film is particularly fitting because the corrido was a preferred genre for criminal or criminalized populations and "outlaw" culture, especially in the US-Mexico borderlands, where corridos often related the experiences of Mexicanos/as living in the United States under oppressive conditions in which they were often seen and portrayed by Anglo-Americans as criminally suspect and untrustworthy, regardless of their actions. In such a context the corrido served as a communal form of protest that revealed the prejudices against Mexicanos/as in the United States. *La jaula de oro* modernizes the corrido and shows the new forms of violence and trauma that Central American transmigrants face in the twenty-first century; in its allusion to the original corrido it also shows that this is part of a much longer history of state-sponsored cruelty that has been expressed through the criminalization and exclusion of certain communities.

The journey in *La jaula de oro*, much as in the original corrido of the same title, is driven by the allure of the modern nation – the United States – which is exoticized and romanticized but not well understood by the protagonists. The United States appears in the film as an abstract idea of a "better place," but the young protagonists seem to have no

---

73   As Quemada-Diez explains, he only places the camera at eye level, thereby "using the camera as an observer of events as close to life as possible" ("A Conversation").
74   Saavedra Luna similarly explores the film as a type of "testimonio colectivo" (290).

sense of where they are going or why; they just know that they cannot stay where they are. Travelling by boat across the Guatemala-Mexico border, for example, Juan, the self-appointed leader of the group, asks the driver, "Y para el norte, ¿para dónde es?,"[75] and the driver gestures to the right. Juan follows his motion, and his response is as much a question as it is an affirmation: "Hacia allá. ¿Caminamos hacia allá?"[76] Near the beginning of their journey Sara asks Juan what he wants to do in the United States, and he childishly responds, "Si te digo, no se cumple,"[77] but the viewers have a sense that he himself perhaps does not even really know.

One key scene early in the film reveals this allure of the mythical north for the young migrants. After they have crossed the border from Guatemala into Mexico, Sara and Samuel perform skits for tips in a busy plaza. They buy some snacks and drinks and then decide to spend some of the money on novelty photographs in which they can choose from a variety of backdrops and props. For his photograph Chauk dresses as a Native American with a headdress and an elaborate beaded breastplate, but Juan dresses as a cowboy, complete with a cowboy hat and a golden pistol; he straddles a small plastic horse. The juxtaposition of these two images once again reinforces Juan's sense of difference from Chauk and his own superiority, as he remarks scornfully that "A la verdad sí éste es indio por donde lo mirés, 'mano.'"[78] In the photograph that Sara and Samuel choose, they stand in front of a massive US flag, the Statue of Liberty, and the New York skyline, and they hold a tiny Guatemalan flag, making it appear as if it sits atop a building on the fake skyline. There is a sense of absurdity in the photographs – they are not realistic at all, and the proportions and perspectives are completely inconsistent. But even more than that, they are simplistic stereotypes and images of the United States. When Samuel remarks that this is "his dream," we as viewers are perhaps left confused. What is his dream exactly? To see New York and the Statue of Liberty or to live the American dream? It is never explained (or perhaps completely understood) by Samuel, just as Juan never reveals what his ultimate goals are in the journey. The photographs, costumes, and obviously fake backdrops, for example, paradoxically reveal how the protagonists do not "naturally" fit into these clothes or scenes, even as they also speak to

---

75 "And to go north, what way is it?"
76 "That way. We walk that way?"
77 "If I tell you, it won't come true."
78 "This guy is really an Indian, whatever way you look at him, bro."

the production of desire to possess and inhabit them. This frame within the frame is also a meta-cinematic moment, similar to the metafictional scene in the theatre in *Don Chipote* that I discussed, that asks viewers to reflect on how myths of belonging and exclusion are constructed, and on the deceptiveness but also the allure of such myths.

Chauk's dream, which we see represented visually at several points in the film when he sleeps, appears frustratingly simple but also somewhat magical: from a point-of-view shot we see snow falling against a black background and towards the camera, as if falling in our faces, the snowflakes growing larger as they near the camera/face. In fact, the only Tzotzil word that is clearly translated for a Spanish-speaking audience and for the Spanish-speaking characters in the film is *taiv* ("snow"). It is no surprise that when Chauk chooses the backdrop for his snapshot, he opts for the background with snowy woods; however, he also, perhaps unexpectedly, chooses to put on a Native American headdress, underscoring his own awareness of his racial and cultural differences from the other protagonists. And when they reach Mexico's northern border, there is a scene in which both Juan and Chauk look at a window display containing a toy train with fake snow falling around it. Almost like two small children, they smile and gaze at it with wonder, excitement, and innocence, even as the glass barrier once again marks their distance and exclusion from such a scene. Snow serves throughout the film as a symbol of both the naïveté of the protagonists and the mythical allure of a new and little-understood place (where it snows), the United States. Over and over again, the film highlights the fact that these are barely more than children, drawn to make a perilous journey for which they are ill prepared and for which they barely understand the possible consequences or, perhaps, even the ultimate goal.

The journey of these young protagonists, in other words, is almost irrational; Quemada-Diez in fact uses this exact language, calling the film a depiction of "irrational" migration ("Q & A"). In fact, I think the film's focus on this sort of irrationality moves towards a critical view of the "purposeful" im/migration experience and the accompanying narrative of national integration that many stories of immigration reinforce (intentionally or not). Rather than a carefully planned and well-informed trip, as we see in *Viage* or even to a certain extent in *Don Chipote*, the film depicts what Kirsten Silva Gruesz calls "the accidental or reluctant migrant, the wanderer blown off course, the person at the end of his or her chances" (21). The "errancy" of such migrants, Gruesz argues, demonstrates a refusal to have purpose, pushes back against celebratory narratives of intentionality, and troubles "the way such purposefulness can be used not only to embrace or demonize migrants but also to establish someone's place within a narrative of national and ethnic belonging" (21). She further explains that "errancy – not as a synonym for a mistake, but as a name for a movement that has no idea where it is ultimately headed – captures more of the experience of undocumented people and their relationship to this inscrutable future" (39). Indeed, the fact that the storylines of three out of four protagonists end in disappearance or death – in failure to "arrive" or in errancy, in other words – underscores the commonness of these sorts of migration stories. Along the way, Samuel decides to return home after they are deported to Guatemala; Sara is kidnapped by a gang; and Chauk is murdered, seemingly by a vigilante sniper, on the US side of the border. Juan is the only character from the group to make it to the intended destination. The others all disappear from the film's storyline. The open-endedness, absences, and silences that permeate the film call into question the very idea that there is an ending or goal in this twenty-first-century im/migration story, and not just a constant, present-tense movement, a sense of errancy and improvisation that leaves the majority of such im/migrants and refugees perpetually stateless and "home"-less.

In highlighting the errancy of these protagonists, the film also provokes a questioning of viewers' assumptions about the moral value of purposefulness and about the accompanying blame or responsibility placed on im/migrants for "choosing" to make such a dangerous and irrational journey. Although Juan does decide, on some level, to continue north at each step of his journey, for example, it seems fair to question how much choice any migrants or refugees really have in the matter when, for many of them, there is no liveable, tolerable future in their home countries. Would it be a more rational choice to remain at home and be raped, brutalized, or murdered? Or to stand by and watch these things happen to your families and loved ones? The migration we see in *La jaula de oro* is an example of errancy in the sense that it is, like the migration that Gruesz describes, "less than wholly purposeful, less than fully chosen" (38). The film, in other words, seems to propose the idea that one does not need to be a child – unequivocally innocent – in order to understand a migrant's suffering or death as being not fully chosen, as being undeserved tragedies.

In the very last scene of the film, following a detailed shot sequence in which Juan cleans up bloody meat scraps in a slaughterhouse – made more horrendous by a sickly, greenish tint of artificial light, a complete lack of dialogue, and a sorrowful solo violin playing in the background – we see him walking alone down a dark road in the snow. He looks into a streetlight, and as the camera switches to a point-of-view shot, we see the snow once again falling towards our/his face and the camera against a black background – the very image that Chauk had seen in his dreams and that we also saw in the point-of-view shots interspersed throughout the film. The non-diegetic music shifts from the solo violin to more uplifting piano chords, though still in a minor key. It is a bitter-sweet moment and a reminder of all that the characters have lost, including Chauk's dream to finally see snow. Juan stands, alone and in the dark on a deserted street, representing his isolation and solitude in the United States. But he is there. *La jaula de oro* shows the cruelty of coloniality and border making: coloniality creates the conditions that drive migration and simultaneously makes any attempt to escape those conditions a criminal act, thereby perpetually providing the "irrational" hope of – and simultaneously the impediments to – a better life.

In its dialogue with and evocation of the travel narrative, the coming-of-age narrative, and the corrido – in both form and content – the film speaks to the continuities with these forms, but it also, perhaps more importantly, uses them to underscore how travel, especially for migrants, is experienced and understood differently in the twenty-first century. In the nineteenth and early twentieth century, as I have discussed, travel was often a mode for learning about the "other" and, through comparison, the self – both individual and national identity. In *La jaula de oro*, however, what we see is an evolution of a form – the corrido or even Mexican film itself – that might have once been considered a "folk," national, or nationalist form, and using it to think through the multiplicity of transmigrant identities and how those identities are continually in a process of hybridization and change. Rather than being used, for example, to define a national or regional identity, the film contemplates how the idea of the nation has become completely destabilized, even as the geopolitical borders of the nation have become more rigid in many senses. The borders are less open, more militarized, yet the idea of the border has also expanded. As we see through the eyes of the young protagonists, all of Mexico has indeed become like one giant border that immediately labels and separates the protagonists as "other." While there are important differences between this film and earlier travel narratives like *Viage* and *Don Chipote*, they all reveal how nationhood and geopolitical borders have always operated as much through crossing over and differentiating as through boundary setting and identification.

Conclusions: Coloniality and Neocoloniality in the Age of Trump and Beyond

In his 2016 presidential-campaign-announcement speech, Donald Trump incited and vindicated the xenophobia and racism of his supporters when he explained: "When Mexico sends its people, they're not sending their best. They're not sending you. They're not sending you. They're sending people that have lots of problems, and they're bringing those problems with us. They're bringing drugs. They're bringing crime. They're rapists."[79] Trump's campaign announcement perfectly captures how in the United States brown bodies have come to be understood as always already criminal, and also how the criminalization of such bodies works: the "other" must always be contrasted with "us," as when Trump looks to his audience and repeats, "They're not sending you." During Trump's presidency his administration continued to ramp up the detention,[80] prosecution, and incarceration of (primarily, almost exclusively) Mexican and Central American undocumented immigrants and refugees,[81] while also moving to curtail, if not eliminate, the very few options that these vulnerable populations legally had a right to in the first place, such as applying for asylum or seeking Temporary Protected Status.

Perhaps nothing better illustrates Cacho's idea of social death and the illegibility of undocumented immigrants' personhood better than the so-called border crisis in the United States, as we have witnessed the caging of families, of unaccompanied minors, and of children reportedly as young as two years old who have been separated from their parents or guardians in so-called immigrant detention centres,[82] while lawyers debated if the detainees in such centres had the "right" to essential items such as soap, toothpaste, diapers, feminine hygiene products, and access to showers, beds, and blankets.[83] Not only did the Trump administration continue to criminalize undocumented

---

79 See Amber Phillips's annotated version of Trump's 2016 speech.

80 For more on the increased investment in and development of immigrant detention centres in the United States, see Emily Kassie's exposé "Detained."

81 For more detailed statistics on the large increases in the numbers of people criminally prosecuted for immigration offences during the Trump administration, see John Gramlich's reporting for the PEW Research Center.

82 In an article in *The Atlantic* from June of 2019, children who had been separated from parents or guardians in the detention centres were receiving little to no care, with the younger children reportedly being cared for by other children, some of them only a few years older than the toddlers themselves (Fetters). The youngest child separated from parents or guardians at the border was only four months old, but he was cared for by a foster family (Dickerson and Heisler).

83 The US government argued, for example, that it was not required to provide the detained migrant children with toothbrushes, soap, and showers (Dickerson and Heisler). For more on the legal fight over what constitutes "safe and sanitary" conditions for detainees, see Michael García Bochenek's investigative report and summary for Human Rights Watch.

immigrants and refugees, but it did so in increasingly cruel and punitive ways.[84] In fact, the Trump administration deliberately used the inhumane treatment of detainees, especially the separation of children from parents, as tactics designed to deter people from attempting to enter the United States illegally.[85] Upon crossing borders into the United States, rather than finding relief from precarity and trauma, detainees find that they are even further marginalized and deemed unworthy of basic human necessities and the very right to have any rights at all.

This is strikingly similar to Pratt's discussion of the ways in which neocolonial subjects are driven to be "modern" and subscribe to the values of the "modern" metropole, yet are only admitted as "second-class" members (*Imperial Eyes* 226). As Pratt argues, it is through travel to the metropole that Latin American writers realize and articulate the full extent of the neocolonial condition of their home countries and their perpetual positions as second-class members in a global community. For undocumented im/migrants and refugees, immigration to the United States promises potential relief from poverty, violence, and suffering; yet, what they find is that their travel across these borders brings into sharper focus – and increases – their subalternity. It is not just that travellers and border crossers become marginalized after crossing borders, such as the one between Mexico and the United States, but that such types of travel bring into focus the fact that they were *already* marginalized, neocolonial subjects before they crossed those borders.

The horrific treatment of migrants in both Mexico and the United States, however, is neither a completely new phenomenon nor something for which the Trump administration alone was responsible. Indeed, we must recognize that the criminalization of geopolitical borders and the vilification of undocumented im/migrants is part of a much longer history of coloniality. Borders are socially produced and geopolitically constructed spaces, but "coloniality is the epistemological and material scaffolding for the social construction and reproduction of nation-state boundaries and identities and of national, racial, and sexual

---

84   For a deeper discussion of the intentional cruelty of the Trump administration's immigration policies, see Julianne Hing's essay "For Trump, Cruelty Is the Point," and Adam Serwer's essay, "The Cruelty Is the Point."

85   In an article from June of 2018, Russell Berman notes that lawyers working in border cities like McAllen, Texas, noticed a pattern of specifically targeting for prosecution the adults who crossed the border with children. An article in *The New York Times* from May of 2018 similarly noted the Trump administration's push to "deter new migrants with the threat of jail sentences and separating immigrant children from their parents" (Jordan and Nixon).

borders" (R. Hernández 10–11). In order to see migrants and refugees as people who are deserving of the protections, services, and goods that will help them survive and thrive, we must seriously reconsider not only how borders are constructed, monitored, enforced, and criminalized but also how those borders are a product and symptom of coloniality itself, of the attempt to differentiate between "them" and "us" and to classify those who are recognizable by the nation state and others as valuable and those who are not. To travel across a border, as I have attempted to show in this chapter, is revelatory because it is precisely at the territorial borders of a nation state that coloniality is made visible in all of its cruelty and contradictions.

This chapter, then, like the other chapters in this book, has examined the ways in which *mexicanidad* is tied to coloniality and colonial legacies, but the chapter also expands notions of what we mean by coloniality and even *mexicanidad*, moving outside of Mexican national limits, to its borders and beyond to examine how coloniality is experienced and recognized in new ways by those who cross borders. The next chapter in this book similarly widens our perspective by moving across the Atlantic to examine the ways in which Spain and Mexico remain enmeshed within centuries-old colonial dynamics, and how the history of and popular representation of the Spanish conquest are part of a much larger symbolic power struggle between Mexico and Spain over the identities of both nations since the post-independence era. As we will see in the next chapter, how Mexico's history is understood, represented, and addressed (or not) in the present speaks to the ways in which coloniality has permeated the complex and contested relationship between Mexico and Spain from the colonial period through to the present day.

WORKS CITED

Abbott, Jeff. "Keep Out! How the U.S. Is Militarizing Mexico's Southern Border." *The Progressive*, 2 Oct. 2017, https://progressive.org/magazine/keep-out-how-the-us-militarizes-mexico-southern-border/.

Anzaldúa, Gloria. *Borderlands / La Frontera: The New Mestiza*. 2nd ed., Aunt Lute Books, 1999.

Arendt, Hannah. *The Origins of Totalitarianism*. Harcourt, 1994.

Baggio, Fabio. "Fronteras nacionales, internalizadas y externalizadas." *Migraciones y fronteras: Nuevos contornos para la movilidad internacional*, edited by María Eugenia Anguiano Téllez and Ana María López Sala, Icaria-CIDOB, 2010, pp. 49–73.

Berman, Russell. "85 Immigrants Sentenced Together Before One Judge." *The Atlantic*, 19 June 2018, https://www.theatlantic.com/politics /archive/2018/06/zero-tolerance-inside-a-south-texas-courtroom/563135/.

Bolaki, Stella. *Unsettling the Bildungsroman: Reading Contemporary Ethnic American Women's Fiction*. Rodopi, 2011.

Bonello, Deborah, and Erin Siegal McIntyre. "Is Rape the Price to Pay for Migrant Women Chasing the American Dream?" *Splinter*, 10 Sept. 2014, https://splinternews.com/is-rape-the-price-to-pay-for-migrant -women-chasing-the-1793842446.

Bracken, Rachel Conrad. "Borderland Biopolitics: Public Health and Border Enforcement in Early Twentieth-Century Latinx Fiction." *English Language Notes*, vol. 56, no. 2, 2018, pp. 28–43. *Duke UP*, https://doi .org/10.1215/00138282-6960702.

Butler, Judith. *Frames of War: When Is Life Grievable?* Verso, 2016.

Cabrera, Patricia. "Dialogismo y carnavalización en la primera novela chicana." *The Americas Review*, vol. 22, nos. 1–2, 1994, pp. 168–78.

Cacho, Lisa Marie. *Social Death: Racialized Rightlessness and the Criminalization of the Unprotected*. New York UP, 2012.

Chamberlain, Daniel F. "The Mexican *Corrido*: Identity Configurations, Time, and Truth Claims." *Latin American Narratives and Cultural Identity*, edited by Irene Maria F. Blayer and Mark Cronlund Anderson, Peter Lang Publishing, 2004, pp. 28–38.

Cisneros, Josue David. *The Border Crossed Us: Rhetorics of Borders, Citizenship, and Latina/o Identity*. ProQuest Ebook, U of Alabama P, 2014.

Curry, Richard. "The Migration Genre in *La jaula de oro*: Voids and Virtues." *Studies in Latin American Popular Culture*, vol. 36, 2018, pp. 47–68.

Dickerson, Caitlin, and Todd Heisler. "The Youngest Child Separated from His Family at the Border Was 4 Months Old." *The New York Times*, 16 June 2019, https://www.nytimes.com/2019/06/16/us/baby-constantine-romania -migrants.html.

Dublin, Thomas. *Women at Work: The Transformation of Work and Community in Lowell, Massachusetts, 1826–1860*. E-book, Columbia UP, 1993.

Fallon, Paul. "Staging a Protest: Fiction, Experience and the Narrator's Shifting Position in *Las aventuras de don Chipote o Cuando los pericos mamen*." *Confluencia*, vol. 23, no. 1, 2007, pp. 115–27.

Fetters, Ashley. "Children Cannot Parent Other Children." *The Atlantic*, 24 June 2019, https://www.theatlantic.com/family/archive/2019/06 /immigrant-children-border-parentification/592393/.

Feu López, María Montserrat. "The U.S. Hispanic Flapper: *Pelonas* and *Flapperismo* in U.S. Spanish-Language Newspapers, 1920–1929." *Studies in American Humor*, vol. 1, no. 2, 2015, pp. 192–217. *Scholarly Publishing Collective*, https://doi.org/10.5325/studamerhumor .1.2.0192.

Franco, Jean. *Cruel Modernity*. Duke UP, 2013.

Franco Aguilar, Enrique. "Jaula de oro." *Jaula de oro*, performed by Los Tigres del Norte, Fonovisa, 1984.

García Bochenek, Michael. "In the Freezer: Abusive Conditions for Women and Children in US Immigration Holding Cells." *Human Rights Watch*, 28 Feb. 2018, https://www.hrw.org/report/2018/02/28/freezer /abusive-conditions-women-and-children-us-immigration-holding-cells.

Gramlich, John. "Far More Immigration Cases Are Being Prosecuted Criminally under Trump Administration." *PEW Research Center*, 27 Sept. 2019, https://www.pewresearch.org/fact-tank/2019/09/27/far-more -immigration-cases-are-being-prosecuted-criminally-under-trump -administration/. Accessed 28 May 2020.

Gruesz, Kirsten Silva. "The Errant Latino: Irisarri, Central Americanness, and Migration's Intention." *The Latino Nineteenth Century*, edited by Rodrigo Lazo and Jesse Alemán, New York UP, 2016, pp. 20–48.

Hernández, Kelly Lytle. *City of Inmates: Conquest, Rebellion, and the Rise of Human Caging in Los Angeles, 1771–1965*. U of North Carolina P, 2017.

– "How Crossing the U.S.-Mexico Border Became a Crime." *Conversation*, 30 April 2017, https://theconversation.com/how-crossing-the-us -mexico-border-became-a-crime-74604.

– *Migra! A History of the U.S. Border Control*. U of California P, 2010.

Hernández, Roberto D. *Coloniality of the U-S Mexico Border: Power, Violence, and the Decolonial Imperative*. U of Arizona P, 2018.

Hing, Julianne. "For Trump, Cruelty Is the Point." *The Nation*, 15 March 2018, https://www.thenation.com/article/archive/for-trump-cruelty-is-the -point/.

La jaula de oro. Directed by Diego Quemada-Diez, Animal de Luz Films, Kinemascope Films, and Machete Producciones, 2013.

Jordan, Miriam, and Ron Nixon. "Trump Administration Threatens Jail and Separating Children from Parents for Those Who Illegally Cross Southwest Border." *The New York Times*, 7 May 2018, https://www.nytimes.com /2018/05/07/us/politics/homeland-security-prosecute-undocumented -immigrants.html.

Kanellos, Nicolás. Introduction. *The Adventures of Don Chipote; or, When Parrots Breastfeed*, by Daniel Venegas, Arte Público, 2000, pp. 1–17.

Kassie, Emily. "Detained: How the US Built the World's Largest Immigrant Detention System." *The Guardian*, 24 Sept. 2019, https://www.theguardian .com/us-news/2019/sep/24/detained-us-largest-immigrant-detention -trump.

Kitch, Carolyn. *The Girl on the Magazine Cover: The Origins of Visual Stereotypes in American Mass Media*. ProQuest Ebook, U of North Carolina P, 2001.

Kopelson, Heather Miyano. *Faithful Bodies: Performing Religion and Race in the Puritan Atlantic*. ProQuest Ebook, New York UP, 2014.

Leduc, Julia. "Tragedia en el Bravo evidencia viacrucis que viven migrantes."
    La Jornada, 25 June 2019, https://www.jornada.com.mx/2019/06/25
    /politica/003n1pol.

López, Marissa K. *Chicano Nations: The Hemispheric Origins of Mexican American
    Literature*. New York UP, 2011.

Lowe, Lisa. *Immigrant Acts: On Asian American Cultural Politics*. Duke UP, 2007.

Mexal, Stephen J. "The Logic of Liberalism: Lorenzo de Zavala's Transcultural
    Politics." *MELUS*, vol. 32, no. 2, 2007, pp. 79–106.

Molina, Natalia. "The Power of Racial Scripts: What the History of Mexican
    Immigration to the United States Teaches Us about Relational Notions of
    Race." *Latino Studies*, vol. 8, no. 2, 2010, pp. 156–75.

Ngai, Mae. *Impossible Subjects: Illegal Aliens and the Making of Modern America*.
    E-book, Princeton UP, 2004.

"One of the Deadliest Places on the Southwest Border: Crossing the Border
    Newsletter." *The New York Times*, 18 Apr. 2019, https://www.nytimes.
    com/2019/04/18/us/mexico-border-deaths.html.

Paredes, Américo. *"With His Pistol in His Hand": A Border Ballad and Its Hero*.
    U of Texas P, 1971.

Patterson, Orlando. *Slavery and Social Death: A Comparative Study*. Harvard UP,
    1982.

Paz, Octavio. *El laberinto de la soledad*. 1950. Fondo de Cultura Económica,
    1967.

Phillips, Amber. "'They're Rapists.' President Trump's Campaign Launch
    Speech Two Years Later, Annotated." *The Washington Post*, 16 June 2017,
    https://www.washingtonpost.com/news/the-fix/wp/2017/06/16/theyre
    -rapists-presidents-trump-campaign-launch-speech-two-years-later
    -annotated/.

Pinzón, Claudia. "El presente de la basura en la Ciudad del Futuro."
    Nómada, 14 Jan. 2016, https://nomada.gt/cotidianidad/el-presente
    -de-la-basura-en-la-ciudad-del-futuro/.

Pratt, Mary Louise. *Imperial Eyes: Travel Writing and Transculturation*. 2nd ed.,
    Routledge, 2008.

– "In the Neocolony: Destiny, Destination, and the Traffic in Meaning."
    Coloniality at Large: Latin America and the Postcolonial Debate, edited by Mabel
    Moraña, Enrique Dussel, and Carlos A. Jáuregui, Duke UP, 2008, pp. 459–75.

Pugibet, Veronique. "Cine mexicano y migración: Los pasos perdidos en *La
    Jaula del oro* [sic] de Quemada-Díez [sic]." *Comunicación y Medios*, no. 36,
    2017, pp. 20–32.

Quemada-Diez, Diego. "A Conversation with Film Director Diego Quemada
    -Díez [sic]." Interview by Douglas Valentine. *CounterPunch*, 19 Dec. 2014,
    https://www.counterpunch.org/2014/12/19/a-conversation-with-film
    -director-diego-quemada-diez/.

– "Extended Interview with Director Diego Quemada Diéz [sic] on *La Jaula de Oro* and Migration to the U.S." Interview by Amy Goodman and Juan González. *Democracy Now!*, 15 Sept. 2015, https://www.democracynow .org/2015/9/15/la_jaula_de_oro_new_feature.

– "Q &A with Diego Quemada-Diez." *Americas Quarterly*, 29 Jul. 2014, https://youtu.be/hbsxRm4jZc4. Accessed 15 Nov. 2019.

Quijano, Anibal. "Coloniality of Power, Eurocentrism, and Latin America." *Nepantla: Views from the South* vol. 1, no. 3, 2000, pp. 533–80.

Ragland, Cathy. *Música Norteña: Mexican Migrants Creating a Nation between Nations*. Temple UP, 2009.

Reeves, Benjamin. "The Humanitarian Crisis in Guatemala City's Immense Garbage Dump." *Vice*, 25 March 2014, https://www.vice.com/en_us /article/vdpbxm/the-basurero-is-burning-life-at-the-gates-of-hell -in-guatemala-city.

Rosagel, Shaila. "Muerte, trata, violación … el drama de migrantes en México es peor que el de Europa: ONGs." *Resumen Latinoamericano*, 9 Sept. 2015, https://www.resumenlatinoamericano.org/2015/09/09/muerte-trata -violacion-el-drama-de-migrantes-en-mexico-es-peor-que-el-de-europa-ongs/.

Saavedra Luna, Isis. "Imágenes de la violencia en la frontera norte de México a través del cine contemporáneo: Sangre, exclusión y muerte en una tierra sin ley." *Image et Violence*, Les Cahiers du Grimh, 2016, pp. 285–93.

Said, Edward. *Orientalism*. Routledge, 1978.

Sagert, Kelly Boyer. *Flappers: A Guide to an American Subculture*. Greenwood P, 2010.

Serwer, Adam. "The Cruelty Is the Point." *The Atlantic*, 3 Oct. 2018, https://www.theatlantic.com/ideas/archive/2018/10/the-cruelty -is-the-point/572104/.

Stern, Alexandra Minna. *Eugenic Nation: Faults and Frontiers of Better Breeding in Modern America*. U of California P, 2005.

Stock, Inka, Aysen Üstübici, and Susanne U. Schultz, "Externalization at Work: Responses to Migration Policies from the Global South." *Comparative Migration Studies*, vol. 7, no. 48, 2019, pp. 1–9. *SpringerOpen*, https://doi .org/10.1186/s40878-019-0157-z.

"Stopping Migrant Deaths." *National Network for Immigrant and Refugee Rights*, https://nnirr.org/programs/seeking-border-justice/stopping-migrant -deaths/. Accessed 15 July 2020.

Torre-Cantalapiedra, Eduardo, and José Carlos Yee-Quintero. "México ¿una frontera vertical? Políticas de control del tránsito migratorio irregular y sus resultados, 2007–2016." *LiminaR: Estudios Sociales y Humanísticos*, vol.16, 2018, pp. 87–104.

Urquijo-Ruiz, Rita E. "Estudio onamástico de los personajes en *Las aventuras de don Chipote o Cuando los pericos mamen*." *Nerter*, vol. 5–6, 2003, pp. 64–7.

206   Cara Anne Kinnally

– *Wild Tongues: Transnational Mexican Popular Culture*. U of Texas P, 2012.
Venegas, Daniel. *The Adventures of Don Chipote; or, When Parrots Breastfeed*. Translated by Ethriam Cash Brammer, edited by Nicolás Kanellos, Arte Público, 2000.
– *Las aventuras de don Chipote, o Cuando los pericos mamen*. Edited by Nicolás Kanellos, Arte Público, 1999.
Ventura, Abida. "The Real Cost of Mexico's Violent Revolution." *El Universal*, 22 Nov. 2016, https://www.eluniversal.com.mx/articulo/english /2016/11/22/real-cost-mexicos-violent-revolution.
Zavala, Lorenzo de. *Journey to the United States of North America / Viaje a los Estados Unidos del Norte de América*. Translated by Wallace Woolsey, Arte Público, 2005.
– *Viage a los Estados-Unidos del Norte de América*. Decourchant, 1834. *Sabin Americana, 1500–1926*.

5 On Bad Education and Growing Flowers: Colonial/Imperial Legacies in Arturo Pérez-Reverte, Pedro Almodóvar, and Manolo Caro

ALEJANDRO MEJÍAS-LÓPEZ

Previous chapters have explored ways in which colonial legacies persist in contemporary Mexico, both within and across its porous and often deadly national borders. They have examined how these legacies are engaged, reproduced, and contested, but nonetheless remembered, in a variety of forms ranging from literary fiction and travel narratives to photography, film, and social media. In this chapter I will look at how those legacies are manifested in the relationship between Mexico and Spain in the twenty-first century. Doing so brings up the question of why we should talk about the legacies of colonialism in this context, when decades of postcolonial studies have shown how irrelevant Spain is to the study of Mexico since the nineteenth century. Despite justified criticism of recent Spanish companies and investment operations in Mexico (partially the result of the dynamics explored in this chapter), historically the economic and political flows between both countries are hardly those generally associated with postcolonialism. Even less so are migratory patterns: over the last two centuries many more Spaniards have migrated to Mexico for economic and political reasons than the other way round (Rodríguez Fariñas et al.). And still there is no doubt that the memory of centuries of historical colonialism remains alive.

Two recent and seemingly unrelated examples can serve to introduce how colonial/imperial legacies are indeed continuing to be at work. In December 2018, Alfonso Cuarón's film *Roma* was released in Spain. The movie was filmed in Spanish and Mixtec, but Netflix-Spain released it with subtitles, "translating" so-called Mexican Spanish into Castilian Spanish. Cuarón complained that it was "parochial, ignorant and offensive to Spaniards themselves ... Something I enjoy most is the color and texture of accents ... It's as if Almodóvar needs to be subtitled" (Marshall); others, including Mexican writers Benito Taibó and Jordi Soler, saw it as another example of Spanish colonialism (Marshall). Only a few months later, on 6 March 2019, Santiago Abascal, leader of the Spanish far-right political party Vox, tweeted a picture of himself dressed as Hernán Cortés in preparation for the national elections that would indeed bring his party an important number of seats in the Spanish parliament (Vox).[1] Theatrics aside, I would argue that Abascal's discourse on Cortés is not radically different from the discourse of most mainstream political parties and, indeed, most of Spanish society.

Netflix's Spanish-to-Spanish subtitles and Vox's appeal to the conquest of Mexico are examples of the ways in which colonial/imperial legacies are still active in Spain, although operating differently than they do in Mexico. Their different approaches to historical memory collide from time to time, as they recently did over the commemoration of the fall of Tenochtitlan, causing a diplomatic tension that makes clearly visible Spain's state of what Paul Gilroy calls "postcolonial melancholia," a seeming incapacity to deal constructively with the loss of empire. This persistent Spanish melancholia manifests mainly in the form of imperial nostalgia that reads any historical narrative and any view of the Spanish language that do not have Spain at their centre as an attack on Spain's sense of national self. Dating back to the nineteenth century, imperial nostalgia grew and fuelled the emergence of Spanish fascism in the twentieth century. Embedded in institutions and promoted through the educational system, colonial/imperial legacies became complexly intertwined with Francoism and were assumed, unchallenged, by democratic Spain. As we will see in this chapter, there is also an anxiety in contemporary Spanish cultural discourse over being displaced by Mexican cultural capital, which leads to constant attempts to appropriate and transform it into *Spanish* cultural capital ("españolización"), a process that is seemingly never ending.[2]

---

1   As part of Vox's first election campaign in 2014, Abascal had already used Hernán Cortés in a rather anti-democratic tweet: "Hernán Cortés: 'No pelea el número sino el ánimo. No vencen los muchos sino los valientes.' Así que ¡ánimo valientes!" ("Hernán Cortés: it is not numbers but courage that fights. Not the many, but the brave, win; go, you brave!") #LosValientesVotanVox. @Santi_ABASCAL. Unless otherwise noted, all translations are my own.

2   The anxiety over authority and the appropriation of Mexican and Latin American culture by Spanish writers and cultural producers has a long history that goes back at least to *modernismo*. See Mejías-López, *The Inverted Conquest*. These transatlantic anxieties over authority have long been shaping the field of Hispanic Studies. See Mejías-López's "Hispanic Studies."

This chapter will explore how colonial/imperial legacies are manifested and contested in contemporary cultural discourse in both Spain and Mexico through a reading of literary, filmic, and television works by three globally renowned creators. First, I will briefly expand on the relationship between the legacies of colonialism and imperialism and the legacies of Francoism in democratic Spain. I will then analyse how these legacies are at work in two high-profile Spanish cultural producers at opposite sides of the ideological spectrum: bestseller novelist Arturo Pérez-Reverte and internationally acclaimed auteur Pedro Almodóvar. Finally, I will focus my analysis on Mexican filmmaker Manolo Caro and on what I argue is his opposite approach to colonial legacies and historical memory in his globally successful Netflix series *The House of Flowers* (*La casa de las flores*, 2018–20). Caro offers a critique of colonial/imperial legacies by queering both Mexican and Spanish histories, calling out the Spanish transition's failed memory politics and its legacy in cultural producers like Pedro Almodóvar, with whom Caro has been repeatedly compared.

The Francoist Legacy of Hispanidad

The March 2019 diplomatic tension that resulted from President López Obrador's letter to the king of Spain regarding the crimes committed during the conquest of Mexico serves to illustrate the collision of two profoundly different ways of dealing with the past. In Mexico, on the one hand, the letter provoked an array of diverse reactions and responses, ranging from politicians to social media; in Spain, on the other hand, most voices from the political, media, academic, and cultural establishments reacted with a rather unusual level of agreement based on a common understanding of history. In other words, while in Mexico the meaning and legacy of both the conquest and the colonization have been discussed, argued over, and reckoned with in myriad ways for over two centuries – and, as shown in previous chapters of this book, continues to be – the dominant historical narrative in Spain has remained virtually unchanged, with colonial/imperial legacies being left largely unacknowledged. However, in moments like 2019 this difference becomes plainly obvious and Spanish melancholia is clearly manifest, because there was not only almost universal agreement on a negative answer to the letter but also a general sense of being attacked, offended, and insulted, which generated belligerent, almost violent responses in Spanish political and cultural discourse. Albert Rivera, a centre-right politician, called it "an intolerable offence to the Spanish people," while conservative leader Pablo Casado considered it an "affront to Spain" that should not be permitted (Saiz). A tweet by writer Arturo Pérez-Reverte went viral and made international headlines: "Que se disculpe él que tiene apellidos españoles y vive allí. Si este individuo se cree lo que dice, es un imbécil. Si no se lo cree, es un sinvergüenza." ("Que se disculpe él").[3] The visceral, aggressive tone and insulting remarks to the president, the lack of any argument, and the contradictory reference to Spanish last names are signs of a condescending attitude that can barely hide the fear of confronting a different version of history. The imposition of one historical narrative over all others is what the polemic came to be about, one based on the seemingly unquestionable beliefs encapsulated in the term *Hispanidad*. The official response of the Spanish socialist government, if more measured, was no less based on the same core beliefs, albeit couched in the language of fraternity: "La llegada, hace quinientos años, de *los españoles a las actuales tierras mexicanas* no puede juzgarse a la luz de consideraciones contemporáneas. Nuestros *pueblos hermanos* han sabido siempre *leer nuestro pasado compartido* sin ira y con una perspectiva constructiva, como pueblos libres con una *herencia común y una proyección extraordinaria*" (Gobierno de España; emphasis added).[4] The alleged "common" reading of history is belied by the very act of having to write the communiqué and reimpose a Spanish reading. That the conquest had been denounced already in the sixteenth century is entirely ignored, allowing any judgment to be framed as "contemporary" (i.e., anachronistic). Indeed, the dominant view among politicians, intellectuals, and mainstream and social media was that the Mexican president's letter was based on a "falsification of history" (Rivera, quoted in Saiz).[5] Soon history lessons filled the Spanish media, which published and aired interviews, debates, and articles featuring professors and academics charged with "explaining" the conquest of Mexico and particularly the historical figure of Hernán Cortés. By and large, most of these voices repeated, to different degrees, similar

---

3   "He should be the one apologizing since he has Spanish last names and lives there. If this individual believes what he says, he is an imbecile. If not, he is a scoundrel."

4   "The arrival, 500 years ago, of Spaniards to the lands of present-day Mexico cannot be judged by current considerations. Our brotherly countries have always known how to read our shared past without anger and with a constructive perspective, as free peoples with a common inheritance and an extraordinary projection."

5   The only dissonant political voice in Spain came from the far-left party *Podemos*, whose speaker tweeted her support of AMLO's request.

arguments.[6] The history lesson to the Spanish public seemed a notable push to shore up any possible cracks in the wall of postcolonial melancholia that the letter was perhaps feared to have opened. Such scholarly consensus paralleled the political one, being a product of an education in which Hispanidad held, and still holds, a central place.

After the Spanish Civil War an entire social, economic, political, and cultural structure was developed by the Franco regime to support and perpetuate Hispanidad and thoroughly integrate it into national consciousness via the educational system: from elementary schools to universities and research centres, such as the Consejo Superior de Investigaciones Científicas, and scholarly journals such as *Cuadernos hispanoamericanos*, born in 1948 as a response to Mexico's *Cuadernos americanos*.[7] In fact, Mexico posed a major challenge to Franco's well-crafted neo-imperial imaginary. Mexico's welcoming of Republican exiles, support for the legitimate Republican government, and its unwavering and unbroken refusal to recognize the legitimacy of the Franco regime were forever a thorn in the side of the dictatorship's projection of a unified brotherhood of nations under the leadership of Spain.[8] The democratic transition of the 1970s and 1980s did little to dismantle the solid structure of Hispanidad, and indeed Spain has kept 12 October as its national day. The continuity in attitude, policies, and discourse about Latin America between the Franco regime and subsequent democratic governments has long been well established.[9] Hispanidad, the concept that unifies those continuities, remains profoundly entrenched both in long-standing institutions such as the

6 See, for instance, the series of interviews published by Barcelona's *La vanguardia* ("Hernán Cortés: ¿héroe o genocida?"), *El Cultural* (Díaz de Quijano, "Una reclamación 'absurda' y 'populista'"), and RNE ("Futuro abierto: Hernán Cortés").

7 See Marcilhacy on the institutionalization of Hispanidad in the Franco regime.

8 Hispanism also has a long history in Mexico, although there it was largely a conservative discourse that soon lost ground to liberalism; after the revolution, however, Hispanism was still fuelling both the opposition to *indigenismo* and the unofficial support of Francoism in conservative sectors of Mexican society. See Mora Muro, "En defensa"; Pérez Montfort; Pérez Viejo, *España en el debate*; Sánchez Prado, *Naciones intelectuales*; Sola Ayape, "Al rescate de Franco"; and Urías Horcasitas, "Una pasión antirrevolucionaria." For Hispanism in Latin America, see Moraña, *Ideologies of Hispanism*.

9 See for instance the pioneering studies by Escudero ("Hispanist Democratic Thought") and Pérez de Mendiola ("Universal Exposition"). On broader continuities between dictatorship and democracy regarding national identity, see Aguilar and Humlebaek, "Collective Memory."

Royal Spanish Academy (RAE) or the Royal Academy of History and in newly refurbished and face-lifted versions of Francoist institutions, such as the Instituto Cervantes (IC) and the Agencia Española de Cooperación Internacional para el Desarrollo (AECID), present-day adaptations of the regime's Consejo de la Hispanidad (1940–3) and Instituto de Cultura Hispánica (1943–77), respectively.[10] The long-standing RAE and the IC are well-studied powerful institutions of control and policing of Hispanidad and its glottopolitics, and both are ridden with anxiety to keep Spain's authority over language and culture.[11] The RAE is likely the most pervasive because of its long history as a mechanism of control and policing of language normativity. By the time of Mexican independence any utterance and any scholarly reflection on the rules of the Spanish language were inevitably a citation (in both the Derridean and the Butlerian sense) of that normative discourse in a new context. The naturalization of linguistic norms, coded and recoded over centuries, much like gender norms responding to specific political and ideological contexts, was so successful that they became accepted as "natural." The existence of the RAE only served to confirm it and to police any type of deviance from the norm. If the recent *Diccionario de Americanismos* proves anything, it is precisely the non-marked Castilian nature of the normative *Diccionario de la Real Academia Española* (*DRAE*).[12] The IC, created in 1991 and connected to Spain's planned international projection of the 1992 celebrations, has extended globally the same logic of the RAE and expanded its purview to "Hispanic culture" so that, though only a Spanish institution, it promotes the "patrimonio lingüístico y cultural que es común a los países y pueblos de la

---

10 Franco's Instituto de Cultura Hispánica (ICH) was split into two main bodies: the Instituto Cervantes for language and culture and the AECID for economic development. Those changes made obvious both the continuities between the dictatorship and the democracy and the political and economic drive behind the concept of Hispanidad.

11 José del Valle, a leading scholar on the glotopolitics of Spanish, defines glotopolitics and linguistic ideologies as "sistemas de ideas que articulan nociones del lenguaje, las lenguas, el habla y/o la comunicación con formaciones culturales, políticas y/o sociales específicas" ("Glotopolítica" 39; "systems of ideas that articulate notions of language, languages, speech and/or communication with specific cultural, political and/or social formations") This system is characterized by its specific context, its naturalizing function, and its institutionalization ("Glotopolítica"41).

12 See, for instance, Lope Blanch, "Americanismo," whose argument goes further, calling into question what constitutes a variant and pointing out the inconsistencies behind the RAE's politics of naming.

comunidad hispanohablante" ("La institución") through cultural centres and language schools worldwide.[13]

Domestically, education has also been an effective method of transmission of Hispanidad so that its ossified historical narrative of empire has persisted through regimes and governments, despite an increasing demand for revisions. As Mario Carretero et al. explain, "Spanish textbooks transmit the discoverers as the 'good guys' ... The picture that Spanish textbooks offer agrees with the image of Spain as a great empire where the sun never sets. [And] reinforces the idea of being proud of their past in Spanish students" (662). According to historian Henry Kamen, "la manera de enseñar la historia en la época de Franco no ha cambiado en absoluto, en nada, hasta hoy en día" (Guerrero).[14] What stands out is that, unlike many other legacies of the Franco regime, imperial/colonial legacies have hardly been the subject of any serious public national debate, nor have they been a significant part of the recent effort to address historical memory in Spain, largely centred on the catastrophe of the civil war, the dictatorship's repression, and the political compromises made by the Spanish transition. Hispanidad, which sustained a large part of Francoism, has remained a blind spot, no doubt because, as Pérez Viejo stated regarding the reactions to AMLO's letter, "nadie se disculpa por aquello de lo que se siente orgulloso" ("México-España").[15]

The strong association of Hispanidad with the Franco regime, however, places democratic discourse, particularly that of the political left, in an uneasy situation, having to navigate at times a fine line between its own unquestioned belief in the basic tenets of Hispanidad and the avoidance of expressing them in a language that might evoke Francoism. Most often, the different ministries of education and culture in democratic Spain opted for softening the harshest imperial rhetoric of the regime, while leaving the basic tenets of Hispanidad untouched. In this sense, there are similarities between the teaching of Spanish imperialism, the civil war, and the dictatorship as identified in recent

---

13 "Linguistic and cultural patrimony common to the countries and peoples of the Spanish-speaking community." On the RAE and the IC, see del Valle, *A Political History of Spanish* and "Glotopolítica"; Fernández Mauro, "De la lengua del mestizaje"; Moreno Cabrera, "'Unifica, limpia y fija'"; and Mar-Molinero, "The European Linguistic Legacy."
14 "The way history was taught during the Franco regime has not changed at all until today."
15 "No one apologizes for that of which they are proud."

work by education scholars in Spain. As Raimundo Rodríguez Pérez explains, Spanish textbooks tiptoe through the "painful" parts of Spanish history: "[el alumno] verá [la conquista] de puntillas, y además de una forma en la cual se eviten los aspectos más salvajes, de barbarie o de agresión … Pasa con otras épocas de la historia de España que son polémicas, por ejemplo, la Guerra Civil, el Franquismo, la Transición … Eso se pasa de puntillas o ni se menciona en los libros. Las editoriales en España tratan de evitar las cuestiones polémicas" (Gozzer).[16] Because the core of Hispanidad has remained alive and well in democratic political discourse, the basic storyline of the Spanish imperial past has lingered in an educational system and publishing industry that is in a state of postcolonial melancholia, creating a thread that binds together the Spanish Empire, Francoism, and the Transition, even when that tie remains symptomatic rather than addressed. This is also the case in contemporary Spanish cultural production, of which two otherwise very different figures, Pérez-Reverte and Almodóvar, are paradigmatic examples.

An Imperial Education in Arturo Pérez-Reverte's *Ojos azules* and *La reina del sur*

A bestselling novelist and brashly outspoken member of the Royal Academy of the Spanish Language, Arturo Pérez-Reverte is, without a doubt, an odd man out in the Spanish literary field. It could be argued that no other Spanish writer has managed so successfully to join the lowbrow and the highbrow, to become a public intellectual claiming authority, as he so often does, over language, culture, history, and politics, while writing popular fiction. No other writer of bestsellers has ever become a member of the RAE. As we will see, however, it was precisely after his bestsellers had turned into a didactic machine for the defence of empire and its imperial language that the RAE became interested in counting him in its ranks.

In the late 1990s Pérez-Reverte decided to embark on a new literary project as a "corrective" to what he saw as a school curriculum that was afraid to properly teach about Imperial Spain; it comprised a

---

16 "[The student] goes over [the conquest] on tiptoes and avoiding the most savage, barbaric, aggressive moments. The same happens with other periods of Spanish history that are polemical, like the civil war, Francoism, the Transition. Those are covered on tiptoes or not even mentioned in textbooks. Spanish publishers try to avoid polemical issues." See also Rodríguez Pérez et al., "Construcción."

series of historical thrillers set in the seventeenth century with a soldier as protagonist, the now famous Captain Alatriste. Education and politics go hand in hand, and for Pérez-Reverte, educating Spanish children on empire is a necessary act of memory politics: "Muchos jóvenes españoles conocen mejor la historia de Estados Unidos que la de su país, porque una gran parte de nuestra memoria ha sido sometida a un proceso de negación, y eso nos condena a ser huérfanos sin pasado" (M. Mora).[17] His project is presented as fighting against the "tiptoeing" of textbooks that "have denied" Spanish children their imperial history. He takes upon himself the task of "recuperar sin alharacas un siglo que no es ni tan abyecto como se dice ahora ni tan maravilloso como se decía durante el franquismo."[18] As is increasingly the case in Spanish political discourse, however, Pérez-Reverte's "middle ground" or equidistance is code for a defence of the Francoist version of imperial/colonial history, in which brave and honourable men (and in Pérez-Reverte's novels they are always very "masculine" men) are the true agents of empire, whose greatness is unfortunately hindered by an elite of corrupt and weak politicians, tax collectors, and administrators that (Pérez-Reverte does not hide) are stands-in for present-day politicians. In his populist refurbishing of Francoist imperial history for mass consumption the conquest of Mexico also found a place, as it could not be otherwise, and was imagined by Pérez-Reverte in true imperial fashion in the story *Ojos azules* as a submissive yet rebellious woman who is seduced and impregnated by Spanish masculine power, engendering a mestizo who is always already Spanish.

Published in 2000, *Ojos azules* takes place in Mexico during the so-called *noche triste* when Cortés and his men were driven out of Tenochtitlan by

---

17 "Many young Spaniards know better the history of the United States than of their own country because a large part of our memory has been subjected to a process of negation, and that leaves us orphans of our past." Pérez-Reverte uses another trope of Hispanidad: learning about the Spanish Empire is a necessary part of an imagined imperial rivalry with anglophone culture. Pérez-Reverte has used this trope explicitly in relation to the conquest and colonization of Mexico: "Pero, aun así, sin pretenderlo, preñando a las indias y casándose con ellas –en lugar de exterminarlas, como en el norte harían los anglosajones –, bautizando a sus hijos y haciéndolos suyos." ("Una historia"; "But, even thus, without wanting to, impregnating Indian women and marrying them – instead of exterminating them like the Anglos would do in the north – baptizing and accepting their children.")

18 "To recover without fanfare a century that was not as abject as they say now nor as wonderful as they said under Franco."

the Mexicas.[19] The story coincided with and complemented, I suggest, the fourth instalment of the Captain Alatriste series entitled *El oro del rey* (2000), an adventure involving a network of corruption connected to American gold. *Ojos azules* is narrated from the perspective of an anonymous Spanish soldier who is trying to make it out of Tenochtitlan alive, carrying a sack of gold. In his escape he remembers a Mexica woman who is pregnant with his child. The soldier is captured, and the story ends with his final thoughts as he is sacrificed, wondering if his unborn child will have his blue eyes. The soldier in the story will never know, of course, but the lingering question was answered outside of the fiction by Pérez-Reverte as he explained that the story was inspired by a blue-eyed child carried on the back of a faceless Mexica woman in Diego Rivera's mural *The Arrival of Hernán Cortés* in Mexico's National Palace. The rest of Rivera's painting (the branding, enslavement, torture, and hanging of the Mexicas, the economic transaction in which they are objects, and the forced conversion, etc.) are all ignored by Pérez-Reverte who chooses, instead, to single out the Spanish bicultural legacy metaphorized in the blue eyes of the baby. It is on that legacy – the Spanishness of the baby – that the story is built and finds its purpose and meaning.

As mentioned, *Ojos azules* should be read in dialogue with Pérez-Reverte's Captain Alatriste pedagogical project, not only because, as María Estela Reviriego rightly notes, in both cases he presents history from the point of view of downtrodden soldiers, but also, I argue, because both protagonists embody the values that Pérez-Reverte makes central to his portrayal and validation of imperial history: dominant heterosexual masculinity, sexual violence, and a traditional idea of bravery and honour. These values are often expressed in present-day Castilian slang that is meant to create complicity with the readers.[20] I will argue that it is this

---

19 The story was originally published in 2000 in a journal in Mexico (that I have been unable to identify) and included by Alfaguara in a collection of short stories in 2001. In 2009 it was published by Seix-Barrall in a special illustrated edition as a stand-alone book.

20 Gómez López-Quiñones has noted the story's "sobre-insistencia en una perspectiva extasiada por una violencia sublime, su negativa a cualquier tipo de distancia explicativa y una mirada cómplice con valores *dépassé*, propios del Antiguo Régimen (valentía, honor, arrojo, pundonor, firmeza), que en ningún lugar como en la guerra se plasman con tanta rotundidad" (125; over-insistence on an ecstatic perspective before a sublime violence, its refusal to offer any explanatory narrative distance, and a gaze that is complicit with outmoded values, those of the Ancient Regime [bravery, honour, daring, pride, firmness] that nowhere are more visible than at war). These values do not seem so "*dépassé*" in Pérez-Reverte's narrative and

combination, the way Pérez-Reverte crafts the story to portray the victimizer as *the* victim, as *the* underdog of history, that makes his text so problematic (and yet seemingly so admirable to the general Spanish public).

The protagonist of *Ojos azules* finds himself in a bind when he is unable to let go of a sack of gold that is weighing him down and hindering his escape. Employing a third-person narrator that brings the readers close to the protagonist as a sympathetic character, the story presents him not as a thief but as a survivor taking what is rightfully his ("El peso del oro lo reconfortaba. Había venido muy lejos a buscarlo, había peleado y sufrido y visto morir a muchos camaradas por ese oro"),[21] and as an everyday man, victim of a corrupt and "bloodsucking" elite ("ya no tendría que arar la tierra ingrata en la que había nacido, seca y maldita de Dios, tierra de caínes esquilmada por reyes, curas, señores, funcionarios, recaudadores de impuestos y alguaciles; por sanguijuelas que vivían del sudor ajeno").[22] Thus, the readers are led to see the protagonist as deserving of the gold that will justly bring him a better life ("Con aquel oro tendría para vivir bien y hacer una buena boda, para poseer su propia tierra y su propia casa. Para envejecer tranquilo, como un hidalgo, contándole a sus nietos cómo conquistó Tenochtitlan"),[23] and to agree that he does not owe anyone anything, because rather than being violently stolen from the Mexica, the gold was earned in the hardest way imaginable ("Para morir anciano y honrado sin deber nada a nadie porque hasta el último gramo de oro lo había ganado con su sangre, sus peligros, sus combates, su salud, y su miedo"; *Ojos azules* 9).[24] The faithful readers of the Captain Alatriste series and particularly of the recent *King's Gold* had been taught all too well where their

---

readership, and, I would argue, rather than being taken directly from the ancient regime, they are a recovery of Francoist values, often opposed to what Pérez-Reverte (and many in Spain today) often criticizes as "political correctness." Both Reviriego and Gómez López-Quiñones take the narration of violence in the story at face value and ultimately see the soldier as the victim of unspeakable violence and trauma.

21 "He found comfort in the weight of the gold. He had come from very far to look for it; he had fought and suffered and seen many friends die for that gold."

22 "He no longer would have to work the ungrateful land in which he had been born, dry and cursed by God, a land of Cains impoverished by kings, priests, lords, public servants, tax collectors, and guards, by leeches that lived off other people's sweat."

23 "That gold would allow him to live and to marry well, to own his own land and his own house, to grow old in peace and quiet, like a nobleman, telling his grandchildren how he conquered Tenochtitlan."

24 "To die old and honest without owing anything to anyone because he had earned every gram of that gold with his blood, his health, and his fear, in danger and in battles."

sympathies should lie. In the perverse logic of the story the Spanish soldiers are the true victims of both the bloodsucking Spanish elite and the bloodthirsty Mexica, who are simply depicted as an angry and violent mob, an undifferentiated mass of "mexicanos sedientos de venganza" (7, 11), "vociferantes" (10), "armados y feroces" (11), who take Spaniards to pyramids "donde los sacerdotes no daban abasto y la sangre corría en regueros espesos" (12).[25] It has been difficult, even for critics, not to be lured by a narration that wants us, needs us, to see the Spanish soldier as *the* victim of history. This affective manipulation of the readers makes clear that Pérez-Reverte is interested not in opening a reflection on the many layers of oppression and victimhood in the history of the conquest but rather in justifying the latter by creating empathy *only* with the Spaniards, turning them into "traumatized" victims.

Having first established empathy for the soldier, the narrative turns to the depiction of the Mexica woman, taking the readers to what is, by any standard, a rape scene. Once again without any distance, the narrator seems, in fact, to revel in the description of the rape and continued humiliation of the woman. Moreover, in classic patriarchal fashion, no sooner has the rape taken place than the narrative denies it ever happened, depicting her as willingly submitting to the protagonist's sexual prowess and returning to him time and time again, a depiction that also includes another imperial myth of the conquest: the woman believes the soldier to be a *teule*, a god:

> Solo era una de esas indias. Las había a cientos, y esta no tenía nada de particular. No era ni especialmente bonita ni especialmente nada … Se la había tirado como lo que era: una perra pagana. Se la había tirado disfrutándola, con rudeza. Sin embargo, ella le cobró afición al *teule* barbudo de ojos azules; volvió un día tras otro, y él repetía hembra entre las bromas groseras de sus compañeros. Qué le das, decían socarrones. Aquella mexicana se le quedaba mirando a los ojos y lo acariciaba hablando cosas extrañas en su lengua … Un día, ella le dio a entender que estaba preñada, y él se lo contó a los otros y todos se rieron mucho. Luego se la calzó por última vez antes de echarla a patadas, a ella y al bastardo pagano que llevaba en la tripa. (Pérez-Reverte, *Ojos azules* 10)[26]

---

25   "Mexicans thirsty for vengeance … screaming … armed and fierce … [pyramids] where the priests could not [kill] fast enough and the blood run in thick trails."

26   "She was just one of those Indians. There were hundreds of them and this one was nothing special. She was neither specially pretty nor specially anything … He had fucked her like the pagan bitch she was. He had fucked her, savouring her, with

Like the men, Mexica women are presented in generic, unindividualized terms: she is an "india" like all the others. Nothing in the narration wants to provoke horror in the reader, or empathy towards the victim. On the contrary, narrated in present-day Castilian masculinist sexual slang ("se la había tirado," "se la calzó"), the narrator emulates the "bromas groseras" of the soldiers as if aiming to form the same bond with the readers that the rape generates between the men in the story. At this point and rather out of the blue, the story moves to the terrain of romance when the protagonist, facing possible death in his escape, feels the woman's absence like "un hueco en el corazón" (10, 11, 13), missing her "piel sumisa," "el tono quedo de su voz," and the "mirada oscura" of a woman "inconquistable allá dentro" (11).[27] This rather sudden romantic turn comes to an end as the barbaric Mexicas triumphantly pull his heart from his body, leaving the readers with the man's last hope that his child has "ojos azules" (14).

The commercial and critical success of *Ojos azules*, with its re-edition in illustrated book form by Seix-Barral to great fanfare speaks volumes about the force that imperial nostalgia and masculinist imperial/colonial legacies still have in contemporary Spanish culture. As is often the case in Perez-Reverte's marketing machine, as if the message were not clear enough in the story, he repeats it through Twitter, interviews, and his weekly contributions to *El País*. The exculpation of a soldier who is the heroic agent of empire, his conversion into the "proper" victim of violence and trauma, and his enshrining as the heroic creator of an entirely new world were thus made explicit when Pérez-Reverte explained the connection to Rivera's mural: "Pensé lo bien que reflejaba Rivera el mestizaje y me plantee si sería capaz de hacerlo yo en una pincelada corta … Ese español, que ha ido a México a por el oro, pero *involuntariamente casi*, no se da cuenta de que ha creado un mundo nuevo, una raza nueva para lo bueno y para lo malo" (EFE).[28] In his apparent blindness

---

force. But she took to the blond and blue-eyed *teule*, returning day after day, and he repeated the same female among the vulgar jokes of his mates. What do you give her, they said mockingly. That Mexican woman would look into his eyes and caress him, saying strange things in her tongue … One day, she conveyed to him that she was pregnant, and he told the others and they all laughed. Then he banged her one last time before kicking her out, her and the pagan bastard that she carried in her belly."

27 "A hole in his heart,"… "submissive skin," "the quiet tone of her voice,"… "the dark gaze,"… "unconquerable inside."

28 "I thought that Rivera represented *mestizaje* very well and I wondered if I would be able to do it with a small brush stroke … That Spaniard who has travelled to Mexico for gold but almost involuntarily, he is not aware that he, for good and evil, has created a new world, a new race."

to the violence portrayed by Rivera and, ironically, in his own text, for Pérez-Reverte the rape is almost an involuntary act by a man who, like a Hegelian world-historical individual realizing the will of Spirit, is moving history forward and making the Spanish Empire the creator of the future, of a new world and a new race. Furthermore, Pérez-Reverte's insistence on linking his text to Diego Rivera is ultimately as perverse as is his short story. He uses Rivera as a source of authority seemingly only to compete with him "in a brush stroke," bettering him in a type of *paragone* between the arts and stripping him of that authority. By the end of *Ojos azules*, Pérez-Reverte has rewritten Rivera's mural, transforming it from a critique to an apology of empire and mestizaje. Connected to the image of the baby, now on the cover of mass-market and e-book editions, *Ojos azules* aims to erase for thousands of readers what is otherwise Rivera's scathing criticism of the conquest sitting in Mexico's National Palace. This is the final gesture of Pérez-Reverte's "masterly miniature" (Gimferrer), to "correct" the Mexican master and "Hispanicize" Mexican national history.

For the concept of Hispanidad to function as the sustaining category of Spanish post-imperial / postcolonial dynamics with Mexico, Spain must constantly be asserting its authority. Only two years after writing *Ojos azules*, Pérez-Reverte performed another type of correction and appropriation, this time on what was emerging in the world literary market as a Mexican literary genre: narcoliterature. In 2002 the Spanish novelist published *La reina del sur* (*The Queen of the South*, 2004), his first novel to have a woman as the protagonist, a Mexican mestiza who can be read as a present-day rewrite of both the anonymous Mexica woman of *Ojos azules* and her offspring by the Spanish soldier. In *La reina del sur*, Pérez-Reverte performs the same trick in several ways: character and plot, the appropriation of a Mexican genre, the gendered narrative frame, and the imposition of linguistic norm.

La reina del sur is the story of a Mexican woman, Teresa Mendoza, who works as a money changer in Sinaloa and must flee Mexico to avoid being killed by the cartel that killed her boyfriend, El Güero Davila, a blond, blue-eyed man, which, although he is Mexican, immediately recalls both the anonymous Spanish soldier of *Ojos azules and* his imagined son. Teresa seeks refuge in Spain, where eventually she falls in love with a Spanish man, becomes involved in drug trafficking, and ultimately succeeds as a *capo* known as "the queen of the south." The novel ends when Teresa, pregnant, returns to Mexico to testify against the Mexican drug lord Don Epifanio Vargas, before disappearing and becoming the stuff of legend. Her story is pieced together and imagined by a Spanish journalist-narrator who is meant to be Pérez-Reverte's alter ego.

If constructing a morally justified Spanish legacy was at the core of *Ojos azules*, it can be argued that Teresa Mendoza is the embodiment of that legacy, which is made explicit by the narrator ("era hija de padre español y madre mejicana [sic]"; ch. 1), and by Teresa herself ("mi papa era español"; ch. 5).[29] Teresa may be called *la mejicana* in the novel, but it is soon made clear that, as in the case of her distant sibling in *Ojos azules*, to be Mexican is to always already be Spanish. Therefore, Teresa is often surprised at how at home she feels in Spain, how familiar Spanish cities are to her:

[A]quellos techos altos, las estilizadas columnas, la penumbra y el silencio le recordaron a Teresa las iglesias mejicanas construidas por los conquistadores. Era singular, pensaba, cómo algunos viejos lugares de España le producían la certeza de *encontrarse con algo que ya estaba en ella. Como si la arquitectura, las costumbres, el ambiente justificasen muchas cosas que había creído propias solo de su tierra.* Yo estuve aquí, pensaba de pronto al doblar una esquina, en una calle o ante el pórtico de un caserón o una iglesia. Híjole. *Hay algo mío que anduvo por este rumbo y que explica parte de lo que soy.*[30] (312)

The novel makes this explicit so often that it could be said that, rather than escaping to Spain, Teresa seems to be coming home to Spain, where cultural authority is inscribed in the form of Teresa's re-education. As Gómez Lopez-Quiñones and Juan-Navarro have rightly pointed out, her move from Mexico to Spain is also depicted as a move from low culture to high culture, from barbarism to civilization. Teresa becomes a voracious reader and learns how to dress "properly" thanks to Pati, her Spanish friend, turned associate: "gracias a [Pati] Mendoza descubrió la utilidad de la instrucción ... le inspiró deseos de superarse, de

---

29 "She was the daughter of a Spanish father and a Mexican mother" (26); "my father was Spanish" (132).

30 "The high ceilings, stylized columns, shadowy interiors, and the silence reminded Teresa of Mexican churches built by the conquistadors. It was strange, she thought, how some old places in Spain *gave her the [certainty] that she was coming face to face with something [that was] already [inside] of her. As though the architecture, the customs, the feeling of place [justified] things she thought belonged only to her own land.* I've been here before, she would think as she turned a corner, or walked down a street, or stood before the portico of a mansion or a church. *Híjole. Something in me has been this way before, and it explains part of what I am.*" (ch. 10; translation amended and emphasis added)

cambiar. Leyó, estudió" (214).[31] However, if Pati is a civilizing force for Teresa, it is Teresa's knowledge of people and her skills with money that not only save her and Pati from being killed by the Russian mafia but also turn what is as an otherwise small risky business into a full-fledged drug-trafficking emporium. I would argue that this is so because, although *La reina del sur* is explicitly presented as a rewrite of Alexander Dumas's *The Count of Montecristo*, it is also a modern rewrite of a much older story, one already rewritten by Pérez-Reverte in *Ojos azules*. I would argue that, in its bare bones, the story of Teresa Mendoza is the story of Malinche: wronged by her Mexican people, Teresa ends up with the Spaniards, and her life begins to change when she meets Santiago Fisterra, whose name embodies Spanishness and whose green eyes are soon associated in Teresa's heart with the blue-eyed Güero Dávila.[32] As with Malinche, Spaniards "civilize" her but, in turn, benefit from her knowledge, her know-how with people, and her skills. And just as Malinche became Doña Marina, "Teresita" becomes Doña Teresa Mendoza in Spain. The story includes all the elements: her unique skills, her "betrayal" of her own people when she testifies against Don Epifanio, and her pregnancy by a Spanish man, here portrayed by two characters – the drug trafficker Santiago Fisterra, who dies escaping from the police, and Teo Aljarafe, a lawyer whom she meets when she is already on her way to becoming the queen and who will eventually betray her. And indeed, it is after seeing Teo for the first time that the narrative makes explicit the connection with Malinche: "Era esbelto, el pelo muy negro, peinado hacia atrás con fijador, largo y rizado en la nuca … La mandíbula pronunciada y la nariz grande, curva, le daban un interesante perfil de águila flaca. Un tipo con clase, pensó. Como aquellos españolazos que una imaginaba de antes, aristócratas e hidalgos y demás – por algo tuvo que apendejarse la Malinche, a fin de cuentas" (251–2).[33] Both the name Teo (God) and the eagle (empire) connect

---

31 "Thanks to [Patty], Mendoza discovered the usefulness of an education … it gave her the desire to better herself, to change. She read, studied" (ch. 7).

32 The name Santiago refers to the national patron saint of Spain, Santiago Matamoros, and his last name, Fisterra, to the idea of the Iberian Peninsula as the end of the world before Columbus's voyage.

33 "He was thin, with very black hair, slicked back and glistening, long and curly at the neck. He was wearing a dark suit, white shirt with no tie, shiny black shoes. The pronounced jaw and big curved nose gave him an interesting profile, like a skinny eagle. A guy with class, she thought. Like those super-Spaniard types one imagines from days gone by, aristocrats and hidalgos and all that – Malinche must have gone over to the other side for some reason" (ch. 8).

him to the myth of Cortés and so do Teresa's musings about Malinche. In this way, *La reina del sur*, written shortly after *Ojos azules*, functions as its continuation. Like the baby, Teresa is mestiza, daughter of an unknown Spanish man. Like the anonymous Mexica woman in that story, like Malinche, like Teresa's own mother, she once again carries the baby, the legacy, of a Spanish man in what seems to be an endless process of *españolización* of Mexico.

La reina del sur is ridden with anxiety and the need to affirm repeatedly the Spanishness of Mexico and Mexican culture. It can be argued that *La reina del sur* is an attempt to appropriate a Mexican literary genre, to steal the fire from what was in 2002 a narcofiction boom that, although first associated with Colombia, was becoming increasingly so with Mexico. As he did with Rivera, Pérez-Reverte does not hide his debts; he acknowledges them and makes them "Spanish." One of the genre's main and earliest authors, Elmer Mendoza, besides being honoured in Teresa Mendoza's name, appears as a character in the novel, a friend and "guide" of the narrator, "cuyas espléndidas novelas *Un asesino solitario* y *El amante de Janis Joplin* había leido para ponerme en situación. Fueron Elmer y Julio quienes major me orientaron por los vericuetos locales" (45).[34] But *La reina del sur* quickly moves characters, plot, and genre away from Mexico and to Spain in an attempt to "demexicanize/ delatinamericanize" narcoliterature and turn it into a Spanish genre for global consumption (with the help of Alfaguara's powerful editorial machinery displayed at its service).[35] Teresa Mendoza's story is a Spanish contemporary remake of well-known Mexican and Latin American myths (from Malinche to Doña Bárbara to Rosario Tijeras) that end up bringing them back "home" to Spain and on to the global market from there. The extent of Pérez-Reverte's success can be measured by the fact that not only was *La reina del sur* his first truly international bestseller, but the novel has also climbed to the top of the canon of narcoliterature and is even considered a "pioneer" text. Any discussion of narcoliterature is now bound to include Spain.[36]

---

34 "Whose splendid novels *A Lonely Murderer* and *The Lover of Janis Joplin* I'd read for background. It was Elmer and Julio who acted as my guides through that underworld and filled me in on all the local eccentricities" (ch. 2).

35 See García Alvite's and Juan-Navarro's opposite readings of transnationality in this novel, and Juan-Navarro and Gómez López-Quiñones on Alfaguara and the global market.

36 Bialowas Pobutsky, for instance, states without hesitation: "*La reina del sur* (2002) by Arturo Pérez-Reverte (Spain, 1951) is a pioneering contribution to the Latin American narconovel" (273). Although aware of the postcolonial problems that the novel

The framed narrative structure chosen by Pérez-Reverte functions in a similar way: Teresa's story is contained by the Spanish journalist-narrator, and it is only through his story that we have access to hers and, by extension, Mexico's. That this narrative frame is gendered is, of course, also crucial in a literary project dominated by a masculinist view of the conquest. Pérez-Reverte's use of this narrative device works similarly to what Muneeb Hafiz has called in a different context "imperial frame": "a way of substituting what is with another reality in the service of powerful (imperial) interests through the coming together of epistemic and coercive means ... The person we choose not to see or hear cannot exist or speak for themselves and, secondly, must be spoken for so that what they say makes sense in 'our' language(s)" (116–17). The entire discourse of Hispanidad is built on a refusal to see Mexico for "what is" and on the need to substitute it for "another reality," one whose full meaning can only be understood as part of Spain. Thus, the narrative's imperial-frame mediating voice also becomes a linguistic frame containing Teresa's Spanish. Pérez-Reverte explained how in the novel he moved his writing away from his usual "orthodox Spanish" and used instead a "mestiza" language that is full of "mejicanismos [sic], anglicismos, un español fronterizo, mestizo, popular" ("He escrito").[37] For the Spanish author and future member of the RAE, Mexicanisms are not, of course, part of Spanish; they are markers of difference that he incorporates into the larger "español mestizo" of the novel. This linguistic mestizaje is, like the biological one, described in gendered and sexualized terms: "tenía que saltar del narrador a ella sin que hubiera chirridos. Ha sido *gozoso, apasionante y agotador*, pero he visto que hay una parte negociable del idioma, una parte *brutal y muy expresiva*, que enriquece mucho esa otra parte *inviolable*. Ya se sabe que las razas mestizas producen las mujeres más hermosas" ("He escrito").[38] Casually deploying the language of sexual violence, Pérez-Reverte presents "real" Spanish (i.e., Castilian) as "inviolable,"

---

raises, Hugo Benavides dedicates a full chapter to *The Queen of the South* in his book *Drugs, Thugs, and Divas*. See also the recent collection *Crime Scenes*, edited by Lange and Peate, in which Pascale Baker dedicates the first chapter to *Rosario Tijeras* and *The Queen of the South*. Gómez López-Quiñones begins his excellent article by having to remind readers that, in fact, *La reina del sur* is *not* a novel about Mexico.

37   "Mexicanisms, Anglicisms, a border, mestizo, popular Spanish."

38   "I had to jump from the narrator to her without screaking. It has been a *pleasurable, passionate, and exhausting* experience. But I have seen that there is a part of the language that is negotiable, *a brutal and expressive part* that enriches that other *inviolable* part. It is well known that mestizo races produce the most beautiful women" (emphasis added).

pure, universal, and civilized, while Mexicanisms are, like Teresa before arriving in Spain, expressive but "brutal," barbaric, one might say. Nonetheless, however mestizo Pérez-Reverte claims his Spanish to be in the novel, it is Castilian Spanish that, like the masculine frame that imagines and contains Teresa, is imposed on a text in which, even when Mexican characters are speaking, the old-fashioned, and indeed anti-Mexican *j* spelling (as in *mejicana*) is used, rather than the Mexican preferred and truly universally used *x*. This might seem to be a minor detail but one known to have immediate political/imperialistic implications, and, in *La reina del sur* the Castilian devil is in the details.[39] In 2003, in the wake of the Captain Alatriste series and the success of *La reina del sur*, Arturo Pérez-Reverte was surprisingly nominated and accepted to the very elitist and conservative RAE and has since become one of its most vociferous defenders. Never before had a member of the RAE been a foul-mouth, mediatic, mass-market writer, but, then again, never before had the RAE had such a powerful speaker defending "inviolable" Spanish and disseminating Hispanidad.

Rape, violence, language, and gender are the elements of postcolonial melancholia's manifestation in another well-known Spanish cultural producer, Pedro Almodóvar, who has also proven to have a problematic relationship with Mexican culture. To be sure, Pérez-Reverte and Almodóvar are a world apart in most regards, but, then again, Hispanidad makes for strange bedfellows. In what follows, I will focus on Almodóvar's film *La mala educación* (*Bad Education*, 2004). I will show how the casting and production of the film reveal a filmmaker who is competing with, punishing, and appropriating Mexican cinema's symbolic capital and how Almodóvar's constant conflation of actors and characters opens the film to a reading in which the legacies of Francoism in the Transition remain ambiguously addressed. Seemingly transferring blame to characters who are defined by the *mexicanidad* of the actors embodying them, *La mala educación* is a symptom of leftist postcolonial melancholia, as Almodóvar enters into an endless loop in which the incapacity to reckon with the legacy of Francoism makes the

---

39 The RAE refused to acknowledge and accept the letter *x* for almost two centuries. It may seem hard to believe but it was not until 1992 (and likely caused by Spain's polemical celebration of the fifth centenary) that the RAE begrudgingly accepted the use of the letter *x* in the word *Mexico*, albeit strongly recommending the use of *j*. Only in 2001 did the RAE finally recommend that *México* be written with an *x*. Despite the RAE's final acceptance of defeat, Pérez-Reverte (and Alfaguara) preferred to stick to the old imperial ways.

filmmaker apparently unaware of his own imperial impulses, which, in turn, contribute to his failed engagement with Francoism.

On *La mala educación*, Abuse, and Silencing the Discourse of Others

Pedro Almodóvar is the best-known Spanish filmmaker today. His filmography, born out of the Spanish democratic Transition and concomitant cultural movida of the 1970s and 1980s, of which he became the poster child, brought about a radical new type of film best known for explorations of desire, gender and sexuality, kitsch aesthetics, and the use of melodrama, a genre that has a long tradition in Mexican music, film, and television. Although Almodóvar has spent much of his career highlighting his debt to Hollywood cinema, many of his films are strongly marked by Mexican culture, particularly the Mexican bolero. Boleros populated most of his films in the 1990s, and, as Almodóvar explains, "en mis películas las canciones son una parte activa del guión, forman parte del diálogo y nos dicen muchas cosas de los personajes, no son canciones que se cantan porque son bonitas … la música tiene una importancia narrativa" (Strauss 85, 126).[40] When Almodóvar was asked about the presence of Mexican music in his films, his response was a classic example of the difficulties that associations between imperialism and Francoism have created for the leftist version of Hispanidad:

> A mí es una música que me apasiona y estoy muy contento, además, de haber ayudado a que todos estos artistas hayan sido editados con bastante éxito. Ahora, en España, el bolero se mira de otro modo, incluso se ha puesto un poco de moda. España es muy injusta con los países de habla hispana, siente una especie de superioridad poco solidaria. En la celebración del quinto centenario del descubrimiento de América había mucha hipocresía. Las cosas las descubro de modo sentimental y es muy agradable ver después que eso funciona en el mercado, porque me parece que restablece la justicia. (Strauss 126)[41]

---

40 "In my movies, songs are an active part of the script, part of the dialogue, and tell us many things about the characters; they are not just pretty songs … music has narrative importance in my movies."

41 "I am passionate about that music, and I am also very glad to have helped all these artists to be successfully published. Now, in Spain, bolero is seen differently, it is even fashionable. Spain is very unfair with the Spanish-speaking countries; it feels a kind of superiority with little solidarity. In the celebration of the fifth centenary of the discovery of America there was a lot of hypocrisy. I discover things in a sentimental manner and it is very nice to see when that works in the market because I think it restates justice."

It is symptomatic that in a conversation about Mexican music Almodóvar ends up talking about the "discovery of América" and criticizing the 1992 celebrations. In this apparent non-sequitur Almodóvar feels compelled to criticize the state-sponsored events of the fifth centennial for the very language of discovery and superiority he has just used to describe his own relationship to Mexican music. As Katherine Vernon has rightly noted, Almodóvar's "discovery" is untrue because Mexican (and Latin American) music has had an important and documented presence in Spain throughout the twentieth century ("Almodóvar's Global Musical Marketplace" 395–6). While Vernon excuses it as a sort of temporary amnesia, I suspect that the Spanish filmmaker, instead, chooses to ignore (rather than forget) this long-standing presence, not only to present himself as the discoverer of music from Mexico and the "Spanish-speaking countries" but also as being single-handedly responsible for its success. In other words, it is because of him and his movies that this music matters, that its existence comes to be recognized. His seemingly unnecessary jump to the 1992 celebrations is symptomatic, at a certain level of awareness, of a need to distance himself from an imperialist version of Hispanidad that, as I have discussed, immediately brings the Franco regime to mind. Indeed, Vernon makes that very connection as she ties Almodóvar's alleged musical "amnesia" to his well-known decision to make movies "as if the Franco regime never existed," thus assuming the conflation of both in Almodóvar's mind. Vernon also identifies the odd connection to 1992 but reads it as a critique of Spain. Vernon believes that it is Almodóvar's role as discoverer that turns the market into "the potential source of a kind of justice or reparation for what is just the latest in a series of historical wrongs [i.e., the 1992 celebrations]" ("Almodóvar's Global Musical Marketplace" 396). I believe, however, that rather than being a critique, Almodóvar's non sequitur and his ambiguous use of the term *discovery* is instead paradigmatic of how postcolonial melancholia functions in the Spanish left. While right-leaning populist writers like Pérez-Reverte have openly embraced a defence of the Francoist discourse of Hispanidad, left-leaning artists like Almodóvar must navigate, consciously or unconsciously, the dangers of association with the Franco regime when expressing what is otherwise the same hegemonic understanding of Hispanidad. Like the school textbooks that Pérez-Reverte despises, Almodóvar must tiptoe around "polemical" and "painful" issues, while still reproducing the same discourse.

In an earlier essay Vernon had shown how "en el lenguaje del *marketing*, el éxito de las películas de Almodóvar ha ocasionado un fenómeno de 're-branding' por medio del cual los artistas y la música de Latinoamérica y el Caribe se re-clasifican y se venden como 'las canciones de Almodóvar'" ("Canciones" 173).[42] While I agree with Vernon that the so-called *canciones de Almodóvar* function in multiple, even contradictory ways, Almodóvar's appropriation of Mexican music, its alleged discovery and re-branding, are, at a fundamental level, prime examples of the legacies of coloniality and empire embodied in Hispanidad and one of its modus operandi: taking Mexican and Latin American symbolic capital, to make it Spanish and to bring it to its proper "home" in Spain, thus stealing and appropriating that symbolic capital as its own, making money in the process, and trying to make Mexican culture dependent on Spanish culture. Not much may unite Pérez-Reverte and Almodóvar, but colonial/imperial legacies are at work in both in strikingly similar ways, be it *españolizando* narcofiction or boleros.

If gender, language, and power are three of the ways in which colonial/imperial legacies manifest in Pérez-Reverte's educational literary project, all three sustain a similar attitude at the opposite side of the ideological spectrum, as became apparent on the set of Almodóvar's film *La mala educación*, his first movie dealing explicitly with the Franco regime period and, perhaps not surprisingly, with education. While Pérez-Reverte's preferred trope is mestizaje as an affirmation of the always already Spanishness of Mexico through an unapologetic performance of masculinity and violence, Almodóvar's gender-fluid and apparently non-normative narrative turns out to be just as violent, albeit based on a different trope, the metaphor of fraternity. Generally preferred by the political left, the trope of brotherhood also resonates with the director's own understanding of family dynamics and melodrama: "Adoro el sentimiento de fraternidad … A veces la relación fraternal se complica (¡como no!) cuando hay sexo … La fraternidad es un sentimiento en desuso, sustituido en la vida actual por la amistad, pero no es exactamente lo mismo: la fraternidad participa de dos grandes sentimientos, el amor y la amistad, unidos por algo tan insondable como la consaguineidad" (Duncan 318).[43] Sex, of course, permeates *La mala*

---

42   "In marketing language, the success of Almodóvar films has caused a rebranding phenomenon by which Latin American and Caribbean artists are reclassified and sold as 'Pedro Almodóvar's songs.'"

43   "I adore the sentiment of fraternity … Sometimes, fraternal relations get complicated (how not!) when there is sex …Fraternity is a sentiment in disuse, substituted in the present by friendship, but they are not exactly the same: fraternity partakes of two great sentiments, love and friendship, united by something as impenetrable as consanguinity."

educación, and the fraternal consanguinity turns out to be deadly. In a film with two Mexican actors in central roles playing Spanish characters (each of whom, in turn, passes as someone else), fraternity takes on added meaning, much like Almodóvar's discovery of Mexican boleros. Both characters are indeed deadly figures in the film: Father Manolo, a child rapist (played by Mexican actor Daniel Giménez Cacho), and Juan/Ángel, an impostor and fratricidal brother (played by Mexican star Gael García Bernal). The choice of actor may seem irrelevant to the story filmed, but in Almodóvar's *La mala educación* intra- and extra-filmic elements were often publicly confused as García Bernal's *mexicanidad* became a much-commented point of contention. While *La mala educación* certainly confronts some of the legacies of Francoism, as we will see through a reading of the movie's ambiguous memory politics, its production and filming made apparent the unchecked pervasiveness of colonial/imperial legacies.

"A la dificultad de cambiar de sexo, y no resultar grotesco, se le unía el que yo quería que hablara español" (Silvestre).[44] This statement refers to what was (and remains) the most commented aspect of Pedro Almodóvar's filming of *La mala educación*, the strained relationship between the Spanish filmmaker and the Mexican leading actor Gael García Bernal. That Almodóvar has always had a complicated relationship with his male and female actors is well known, as is his alleged obsession with controlling every aspect of his movies. In the case of *La mala educación*, however, the tension seemed to have bordered on abuse, as García Bernal was reportedly crying on set and the high level of stress repeatedly threatened the completion of the film.[45] In her very insightful article on brotherhood in Almodóvar's filmography Marsha Kinder convincingly argues that Almodóvar's choice of actor and abusive treatment of García Bernal may have been motivated by "the young actor's global stardom in Spanish-language works that rival Almodóvar's unique success in the transnational market. [García Bernal's previous] films featured homosocial characters in plots that are explicitly political beyond the registers

---

44 "The difficulty of changing sex without being grotesque was compounded by the fact that I wanted him to speak Spanish."

45 "Según algunas fuentes, Gael acabó 'llorando por los pasillos,' y su estrés llegó a tal punto que Almodóvar tuvo que parar el rodaje durante una semana para que se repusiera" (García; "According to some sources, Gael ended up 'crying in the hallways,' and his stress reached a point that Almodóvar had to stop filming for a week so that he could recover"). According to *The New Yorker*, "There were plenty of times when Almodóvar was afraid he wasn't going to be able to finish the movie" (Max).

of sexuality and gender, where Almodóvar has reigned supreme" (287).[46] For Kinder, Almodóvar seems to enjoy punishing the Mexican actor (and Mexican cinema, I would add) for daring to compete: "Despite, or possibly because of García Bernal's own growing stardom, Almodóvar seems to take pleasure in making the power dynamics of their collaboration very clear, even while mocking his own tyranny ... Even when praising Bernal for his hard work, Almodóvar claims that he gave him the most challenging role that he had ever had, as if his earlier parts were easy" (288). To Kinder's perceptive observation, I would add that Almodóvar's choice of actor also had the double purpose of capitalizing on García Bernal's (and Mexico's) rising symbolic prestige in film (not unlike his capitalizing on Mexican music, or Pérez-Reverte's capitalizing on narcoliterature).

Kinder goes as far as to suggest that the sibling rivalry portrayed in the film between Ignacio and Juan (played by García Bernal), which was grounded in the latter's resentment towards the former for doing everything better than he did, mimics the transnational tension she describes: "[Almodóvar] seems to fuse the actor Gael García Bernal with the opportunistic actor and femme fatale that he plays in the movie, finally asking himself, 'Is Gael the evil one in this story?'" (288). Kinder's reading of *La mala educación* (the filming and the film) in relation to transnational cinema is not only compelling but also opens the field of signification of both the difficult filming and the complex film to larger postcolonial dynamics between Mexico and Spain. It is not a stretch to see the widely commented abuse of Gael/Juan/Zahara by Almodóvar, based on Gael's *mexicanidad*, as an iteration of Pérez-Reverte's violently masculine and glottonormative mestizaje in which García Bernal/Zahara plays the part of Malinche to Almodóvar's Cortés. Almodóvar is not Pérez-Reverte, however, and whatever the similarities of their imperialist nostalgia, Almodóvar's narratives are hardly ever simple or obvious. In *La mala educación* the rhetoric of violence and mestizaje becomes entangled with and complicated by a less heteronormative but no less glottonormative and violent use of fraternity, a rivalry between brothers that cannot but recall the *paises hermanos* of Hispanidad.

When speaking about the filming of *La mala educación*, García Bernal himself made explicit the colonial/imperial dynamics haunting the movie. Conflating linguistic and gender performance, he explained: "[W]hat was most difficult was losing my Mexican accent. Pedro insisted

---

46   I believe that in addition to García Bernal's stardom, there is a larger connection to the international success of Mexican cinema and Mexican directors (Cuarón, Iñarritu, del Toro) who are equally at home filming in English and in Hollywood, something Almodóvar has often expressed interest in doing but finds himself unable to do.

on that, and frankly, I thought it was ridiculous. He wanted a Spanish accent and that is a colonialist thing ... Everyone has their inner transvestite, but my inner transvestite is Mexican-Caribbean, and that's a very different way of putting on a show than Pedro's" (Hirschberg). Not only does García Bernal make explicit the assumptions behind Almodóvar's normative understanding of Castilian as Spanish, calling him out for his "colonialist" attitude, but this attitude extends also to gender performance and cultural difference. It is in this light that what may sound as an odd thing for non-normative Almodóvar to say ("change sex without being *grotesque*") may take on a new meaning: he wanted García Bernal to become Spanish in both language and gender/sex because any other culturally inflected linguistic/gender performance would be "grotesque." What is implicit in Almodóvar's statement becomes explicit in García Bernal's: normativity and deviance in Spanish are the result of colonial legacies that continue to inflect Mexican/Spanish relations even in the most unsuspected places.

Although these postcolonial/post-imperial dynamics seemed to be immediately apparent to the Mexican actor, the Spanish director seemed oblivious to the imperialist undertones of his otherwise absurd request that García Bernal, from the country with the largest number of Spanish speakers in the world, speak Spanish. Almodóvar's use of words is a symptom of the hegemonic understanding of the central place of Spain and *its* central linguistic variant within the larger community of Spanish-speaking countries. Implicit in this way of thinking, best represented by the RAE, the Castilian or central Spanish variant of the language is not a variant (or "accent") at all, but the norm against which all other forms are considered deviations. In other words, according to this logic only Castilian *is* Spanish (the "inviolable" part of the language according to Pérez-Reverte's sexual metaphor). In an interview in which he was praised for "neutralizing his accent," García Bernal addressed again the imperial normativity behind Almodóvar's (and Spain's) linguistic fixation: "Estoy muy en desacuerdo con esa palabra, *neutralizar* (risas). Más bien *hice un acento*. Si yo le quitara mexicanidad a mi acento, hablaría como un robot. Procuré *hacer un acento español*, que consiste más bien en poner que en quitar. *En España piensan mucho así*: que tú vienes con tu acento y lo que tienes que hacer es rebajarlo" (Ponga; emphasis added).[47] The Mexican actor shows the fallacy

---

47 "I completely disagree with that word, *neutralize* (laughter). Rather, *I did an accent*. If I took Mexicanidad away from my accent, I would speak like a robot. I tried to *do a Spanish accent*, which means putting on rather than taking off. *There are many who think like this in Spain*: that you arrive with your accent, and you have to get rid of it."

behind the idea that he had to *take off* his accent (the "mejicanismos" of Pérez-Reverte and the RAE) so that an alleged "neutral" Spanish came through, "neutral" meaning, of course, Castilian Spanish. Rather, he turns Castilian into another accent that he learned to "put on." Not only does García Bernal decentralize Spanish, but he also denaturalizes Castilian normativity, which has been sustained by centuries-long colonial structures, and turns it into another accent or variant.

More broadly, García Bernal exposes the mechanism behind linguistic normativity in a way that resonates with Judith Butler's theory of gender. Implied in his critique is the idea that *all forms of Spanish* are but equal variants without a centre, for to speak without an accent is to speak not like a human but like a "robot." Much like gender is inscribed in the body by centuries of social, cultural, and political forces performed and sedimented over time, Castilian Spanish has been naturalized as Spanish over centuries of colonial and centralist structures, institutions, and practices. In this context the tensions on the set, Almodóvar's remark regarding language, and García Bernal's response are all symptoms of a larger historical problem regarding the nature and politics of the Spanish language, its history, its coexistence with other languages, and its ties to a nostalgic imaginary of empire. This imaginary, however, extends well beyond language, of course, and the fact that both director and actor continually conflated language and gender performance is also revealing, as it recalls a long history in which the iconography of empire has been populated by female representations of America and by male conquistadors, an iconography still performed in the present, as in the case of Pérez-Reverte's fiction. In the context surrounding the making of the film, Almodóvar's anxiety over Gael García Bernal and Mexican cinema's symbolic capital should be read, then, as a manifestation of a pervasive postcolonial melancholia in Spain. Like the case of Pérez-Reverte, this anxiety often leads to violent reactions and to the paradoxical need to both capitalize and *españolizar* Mexican cultural capital.

Regarding the film itself, Marsha Kinder rightly suggests that the relationship between the director Enrique and the actor Juan in *La mala educación* parallels that of Almodóvar and García Bernal, and Paul Julian Smith (*Desire Unlimited*) correctly sees a parallel between the rapist Father Manolo / Señor Berenguer and Enrique's obsession with (and rape of) Juan. These connections deserve further exploration in the context of the legacies of the past and the memory politics of *La mala educación* and require a brief summary of what is otherwise a very complex plot.

Set in 1980, *La mala educación* starts with film director Enrique Goded being visited by a man (García Bernal) who claims to be his longlost childhood best friend and love Ignacio, although now he goes by the name Ángel. He brings Enrique a story he has supposedly written, called "La visita," about their time in a Catholic boarding school in the 1960s and about the sexual abuse Ignacio suffered by Father Manolo. We learn later that the story ends with the adult Ignacio, now transgender Zahara, exacting revenge on Father Manolo and demanding a monetary reparation that allows her to finish her gender transition and become the woman she wants to be. Ángel asks Enrique to turn the story into a film and cast him in the role of Ignacio/Zahara. Enrique's misgivings about Ángel lead him to discover that Ignacio is dead and that Ángel is in fact Ignacio's brother, Juan. Angry, but curious about Juan, Enrique does not expose Juan/Ángel but chooses instead to punish him by raping him repeatedly, which Juan endures, hoping to be cast in the film. At this point Enrique decides to change the ending of Ignacio's "La visita" from happy to tragic. In Enrique's film *La visita*, rather than letting Ignacio/Zahara succeed in her revenge, Enrique has Ignacio/Zahara killed when she tries to blackmail Father Manolo. In doing so, Enrique unknowingly ends up replicating in his fictional version what actually happened to the real Ignacio, as he and the audience later learn: Ignacio was, in fact, killed in 1977 by Señor Berenguer (the new persona of Father Manolo in democratic Spain) and his own brother, Juan (now the sexual object of Berenguer's desire).

In his film Enrique performs yet another type of violence on the real Ignacio/Zahara: he strips her of her authorship/authority. Enrique deems Ignacio's happy ending to be unrealistic, utopian perhaps, and overwrites it with his own version, therefore killing not only the fictional Ignacio but also Ignacio the author. Ignacio chose to write herself and imagine her own future as a drug-free woman thanks to the money that she believes is owed to her by Father Manolo as reparation for the abuse and rape. The empowerment that authoring her own story brings to Ignacio, imagining herself as the free woman she wishes to be, is emphasized in Ignacio's final written words in a letter to Enrique: "Creo que lo he conseguido ..." Though she is killed, her story lives on and is brought to Enrique by Ignacio's brother, Juan, who wants to be called Ángel, that is, "messenger" – thereby loading Ignacio's manuscript with Christian echoes. If Father Manolo / Señor Berenguer choose to kill Ignacio rather than pay for his past crimes, Enrique is given the chance to extract that reparation through narrative and honour that empowerment: he is given the chance to tell Ignacio's story, to enable her resurrection as it were on the screen and her becoming the woman she is. Instead, he eliminates Ignacio's voice and self-narrative and imposes his own in what he sees as a righteous act, while he takes advantage of her story to relaunch his stagnant career.

In the preproduction phase of the film *La visita*, Enrique parallels Father Manolo in his repeated raping of Juan/Ángel, as Smith rightly notes (*Desire Unlimited* 286), and Almodóvar's abuse of García Bernal, as Kinder points out. Yet nothing in the film seems to condemn Enrique/Almodóvar for these abuses or for the symbolic killing of Ignacio in a film that allows Enrique to continue living in his grand suburban house with a pool, reaping the symbolic and economic benefits of Ignacio's murder as he launches a successful career as a filmmaker. Likewise, while the film condemns Father Manolo's violent abuse of young Ignacio, his "democratic" persona, Señor Berenguer, who now works in a publishing house, is instead presented as *the* victim of Juan/Ángel by Almodóvar:

> [C]uando al Padre Manolo lo interpreta Daniel Giménez Cacho, la pasión que siente por el niño y su abuso de poder hacen de él un verdugo. Cuando se hace llamar señor Berenguer y ha dejado los hábitos y se enamora de Juan, el mismo terrible personaje juega el papel contrario en la ruleta de la pasión: ahora es una víctima. La película es inconcebible sin estos dos personajes, que son uno solo, y sin la encarnación que de ellos hacen Daniel Giménez Cacho y Lluis Homar, respectivamente. (Duncan 314)[48]

Considering the only character undeniably connected to the Franco regime in the movie as both victimizer and victim, and equating the abuse and rape of young Ignacio with being rejected by the young man he desires (whose "love" he had to buy to begin with), is not only morally problematic but also dangerously close to the conservative theory of equidistance that has gained ground in Spain and that Pérez-Reverte embraces in his own memory politics. Notably, this politically ambiguous stance towards the Franco regime is also connected to the geocultural politics of the film. As he repeatedly does when talking about this movie, Almodóvar conflates actors and characters, in this case making explicit that Father Manolo is a victimizer *when played by the Mexican actor* and a victim *when played by the Spanish actor*, and that the film

---

48 "When Father Manolo is interpreted by Daniel Giménez Cacho, the passion that he feels for the boy and his abuse of power make him a victimizer. When he goes by Señor Berenguer and has left the Church and falls in love with Juan, the same terrible character plays the opposite role in the roulette of passion: now he is a victim. The movie is inconceivable without these two characters, that are only one, and without their embodiment by Daniel Giménez Cacho and Lluis Homar respectively."

is unthinkable without those specific actors in those roles. In his comments on the movie Almodóvar may say that he does not judge his characters (Duncan 314), but his subsequent lengthy description of "el personaje *de Gael*" (315; emphasis added) is merciless, comparing him to Patricia Highsmith's psychotic characters and concluding that "el personaje de *Gael* representa a la típica femme fatale (en su caso *enfant terrible*) porque a todos los personajes que entran en contacto con él les lleva a la perdición" (315; italics in original).[49] Enrique and Señor Berenguer (both played by Spanish actors) are exonerated, while Father Manolo and Juan/Ángel (both Mexican actors) are condemned. Despite (or perhaps because of) Almodóvar's insistence that *La mala educación* is not about the Catholic Church, the Franco regime, the Transition, or *la movida*, it is impossible not to see it that way, so why does Almodóvar feel so compelled to deny it? It is pointless to speculate about what the filmmaker may or may not have had in mind when creating the film, but an analysis of his creation reveals a problematic approach to both Spanish historical memory and the long legacy of coloniality/empire that it mediates. In fact, one may be the source of the other. Seemingly incapable of fully reckoning with the legacy of Francoism, the filmmaker and the film deploy the metaphor of brotherhood ("paises hermanos"), of sameness in difference ("españoles de los dos hemisferios"), of Hispanidad to blame a "Mexicanness" that is both erased and constantly remembered, exonerating the Spanish "sibling" and shifting the blame onto the Mexican one. As in the case of Almodóvar's statement on the Mexican boleros, there seems to be a jump or a non sequitur in how Almodóvar talks about this film, an ideological short circuit through which we can glimpse the workings of postcolonial nostalgia in leftist discourse: unable to fully engage with the legacies of Francoism, the director and his film reproduce an imperialist discourse of Hispanidad while remaining oblivious to doing it because showing awareness would imply guilt at perpetuating the legacies of Francoism, legacies that remain unaddressed and that lead to the perpetuation of imperialist nostalgic discourse in an endless loop.

---

49 "The character of Gael represents the typical femme fatale (*enfant terrible* in his case) because he brings perdition to all the characters that enter into contact with him."
   In his introduction to the film in *Los archivos de Pedro Almodóvar*, Gustavo Martín Garzo goes as far as to consider García Bernal's character "la encarnación más pura del mal que se haya llevado a cabo en nuestro cine" (307; "the purest incarnation of evil ever carried out in [Spanish] cinema").

Almodóvar has denied that his film is autobiographical. Nonetheless, "La visita," the story that Ignacio wrote and Juan delivers to Enrique as his, seems to be based on a real story of the same title written by Pedro Almodóvar early in his career and, according to Paul J. Smith, currently kept at Spain's National Library (*Desire Unlimited* 285). This adds another layer to the seemingly unending mise en abyme that is *La mala educación*, one that may further clarify the apparent need to shift blames, while at the same time revealing a certain degree of awareness. Almodóvar, author of "La visita," is split into two characters – Ignacio (author of the story) and Enrique (author of the film) – both embodiments of the movida so strongly associated with Almodóvar. It is not a stretch to see the two friends, Enrique and Ignacio, as two different outcomes of the repressive and abusive Catholic boarding school that was the Franco regime and as embodiment of Spain at the crossroads of the 1970s and 1980s. Spain could confront its past and hold those responsible accountable, or ignore it and benefit from its legacies. On the one hand, Ignacio chose to confront the past, face his abuser, ask for reparation, and complete his (political/gender) "transition"; he was killed as a result. On the other hand, in 1980 (the year of Pedro Almodóvar's first feature film), Enrique does not truly investigate the past (he never tried to get back in touch with Ignacio) or seek reparation, leading him to reproduce Father Manolo's violence on Juan and actively silence Ignacio's transition narrative and authority/authorship of "La visita" for his own benefit. He seems content with Father Manolo's / Señor Berenguer's account of history. Notably, Enrique, Señor Berenguer, and Almodóvar all place the blame on the messenger, Juan/Ángel, who dared to bring Ignacio's alternative utopian future to Enrique's attention, forcing him perhaps to face his own complicity in the legacy of oppression. As both *La mala educación* and the filming of *La visita* come to an end, Enrique meets Señor Berenguer (Father Manolo) on the movie set and has a chance to confront him. But he does not, choosing instead to listen to his story. Perversely, it is the Francoist Father Manolo, now refurbished as the "publisher" Señor Berenguer, who takes control of the film narrative at the end of *La mala educación*. That is, it is through the character of Ignacio's abuser and murderer that Enrique and the viewers learn the alleged truth of what happened to Ignacio.

In *La reina del sur* it is the journalist alter ego of Pérez-Reverte who tells the story of Teresa Mendoza, and in *La mala educación* the authorial voices are Almodóvar's, Enrique's, and Señor Berenguer's. Like in Pérez-Reverte's novel, the many narrative devices of *La mala educación* function as a sort of imperial frame, "substituting what is with another reality ... through the coming together of epistemic and coercive means ... The person we choose not to see or hear cannot exist or speak for themselves and, secondly, must be spoken for" (Hafiz 116–17). The narrative complicity of Enrique, Berenguer, and Almodóvar is the imperial frame that silences Ignacio and lays the blame exclusively on his Mexican brother, Juan. If this has to do with Almodóvar's own demons about his place in the movida, we may never know, but, as his first film explicitly dealing with historical memory, *La mala educación* is a validation of the Transition's "Pacto de olvido" and of Spain's subsequent neoliberal turn. But in the Spanish Pact of Forgetting, more than the crimes of the Franco regime were disremembered; so too were the imperial/colonial legacies of Francoist Hispanidad, which were not only institutionalized and normalized in society, politics, economics, and culture but also perpetuated in Spain's own "bad education." As a result of the national refusal to reckon with the crimes of its imperial past, Almodóvar, like Enrique, punishes the body of García Bernal (and Mexican cinema with him), exerting his authority and imposing his linguistic, gender, and cultural normativity. Almodóvar may stay away from Perez-Reverte's misogynous, violent, heteronormative narrative of mestizaje and may appeal instead to the apparently less confrontational metaphor of fraternity. This proves to be no less violent, however. It is proof of the strength of Spain's postcolonial melancholia across the ideological spectrum that an otherwise progressive, visionary, and groundbreaking filmmaker like Pedro Almodóvar remains seemingly oblivious to and complicit with Spain's problematic post-dictatorial memory politics.[50]

Building on Annabel Martín's argument that "Francoism finds its kindred spirit in the hyperbolic language of melodrama, its moral Manichaeism" (quoted in D'Lugo 370), Marvin D'Lugo affirms that *Bad Education* denies its viewers the satisfaction of melodrama's simplistic division between good and evil, offering instead an "underlying personal and collective structure ... within which characters are no longer

---

50 In his more recent film, *Dolor y gloria* (*Pain and Glory*, 2019), Almodóvar returns to his past and once again uses the trope of an "old story" that is actualized in the present (in the form of a play rather than a film, this time). Titled "Addiction," the story also starts in 1980 when Salvador/Almodóvar is doing his first film, and it has strong echoes of Enrique's and Ignacio's story in *La mala educación*. Not surprisingly, Mexico plays a central part as well. This time, however, in this rather openly autobiographical text and film, Almodóvar/Salvador acknowledges that Cuba and Mexico were his "mejor escuela. En esos viajes encontré la inspiración para escribir las historias que años después contaría" (*Dolor y gloria*; "my best school. In those trips, I found the inspiration to write the stories that I would tell years later").

perceived as being simply good or bad but as occupying the shifting middle ground of moral and political ambiguity. Such recognition may finally be the guiding objective of the film's post nostalgic turn" (381). Such reading runs the risk of turning melodrama into a mere Francoist device, void of its long transatlantic history; I would argue that, rather than post-nostalgic, the moral and political ambiguity of Almodóvar's films is, in fact, imbued with imperial nostalgia. In contrast, the television streaming series *La casa de las flores* (*The House of Flowers*, 2018–20) by Mexican director Manolo Caro offers a celebration of the moral stance of melodrama in which some actions, some regimes, and some ideologies and structures of power are quite simply morally wrong, highlighting in the process that melodrama does certainly not belong to the Franco regime, that it has a history that predates it, and that it is by no means exclusively Spanish; it is hugely Mexican and indeed fully transnational. Through its own story of Mexican and Spanish siblings, *La casa de las flores* affirms that neither melodrama nor morals should be held hostage by the long shadow of either Hispanidad or the Franco regime. As we will see, Caro's critique of Mexican history and of its own form of political and cultural *hispanismo*/Hispanidad goes hand in hand with a critique of Spain's inability to address its imperial ghosts and its reproduction of imperialist discourses. Also playing with language and gender, and queering both Mexican and Spanish histories, *La casa de las flores* creatively pushes back, rereading postcolonial/post-imperial narratives as a telenovela.

Queering Colonial/Imperial Histories: Language, Gender, and Historical Memory in Manolo Caro's *La casa de las flores*

Director Manolo Caro came to prominence in Mexico after the release of his films *No sé si cortarme las venas o dejármelas largas* (2013) and *La vida inmoral de la pareja ideal* (2016). In 2018, he released the first season of a Netflix series called *La casa de las flores*, which after three seasons, brought him to international acclaim. Building and queering the long tradition of Mexican melodrama and telenovelas, Caro tells the story of a well-to-do Mexican family, incorporating a pair of Spanish siblings (sisters now rather than brothers). In a story that is also about engaging the past, confronting family traumas, and reimagining the future, Caro, as did García Bernal, tackles historical memory and the colonial legacies still hindering Mexican-Spanish relations. Unlike Enrique/Almodóvar, Caro allows for silenced narratives to be told and chooses to imagine possible futures, unafraid of what confronting the past may reveal.

Divided into three seasons, *La casa de las flores* traces the story of the De la Mora family, a once powerful and wealthy traditional family living in the well-off neighbourhood of Las Lomas de Chapultepec in Mexico City. Recognized as a playful homage to Mexico's long tradition of telenovelas, *La casa de las flores* is melodramatic, full of improbable plot twists and turns and the classic themes of love, betrayal, class, and family relations, as well as anagnorisis, forgiveness, and secrets. Secrets are indeed central to the story, but in Caro's hands they take on a larger significance than a mere plot device for the creation of suspense and become a driving force behind a reckoning with the past. In telling the story of the De la Mora family, *La casa de las flores* takes colonial legacies head on and offers a rewriting of postcolonial Mexico and post-imperial Spain, opening new ways to imagine and articulate a new Mexican and Spanish narrative in the twenty-first century. It would be inaccurate and misleading to say that *La casa de las flores* is an allegory because, in fact, the series resists allegorical readings. However, the story, the characters, the plot, and the sound track all create both explicit and implicit connections and unfold metaphorical significations that encourage us to reflect on and question naturalized normative discourses. Ultimately, *La casa de las flores* performs a queering of hegemonic historical narratives while resisting the totalizing impulse of a satisfying allegory. In this sense, Manolo Caro's series rewrites the glottopolitics and masculinist violence of Hispanidad so successfully rehabilitated in Pérez-Reverte's fiction, as well as the less obvious but not necessarily less violent glottopolitics and discourse on fraternity that transpired in Almodóvar's *La mala educación*. As we will see, *La casa de las flores* is also an exercise in historical memory and the confrontation of past legacies, both of which, the show seems to tell us, require time. It is through serialization, narrative time, and flashbacks that *La casa de las flores* accomplishes this, so an analysis of the series is required, to an extent, for sensitivity to the timing of events and plot.

The story begins in 2018 at the De la Mora's mansion in Las Lomas where the family is celebrating a large birthday party for Ernesto, the father. The family owns an expensive flower shop called La casa de las flores, located next to the family home and run by the mother, Virginia. The series opens as Roberta, the narrator, arrives at the party uninvited and enters the shop unnoticed. Despite the glamour and glitter of the place and the party, Roberta tells us, nothing is what it seems: the De la Mora's projected image as the perfect family is a lie. Roberta, we soon learn, is Ernesto's lover and the owner of a drag-show cabaret in Mexico City that is also called La casa de las flores. In the flower shop she leaves an envelope addressed to Ernesto's wife, Virginia, and, after stating that it is time to "tell the truth," she hangs herself. Guided by this dead narrator whose death is the catalyst of all subsequent events, the series follows the lives of De la Mora children. Paulina is the oldest and most concerned, at first, with the family's reputation; she is also the only one who knew of her father's "second family" and the cabaret. Paulina is divorced from her Spanish husband, José María, a criminal lawyer who is now back in Spain and is now a woman, María José. Paulina and José María have a child, Bruno, who stayed with his mother in Mexico. Elena, the middle child, studied architecture and got engaged to Dominique in the United States, whence she and Dominique have arrived at the start of the show. Caught in the family drama, Elena does not want to return to the United States, breaks her engagement, and stays in Mexico, where she has affairs with men of all nationalities including a Mexican priest. Finally, Julián, the youngest of the three, has commitment issues as he navigates his bisexuality and his secret relationship with Diego, the family accountant. With the secret help of Virginia (who re-evaluates her own life after reading Roberta's letter and who will soon leave her family) and the not-so-secret help of the live-in housekeeper, Delia, the De la Mora children soon embark on opening the family secrets, including those they have kept from each other. As the series ends, the De la Mora siblings have travelled a long way in coming to terms with their family's traumatic past, working out their own issues, and reinventing themselves and their own families into the future: Paulina and María José will remarry and re-form their family with Bruno in Mexico, away from María José's evil sister, Puri. Julián will come out of the closet and finally commit to his boyfriend, Diego, with whom his sister Elena eventually agrees to have a child. Finding love unexpectedly in Pablo, an ex-architect colleague turned delivery guy, Elena moves with him into an apartment next door to Julián and Diego, and the four of them form one new nuclear family as the four parents of baby Patricio.

The very first episode contains several elements that already signal a larger scope than just the ins and out of a particular family, pointing instead to Mexico's own secrets and national family dramas. The first of those elements is the ghostly narrator. Despite her many obvious differences, Roberta cannot but remind the viewers of the most famous dead narrator in Mexican literature, *Pedro Páramo*'s Juan Preciado, and his search for his father in a ghostly town that is tormented by its past.[51]

---

51   Piñeiro Otero rightly points out to another intertextuality: Roberta's ghostly voice connects Caro's series with shows like *Desperate Housewives* (247).

While Las Lomas and Mexico City in Caro's series are far from ghostly towns, they certainly are haunted by the past, and, as in Rulfo's novel, the haunting has to do with fatherhood. Indeed, the De la Mora children are marked by a traumatic family history originating in the connected murders of two fathers forty years prior, one of which resulted in the wrongful conviction of a housekeeper; the other was not truly investigated in a society that preferred to blame the victim, a homosexual man, for his own murder.

The second element is the mariachi band. As the first episode ends, the party is over, and the family is gathered, trying to process all that has transpired after Roberta's suicide. Suddenly a mariachi band enters the house, beginning to play a tune that is interrupted when Paulina laments that she forgot to cancel the band. Nonetheless, we will see and hear the mariachi band play in the last episode, as the series ends with Paulina's second wedding. The mariachi band and the song "Viva Mexico" will have radically changed their meaning by the end of the show.

The third element is the chronology of events, which is made explicit when Roberta, upon entering the flower shop in the present, 2018, states, "En esta casa tampoco crecen flores; al contrario, se han vendido por casi 50 años millones de ellas" (season 1, episode 1).[52] In Mexico's history, those fifty years recall what was arguably the main and most traumatic historical event after the Mexican Revolution: the 1968 student protests and the state's violent response to them, known as the Tlatelolco massacre. Beyond Mexico, 1968 was also a year of massive protests across the West and other parts of the world and has since been understood as a turning point in the twentieth century in terms both of what they achieved and, perhaps more so, of what they did not – their unrealized potentialities. It is in this light that Roberta's passing comment about the flower shop takes on wider political meaning: since 1968, there has been no growth of life, only the commodification of life.

In season 3, through flashbacks, the series delves into Virginia de la Mora's youth and the events that led to the killing of her homosexual friend (and the father of Paulina) Patricio, "Pato," on 1 January 1980. This means, however, that the family story depicted in the show (1979–2018) does not neatly follow the chronology of the flower shop stated by Roberta, and its historical echoes (1968–2018). There is a gap of ten years. I suggest that this gap is implicitly bridged by one of the key moments of Virginia's youth, her participation with her friends Pato,

---

52   "Flowers don't grow in this house either; on the contrary, millions of them have
      been sold for almost fifty years."

Ernesto, and Salo in the first LGBT+ march in Mexico City in 1979, of which Pato was an organizer. Although this is generally considered the first Gay Pride march in Mexico, in truth, gay and lesbian activist groups had participated on 2 October 1978 in a demonstration commemorating the tenth anniversary of the Tlatelolco massacre, in what Carlos Monsiváis considers a watershed moment in Mexican LGBT+ history (196–7). In the show the participation in public view (newspaper cover photo included) of Virginia, Ernesto, and Salo, all of them identified as heterosexual, in the 1979 LGBT+ march is certainly presented as a moment of progressive politics, no less because of the upper social class of Pato's friends. As Pato, dressed in drag, tells his well-to-do friends in a later scene, "lo que pasa es que estaban viviendo en su burbujita de Las Lomas, pero se la vamos a reventar" (season 3, episode 4).[53] I believe, then, that it is through the LGBT+ movement, and not directly, that *La casa de las flores* makes the connection to 1968, and in doing so, it queers it, for queering history is what the series sets out to do from the moment that Roberta hangs herself in the name of truth.

Mexican history, or the landmarks and monuments that are its physical signs, is what the camera focuses on in some of the following scenes. After narrating her own suicide, Roberta takes us back to the few hours before her death and the discovery of her body, and the sound track turns to the song "Me colé en una fiesta" ("I Crashed Your Party") by the 1980s Spanish pop band Mecano. With the sound of Mecano in the background, the camera shows Elena and her fiancée, Dominique, on their way from the airport to the party, driving through the well-known Paseo de la Reforma. Rather than moving with the car, the camera shot starts and ends, lingering on El Ángel, Mexico City's famous monument to independence; a few scenes later, through a note left by Roberta to her children (Claudio and Micaela), the camera makes a point of showing the address of the De la Mora family home: "Boulevard of the Viceroys, 1652" in Las Lomas. Seemingly unimportant to the plot and easy to miss, these two lingering moments of the camera recall several key events in Mexico's history. In chronological order they are the Viceroyalty of New Spain (where the De la Mora family seems to still live symbolically, as we shall see), independence, the Juárez Reform, the Porfiriato, the Mexican Revolution, and the neoliberal era ushered in

---

53 "The thing is that you were living in your little bubble in Las Lomas, but we are going to burst it." Pato's family also lives in Las Lomas, but they threw him out when he came out of the closet.

during the 1980s. The presence of El Ángel may also be calling attention to the ghosts of *both* independence and the revolution because the monument is also a mausoleum. Finally, the camera is painstakingly careful to linger on the surrounding high-rises: the luxury hotel St Regis by Marriot, HSBC (the British multinational investment bank), and Torre Reforma, itself a monument to neoliberalism. The early 1980s evoked by Mecano's music further connects the banks, hotels, and shopping centres surrounding El Ángel to the explosion of neoliberalism in Mexico beginning in that decade. Masterly, Caro is able to seamlessly encapsulate Mexican historical landmarks in a couple of short shots.

The Mecano sound track of these first scenes has other significant connections to the De la Mora family story.[54] In its immediate context Mecano's song ("Me colé en una fiesta") contributes to the dark humour of the scene because crashing Ernesto's party is literally what Roberta is about to do. But there is more to it. Mecano's music is associated with the breaking of gender norms, which in addition to being a politically driven central theme in *La casa de las flores*, is associated with the Spanish movida of the late 1970s and 1980s, the breeding ground of Pedro Almodóvar.[55] Like the year 1968, the movida is a historical and cultural moment that has been connected to the end of utopia and to historical forgetting, an expression of the Spanish *pacto de olvido*, and the path towards neoliberalism. This musical connection to Spain also prefigures the arrival of María José (formerly José María) Riquelme, the Spanish lawyer and ex-husband of Paulina de la Mora, who called her to Mexico to help with the family's legal problems. María José plays a central role in the series, and she, her sister Puri, and other characters and plot devices are enmeshed in the queering of national and transnational narratives and postcolonial/post-imperial discourses that the series undertakes.

The marriage of Paulina and José María was the marriage of two families who shared a common understanding of Hispanidad and colonial/imperial history. José María / María José and Puri, siblings and lawyers, visually and thematically connected in the series to the royal palace and the Spanish royal family, embody the continued colonial/

---

54 See Ávila for an early reading of the first season's sound track.

55 Jorge Pérez affirms: "The subtexts of [Mecano's] songs and their aesthetics hardly favored a heteronormative social structure, but rather pinpointed its fissures and gaps. It is in this ambivalent terrain, in the enactment of potentialities that are not explicitly articulated, in highlighting the instability rather than unitary gender and sexual identity that the queer edge of Mecano's music unfolds" (137).

imperial legacy I examined earlier as it pervades both right- and left-wing politics, both populist bestsellers and melodramatic *cinéma d'auteur*, and both masculinist and gender-defiant discourses in Spain. Such a family finds its match in the De la Mora family, with its symbolic connection to the Viceroyalty, part of a conservative class that is unhappy with post-revolutionary politics. As Beatriz Urías explains, between 1920 and 1960 "los hispanófilos lograron articular un modelo social alternativo que fue interiorizado por las clases alta y media" (599).[56] Among the tenets of that model was understanding "el fenómeno revolucionario como origen del acrecentamiento del poder estatal; la erosión de la moral y las costumbres tradicionales que afectaban particularmente a las mujeres, y la desarticulación de una estructura familiar profundamente arraigada en la sociedad mexicana" (601).[57] Connected to the ideology and politics of Franco's Spain despite Mexico's official opposition to the regime, "la propuesta hispanófila apeló a lo religioso, a los valores de la España imperial y al mantenimiento de un sistema organicista fundado en jerarquías naturales que 'armonizaban' el espacio social desde la cúspide de la pirámide social hasta la familia (623).[58] As historian Cosío Villegas would ironically put it, Hispanidad was the discourse of "gente decente" (quoted in Urías 600).

"Decent people" is precisely what the De la Mora family in their neighbourhood of Las Lomas de Chapultepec have always thought themselves to be, from Grandmother Victoria forty years ago all the way to Paulina de la Mora at the start of the series. In a series in which the engine that moves the story forward is historical memory and the working through of family secrets and past traumas, whose first few shots call our attention to Mexican and Spanish histories through the monuments and sound track, one must certainly read in another key not only Paulina's marriage to a Spanish lawyer, José María Requelme, but also his return to México as María José and the central role that María José and her sister Puri have in the unfolding of the De la Mora drama. The De la Mora family is indeed one of those upper-class

---

56 "Hispanophiles managed to articulate an alternative social model that was internalized by the middle and upper classes."

57 "The revolution as origin of the enlargement of state power; the erosion of traditional morals and habits particularly affecting women, and the disarticulation of a family structure deeply rooted in Mexican society."

58 "The Hispanophile position appealed to religion, the values of imperial Spain, and the keeping of an organicist system of natural hierarchies that 'harmonized' social space from the apex of the social pyramid to the family."

families who are seduced by Hispanist discourse and see their worth as attached to traditional Spanish values, social hierarchies, and race and gender structures. And it is upon this long colonial/imperial legacy that *La casa de las flores* reflects. Postcolonial narratives, Manolo Caro seems to be telling us, are not unlike telenovelas, and *La casa de las flores* is a telenovela that sets out to queer colonial/imperial legacies as family melodrama, from the glottopolitics of language to the narrative of the conquest.

As the ex-wife of José María (and later the wife of María José), Paulina is certainly not any kind of allegorical Malinche figure. However, after centuries of competing symbolic narratives about the conquest, and after its explicit and implicit re-enactment in art, literature, and film, it is fair to say that a relationship between a Mexican woman and a Spanish man, with a son, is bound to evoke the Malinche-Cortés-Martín triad. But while Teresa Mendoza felt "at home" in Spain in *La reina del sur*, on the contrary there are constant reminders of the differences between Spaniards and Mexicans in *La casa de las flores*. Early in the first episode, as Paulina greets Dominique, she explains to him that Mexicans only kiss once because "we are not Europeans," and when Paulina greets María José at the Mexico City airport after five years of their not seeing each other, the double/single kissing confusion between them is made explicit once again. At the end of the first season María José needs to return to Madrid, and despite Bruno's opposition, she takes him with her. At the eleventh hour, though, encouraged by her mother, Virginia, who warns her not to repeat her mistakes, Paulina joins María José and Bruno at the airport and they agree to give their relationship a chance. Season 2 begins after a year has elapsed, during which time Paulina, María José, and Bruno have been living in Madrid together with María José's sister Puri, short for Purificación, a barely disguised association with the "purity of blood" laws of imperial Spain. Puri, indeed, will live up to her name and its inquisitorial connotations both in Madrid and in the unfolding of the De la Mora family drama in Mexico.

Season 2 starts with Roberta's voice reminding us: "No siempre las historias son como nos las han contado. Por eso es hora de que juntos descubramos la verdad" (season 2, episode 1).[59] After the credits and to the telling sound of the song "Disintegration" by the band Monarchy, we see Paulina de la Mora in Madrid. Unable to sleep, she comes

---

59 "Histories are not always as we have been told. That's why it's time for us to discover the truth together."

out onto a balcony of their downtown apartment and sees a Spanish stranger smoking in the balcony next door, who says, "¡Ay! ¿te robe el sueño?" to which Paulina replies, "Yo, la verdad, que ya no tengo nada que me puedan robar."[60] Given the setting, the interlocutors, the sound track, and Paulina' subsequent "Soy de México," this first scene and dialogue in Madrid is loaded with colonial meaning. If "robbing" Mexico of its riches is no longer possible, linguistic imposition remains: "Te lo he notado. Por el acento, claro," replies the man to Paulina.[61] This is the first time that the issue of speech and accents comes up, and it should not be a surprise that it takes place in Madrid and in the form of the dominant Castilian view of itself as "normal" and every other speech as marked by difference, "accented." Like Teresa Mendoza's and García Bernal's, Paulina's speech is marked by the Spanish man for whom an accent embodies an obvious sign of difference and a vehicle to stereotyping. Despite having heard about Paulina's homesickness, the flower shop, and her family problems, the neighbour enters his apartment and tells his friends: "Oye, aquí hay una mujer que se quiere suicidar, ¿eh? No sé, dice que es de México. Yo creo que tiene problemas con el narcotráfico" (season 2, episode 1).[62] None of this remotely resembles his and Paulina's conversation but easily turns her into a version of the queen of the south. At some point the proxemics of the scene place Paulina as caught between the stranger in the balcony to the left and Puri, who is eavesdropping in the balcony to the right, and thus Paulina is symbolically framed by the continuity between left and right, the Spanish present (the young man) and past (Puri as purity of blood or linguistic purity). Puri's metaphorical name becomes clear only a few scenes later when, needing the family to return to Mexico, she secretly burns María José's and Bruno's passports so that they do not go with Paulina.

When María José can finally obtain new passports and join Paulina in Mexico, Bruno loves being back in his family's home: "Oye, pero, qué guay que es esta casa. En serio, que mola un mogollón."[63] Bruno's speech (his use of Castilian pronunciation and slang) catches the attention of not only the viewers but also the family and friends. When Bruno

---

60 "Ay, did I rob you of your sleep?"; "The truth is that I no longer have anything that can be robbed."
61 "I've noticed. By your accent, of course."
62 "Listen here, there is a woman who wants to kill herself. What? I don't know, she says she is from Mexico. I think she has problems with drug trafficking."
63 "Listen, this house is wicked; seriously, bloody brilliant."

sees Micaela, his aunt who is younger than he is, she looks puzzled and asks, "¿Por qué hablas así?" Bruno answers: "Bueno, pues niña, cuando vas a España y la gente habla con este acentazo, pues, se pega, ¿sabes? O sea, que no hay nada que yo pueda hacer."[64] At some point Micaela has to remind Bruno of his own family history (that Salo is allegedly his real grandfather) because, although he has been in Madrid for only a year, Bruno is already suffering amnesia: "Ostia, es que ya me había olvidado, ¿eh?" "Bienvenido a casa, Ana Torroja," concludes Micaela.[65] In a show in which a drag-queen cabaret (run by her mother, Roberta) both made possible and brought down the lifestyle of the well-to-do De la Mora family, Micaela's identification of Bruno with the lead singer of Mecano, Ana Torroja, produces two immediate effects. First, it connects the viewer back to Mecano's sound track, strengthening the references to Spain's movida, the amnesia it represents, and its legacy in the present, which is metaphorized in Bruno's forgetting after living in Spain. Second, this exchange makes explicit for the first time a connection between language and gender normativity. The viewers are here placed in a similar but reversed scene from the one on the balconies in Madrid. When the neighbour identifies Paulina as Mexican because of her accent, he is reproducing the dominant linguistic ideology behind the Spanish language that has kept Spain and the RAE at the centre of linguistic authority (not without the help of precisely the type of Mexican Hispanist discourse that sustained the world-view of families like the De la Mora). As Lope Blanch points out, the absence in the *DRAE* of the term *españolismo* makes obvious the linguistic naturalization that equates normative Spanish with Castilian Spanish. Caro makes sure to have Bruno use, in rapid succession, words and expressions that are mostly unique to Castilian Spanish (*guay, molar, mogollón, tío* or *tía*, etc.), all of which can be found in the *DRAE* without any reference whatsoever to their specific locality. As discussed in the case of Pérez-Reverte and Almodóvar, the naturalization of Castilian Spanish as "Spanish," as the paradigm that governs the entire glottopolitical structure of the language, is alive and well in Spain beyond the borders of the RAE. In the scene between Bruno and Micaela in Mexico, however, there is a small but very significant difference from the one on the balconies of Madrid. Bruno refers to Madrid's speech as an "acentazo," and in

---

64 "Why do you speak like that?"; "Well, mate, when you go to Spain and people speak
    with such huge accent, well, it sticks to you, you know. There is nothing I can do."
65 "Fuck, I already forgot, see?"; "Welcome home, Ana Torroja."

doing so, as García Bernal had done, he denaturalizes Castilian Spanish as norm and turns it into just another accent, another variant of the many. In the conversation between the youngest members of the De la Mora family there is nothing essentializing about language at all: Castilian is but another "accent," one that "sticks to you" when you live surrounded by people who have it. In connecting it to gender, Micaela's gesture suggests that, like gender norms, linguistic norms are merely the result of naturalization processes sedimented by performative practices learned and reproduced in social contexts. If gender/sex is not an essence but is imposed, learned, internalized, or performed on bodies, is something "that sticks to you," we could say that with Bruno, language functions in much the same way. While the series ridicules the Madrid neighbour's attitude and the stereotypes it produces, Bruno and Micaela's short exchange more radically undoes the normative judgment of the Spanish neighbour who immediately associated accent, nationality, and belonging.

Bruno de la Mora's Madrid accent will continue to be noticed at different points, but ironically the only person to become upset about it is his own Spanish mother. In the middle of an argument between Paulina and María José, Bruno says that he needs to buy Micaela a "ratonzuelo," at which point María José explodes: "¡Yo no sé por qué hablas así! ¡Los españoles no decimos 'ratonzuelos'!" "¿Cómo dicen, entonces?" asks Bruno. "Hamster," replies María José, and Bruno repeats it with an English pronunciation.[66] The humour in this exchange is multilayered. When confronted with a word he does not know, Bruno opts for the most Castilian Spanish–sounding, related word he can imagine by using the suffix -*zuelo*, with its Castilian and old-fashioned-sounding echoes; that is, he chooses what seems to him to be the most *castizo* word, as this idea of "pure" language is called in Madrid. Ironically, it turns out that in Spain they use the least *castizo* term possible, the word *hamster*, of German origin but likely to have entered Spanish through English, a point underscored by Bruno's pronunciation. The irony is furthered because of the perception in Spain, made explicit by Pérez-Reverte in talking about *La reina del sur*, that Mexican Spanish is full of Anglicisms. What seems an otherwise minor joke is also a stab at the heart of what we could call linguistic "purism," and a more playful take on the porosity and hybridity of language. It is also ironic, considering the previous association of gender and language, that María José cannot make that

---

66   "I don't know why you speak like that! We Spaniards don't say *ratonzuelo*!"; "How do you say it, then?"; "Hamster."

association herself and turns to an essentializing concept of language, nationality, and belonging: "We Spaniards don't say ..." Shortly after the exchange about pets, María José and Bruno, now at home, will have a similar confrontation. As soon as Bruno speaks, María José throws a fit again: "Para empezar, ¡deja de hablar como si fueras español porque me pone de una mala ostia que no sabes!"[67] As a transgender woman who, as the show makes explicit, fights for the rights of people to define their own gender, María José, however, keeps conceiving of language in an essentialist, imperialistic way: Mexicans speak the Mexican variant, and Spaniards speak (normative) Spanish. Hearing Mexican Bruno perform a Spanish accent in Mexico discombobulates her. In this light we could say that Bruno is setting into motion something akin to what, in another context, Judith Butler calls "performative contradiction," when "subjects who have been excluded from enfranchisement by existing conventions governing the exclusionary definition of the universal seize the language of enfranchisement and set into motion a 'performative contradiction,' claiming to be covered by that universal, thereby exposing the contradictory character of previous conventional formulations of the universal" (*Excitable* 89). By using the "universal" Spanish norm, Bruno, a Mexican, ultimately shows the contradictory and exclusionary formulation of that alleged norm, and María José seems to be profoundly unsettled by his performative act. It can be argued that it is here that María José's motherhood takes on a different aspect: that of the *madre patria* or motherland/fatherland. Bruno as a Mexican can speak as he wants so long as he speaks "differently" and can be classified as such; otherwise, the entire system built around the balance between normative, standard, or universal Spanish and all its "deviations" or "variants" would fall apart and show itself for what it is, a power structure of dominance, of inclusion and exclusion. Although she is clearly attuned to and willing to unsettle gender norms, Maria José, like Almodóvar, imposes normativity when it comes to the Spanish language.

In contrast to what we could call the linguistic policing enacted by María José and the Spanish neighbour, the many comments in Mexico about Bruno's Spanish accent are meant to subvert the basis of that policing, the very idea of the normativity of Castilian. By continually calling attention to the way he speaks, *La casa de las flores* reveals Castilian Spanish as just another performance, simply another "variant" of Spanish, an *españolismo*: the locality, the "difference" that is everywhere yet nowhere in the *DRAE*. It is not until episode 4 of the third season that

---

67   "For starters, stop speaking as if you were a Spaniard because it makes me really mad!"

Bruno is finally released from this "accent" that has stuck to him. Further highlighting performativity, it happens during a meeting of the lip-sync band that Bruno has formed with Micaela and his friend and love interest Rosita, when their manager, Xavier, stops Bruno in his tracks:

BRUNO: "El lip-sync está *de puta madre, tía, hombre.*"
XAVIER: "'De puta madre.'"
BRUNO: "Está *muy guay.*"
XAVIER: "Sí caón, y de nueva vez, este, antes de que se me olvide, Bruno, por favor *ya quítate ese acento de español,* no somos los Hombres G, papá."
BRUNO: "Ya ¿no pasa nada si hablo así, *normal?*
XAVIER: Sí, por favor.[68]

Xavier and Bruno reverse the hegemonic mechanism of Spanish by using *normal* in a non-normative context, making a Mexican accent the norm, and ultimately calling attention to the absurdity of normativity. Language is never too far from gender and from imperial/colonial discourses in *La casa de las flores*, and, thus, the musical reference here ("no somos los hombres G") is also meaningful. Like Mecano, Hombres G was a 1980s Spanish band of the movida, but one on the opposite side of the ideological spectrum: Hombres G was associated with preppy, conservative, and masculinist Spanish culture, was famous for traditional, heteronormative lyrics of (sometimes violent) rivalry between men over women, and was openly homophobic.[69] Xavier associates

---

68 "Bruno: the lip-sync is *wicked, mate!* Xavier: Wicked. Bruno: It's *brilliant.* Xavier: Yes, dude, but before I forget, Bruno, please *take off that Spanish accent already,* we are not *Hombres G,* man. Bruno: Is it ok if I speak like this, *normal?* Xavier: Yes, please." (Emphasis added.)

69 Led by singer David Summers, Hombres G had an ambivalent connection to the movida. Summers himself recalls: "La Movida lo que pasa es que era una especie de movimiento gay. Era muy gay. Nosotros no nos sentíamos ahí. Nunca hemos sido gays. No nos sentíamos en ese ambiente ... Nos acusaron de homófobos. Yo flipé, pero de eso me di cuenta años después. También un día, como hace 10 años, estábamos tocando en México y oímos que un grupo se había quejado de que había un grupo homófobo en el Festival. ¡Cómo! ¡Por qué! Claro, ya empezaba la tontería de la corrección política y eso." (Colmenero; "The movida was a kind of gay movement. It was very gay. We did not feel right in it. We have never felt gay. We were never at home in that (gay) environment ... They accused us of being homophobic. I flipped, but I only realized all this years later. Also, one day, like 10 years ago, we were playing in Mexico and we heard that a group had complained that there was a homophobic band in the Festival. What! Why? Of course, it was the beginning of that whole political correctness nonsense.")

Bruno's Castilian accent directly with this type of masculinist glotton-ormativity/heteronormativity that, as we have seen, also pervades Spanish imperial nostalgia, suggesting that laying bare that association is what makes Bruno stop using the accent.

Manolo Caro's subversive linguistic/gender plays are indeed multilayered in *La casa de las flores* and aim to dismantle an entire belief system. If the musical references are loaded with meaning, Caro's casting of the two Spanish sisters goes beyond their recognition as actors. Paco León (José María / María José) and María León (Puri) are not only well-known and acclaimed Spanish actors but also siblings in real life who, though not twins, have a very striking physical resemblance. This similarity is important if, as I will argue, they are made to embody two sides of the same Spain. Linguistically speaking, the León siblings are both Andalusian. The added irony of María José's (Paco León's) chastising of Bruno for speaking "as if he were Spanish" is that she herself does not speak Castilian Spanish and even less so does her sister Puri (María Leon), whose speech is ironically never "pure." Both actors/characters speak Andalusian Spanish. Caro thus foregrounds the way in which Castilian linguistic hegemony functions within the political borders of Spain itself, where Andalusians are thought to speak a variant of Spanish, marked as local and different from the norm and also laden with stereotypes.[70] Many Andalusians, nonetheless, often project a Castilian normative gaze over non-Peninsular speakers of Spanish. Within this framework of internal Spanish linguistic politics, one last glottopolitical twist of the series is the presence of Alejo, Virginia's Spanish lover whom she met after leaving her family and before dying of cancer. Alejo comes to visit the family and falls in love with Paulina. He is the only Spanish character whose speech most viewers could arguably associate with Castilian; yet, ironically, when Elena asks if he is Spanish, he replies, "Absolutely not. I'm Catalan" (season 2, episode 4).

In stark contrast to *La mala educación*, in which Pedro Almodóvar's revelling in the performativity of gender hides the performativity of language, in *La casa de las flores* Caro maintains a constant play with gender, language, performativity, and identity that exposes, rather than hides, the mechanisms by which imperial/colonial legacies keep articulating Spanish hegemonic discourse. Caro's juxtaposition of gender and language, and the foregrounding of the performative nature

---

70 Pedro Almodóvar, in fact, employs southern stereotyping in his movies, in which there is often a linguistically southern character (Candela, Agrado, Paca) functioning as a *graciosa* stock character.

of both, expose the ideological and political sediments that have constructed glottonormativity/heteronormativity over the centuries. In a larger historical sense, *La casa de las flores* is also revealing the broader economic and political drive behind such normativities as alienating and barren. The show begins with an epigraph attributed to Van Gogh: "La normalidad es un camino pavimentado. Es cómodo para caminar, pero nunca crecerán flores en él."[71] Roberta refers to this epigraph when she starts her narrative: "En esta casa *tampoco* crecen flores" (emphasis added). In this house, as in the regime that sustains it, flowers do not grow; they are commodities, bought and sold. The questioning of linguistic and gender norms in *La casa de las flores* goes, indeed, to the core of a language hegemony that is both the result and the raison d'être of conservative Hispanism and Hispanidad on both sides of the Atlantic, a pervasive colonial/imperial legacy that, to an extent, also made possible and sustains the structures that support the De la Mora family in Mexico.

In season 2, María José runs into Gloria, a transgendered woman and one of the drag performers at the cabaret. María José learns of the discrimination suffered by Gloria at her gym, where they insist on using her male name. María José offers to accompany her to the civil registry and help her legally change her name to Gloria. "Es un derecho que tenemos todas. Si no fuera por nosotras, ¿qué sería de nosotras?" says María José (episode 4) as they wait in line at the central civil registry.[72] The camera shots are meaningful. The frame shows María José against the back-drop of the colonial church Nuestra Señora de Belén, located near the civil registry, thereby associating María José with the colonial period, a connection that will indeed become explicit a few scenes later. Additionally, the name of the church in the context of a scene about gender normativity humorously refers to the non-normative family that is at the core of Christianity and that is, of course, inscribed in María José's own name. Located midway between Cuauhtémoc and Isabel la Católica subway stations in Mexico City, the location of the scene also evokes the conquest and the national myths of Mexico and Spain. Only a few scenes later, having successfully changed her name, Gloria takes the microphone at the cabaret to publicly thank María José for helping

---

71   "Normativity is a paved path. It is comfortable to walk on, but flowers will never grow in it."
72   "It is a right that we all have. If we didn't do anything, what would become of us?"

her, calling her "la abogada más chingona" (episode 4).[73] Hearing that, Amanda, another drag performer, says to her friend, "La Gloria bien colonizada. Así cayó la Malinche," to which her friend replies, "¡Qué perra eres!"[74] Closing the chain of meaning that began in the previous scene, *La casa de las flores* conjures the postcolonial narrative as it rewrites it, queering it. As is often the case in Caro's series, this type of quick and humorous reference needs some unpacking. Obviously, in Amanda's comment, Gloria is Malinche, the "colonized" traitor to her people, but that view is subsequently presented as mean and unfair by the friend's scolding reply. The chain of signification has been set in motion, however. If Gloria is Malinche, María José is Hernán Cortés who Gloria just called "la abogada más chingona," thus turning herself into Malinche, *la chingada*. To the extent that Amanda is self-identifying as belonging to the group that resisted colonization and was betrayed by Gloria/Malinche, she aligns herself with the non-traitor Cuauhtémoc, indirectly alluded to earlier. Resisting the neat impulse of allegory, however, Amanda's comment creates a domino effect, producing a network of possible connections that are left for the viewer to establish and in which interpretations complement rather than cancel each other, creating subversive "queer" readings of colonial continuities and of the many versions of the story of origin in both Mexican and Spanish identity myths. It asks us to "queer" Malinche, Hernán Cortés, Cuauhtémoc, the Virgin Mary, and Isabel la Católica. This new transgender version of Cortés who is María José is the most *chingona* ("very good, competent, great") because she helps Gloria rather than screw (*chingar*) her; and to the extent that Mexico's civil law is largely a result of Spanish colonization and thus of Spanish laws, María José is undoing the legacy of the old, male Cortés. Playing again with language and gender, Caro refuses to present Malinche as *chingada* and instead transforms Cortés into a *chingona* woman, helping undo what her male patriarchal other had done.

If Gloria is Malinche in the chain of associations unleashed by Amanda's comment, so is Elena, who only a few minutes earlier had been called a traitor by her own sister Paulina because she was working for the "enemy" who now owns the flower shop. (The new owners are the children of Agustín Corcuera, the very person who murdered

---

73 "The greatest lawyer."
74 "Gloria is totally colonized. That's how Malinche fell"; "You are such a bitch!"

Paulina's biological father, Pato, although neither she nor the viewers are yet aware of this.) Julián is also called a traitor by Paulina because of his continued relationship with Diego, who now owns the cabaret. Ultimately, of course, it is Paulina herself (caught by the demands of the contending worlds of the cabaret workers, of her family, and of her Spanish transgender ex-husband and her psychotic sister) who can also be read as a more contemporary version of Malinche: smart, savvy, diplomatic, and always strategizing and negotiating. It is Paulina who moves more than anyone else between spaces, *jarchando* (to use Yuri Herrera's neologism) between the big and small houses of flowers, between Mexico and Madrid, between Las Lomas de Chapultepec and prison, where she eventually ends up and where she meets La Chiva / Silvia, the scapegoat of her family's crimes. By the end of the show, Paulina will have learned to dismiss normativity, face her family secrets, resolve the unfinished business of their ghosts, and reimagine an entirely new, decentralized, non-normative, non-patriarchal conception of family, gender, linguistic, and postcolonial relations. In this multiplicity of Malinches, however, each with her/his own set of Corteses, no one really is either, but everyone is connected to both, a move that deepens the series' questioning of heteronormative and glottopolicial national and transnational myths.

It is only in the third and final season that the past and the present of the De la Mora family begin to fully collide when Paulina is forced by La Chiva / Silvia to reckon with her family's crimes. La Chiva / Silvia has spent the last forty years in prison for a crime that she did not commit – the murder of Virginia's father, Paulina's grandfather. As Paulina eventually learns, Silvia was hired by Virginia's mother, Victoria, to help her care for her allegedly sick husband (whom Victoria is secretly killing). The series strategically pairs that reckoning with the past and Paulina's problems with Puri in the present. Puri is doing all she can to keep Paulina in prison, and her psychotic tendencies, glimpsed during the episode of the passport burning in Madrid, become murderous as she tries to get María José and Bruno back to Spain.

Puri Riquelme and Victoria Aguirre, Paulina's grandmother, can be read as two versions of the same ideology with different hairdos and styles: the short-haired, hipster-looking Puri and the traditional and proper Victoria are in many ways two sides of the same coin, the two faces of conservative Hispanidad, of the legacies of Mexican and Spanish colonial/imperial histories on both sides of the Atlantic, past and present. As mentioned, Purificación embodies a connection to the purity-of-blood discourse of the Spanish Empire and its post-imperial manifestations, including linguistic purity. It is thus within the ever-shifting network of metaphorical connections that Hernán Cortés, imperial discourse, and Hispanidad can metaphorically become both a transgender-woman lawyer helping drag queens and her cisgender sister obsessed with sameness, endogamy, and indeed incest (as we see Puri passing as María José while having sex with a stranger, enamoured of her sister as a mirror image of herself). Caro's casting of the Spanish León siblings, then, if meaningful linguistically, is also meaningful symbolically. Puri can thus be read as embodying the pervasive legacies of Francoist institutionalized Hispanidad in democratic Spain. Behind her hipster, modern look, Puri hides the same old Spanish myth that is infatuated with itself, not unlike the ways in which the refurbished look of the Instituto Cervantes hides the Francoist Instituto de Cultura Hispánica; the popular bestsellers of Pérez-Reverte are but the unencumbered actualization for the twenty-first century of the same old masculinist defence of empire; and Almodóvar's problematic relationship with Spanish, García Bernal, and Mexican cinema manifests in a film about a resentful and murderous brother often called Gael. It takes time for María José to accept that her sister Puri is psychotic and dangerous and must be stopped. It takes three seasons for María José not to be defensive and to accept, unlike her sister, that other narratives are possible; to finally understand that what Paulina wants to do is the right thing; to believe her narrative and help her uncover the truth, as Roberta has enjoined her to do. But eventually she does. This new transgender, female version of Cortés frees herself from her evil sister Purificación, leaves Spain behind, places her sister in a mental health institution, and chooses to stay with Paulina and Bruno.

Simultaneously the flashbacks take the viewers to 1979 with Virginia's mother, Victoria, playing the part of the perfect Las Lomas housewife and socialite, and owning a flower shop that is set for success after having been commissioned for the president's daughter's wedding. In secret, however, Victoria is poisoning her husband drop by drop, keeping him locked in a room in a perpetual slumber from which he cannot wake, and keeping their daughter Virginia away from him by insisting that her father has a very contagious disease.[75] For her part, Virginia

---

75   The character of Virginia's father remains elusive throughout the entire series, and we never really know his story or the reason why Victoria kills him. As such, we could consider him a sort of "empty signifier," and, given the politics of memory of Caro's series, his killing could be connected to the revolution and to the potentialities embodied in the 1968 student movement. This is reinforced by the connections between the father, Pato, and Silvia.

finds herself at the cusp of liberation, escaping with her male friends for a weekend of sex and drugs in Acapulco, a liberation that Victoria will do anything to prevent. She dislikes all Virginia's male friends: Ernesto de la Mora because his family's ruin has disgraced him; Salomón (Salo) because he is Jewish; and Patricio (Pato) because he is gay. Victoria, like Puri and like the myth of Hispanidad, is obsessed with self-preservation and rejects difference. She is set on having Virginia married as soon as possible, pushing her daughter to marry Agustín Corcuera, the son of another well-to-do family, unaware of the fact that, although he is in the closet, Agustín is in fact Pato's lover. Pressured by her friends and neighbours, Victoria tries to stop Virginia's freedom, her "deviations," and sends her to a "school for young ladies," where she hopes Virginia will be "normalized" into a proper woman of her class, that is, *gente decente*. But Virginia, who wants to marry Salo, starts enquiring more often about her father's disease, insisting on seeing him, which Victoria forbids. With the help of Silvia / La Chiva, Virginia manages to do two important things: first, see her father alive although he is in a daze; second, after learning that she is pregnant, figure out that her baby is likely Pato's.[76] Virginia's pregnancy requires Victoria to accelerate events: she finally kills her husband, making sure that Silvia / La Chiva, the only one who knows the truth, is blamed for stealing and sent to jail, and she arranges Virginia's marriage to Agustín. Things go downhill from there as the first murder, that of Virginia's father, will soon be followed by another, Pato's. Shortly before Silvia is sent to jail, Pato learns from her what really happened to Virginia's father and convinces her to call the police, promising that he and Virginia will help her. At the New Year's Eve party Pato tries to tell Virginia the truth of her father's death, but she refuses to listen. Pato, upset and drunk, approaches the closeted Agustín at the party in front of his male friends, and Agustín reacts violently. He and his friends take Pato outside, abuse him verbally and physically, and finally beat him to death, leaving him in the street. His murder will have two victims, both underdogs: Pato himself and Silvia / La Chiva whom Pato can no longer save from being framed by Victoria. Pato's murder is considered unworthy of a full investigation because he was a homosexual and Agustin is from the upper class. Silvia spends the rest of her life in prison, where she will become La Chiva,

---

76 Salo is too drunk to have sex, and Pato has been rejected by his companion, who turned out to be homophobic, so he and Virginia decide to playfully explore having sex together.

resenting both Pato and Virginia, unaware that Pato is dead and that Virginia does not know the truth about her father.

Rather than marrying Agustín, whom she knows to be in the closet and, more importantly, to be Pato's killer, Virginia decides to propose a marriage of convenience to her best friend, Ernesto de la Mora: he gains the money and status that his family has lost, and she gains a husband, a father for her child, and the preservation of the family reputation that her mother, Victoria, wants. Delia is hired by Victoria to replace Silvia as a live-in housekeeper, and life goes on. Whatever possibilities were open in Acapulco, or at the LGBT march in Mexico City attended by Pato and his heterosexual friends, were lost when Virginia's father and Pato were murdered and Silvia wrongly accused; they were lost when Ernesto gave up his own love for Carmela and accepted Virginia's proposal, and both chose to live the scripted life of *gente decente* in Las Lomas, performing the "perfect" Mexican family. Not unlike Mexico in the aftermath of the Tlatelolco massacre, the neoliberal De la Mora family was born out of the ashes of utopia, a utopia imprisoned with Silvia / La Chiva and murdered in the bodies of Virginia's father and Pato, Paulina's father.

Though perhaps not utopian, the de la Mora children's coming to terms with themselves and with their past, helped by Delia, whom they trust and to whom Virginia gave reparation in her will, is a sign that things are changing in the family, that old patterns are being broken, and a different future is possible. But neither Puri nor Victoria will have any of it, and both stage returns to block that reckoning, to block those changes. Victoria, now old, returns to Las Lomas to reclaim the house and the flower shop, as Puri flies to Mexico and begins plotting so that María José can return "home" to Spain. When both fail in their attempts, Victoria and Puri resort to murder. As she did with her husband, Victoria starts poisoning her pregnant granddaughter, Elena, who has refused to marry one of Agustín Corcuera's children. Like Silvia tried to do forty years earlier, it is now Delia who stops Victoria from killing Elena and repeating history. Whether it is by accident or by Delia's hand is unclear, but Victoria falls down the stairs and dies. This time around, however, there is no framing or blaming of Delia. Paulina and María José do what Pato could not: shield her from the police. Elena has the baby she planned with Diego and Julián, gets over her own class prejudices, and starts a relationship with Pablo, ex-architect turned delivery guy. After rescuing Diego from a gay conversion clinic (a present-day version of Virginia's school for decent ladies) with the help of Elena, Julián is ready to commit and raise their child together with Elena and Pablo. All four and the baby set out to try the experiment of a non-normative family. This time there is neither a murdered father nor a secret father but an abundance of fathers, and little Patricio will not have to choose or figure out who they are. Paulina eventually manages to close her own paternal enigmas/wounds by searching for and learning about Pato. Only now, after her reckoning with her family history and the resolution of past violence, she can finally move on and reset things with María José, declaring her love and asking her to marry her, again, to start anew.

The world of the De la Mora family is changing, indeed, but the threat of Puri's violence lingers until the very end. In the final scene of the last episode, as Paulina and María José declare their love in a ceremony in front of family and friends, after letting go of both their family house and the flower shop, Puri, who has escaped from the mental-health clinic where María José had finally placed her, lurks with a gun behind a window, ready to kill Paulina. But the ghosts of the past have been exorcised and no longer hold the family back. On the contrary, they come to their aid: Puri shoots the gun but misses Paulina, as Virginia's ghost appears and hits Puri on the head, knocking her out. Virginia and Delia have finally set right what Virginia and Silvia would not or could not do in the past.

The De la Mora children say goodbye to the old house, the shop, and their family secrets. They are all ready to move on. As the wedding celebration continues and the mariachi band, interrupted in the first episode, can finally play its tune, Paulina ends the series with a resounding "¡Viva México!" Pedro Galindo Galarza's famous song "Viva México, Viva América" has in its very middle the following stanza: "Que México es valiente / y nunca se ha rajado / viva la democracia / y también la libertad." In the very first episode of the series this song was meant to be sung at Ernesto's birthday party, yet Roberta's suicide and the search for truth and justice that it set into motion stopped it. In the context of *La casa de las flores*, it can be argued that the song was initially meant as an empty repetition of national rituals rendered meaningless by what they hide rather than by what they say. It is not until a new narrative emerges, after the De la Mora family has finally stopped hiding secrets and has, instead, reckoned with the ghosts of the past, properly burying them, and confronting postcolonial/post-imperial narratives of glotto- and heteronormativity, that things can begin to change and that the signifiers Mexico, democracy, and liberty in the song may begin to signify anew. In the wake of all the changes that have taken place in the family narrative, "¡Viva Mexico!" can only now begin to be articulated with a new set of meanings and possibilities. In this newly configured, decentred, non-normative Mexican family story,

"¡Viva Mexico!" can be heard as a refusal to *rajarse*, to give up, and as a desire to look for ways, however flawed, to create new narratives of inclusion that can begin to dismantle normative structures put in place five hundred years earlier – in other words, a desire to start growing flowers rather than selling them.

Conclusion: Engaging Contemporary Colonialities

No one ever labelled Pérez-Reverte the Spanish Elmer Mendoza after he wrote the novel that would catapult him internationally, but as soon as Manolo Caro began to make a splash in cinema, Caro was called the Mexican Almodóvar. It has indeed become common to compare Manolo Caro with Pedro Almodóvar, and in the very proliferation of that comparison lurks once again an unspoken but stubbornly present imperial/colonial legacy, that of the directionality of influence. In his review of *La casa de las flores* Paul J. Smith connects the series to creative Mexican cinema and directors like Alejandro González Iñarritu and Alfonso Cuarón and astutely identifies a progressive legacy of Mexican telenovelas produced by Argos and broadcast by TV Azteca, a lineage within which we should understand Caro's *La casa de las flores*. Nonetheless, he frames his review with what he reads as Caro's apparent debts to Pedro Almodóvar, starting with his description of Caro's "appeal to a lush 'Almodovarian' style" and nearly ending with his criticism that "the series' tone comes too close to early Almodóvar for comfort" ("Netflix's *The House of Flowers*," 60). For Smith, Mexican creator Manolo Caro even signals his allegiance to the Spanish director through his sound track, featuring campy pop hits from Spain like Baccara's "Yes, Sir, I Can Boogie" (60). This critique is curious, given that the films of the early Almodóvar are full of Mexican boleros and the use of melodrama, which has a long Mexican history, no less in telenovelas; yet no one felt uncomfortable with those Mexican connections, which, if anything, became Almodóvar's discovery. Such is the power of imperial frames that often function unexpectedly and probably unwittingly. Other readings of intertextuality are not only possible, but desirable, as Caro himself reminds us through his telenovela.

In a series like *La casa de las flores*, in which the movida, Mexico's LGTB+ movement, and Tlatelolco are an integral part of the fabric of Caro's reflection on and queering of historical memory, the intertextuality with the early films of Almodóvar, precisely those that are the most Mexican and likely the most groundbreaking in the context of the 1980s and 1990s, is certainly not just a mere debt or infatuation with his style but an integral part of Caro's critique. Indeed, in *La casa de las flores* there is both a homage to and a powerful critique of Almodóvar's films. Through Caro's lens we see not only the many groundbreaking achievements of the Spanish filmmaker and the movida but also the limits of those achievements and their incapacity, caught in the loop of postcolonial melancholia, to fully engage with historical memory and colonial/imperial legacies.[77] In *La casa de las flores*, moral and political ambiguity or equidistance is an excuse to not confront the past, as Virginia and Ernesto ultimately did for many years in Mexico: they compromised and chose to forget. But Roberta, the ghostly narrator, will have none of that and will force the De la Mora family to dig deeper into the past, to confront it, to face the traumas of history, to acknowledge responsibility, and to try to right past wrongs as part of self-discovery and looking forward. *La casa de las flores* certainly returns to the 1960s, 1970s, and 1980s, yet, unlike Almodóvar's films, it does not understand the events of those years as the original trauma but as iterations of a much longer wounding inscribed in centuries of Mexican and Spanish histories and in legacies of coloniality and imperialism that are still haunting Spanish contemporary culture. It is this postcolonial melancholia that prompts a type of acting out in the glottopolitics of the ever-policing RAE and the constant reimposition of an ossified understanding of Spanish and Mexican histories. It is also this postcolonial melancholia that turns a violent heteronormative and glottonormative literary project like Pérez-Reverte's into mainstream bestsellers in a country in which a politician can dress like Hernán Cortés and win votes. It is the same postcolonial melancholia, though, that also lies behind the progressive politics of a filmmaker like Almodóvar, attenuating any reckoning with the past and, thus, leading him to reproduce the same masculinist (and imperialist) discourse that he means to critique.

As the previous chapters of this book have clearly demonstrated, however many legacies of coloniality still persist in Mexico and in notions of *mexicanidad*, contemporary Mexican culture – from literature to photography to film to social media creations – continues to engage

---

77 In October 2020, after the writing of this chapter, Netflix released a miniseries by Manolo Caro, *Alguien tiene que morir* (*Someone Has to Die*), starring Carmen Maura, a choice of actor seen by many as once again too close to Almodóvar for comfort, missing perhaps that making Spanish viewers "uncomfortable" may be part of the point of the series. Set in Spain during Francoism, Carmen Maura's role is closely related to that of Purificación and Victoria in *La casa de las flores*, and the engagement of the series with queerness, Mexico, and Franco Spain brings home, in many ways, some of the central points of *La casa de las flores* discussed in this chapter.

with them, asking us, if anything, to reflect on those continuities, requiring us not to forget. Manolo Caro's *La casa de las flores*, continuing a very Mexican tradition through humour and melodrama, does the same, while exposing Spain's persistent incapacity to acknowledge the traumas of the past and engage its history across the Atlantic.

WORKS CITED

Aguilar, Paloma, and Carsten Humlebaek. "Collective Memory and National Identity in the Spanish Democracy: The Legacies of Francoism and the Civil War." *History and Memory*, vol. 14, no. 1–2, 2002, pp. 121–64. *JSTOR*, https://doi.org/10.2979/his.2002.14.1-2.121.

Ávila, Jacqueline. "'La música en las casas': Musicalization in *La casa de papel* and *La casa de las flores* and Netflix Global Audience." *American Music*, vol. 37, no. 4, 2019, pp. 472–92.

Baker, Pascale. "Avenging Assassins: Women and Power in *Rosario Tijeras* (1999) by Jorge Franco and *La Reina del Sur* (2002) by Arturo Pérez Reverte." *Crime Scenes: Latin American Crime Fiction from the 1960s to the 2010s*, edited by Charlotte Lange and Ailsa Peate. Ebook, Peter Lang, 2019, pp. 25–43.

Benavides, Hugo. *Drugs, Thugs, and Divas: Telenovelas and Narcodramas in Latin America*. U of Texas P, 2008.

Bialowas Pobutsky, Aldona. "Perez Reverte's *La reina del sur* or Female Aggression in Narcocultura." *Hispanic Journal*, vol. 30, no. 1, 2009, pp. 273–84.

Butler, Judith. *Bodies That Matter*. Routledge, 1993.

– *Excitable Speech: A Politics of the Performative*. Routledge, 1997.

Carretero, Mario, Liliana Jacott, and Asunción López Manjón. "Learning History through Textbooks: Are Mexican and Spanish Students Taught the Same Story?" *Learning and Instruction*, vol. 12, no. 6, 2002, pp. 651–65.

La casa de las flores. Directed by Manolo Caro, Netflix, 2018–20.

Colmenero, Ricardo F. "Nos echaron de la movida por pijos, por envidia, y por no ser gays." *El Mundo*, 7 Nov. 2017, https://www.elmundo.es/papel/todologia/2017/07/11/595f9e44268e3edc1a8b4589.html.

Del Valle, José. "Glotopolítica, ideología y discurso: Categorías para el estudio del estatus simbólico del español." *La lengua, ¿patria común? Ideas e ideologías del español*, edited by José del Valle, Verbuert-Iberoamericana, 2007, pp. 19–52.

–, editor. *A Political History of Spanish: The Making of a Language*. Cambridge UP, 2013.

Derrida, Jacques. "Signature. Event. Context." *Margins of Philosophy*, translated with notes by Alan Bass, U of Chicago P, 1982. pp. 307–30.

Díaz de Quijano, Fernando. "Una reclamación 'absurda' y 'populista.'"
El Cultural, 26 Mar. 2019, https://www.elespanol.com/el-cultural
/letras/20190326/reclamacion-absurda-populista/386213268_0.html.

D'Lugo, Marvin. "Post Nostalgia in *Bad Education*: Written on the Body of Sara
Montiel." *All About Almodóvar: A Passion for Cinema*, edited by Brad Epps
and Despina Kakoudaki, U of Minnesota P, 2009, pp. 357–85.

Dolor y gloria. Directed by Pedro Almodóvar, Sony Pictures, 2019.

Duncan, Paul. *Los archivos de Pedro Almodóvar*. Taschen, 2017.

EFE. "Pérez-Reverte se inspiró en Diego Rivera para su relato 'Ojos azules.'"
Público. 25 Jan. 2009, https://www.publico.es/actualidad/perez-reverte
-inspiro-diego-rivera.html.

Escudero, María. "Hispanist Democratic Thought versus Hispanist Thought
of the Franco Era: A Comparative Analysis." *Bridging the Atlantic: Towards
a Reassessment of Iberian and Latin American Cultural Ties*, edited by Marina
Pérez de Mendiola, State U of New York P, 1996, pp. 169–86.

Fernández, Mauro. "De la lengua del mestizaje al mestizaje de la lengua:
Reflexiones sobre los límites de una nueva estrategia discursiva." *La lengua,
¿patria común? Ideas e ideologías del español*, edited by José del Valle, Verbuert-
Iberoamericana, 2007, pp. 105–54.

García, Yago. "Los rodajes más conflictivos del cine español." *20 minutos*.
25 Oct. 2011. https://www.20minutos.es/cinemania/noticias/los-rodajes
-mas-conflictivos-del-cine-espanol-5416/.

Garcia-Alvite, Dosinda. "De la frontera de los EEUU-México al estrecho de
Gibraltar y de vuelta: Procesos de transculturación en *La reina del sur* de
Pérez-Reverte." *Cincinnati Romance Review*, no. 25, 2006, pp. 81–98.

Gilroy, Paul. *Postcolonial Melancholia*. Columbia UP, 2006.

Gimferrer, Pere. "Prólogo." *Ojos azules*. Arturo Pérez-Reverte. E-book,
Penguin-Random House, 2017, pp. 4–5.

Gobierno de España. "Comunicado del Gobierno de España sobre México."
25 Mar. 2019, https://www.exteriores.gob.es/Embajadas/mexico/es
/Comunicacion/Noticias/Paginas/Articulos/Comunicado-del-Gobierno
-de-España-sobre-México-.aspx.

Gómez López-Quiñones, Antonio. "La conquista y el problema de la
modernidad hispánica: Dos discursos sobre el pasado (post)colonial en la
democracia española." *Anales de la literatura española contemporánea*,
vol. 36, no. 1, 2011, pp. 101–32.

Gozzer, Stefania. "¿Por qué en España se enseña tan poco sobre la conquista
y colonización de América?" *BBC News Mundo*, 4 Apr. 2019, https://www
.bbc.com/mundo/noticias-internacional-47784188.

Guerrero, Catalina. "Henry Kamen: En España se enseña aun la conquista
como con Franco." *La vanguardia*, 8 Nov. 2014, https://www.lavanguardia
.com/cultura/20141108/54419071253/henry-kamen-en-espana-se-ensena
-aun-la-conquista-de-america-como-con-franco.html.

Hafiz, Muneeb. "Smashing the Imperial Frame: Race, Culture, Decoloniality." *Theory, Culture, Society*, vol. 37, no. 1, 2020, pp. 113–45. *Sage Journals*, https://doi.org/10.1177/0263276419877674.

"He escrito desde el corazón de una mujer." Entrevista: Arturo Pérez Reverte. *El País*, 6 June 2002, https://elpais.com/diario/2002/06/06/cultura/1023314406_850215.html.

"Hernán Cortés." Futuro Abierto, *Radio Nacional de España*, 15 Dec. 2019, https://www.rtve.es/play/audios/futuro-abierto/futuro-abierto-hernan-cortes-15-12-19/5465448/.

"Hernán Cortés: ¿héroe o genocida?" Los expertos responden, *La vanguardia*, 16–18 Oct. 2019, https://www.lavanguardia.com/historiayvida/edad-moderna/20191017/471009889022/hernan-cortes-heroe-genocida-ii.html.

Hirschberg, Lynn. "The Redeemer." *The New York Times Magazine*, 5 Sept. 2004, vhttps://www.nytimes.com/2004/09/05/magazine/the-redeemer.html.

"La institución." *Sobre nosotros*, Instituto Cervantes. https://cervantes.org/es/sobre-nosotros/institucion. Accessed 5 Oct. 2023.

Juan-Navarro, Santiago. "Narco-culturas transatlánticas: Espacios fronterizos y globalización en *La reina del sur*." *Diálogos Latinoamericanos*, no. 27, 2018, pp. 22–44.

Kinder, Marsha. "All about the Brothers: Retroseriality in Almodóvar's Cinema." *All About Almodóvar: A Passion for Cinema*, edited by Brad Epps and Despina Kakoudaki, U of Minnesota P, 2009. pp. 267–94.

Lange, Charlotte, and Ailsa Peate, editors. *Crime Scenes: Latin American Crime Fiction from the 1960s to the 2010s*. E-book, Peter Lang, 2019.

Lope Blanch, Juan. "Americanismo frente a españolismo lingüísticos." *Nueva Revista de Filología Hispánica*, vol. 43 no. 2, 1995, pp. 433–40. https://doi.org/10.24201/nrfh.v43i2.2637.

La mala educación. Directed by Pedro Almodóvar, Sony Pictures, 2004.

Marcilhacy, David. "La Hispanidad bajo el franquismo: El americanismo al servicio de un proyecto nacionalista." *Imaginarios y representaciones de España durante el franquismo*, edited by Stéphane Michonneau and Xosé M. Núñez-Seixas, Casa de Velázquez, 2014, pp. 73–102.

Mar-Molinero, Clare. "The European Linguistic Legacy in a Global Era: Linguistic Imperialism, Spanish, and the Instituto Cervantes." *Language Ideologies, Policies and Practices: Language and the Future of Europe*, edited by Clare Mar-Molinero and Patrick Stevenson, Palgrave, 2006, pp. 76–88.

Marshall, Alex. "Mamá to Madre? Roma's Subtitles in Spain Anger Alfonso Cuarón." *The New York Times*, 11 Jan. 2019, https://www.nytimes.com/2019/01/11/movies/roma-spanish-subtitles-alfonso-cuaron-netflix.html.

Martín Garzo, Gustavo. "No hay placer verdadero." *Los archivos de Pedro Almodóvar*, by Paul Duncan, Taschen, 2017, pp. 203–7.

Max, D.T. "The Evolution of Pedro Almodóvar." *The New Yorker*, 27 Nov. 2016, https://www.newyorker.com/magazine/2016/12/05/the-evolution-of -pedro-almodovar.

Mejías-López, Alejandro. "Hispanic Studies and the Legacy of Empire." *Empire's End: Transnational Connections in the Hispanic World, 1808–1898*, edited by Akiko Tsuchiya and William Acree. Vanderbilt UP, 2016, pp. 204–21.

– *The Inverted Conquest: The Myth of Modernity and the Transatlantic Onset of Modernism*. Vanderbilt UP, 2010.

Monsiváis, Carlos. "Ortodoxia y heterodoxia en las alcobas. (Hacia una crónica de costumbres y creencias sexuales en México)." *Debate feminista*, no. 11, 1995, pp. 183–210. https://doi.org/10.22201/cieg.2594066xe.1995.11.1833.

Mora, Miguel. "Arturo Pérez-Reverte bucea en el Siglo de Oro para novelar la 'memoria que se nos niega.'" *El País*, 3 Dec. 1996, https://elpais.com /diario/2004/11/20/cultura/1100905203_850215.html.

Mora Muro, Jesús Iván. "En defensa de la tradición hispánica : La Academia Mexicana de la Historia en el contexto revolucionario, 1910–1940." *Tzintzun: Revista de Estudios Históricos*, no. 65, Jan.–June 2017, pp. 180–208.

Moraña, Mabel, editor. *The Ideologies of Hispanism*. Vanderbilt UP, 2005.

Moreno Cabrera, Juan Carlos. "'Unifica, limpia y fija': La RAE y los mitos del nacionalismo lingüístico español." *El dardo en la Academia: Esencia y vigencia de las academias de la lengua española*, vol. 1. Mesulina, 2011, pp. 157–314.

Pérez, Jorge. "Queer Traces in the Soundtrack of la Movida." *Towards a Cultural Archive of La Movida: Back to the Future*, edited by William J. Nichols and H. Rosi Song, Fairleigh Dickinson UP, 2013, pp. 135–54.

Pérez de Mendiola, Marina. "The Universal Exposition Seville 1992: Presence and Absence, Remembrance and Forgetting." *Bridging the Atlantic: Towards a Reassessment of Iberian and Latin American Cultural Ties*, edited by Pérez de Mendiola, State U of New York P, 1996, pp. 187–204.

Pérez Montfort, Ricardo. "Hispanismo y falange: El México conservador que recibe a los transterrados." *Omnia*, vol. 5, no. 13–14, 1989, pp. 45–51. *Universidad Pedagógica y Tecnólogica de Colombia*, https:// doi.org/10.19053/20275137.n15.2017.5585.

– *Hispanismo y falange: Los sueños imperiales de la derecha española y México*. Fondo de Cultura Economica, 1992.

Pérez-Reverte, Arturo. "Una historia de España (XX)." *XL Semanal*, 10 Mar. 2014, https://www.perezreverte.com/articulo/patentes-corso/817/una -historia-de-espana-xx/.

– *Ojos azules*. E-book, Penguin-Random House, 2017.

– *The Queen of the South*. Translated by Andrew Hurley, E-book. Penguin, 2005.

– *La reina del sur*. Alfaguara, 2002.

— [@perezreverte]. "Que se disculpe él, que tiene apellidos españoles y vive allí. Si este individuo se cree que lo que dice, es un imbécil. Si no se lo cree, es un sinvergüenza." *Twitter*, 25 Mar. 2019, https://twitter.com/perezreverte/status/1110322280310153216.

Pérez Viejo, Tomás. *España en el debate público mexicano,1836–1867: Aportaciones para la historia de una nación.* El Colegio de Mexico, 2008.

— "México-España, la historia que nos divide." Babelia, *El País*, 7 Aug. 2021, https://elpais.com/babelia/2021-08-07/mexico-espana-la-historia-que-nos-divide.html.

Piñeiro Otero, Teresa. "Nuevas perspectivas de las voces en *off* femeninas en las producciones televisivas contemporáneas: Poder, libertad, y ambigüedad en serie." *Investigaciones feministas*, vol. 10, no. 2, 2019, pp. 239–56.

Ponga, Paula. "Gael García Bernal." *Fotogramas*, 2 June 2008, https://www.fotogramas.es/noticias-cine/a118226/gael-garcia-bernal/.

Reviriego, María Estela. "Un momento histórico como piedra de toque en la memoria: *Ojos azules* de Arturo Pérez-Reverte." Actas del VII Congreso Internacional Orbis Tertius de Teoría y Crítica Literaria, 18–20 May 2009, La Plata, https://www.memoria.fahce.unlp.edu.ar/trab_eventos/ev.3602/ev.3602.pdf.

Rodríguez Fariñas, María Jara, Juan Manuel Romero Valiente, and Antonio Luis Hidalgo Capitán. "Los exiliados económicos: La nueva emigración española a Mexico (2008–2014)." *Scripta Nova: Revista Electrónica de Geografía y Ciencias Sociales*, vol. 20, no. 531, 2016, pp. 2–29, http://www.ub.es/geocrit/sn/sn-531.pdf.

Rodríguez Pérez, Raimundo A., and María del Mar Simón García. "Construcción de la narrativa nacional española en los manuales escolares de educación primaria.. *Ensayos: Revista de la Facultad de Educación de Albacete*, vol. 29, no. 1, 2014, pp. 101–13.

Rulfo, Juan. *Pedro Páramo.* Translated by Margaret Sayers Peden. Grove Press, 1994.

Saiz, Eva. "Casado responde a la carta de López Obrador: 'El gobierno tiene que decir que no acepta esa difamación.'" *El País*, 26 Mar. 2019, https://elpais.com/politica/2019/03/26/actualidad/1553595074_910466.html.

Sánchez Prado, Ignacio. *Naciones intelectuales: Las fundaciones de la modernidad literaria mexicana.* Purdue UP, 2009.

Silvestre, Juan. "12 razones por las que seguimos amando *La mala educación.*" *Fotogramas*, 18 Mar. 2019, https://www.fotogramas.es/noticias-cine/g26819326/la-mala-educacion-pedro-almodovar-aniversario/.

Smith, Paul J. *Desire Unlimited: The Cinema of Pedro Almodóvar.* Verso, 2014.

— "Netflix's *The House of Flowers* and the New Telenovela." *Film Quarterly*, vol. 72, no. 3, 2019, pp. 59–61. *U of California P*, https://doi.org/10.1525/fq.2019.72.3.59.

Sola Ayape, Carlos. "Al rescate de Franco y del franquismo: El hispanismo mexicano en la encrucijada de la segunda guerra mundial." *Secuencia*, no. 95, 2016, pp. 91–114. *Instituto Mora*, https://doi.org/10.18234/secuencia .v0i95.1379.

Strauss, Frédéric. *Pedro Almodóvar: Un cine visceral. El País*/Santillana, 1995.

Urías Horcasitas, Beatriz. "Una pasión antirrevolucionaria: El conservadurismo hispanófilo mexicano (1920–1960)." *Revista Mexicana de Sociología*, vol. 72, no. 4, 2010, pp. 599–628.

Vernon, Katherine. "Almodóvar's Global Musical Marketplace." *A Companion to Pedro Almodóvar*, edited by Marvin D'Lugo and Katherine Vernon, Blackwell, 2013, pp. 388–411.

– "Las canciones de Almodóvar." *Almodóvar: El cine como pasión*. Actas del congreso internacional "Pedro Almodóvar," 26–29 Nov. 2003, Cuenca, coordinated by Francisco Zurián Hernández and Carmen Vázquez Varela. Ediciones Universidad de Castilla–La Mancha, 2005, pp. 161–76.

Vox [@vox_es]. "Pablo, no das el perfil para apuntarte a la vanguardia de la reconquista como nuestro presidente @Santi_ABASCAL, pero sigue intentándolo." *Twitter*, 6 Mar. 2019, https://twitter.com/vox_es /status/1103337441723904000?lang=es

Index